Community Structure and Change

Community

LOWRY NELSON, Ph.D.
Professor of Sociology, Emeritus
University of Minnesota

CHARLES E. RAMSEY, Ph.D.
Associate Professor of Rural Sociology
Cornell University

COOLIE VERNER, Ed.D.
Professor of Adult Education
Florida State University

Structure and Change

THE MACMILLAN COMPANY - NEW YORK

Preface

The aim of the authors in writing this book is to provide a meaningful theoretical framework for community analysis and to demonstrate its practical application to community development. The book should prove helpful to citizens participating in local community affairs; to professional workers in health, recreation, education, welfare, or similar work; and to students in college and university courses.

As a textbook, this volume should be appropriate for courses variously called "The Community," "Community Organization," "Community Development," and "Rural-Urban Sociology." The authors kept in mind that these courses are offered in departments of sociology, education, and social work. It is hoped that the approach is equally fruitful for the courses offered in each of these departments. Although the problems encountered by persons with differing professional orientations vary, the principles and generalizations presented here are applicable to all types of interest.

In presenting this material, three main features have been employed that differ from those used by most other books on the community.

First, there is a complete dependence upon theoretical concepts. The concepts which have been found to be so fruitful in the study of social structures generally are used here in analyzing the factors involved in community behavior.

A second feature is our attempt to maintain, as far as possible, a simple, familiar terminology, without diluting or materially altering the basic theoretical approach. In this way we hope to accommodate the general reader with no previous social science education as well as the more advanced student. The only characteristics of the reader assumed by the authors are those of intelligence and interest in community behavior.

The third feature is the wedding of theory and practice. If science and education have any role in community action it is through the application to community problems of the best tested theory available. This purpose is not fulfilled merely by the study of problems within a common sense frame of reference such as any intelligent person might accomplish. In the study of community, a problem is not something to which a theory is applied but indeed a fact of the theory itself. A theory of human behavior must have, as a central focus, the problematic situations to which humans direct their behavior.

These three features lend stability and validity to understanding the community in a way appropriate for students and those who are or will become involved in the life of their local community as teachers, health and welfare workers, cooperative extension agents, adult educators, and as citizens.

Perhaps not all people using this book will find every chapter appropriate to their specific needs. In anticipation of this, the book has been so organized that certain chapters may be omitted. Where a principle or generalization of one chapter is crucial to another it is restated, or suitable reference is provided. This makes the book particularly adaptable for use in a variety of situations, and especially as a text in a college course, or as a source book in a community discussion group.

Since the material presented here is introductory in nature, adequate and carefully selected references are provided for more intensive study of any one topic. Initials are used for certain journals which are quoted frequently: *American Journal of Sociology, American Sociological Review,* and *Rural Sociology.*

We gratefully acknowledge the help in the preparation of the manuscript given by Mrs. Ting Thomas, Mrs. Susan Loberg, Mrs. Diane Friedman, Mrs. Rosalie Goodman, Mrs. Florence Nelson, Mrs. Alberta Ramsey, Mrs. C. Mayfield and Thomas A. Van Sant III. We also wish to thank Gelia T. Castillo and W. Keith Warner for valuable suggestions.

Lowry Nelson
Charles E. Ramsey
Coolie Verner

Table of Contents

CONTENTS

CONTENTS

LIST OF FIGURES

LIST OF TABLES

Community Structure and Change

PART ONE

The Community and its Setting

The term "community" refers to different things, depending upon who is using it and upon the context in which it is used. Sometimes it is used to refer to a geographical area, such as Atlanta, Peoria, or Podunk Hollow. Other uses imply an emphasis upon the individuals who live in the area or upon their psychological identification with the name of the local center of population. The concepts of the community just described are usually simple and easy to communicate. Simplicity and ease of communication are to be valued, unless they also bring about oversimplification. By oversimplification is meant the elimination of some very important ideas about a thing in order merely to achieve understanding more quickly. In such a process, the emphasis is really upon speed, since the "understanding" is actually only pseudo-understanding when important aspects of an idea are eliminated.

The social purpose or function of the study of the community ultimately is to understand how it behaves, how it can be changed to solve human problems (without creating more problems), and to

1

furnish people information leading to some control of the community process and change for their welfare and happiness. The simple concepts of area, individuals, and psychological identification (as well as a multitude of others) all contribute toward this end. Taken alone, however, they represent oversimplification and are not sufficient in any sense to understanding or predicting the community process and change.

The view of the community in the present book is that it operates as a unit, and to do this, it has a system or structure of interrelated parts. It follows that understanding the nature of the community as a unit, the interrelationship of the parts (not to mention the relationship between one community and another and between the community and the mass society about it), is necessary to the understanding and prediction of community behavior. The community, then, is a type of social structure. It is in this sense from the same genus as the society, the group, the institution, and the like. It is also different from these other examples of social structures in important ways.

The community is not an event which is easily grasped, but a complicated and often mysterious set of relationships among people, groups, and institutions. Many concepts of human relationship are necessary to aid in understanding and prediction. In Chapter 1, the importance and nature of these concepts are presented. Included are the nature of the community, the nature of the interrelated parts, and the implications of these for community action. These concepts are used as tools for analysis throughout the book, although the technical words are often not made explicit. The more advanced students in colleges and many professionals in the field will already be using these concepts in their own thinking. The person who is unacquainted with them will find much help, eventually, if he attempts to learn

2

and make them explicit in his own analysis as well as in the analysis found in the present treatise.

Since the community is to be viewed as a social structure, it is important to see how areas and individuals, as external forces, shape community behavior. The second chapter is a consideration of the space relations within the community as a conditioning factor. The confusion of space with the community itself is doubtless a result of the strong influence of space upon human relations. Spatial relations differ from one community to another, and the results in community structure are therefore different. The nature of this influence is seen in the large community where the center is of greatest interest and in the small community where the hinterland takes on significance equal to that of the population center.

Space relations also influence the community from the broader perspective of regions. Southern and Northeastern communities differ from one another, and both types differ from those in the Midwest and Far West. The regional aspects of community analysis are "pan-community," that is, they represent some of the influences exerted on the community by mass society. Such a regional analysis of community is included in Chapter 3.

Many of the definitions of the community involve only individual reactions to a symbol (such as the name of the community or the local basketball team), to a specific area, or to the institutions. The community is a superstructure built upon the relations and feelings of individuals, and it cannot be predicted from knowledge of these individuals only. However this does not mean that individuals, either in terms of numbers or characteristics, do not strongly influence community behavior as such. Demonstration of this principle can be made merely by showing the difference in community structure brought about by great differences in population size; the popula-

3

tion (or demographic) factor influencing community structure is described in Chapter 4. This influence is brought about not only by size but by the movement of people to and from the community area, called migration.

CHAPTER 1

The Community: its Study and Meaning

Every serious student of the community, whether he be of practical or scientific bent, has two predispositions which influence the conclusions he will make and the way he will arrive at them. The first predisposition is a system of attitudes about the relationship between science and practice. If the student is unwilling to integrate the generalizations from the science with the problem situations, his practical program or his science, as the case may be, will take a different form than it will if he effects the integration. Therefore, the first purpose of the present chapter is to discuss some barriers frequently found in integrating scientific generalization and practical judgment as this relationship bears upon the study of the community.

The second predisposition which influences the method and conclusions of the student of the community is a system of concepts. These concepts sensitize him to seek specific types of information and blind him to certain other types. The concepts are derived from common-sense experience and from sociology and related sciences. Therefore, the second purpose of the present chapter is to clarify the concepts from sociology which are essential to the understanding, prediction, explanation, and control of community behavior. These concepts are more useful than common-sense concepts alone, even though they often lack the precision of concepts found in some of the other sciences. Perhaps more important, these concepts represent a system, howsoever incomplete, for solving community problems. In their application to community situations, however, they have to be supplemented with common sense and experience.

THE STUDY OF THE COMMUNITY

There are two distinct areas of interest in the study of the community, the practical and the scientific. The relationship between science and practice is a complicated one, but its importance can hardly be overestimated.[1] Not all the problems involved in this relationship are even now recognized as problems, much less solved. However, the misunderstanding and lack of sympathy often found between the man of action and the man of science demand some attention in a book where the concern for both action and knowledge converge.

The problem of communication between scientist and layman is an ancient one. These seem to be the major reasons for inadequate communication: (1) the language of science in general is obscure to the layman; that of social science often employs terms in common usage, but with different meanings (e.g., "community," "society," "crowd," "group," etc.); (2) social science is abstract and theoretical; (3) it is not always immediately practical; and (4) it appears too often to be elaborating the obvious. A moment's thought will convince anyone that these charges may also apply to other thoughtways as well; religion, common sense, and various systems of philosophy. But the question for the student of society is to find ways in which the impediments to articulation between science and practice can be overcome.

Technical Language

Why does social science, or any science, have to have a specific terminology, a jargon? The answer is in order to promote clarity and economy in communication.[2] This specialized terminology is the first characteristic of any thoughtway, scientific or otherwise. A term, or word-symbol, is a short form for expressing a definition. Once the term becomes accepted as having a specific meaning, it is then no longer necessary to use the definition. This is true of all communication by language, common sense as well as scientific.

In science, a term must perform essentially the same functions as in common sense. That is, the term must be defined so that it places the events to which it refers in some kind of class. This brings generalizations from other members of that class of events as tentatively applicable to the events under study. For example, for purposes of the science of medicine,

---

[1] W.A. Anderson, "Rural Sociology as Science," *RS*, 12:347–56, 1948; Charles E. Lively, "Rural Sociology as an Applied Science," *RS*, 8:331–42, 1944; Carl C. Taylor, "Social Theory and Social Action," *RS*, 5:17–31, 1941; Carl C. Taylor, "Sociology and Common Sense," *ASR*, 12:1–12, 1948; and F. Stuart Chapin, "Social Theory and Social Action," *ASR*, 1–11, 1936.

[2] George A. Lundberg, "The Thoughtways of Contemporary Sociology," *ASR*, 1:703–23, 1936; P.W. Bridgman, *The Logic of Modern Physics*, The Macmillan Company, New York, 1932.

man may be defined as "an animal which . . ." This places man in the class of events known as animals, and the generalizations arrived at through experiment with animals placed near an atomic explosion may be transferred to humans. The practical utility, the necessity of using animals, and the necessity of classifying humans and animals as reacting in the same way cannot be denied in this example. Obviously, a religious thoughtway would not want to classify man along with animals, since most religions distinguish between man and animal on the basis of their major concerns, namely, immortality, morality, and spiritual issues. The community will be defined as "the structuring of sociocultural elements and dimensions which . . . ," and this will bring tentative generalizations from all types of social structures immediately to bear upon the community. This function of terminology brings insight, so necessary both to science and practice. It also helps in determining whether generalizations from one class of events are valid for another.

In addition to classification the definition must distinguish among members of the same class. For example, if man were defined as "an animal which has two legs," man would not be distinguishable from some other members of the class "animal." This point is extremely important in the study of the community, because many definitions fail to distinguish community from society. This means that the application of generalizations about the community to a given case is largely a matter of judgment of the person making the application. This type of guessing must be minimized when inappropriate use of a generalization may bring human misery. Thus, it may be seen that this function of a term, as a short expression of a definition, brings insight as to the generalizations which may be applicable and precision as to whether or not they actually are applicable. By placing the community in the general class of social structure, any principles of structure are subject to application to the community. However, by distinguishing the community from other social structures, certain generalizations can be eliminated immediately.

Limitations of Common Sense

Common-sense words not only call forth the image of certain events, as is required of words, but also call forth connotations of "good" and "bad." When the analysis of relationships is made, these connotations of good and bad enter into the method and conclusions in subtle ways. This makes the conclusions less trustworthy, and therefore less practical. Further, common-sense words have a notorious lack of precision. This brings the difficulty of determining whether a generalization may be applied to a given situation. The field of medicine is a good example. The term "measles" brings a generalization that the person will have to be in bed for a certain length of time. Not until measles were separated into types, one of which is the three-day measles, could more accurate predictions be made. Of course, this example would be more pertinent if the term were in the area of human relations where many common-sense terms are much more ambiguous than the example used. It is therefore worth noting that the chief negative criticism that can be brought against the scientific study of the community is the use of too many common-sense words. This results in inaccurate prediction, lack of precision, and a serious question as to the appropriateness of a generalization in a particular situation. It also makes necessary the attempt to establish a more precise terminology.

Abstract Thinking

A second characteristic of any thoughtway, including sociology and common sense, is that certain features of the empirical world are abstracted for certain purposes.[3] But such abstraction does not necessarily make for impracticality. There is probably nothing more abstract than the concepts "atom" and "gene." Yet these concepts are quite useful in explaining observations in the fields of physics and biology, respectively. The question for a student of the community is not how abstract a concept may be, but how useful it is. Phrased another way, the question is one of selecting which abstraction is to be used, common sense or scientific. Unfortunately, what is usually meant by the term "abstract" or "theoretical" is neither abstract nor theoretical at all, but "new to the student."

The Practical and the Scientific

A third characteristic of scientific thoughtways is that much of the work is not immediately practical. This may be true from a short-term perspective. The physical sciences abound in examples of completely "pure" scientific findings which serve as a base for practical research and decision. Practicality is not, however, a criterion of scientific work. Pure science is not unrelated to practical judgment even though the practical implications of scientific work may not be immediately discernible. For example, the success of a community development project may succeed or fail depending upon the power structure of the community; however, so little is known about the relationship between power and other community phenomena that

---

[3] Herbert Blumer, "Science Without Concepts," *AJS*, 36:515–34, 1931.

the man of practice is forced to operate by guesswork in his relations with the community power structure. The study of the relationship between power and other community phenomena requires a precise analysis and measure of power which is probably more than a lifetime's work to achieve. Therefore, community development could benefit greatly from the work of a sociologist interested in developing a dependable measure of power, and his measurement would be ultimately more useful if he were allowed to concentrate on the development of a measure, with no concern for its practicality.

Elaboration of the Obvious

The fourth problem in the field of community study is that so often the results seem to be an elaboration of the obvious. Only two points need to be made with respect to this criticism. In the first place, since human relationships are the subject matter for the study of the community, it is no wonder that some of the generalizations about these relationships coincide with individual experience. A second point is that anything is obvious once it has been learned. Calculus is quite obvious to a competent mathematician. The discussion presented so far in this chapter is obvious to the authors. The conclusion is also obvious: the four questions discussed do not involve negative criticisms, but are essential to the development of the kind of knowledge needed in order to integrate science and practical work in communities.

CONCEPTS OF COMMUNITY STRUCTURE

The Common-Sense Concept

What is a community?[4] This question is probably one which only the student will ask; the citizen in general takes his community for granted. The community to the ordinary inhabitant is where he lives, and probably works. It is identified with a place and a name in his mind. It is an aggregation or collection of houses for living and buildings for working. It may have factories, shops of various kinds, no doubt a Main Street, along which are arrayed the chief business establishments. Main Street to him means "downtown," the hub, the center of activity. It is where he goes to shop, to attend a show, to meet friends, or simply to loaf.

---

[4] For a consideration of many definitions of community see: George A. Hiller, Jr., "Definitions of Community: Areas of Agreement," RS, 20:111–23, 1955.

Thus, to the mythical man in the street, the word "community" conveys a meaning which is clear enough for some practical purposes. The difficulty comes either when a student of community behavior wishes to discover more exact knowledge of the community or when a man of action wishes to apply generalizations established concerning communities.

Do these generalizations apply to a hamlet at a crossroad? Or at the other extreme, is the great metropolis a community, or a complex of many communities? Is it necessary, in order to be called a community, for all the members to inhabit a limited area? Is the American Sociological Society with members in all states of the Union and many foreign countries a community? In short, how may a community be defined so that it becomes distinguishable as a concept from other kinds of social groups?

The concept of the inhabitant who takes his community for granted is worth more than a passing thought. His day-by-day round of activities along with those of others like him living within a certain area, constitute what the social scientist must recognize as the community. In trying to fashion a definition which will bring more insight and precision into the later analyses, it is helpful to begin with a description of the events which are generally called a community.[5]

The Local Area

The most obvious fact about the common-sense concept of the community is that it involves an area.[6] There are other social phenomena which are also area concepts, the neighborhood and society. However, the neighborhood is smaller in area than the community. The neighborhood also serves fewer needs than the community.[7] Also the neighborhood is an intimate face-to-

[5] Emile Durkheim, *The Rules of the Sociological Method*, University of Chicago Press, Chicago, Illinois, 1938, p. 14.

[6] See Albert J. Reiss, *A Review and Evaluation of Research on Community*, Vanderbilt University, Nashville, Tennessee, 1954, Chapter II. See also Harold F. Kaufman, Willis A. Sutton, Jr., Frank D. Alexander, and Allen D. Edwards, *Toward a Delineation of Community Research*, Social Science Research Center, Mississippi State College, State College, Mississippi, 1954.

[7] John H. Kolb and Douglas G. Marshall, "Neighborhood-Community Relationships in Rural Society," *University of Wisconsin AES Research Bulletin 154*, Madison, Wisconsin, 1944. The differences between neighborhood and community may be viewed less as a qualitative difference by classifying ecologically based entities; for example, see John H. Kolb, "Service Relations of Town and Country," *University of Wisconsin AES Research Bulletin 58*, Madison, Wisconsin, 1923; Dwight Sanderson and Warren S. Thompson, "The Social Areas of Otsego County," *Cornell University Agricultural Experiment Station Bulletin 422*, Ithaca, New York, 1923; and Frank D. Alexander and Lowry Nelson, "Rural Social Organization in Goodhue County, Minnesota," *Minnesota AES Bulletin 401*, St. Paul, Minnesota, 1949.

face group, while the community, *per se*, is not. Therefore, the generalizations made about neighborhoods will not apply to communities.

Societies are much more autonomous and usually much larger than communities. Society must be organized to satisfy all the needs of man, while the community may leave part of this organization to society. Therefore, the generalizations which apply to society will not usually apply to the community.

The community, then, is between the neighborhood and society, both in size and in the number of needs it satisfies. But more precision is needed in indicating the community area.

Most of the basic needs of man must be served at places within easy daily traveling distance. His work, his place of worship, his place of purchasing goods, and the school for educating his children must all be within a radius easy to reach from his home. Usually these services are all located in a village or urban center. The area within which most of the basic human needs are satisfied is generally what is meant by the community area. Not all the needs must be satisfied in an area for the area to be a community, but most of them must be. Those which are not will vary somewhat, but those listed as examples above are usually included.

The area within which most of the basic human needs are satisfied within daily traveling distance will be referred to in this book as the *local area*.

Area and People

Is the local area itself a community? Obviously not, since a community disappears when all the people leave an area, even though the area remains unchanged. Therefore, a sharp line drawn around an area to indicate a community, found in most research on the community, may be misleading. The area within this line is not the community. The line indicates the area within which the community exists for the most part.

Do the people living within this area represent the community? Again the answer is no. This may be demonstrated by noting that the one population may be replaced by succeeding generations without any essential change in the community. Conversely, the community may change considerably without any change in the population composition.

If the essence of the community is neither area nor people (although both are necessary conditions) what then is the community? The answer is that the community is composed of the relationships among the people living in the local area. These relationships may be abstracted for separate study for two empirical reasons. First, changes in area and population may occur without changes in these relations. For example, the domination of one family over church, school, business, and local government may continue through several generations. Second, changes in the human relations may occur within a single generation and with no change in area. For example, the overthrow of the domination by one family may be brought about over a short period of time by the combined strength of other families.

It is important to point out that changes in population, such as the influx of non-farmers into a farm community, and changes in area, such as the rise of a new center, also produce changes in human relations. These factors will be analyzed in later chapters. The important point in arriving at a concept of the community is that variations in area and people are conditions affecting community but are not the community *per se.*

Elements of Structure

The community is the complex of relations among people within the local area. However, more precision is needed before a useful definition may be given. The concept and its implications are most easily understood by building up to the general, over-all concept from those aspects close to the daily experience of the student.

Groups

In the relationship between two persons, some predictable patterns emerge over a period of time. For example, one person may usually suggest activities, and the other may usually agree. Intimate knowledge of each other in the pair relation may lead to trust or distrust, affection or dislike, cooperation or conflict. The student may most easily see this by listing the "personality traits" of a close friend. However, the predictable behavior patterns often are not personality traits. A given person may be trustworthy, passive, and cooperative with an intimate friend but quite the opposite when interacting with a third person.

Another interesting feature of pair relations is that found between complete strangers. Given certain age, sex, and occupational characteristics and the purpose of the meeting, the relationship between two persons can be predicted within a very narrow range of alternatives. Examples are the casual meeting, the job interview, and student-professor conferences.

The predictable nature of these pair relations is elaborated for two reasons. It represents the first step in building the general concept of structure. It also furnishes an undeniable answer to the frequent and crucial question of whether human relations can be predicted.

The predictable nature of the human relations just discussed depends upon the fact that people usually conform to what is expected of them. These expected patterns of behavior are called *roles*.[8] Such roles are sometimes specific to a given situation, as in the case of a talkative student who will patiently listen to fifty minutes of lecture in a classroom without saying so much as a word.

That people live up to these roles cannot be denied. However, the individual is also a factor in selecting from alternative roles. In the example just mentioned, one person may never ask questions in a classroom, while another may ask frequent questions. These represent alternative roles, and they also show that the individual is not entirely without freedom of action. However, the important feature of the concept at this point in the present treatise is that in the selection of roles, the individual is not entirely free to choose. For example, he cannot dominate the classroom if the person who is playing the role of professor selects the more authoritarian alternative.

The roles that emerge from the interaction of people in the pair relation are often arrived at informally through mutual, implicit agreement. These relations which are predictable and informal are called *group* relations.[9] The discussion of the pair and the college classroom were for the purposes of helping the student understand the concept. Actually, the college classroom is not best understood in terms of the concept of the group, since the classroom is more formal. That is, relations in the classroom are largely, although not entirely, explicit and prescribed. While the pair is usually a group, there are other groups. The maximum number of persons who can interact informally is not known. The number probably varies with the purpose of the interaction. It is evident, however, that of all types of relations, groups involve the smallest number of individuals.

The assumptions underlying structure described here are: (1) Human relations are predictable, (2) one form of predictable behavior is the emergence of informal, implicitly understood patterns, which are called

[8] Ralph Linton, *The Cultural Backgrounds of Personality*, D. Appleton-Century Company, New York, 1945; and Theodore M. Newcomb, *Social Psychology*, The Dryden Press, New York, 1950, especially pp. 264–97.

[9] Charles Horton Cooley, *Social Organization*, Charles Scribner's Sons, New York, 1927; and Paul Hare, Edgar F. Borgatta, and Robert F. Bales, editors, *Small Groups*, Alfred A. Knopf, New York, 1955, and bibliography contained therein.

group relations, and (3) the predictability of these relations depends upon the fact that individuals usually select their roles from a narrow range of expected behavior patterns.

Formal Organization

In many situations, such as the college classroom, roles are formally prescribed. These are organized in such a way that one role may be highly specialized, but taken in toto, they represent a single organization capable of unitary action. For example, the army consists of various specialized roles such as chief of staff, field general, radio operator, and so on. None of these roles involve actual fighting, but they are considered necessary to winning. They operate together in an interdependent way to permit unitary action. Thus, decisions of the chiefs of staff would be meaningless without the field general to see that the decision is implemented. The communications system is also necessary to give instructions to the individuals who implement the decision in the field. It is obvious that some roles are essential, such as the fighting man in the army. But fighting would be less effective, often ineffective, without the roles of planner, communicator, and so on.

Roles are formalized when it is felt that the informal emergence of each role cannot entirely be depended upon to occur. Therefore, for jobs that require the interdependence of more than one role, a formal description of roles, usually written, comes about. Not only is each role described but relations between and among roles are prescribed. This type of interdependence of roles is called *formal organization.* Outstanding examples are bureaucracies [10] and "organizations," [11] such as the Parent-Teachers Association, the Farm Bureau, and a Civic Association.

The features of social structure brought out in the description of formal organization, in addition to those described in the previous section, are: (1) more than one specialized role may be required for a single task in society, and yet (2) the assigned task may require all of these roles to act as one; (3) the roles may then be assigned specialized responsibilities to the larger whole and to assure performance; (4) these responsibilities may

[10] Hans H. Gerth and C. Wright Mills, editors, *From Max Weber: Essays in Sociology,* Oxford University Press, New York, 1946; and Robert K. Merton, Ailsa P. Gray, Barbara Hockey, and Hanan C. Selvin, editors, *Reader in Bureaucracy,* the Free Press, Glencoe, Illinois, 1952.

[11] Dwight Sanderson and Robert A. Polson, *Rural Community Organization,* John Wiley and Sons, New York, 1939, Chapter 7; and Dwight Sanderson, *Rural Sociology and Rural Social Organization,* John Wiley and Sons, New York, 1942, Chapters 22, 23, and 24.

be prescribed in detail, often in writing; (5) this permits the performance of role patterns not directly involved in the assigned task but helpful to accomplishing the task.

Institutions

Some complexes of roles performing a single task are considered more important than others. In fact, some are considered so important that a failure to perform the assigned function would threaten the survival of the whole system of human relations. When this condition is considered to exist, the role expectations take on added characteristics which make them operate under different generalizations. The role, as a code of conduct, becomes mandatory. In addition, no alternative roles are presented to the person. The differences between these mandatory, single-alternative roles and the less mandatory roles previously described are so great that another concept is necessary, namely *mores*. When the codes of conduct for any given job and for relations between jobs take on these characteristics, the complex of roles (i.e. *mores*) are called *institutions*.[12]

However, because of the extreme importance of the tasks performed by institutions, the interrelated parts of the institution take on still more characteristics which reinforce them. Rewards and punishment are included in the codes of conduct, and are meted out for conformity and violation, respectively. Ceremony and rituals are included to give an air of reverence to the codes of conduct. These features further assure conformity, and therefore predictable patterns of behavior. This means, then, that each individual involved in institutional behavior can play his roles, and can depend upon others to play their roles.

The dependence upon others to play their roles is one of the most important features of social structure. The role of the homemaker is important to the maintenance of the family. But the role of homemaker, taken alone, is inconceivable, because there must be the role of bread-winner. Conversely, the role of bread-winner can be played fully only if the role of homemaker is being played. That is, the man can go to the office or plant only if someone can be depended upon to give close supervision to the children, to cook meals, and so on. This is what is meant by "interdependent parts" of structure.

The additional features of structure discussed in this section may be enumerated as follows: (1) playing any one role often depends upon the

[12] F. Stuart Chapin, *Contemporary American Institutions*, Harper and Brothers, New York, 1933; and Joyce O. Hertzler, *Social Institutions*, University of Nebraska Press, Lincoln, Nebraska, 1946.

prediction that others will play their roles; (2) when the task for which these roles are organized is considered crucial to the survival of the whole system of human relations, the role definitions and the definitions of the interrelationships among specialized roles take on additional characteristics; (3) they become mandatory; (4) they are accompanied by severe rewards and punishments for conformity and violation; and (5) are given a sacred connotation, demanding reverence, through ceremony, ritual, and symbols.

Division of Labor

The discussion this far has been concerned with the internal *structure* of group relations, formal organization, and institutional relations. Each of these three types represents structure. That is, behavior is patterned, prescribed, and predictable. Further, the patterns are interdependent, so that one pattern supplements another in working toward a larger purpose. This interdependence allows several patterns to become integrated into a single unit, capable of unitary decision and activity. An institution, for example, may involve thousands of persons, playing thousands of specialized roles, with thousands of prescribed relationships among these roles. The state involves a legislative branch to pass laws, an executive branch to implement these laws, and a judicial branch to judge the consistency of the laws with more fundamental policy and to punish infractions. Each of these branches is in turn divided into subbranches, and still further into smaller divisions. A federal law is no better than the local, say, county, administration of that law. Conversely, local administration is no better than the law which it administers. There is perhaps no better example of the definition of relationships among roles than jurisdiction.

The interdependence of parts may also be seen clearly in the occupational field. A person's work does not directly satisfy all of his own basic needs, but rather satisfies a single need for several people. He receives some medium of exchange for his specialized services, and in turn purchases the other satisfactions he does not produce for himself. In other words, he depends upon others, or he has the expectation that others will "do their job." The dependence placed upon others again implies structure, so that there is some person or persons satisfying every need. The interdependence of specialized roles applies to the work world, where, for example, the role of school teacher could not be performed if someone else were not playing the role of food producer, house builder, and clothing manufacturer. But the organization of roles applies to other needs than the work world. Examples are the role of minister, the role of money handler, and the role of active participant in the solution of problems for which there is no formal organization. The organization of these roles is referred to as the *division of labor,* and varies according to the amount of *specialization.*[13]

Values

People who live in the same area tend to share the same beliefs. These beliefs are of two sorts, goals toward which individuals should strive and the codes of conduct for reaching those goals. Many of these beliefs are almost universal, such as the belief about incest, and some vary from place to place, such as the belief in material comfort in American society. Other beliefs may be held by only some people living in an area, as for example a social class. These beliefs are variously called *mores, folkways, laws, customs, values,* and *norms.*[14] The terms given here differ from one another according to whether a code of conduct is written or implicitly understood, whether the code is held to be crucial to the group survival, and whether the belief characterizes a goal or a means of reaching that goal.

The codes of conduct include rewards and punishment for conforming to or violating socially acceptable behavior. In the case of laws, the rewards and punishments are represented by fines and jail sentences. In the case of unwritten codes, the rewards and punishments come through social pressure and loss of self-respect. No matter whether the rewards and punishments are written or implicitly understood, they are referred to as *social sanctions.*

It has already been mentioned that the concept of *values* encompasses the definition of roles, the relationship among roles, and the sanctions for conformity. In this sense, values represent an integral part of structure. They are, as one author puts it, the blueprint for structure.

Social Differentiation

The role is the set of expectations describing patterns of behavior required to satisfy the need assigned to the role. The pattern of behavior is performed by someone in a particular position in the social structure.

[13] Emile Durkheim, *The Division of Labor in Society,* The Macmillan Company, New York, 1933; Theodore Caplow, *The Sociology of Work,* University of Minnesota Press, Minneapolis, 1954; and Edward Gross, *Work and Society,* Thomas Y. Crowell Co., New York, 1958.
[14] William G. Sumner, *Folkways,* Ginn and Company, Boston, 1906; Robin Williams, *American Society,* Alfred A. Knopf, New York, 1952.

These positions are called *statuses*.[15] Some statuses are assigned higher rewards than others. Some rewards are necessary to the performance of the role obligations, as in the case of a profession in which the job requires irregular office hours. Since the rewards are given differentially, a status system, or *stratification*, develops.[16]

Stratification has other elements important to understanding community behavior. Some roles are assigned to oversee other roles, and, insofar as these are formalized by the value system, these overseeing roles are *authority* roles. Thus a bank president has the authority role over the teller and the janitor. Similarly, some roles are so important that they allow the individuals or groups of persons filling them to transfer the ability to make others act against their own wishes. If this is not formally recognized in the value system, it is referred to as *power*.[17]

Rights and duties also differ with regard to other characteristics. Of particular importance are *age* and *sex*.[18] For example, the division of labor is largely based upon age and sex.

Structure and Function

The internal structures of group relations, formal organizations, and institutions have certain characteristics which allow each of these social entities to act as a unit. It is the array of roles and their interrelationships which allow a rather complicated task to be performed by these social entities. This is essentially what is meant by structure. Each role is patterned to perform a specialized duty. The meaning and often the very existence of a role depend upon the total structure within which it operates.

The variations in structure are great.[19] For example, a formal organization may be structured so that democratic action is necessary for any single decision to be made by the organization. Or the structure may be such that the leader and committees make decisions without discussion and compromise occurring within the membership as a whole. These variations in structure are conditioned by several factors. Tradition, purpose, and the

[15] Ralph Linton, *The Cultural Background of Personality*, D. Appleton-Century Company, New York, 1945.
[16] John F. Cuber and William F. Kenkel, *Social Stratification in the United States*, Appleton-Century-Crofts, New York, 1954; and Reinhard Bendix and Seymour M. Lipset, editors, *Class, Status and Power*, the Free Press, Glencoe, Illinois, 1953.
[17] Gerth and Mills, *op. cit.*, Part II.
[18] Talcott Parsons, "Age and Sex in the Social Structure of the United States," *ASR*, 7:610–13, 1942.
[19] E. T. Hiller, *Social Relations and Structures*, Harper and Brothers, New York, 1947.

orientation of members as well as the greater society within which the organization exists all have influence upon variation in structure.

One of the most important factors influencing variation in structure is the purpose for which the group, formal organization, or institution exists. For example, a small group relation among seven people may arise for the explicit purpose of recreation. The leadership role may change frequently and there may be little obligation of followership role to leadership. One might think of this group as "loosely structured," but this would be misleading. Actually, the group may be dogmatically and rigidly democratic or even *laissez faire*. The explicit purpose is recreation, and the structure is modeled to satisfy the whims of the members at the moment. The fulfillment of the recreational need for which this group is structured is its *function*.[20]

These same seven persons may meet for a different purpose, say, as a committee. The group relations may take an entirely different form. They may elect a chairman who will remain in the leadership position for a long time. They may divide into subcommittees with strong obligations for certain specialized tasks. This difference in structure is brought about by the difference in function.

But suppose that these seven persons meet as a group for both the recreational and the committee functions. The *laissez faire* structure of their recreational activities may inhibit the more formalized structure characteristic of their committee function. This means that structure of the committee is influenced by the structure of the friendship relationship. This, in turn, means that the recreational group in this example has two functions. Its deliberate or *manifest function* is recreation. Its influence over the committee is obvious, but the members are not aware of it nor do they purposely bring it about. This type of function is present, but is different from the function for which the relationship is structured. This is called a *latent function*. There are, of course, many types of latent functions arising which represent an extremely important subject matter for sociological analysis. They extend far beyond the group example, which is used here for purposes of understanding the concept.

There is never a perfect matching of structure to function. This has two implications. It means that there are other conditions affecting structure besides function. It also means that variations in structure, in turn, influence variations in function. The type of structure will affect function in two ways:

[20] Robert K. Merton, *Social Theory and Social Structure*, the Free Press, Glencoe, Illinois, Chapter I.

(1) it will condition the effectiveness of manifest function, and (2) it will condition latent function.

THE MEANING OF COMMUNITY STRUCTURE

Within the local area, any given person knows how to act to avoid criticism and achieve his ends. Further, it is not new to the student to know that people do not act at random, but act pretty much the same every day. This patterning of behavior allows one person to predict the behavior of another in almost any situation. For example, it is interesting to note that in a college classroom where seats are not assigned, almost everyone will sit in the same seat every day. Add to this tendency the fact that disrespect from others accompanies deviation in behavior and the meaning of structure or patterning of behavior is clear.

Not only do individuals pattern their behavior, but groups and institutions do also. For example, the family and the school vary from community to community in the way they cooperate, but in any given community their interaction is pretty much the same over a period of years. If it changes, the change is predictable, and the new pattern will continue for a long time.

Families interact with schools, stores, churches, governments, and so on. They interact within a framework of tradition, expectation, and status. These many patterns of interaction occur more frequently within the local area than between a given local area and outside it. While each interaction, say, family and store can be separated for study, the family-store interaction is influenced by other interactions. For example, it may be influenced by the fact that the head of the family is in the same friendship group as the store manager or in the same church. This network of interactions, influencing one another, may be built up until the community may be considered a galaxy or network of patterns. This network is what is meant by structure.

Elements of the Community

As a unit for analysis, a community is a discrete social structure. It is a useful unit for study because it acts as a single unit and these actions are distinguishable from actions of other social units such as an individual, a family, or a political unit. Although the community is a discrete social structure, this does not imply necessarily that all communities are alike, even though there are certain identifiable characteristics that are common to all communities. Common to all communities, for example, is a system of organizations, but one community may have a Parent-Teachers Association and another not. This is a difference in the kinds of formal organizations, not a difference in structure as such.

If the word "community" is to have meaning as a discrete term beyond merely being a substitute for some other term, then it must describe social phenomena not otherwise designated. There are two such phenomena incorporated in the concept of the community. First is the *relationship* among institutions, groups, formal organizations, or other component units within the community. These relationships are designated as *elements* in this book and they are described in terms of *functions*. Thus, the relationship between the educational institution and the family may be centered around the training of the child which can be either through close cooperation, or by each performing the same function independently of the activity of the other.

Dimensions of the Community

The second phenomenon incorporated in the concept of the community is the variable influences of these elements extending through the breadth and depth of a community. The relationship between the educational institution and the family is an element of the community, but it does not pervade the entire community structure. A change in the relationship between these two, for example, through the action of a P.T.A., may leave most other relationships unaffected. A community may be oriented toward tradition, and this traditionalism will be seen as influencing decisions within a family, between the family and the school, and among all the institutions. It will permeate the entire structure of the local area. Likewise, persons and groups pattern their behavior according to status; that is, the person of higher status will receive deference, will get his way more often, and will enjoy success more often because he is higher in status. This will be seen within a family, e.g., the status of father versus son, or in the relations between the family and the school, and among all the elements of the community. These all-pervasive patterns will be referred to as *dimensions*.[21]

Elements and *dimensions* make up the community *structure*. One com-

---

[21] There has been no term in common usage to refer to these all-pervasive structures which are expressed throughout the other structures in the social world. The term "dimension" was chosen because it has been closest to the meaning intended by the authors. The terminology used is for purposes of distinguishing three types of relations: (1) the component, such as the family, the school, and so on; (2) the element, such as the relationship between the family and the school; and (3) the dimension, such as the relative power of family and school, respectively, in their relations with each other.

munity structure may be characterized as familistic. This means that the elements exhibit a tendency for the family to have higher status, more power in relations with other institutions when a conflict issue is present. This is deemed morally right regardless of the situation or the other institution involved. Thus, it is seen that dimensions condition elements. But also elements qualify dimensions. Status may condition relations between family and school. For example, the higher-status family head may get more attention for his boy than would a lower-status family head. But in the relations between family and church, status may not be a consideration.

Needs and Problems

To understand the nature of the community it is necessary to discuss briefly the nature of needs. There are many attempts to give a listing of fundamental needs, for example, the "four wishes" [22] or "seven instincts." [23] Whatever lists are finally demonstrated empirically, at least it may be said that a need is a state of affairs defined in the value system as desirable. Some of these needs are nearly universal, and are often mistaken as being instinctive rather than being derived from the value system (or culture).[24] The test comes in whether there is a choice between alternative goals. One must have nourishment to live, but one need not eat to live, since pills will furnish nourishment. Even the goal to live is not universal; it is sometimes superseded by its alternative, self-annihilation, more often in some societies than in others.

There are orders of needs or values which vary with structure. These orders may be called the hierarchy of values. In one value system the avoidance of pain and death will take precedence over every competitor, while in another, and in all value systems in times of war, honor will take precedence.

At a less important level in the hierarchy, variation in need and value becomes extremely important in understanding community behavior. For example, in one community, material comfort is of paramount importance, while in another it rates low in the hierarchy.

The definition of needs in terms of the value system leads to at least four types of problems:

[22] W.I. Thomas, *The Unadjusted Girls*, Little, Brown and Company, Boston, 1923.
[23] William McDougall, *Introduction to Social Psychology*, Methuen, Ltd., London, 1908.
[24] L.L. Bernard, *Instinct: A Study in Social Psychology*, Henry Holt and Company, New York, 1924.

The first is the contradiction between two or more values. As a case in point, the school is expected to function in the community to meet the needs defined as educational. Likewise, the school budget is extremely large, often the largest single budget in a small community, which brings the American value on efficiency into the picture. When a judgment is made as to whether to pay a higher salary to obtain teachers with better training, the criteria of budget efficiency and community purpose come into conflict. This is particularly so when the amount of added talent obtained for the extra salary cannot be precisely measured and compared to the extra tax money spent. Another example of conflict in values is the difficulty found in community change when a problem calls for new social forms but strong social sanctions are placed on conformity to traditional ways of behaving.

A second type of problem relevant to the understanding of the community is the contradiction between a value and social structure.[25] An example of this is the value placed on a high level of living in most American communities while the structure prevents a proportion of families from reaching the goal. Someone must collect garbage and clean streets, but there is little reward given for such roles. This presents the problem of the underprivileged, which exists in almost all communities the world over.

A third type of problem is the conflict of values between two subcultures. The parents of school children and the taxpayers represent an example. When new school buildings of a particular sort are felt to be needed by those whose interests are in "better schools," there is often a well-organized opposition to spending the necessary tax money. Often the need is ill-defined, and further, the interests are value judgments in both cases. This problem is usually solved by a majority vote, although this does not solve the taxpayer's need of reaching the community goal of a higher level of living and more money in the bank for security. Of if the vote goes the other way, it does not solve the problem of the community value on "good schools."

The fourth type of problem results from poorly defined roles and functions.[26] The role expectations of the minister may demand a great amount

---

[25] Don Martindale and Elio D. Monachesi, *Elements of Sociology*, Harper and Brothers, New York, 1951, Chapter 23.

[26] Samuel W. Blizzard, "The Roles of the Rural Parish Minister, The Protestant Seminaries, and the Sciences of Social Behavior," *Religious Education*, 1955, pp. 1–10; E.A. Wilkening, *Roles of County Extension Agents*, Preliminary Report No. 2, Department of Rural Sociology, University of Wisconsin, Madison, Wisconsin, 1956; and Emory J. Brown and Albert Deekens, "Roles of the Extension Subject-Matter Specialist," *RS*, 23:263–76, 1958.

of time spent in visiting, if his parishioners have their way; however, the authorities in the church may expect that more time be spent in studying theological matters and in the preparation of sermons.

The Definition of the Community

The components of the community have now been made explicit. First, people learn to desire certain goals which are commonly held and sanctioned by their friends and acquaintances. Second, most of these goals must be satisfied at a place within easy daily traveling distance from each person's home. Third, social structure exists for purposes of solving problems within the local area.

The *community* may therefore be formally defined as *the structuring of elements and dimensions to solve problems which must be or can be solved within the local area.*[27] This definition makes possible several generalizations if the foregoing discussion and definitions are clearly understood.

PRINCIPLES

1. *The generalizations established for society and the neighborhood do not necessarily apply to the community, but are always hypotheses for testing in terms of their application to the community.*

The definition places the community in the general class of social structures based upon the common problems held by people living in a given area. Society is also this type of concept. However, in the world today, societies are autonomous and, except for the exchange of some resources and for international relations, are relatively independent of one another. This means that all the needs of men are problematic to the society, but only needs which require daily or weekly satisfaction are the concern of the community. Thus, generalizations made about society are hypotheses for applications to communities, but need to be tested in each case.

Similarly, the neighborhood is an area concept, but the needs satisfied by the neighborhood structure are fewer. Thus, many generalizations found for neighborhoods, such as those surrounding interaction, identification, and affection, are candidates for community theory, but again must be tested to see if they hold under the different situations set by community living.

[27] See Hiller, *op. cit.*

2. *The community is a general social phenomenon, with school districts, political units, and trade areas representing interdependent parts.*

The concepts of the school community,[28] the trade community,[29] and so on have been isolated for analysis and also are often treated in isolation in the world of practical affairs. The definition of the community shows that while such isolated treatment is permissible and sometimes necessary, the elimination of the remainder of the total community structure from consideration in, say, a school problem is dangerous. This follows from the fact that since the school is organized in relation to other structural elements, a program developed for the school will fail or succeed depending upon the nature of the changes in the other elements of the community: for example, the changes brought about in the taxes of a person by the building of schools. From the point of view of the educational institution, there may be no question as to the need for new schools, but it may still bring about changes in other community elements and dimensions deemed undesirable by the community.

3. *The boundaries of the community are not precise, since they are different for each element of sociocultural organization.*

The school district may differ slightly from the governmental district, and both will differ from the several trade areas. This fact has been established so many times and under such varying conditions that it might safely be called a law of community organization. It has seemed to annoy some students, but this perhaps results from the fact that they have over-emphasized the area aspect. It is true that the definition limits community structure to those problems which must be or actually are satisfied within easy commuting distance of each person's home, but the essence of the community is not area but structure. Area is the distinguishing feature. This will be clearer from the two following principles.

4. *The test of whether a given person or family is a member of any particular community is the amount of influence exerted over him by that community.*

If a person lives in a given area he will almost always purchase his food and clothing, work, go to church, and so on in that area. The prices, sales taxes, wage rates, and church affiliations, respectively, influence his be-

---

[28] See Chapter 17.
[29] See Chapters 3 and 18.

havior and his ability to satisfy his needs. Thus, whether or not he participates in voluntary organizations or identifies with the community symbol through loyalty or interest in events, he may be said to be a member of that community. Much more of his basic behavior may be understood in terms of the limitations and opportunities presented by the community than by his unique psychological characteristics. How he adjusts to the social setting depends in part upon his unique psychological attributes. The first fact necessary to understanding whether or not a person participates in a Parent-Teachers Association is whether there is such an organization in his school. If there is one, then it is desirable for predicting to know his place in the social structure; for example, if he is a school teacher he hardly has the alternative of not participating. Likewise, non-parents are not likely to participate. Then, his attitude toward the particular organization and toward participation generally comes into an important position. The example used is obvious, for purposes of making the point clear, but the operation of the principle is not always so obvious. Many books on community structure and many definitions of the community do not set forth the basic principles of social structure in the local area which underlie the procedures more easily controlled and manipulated to bring about deliberate and purposive change.

The emphasis on area and on psychological identification as defining criteria of the community leads to arbitrary judgment as to boundaries. In a given section completely surrounded by roads, five of the ten families will often trade in community A and the other five in community B. Further, some of those who trade in a given center will not feel any loyalty to that community. The question is, then, is this small section completely surrounded by roads part of Community A? To answer this question either "yes" or "no" requires an arbitrary judgment. A more meaningful way of looking at this question is made explicit in the next proposition.

✓ **5. A given person or family may be a member of more than one community and may be a member of a given community at one time but not another.**

A family may participate, trade, and identify with one community while the breadwinner commutes to another community forty miles away for work. The interchange of influence between community structure and the family then occurs in two local areas. If this family happens to be particularly influential, both communities may feel this influence. Likewise, the family will be affected in the satisfaction of basic needs by what happens to the community structure in two local areas. It could hardly be called precision to place this family in one community and not in the other.

Similarly, a given peripheral section of Community A may switch to Community B in all the family-community relations. This means that Community A is no less a community, but that certain variables or characteristics of that community have been affected. One such characteristic is size, both in terms of population and of area. But other community characteristics may remain unaffected, such as conflict, prices, and opportunities for participation.

The emphasis given the organization aspect of community leads to three of the most important principles of the study of the community that could bear upon either scientific or practical work. The last three principles presented here guide the analysis in the remainder of the book.

6. The community is a single unit, acting as a unit through its interdependent elements and dimensions, rather than an arena within which other social entities, such as families and groups, are interacting.

The previous three principles pointed out that the community concept has suffered from its treatment of the community as an arena within which interaction occurs. The point here is that the community acts just as a person does in choosing between job alternatives, as a nation does in declaring war, and as a family does in building a house. The community has a single problem; it reacts to that problem either through apathy or through discussion or through some other process. Lastly, if a decision is made through its decision-making elements, the community will take action to ameliorate the problem. It may pass a law and enforce it through its political institution, judges, police, and so on. It may hire a contractor to build a bypass around a crowded corner in the business district. It does this with the community budget, independently of family contributions. The point is that the real problem of community structure and change is the behavior of the community as a unit. Will it define its problems, consider alternatives, and take action to ameliorate the problem? These are the basic questions.

7. The conception of the community as structure means that a change in one element or dimension will bring about changes in other elements and dimensions.

Structure means that different parts are fitted together so that they do not contradict each other and so that they may act together, producing a new and unpredicted entity. Perhaps the easiest way to explain this concept is in the meeting of two persons. One person who is extroverted, boisterous, and has had broad experiences in the world of affairs may meet another who is introverted, mild-mannered, and limited in experience. The resulting group, if they form one, will not be predictable from the knowledge given. It would be necessary to know the purpose of the group, whether it is friendship or committee work. It would also be necessary to know the social setting in which these two people meet. The group then is more than an addition of the two personalities; it will be a new product. In a two-man group, the personalities will have strong influence on the nature of the group, but will not be the sole determining factor. As the group increases in size, the influence of any one personality over the group usually becomes less, and a product with even greater differences from the mere addition of personalities results. It is not only personalities which combine to produce interdependence but also values, roles, institutions, and the like.

✓ 8. *Community behavior, the existence of problems, decisions about those problems, and implementation of those decisions, is influenced by three general types of factors: characteristics of the community itself, characteristics of the dimensions and elements within the community, and characteristics of the mass society within which the community exists.*

That community factors, such as size, location, unique history, complexity of structure, and amount of specialization, affect community behavior hardly needs elaboration. There is much research to show rural-urban differences, the effect of population density on community behavior, and the effect of specialization.

The prediction of community behavior cannot be made solely from the knowledge of dimensions and elements, but this does not deny that dimensions and elements are variables which affect the course of events in the community. For example, whether the value system is predominantly oriented toward business or religion makes a difference in the way problems will be viewed, which situations will be considered problematic, and the course of action taken to solve these problems. This will be seen clearly in the chapter on value systems.

The community is not autonomous, but exists within a society which exerts pressures, formal and informal, upon community behavior. For example, American communities are split up so that the boundaries may differ considerably, depending upon the element of the community under consideration. The boundaries of school districts, political divisions, telephone exchanges, and trade areas differ so that problems of one element may not be fully considered in solving the problems of another. This is a function of state and federal legislation, and there is little the community can do about it. Likewise, the advance in television, radio, and transportation has brought greater contact with the mass society. Values are internalized from that mass society which may violate unique community values in some instances. Some religiously oriented communities which frown on the use of tobacco and liquor resent the advertising which appears in national magazines and on TV and radio networks.

Community Organization

In the past, the term "community organization" has been used widely by a variety of authors without much general agreement or precision in meaning. For our purposes here we will try to use the term with a precise meaning in mind. Before we do attach a specific meaning to the term it might be wise to examine some of the ways it is used.

In certain fields such as social welfare, recreation, education, and others, where there is a direct concern for the establishment of some form of community action to improve or change existing conditions, the term "community organization" is used to designate the action program. This use of the term implies the establishment of some kind of organizational machinery devoted to one particular aspect of community life. Thus we find a Community Welfare Council, a Recreation Committee, or similar special interest groups established. In this sense the term is usually employed specifically as community organization for social welfare, recreation, or other purposes.[30]

In some instances, particularly in terms of rural areas, community organization is used to designate the formation of a generalized over-all community council type of structure that is concerned with all aspects of community life. In this instance we may find a Community Improvement Council. A Community Club, or other such generalized organization.

In either case the term is used to denote the establishment of some kind of a supra-community organization with the deliberate and purposive intent of changing the community. It would be more appropriate to refer to these programs as "the organization of the community" for the specific purpose for which the community is being organized.

In its original and more precise meaning, community organization is used by sociologists to identify the way in which the community is organized to carry on its functions and activities rather than as some deliberate extra-community action program. In this use it is sometimes employed synony-

---

[30] Wayne McMillan, *Community Organization for Social Welfare*, University of Chicago Press, Chicago, 1945.

mously with social organization, and is identical with the meaning of structure as used here.

The distinction between these action programs and structure is difficult to maintain. First, both are sociocultural organizations, although "community organization" as a deliberate action program is only a narrow part of the total community. Second, the deliberate program at its beginning is an addition to the total structure of the community, and becomes a part of it. Third, the deliberate program is designed to make still further changes in the structure of the community. That is, the deliberate program is centered on some need, such as the need for a sewage disposal unit, which is not being met by existing elements of the total structure. It is also centered on arousing certain social processes, such as spontaneous democratic action, which are latent in the community structure. Thus, the deliberate action program is coterminous with the existing channels of human action prescribed by the value system of the community. Nevertheless, community organization in the special sense is worthy of separate analysis, since the interests of the man of action are predominantly in this field.

Community Development

Community development is a relatively new term in the social sciences that is growing in popularity but it, too, has a confusion of meanings. In the original use, the term included any action program directed toward the progressive development of the community. As a result, it is sometimes used synonymously with community improvement, progress, change, or the more familiar meaning of community organization. In some foreign cultures the term is now used instead of mass education or adult education.

To be precise, community development, as a term, is applied to the process involved in educating community members to take deliberate action for community change, the nature of which is determined by them in terms of their own value systems. This factor of education is the main distinguishing characteristic that differentiates community development from community organization, for it is means- (process-) oriented rather than end- (or product-) oriented.

Education is used here in the broadest and most inclusive sense. It does not refer to formal, traditional, class-type learning experiences, although these are not excluded necessarily. Education for change is an inseparable part of change itself. Members of the community unit learn how and why to participate in the process of change by being actively involved in changing situations in community life.

The professional person has a specific role in community development, although the latter can and does occur without such professionals being present or involved. In community development professional personnel are the agents for change and function in an educative rather than a change-oriented leadership capacity. They are not themselves the determinants of the change but act in the nature of catalytic agents facilitating the process of change by helping the community acquire the knowledge and skills essential to the successful accomplishment of change.

One of the purposes of this book is to help such professional personnel understand better the nature and characteristics of communities and the forces and components inherent in any deliberative social change, so they can fulfill their role as agents for change in community development. For convenience and to maintain clarity we shall use the term "community development" for all deliberate action programs in the community, whether means- or end-oriented.

SELECTED REFERENCES

Angell, Robert C., "The Moral Integration of American Cities," *AJS*, 57: Part 2, pp. 1–140, 1951.

Brownell, Baker, *The Human Community*, Harper and Brothers, New York, 1950.

Brunner, Edmund deS., *The Growth of a Science*, Harper and Brothers, New York, 1957, Chapter II.

Firey, Walter, "Review of Current Research in Demography and Human Ecology," *ASR*, 17:212–15, 1952.

Hiller, George A., Jr., "Definitions of Community: Areas of Agreement," *RS*, 20:111–23, 1955.

Hughes, Everett C., *Human Communities: The Collected Papers of Robert E. Park*, The Free Press, Glencoe, Illinois, 1952.

Hunter, Floyd, Ruth Connor Schaffer, and Cecil G. Sheps, *Community Organization: Action and Inaction*, University of North Carolina Press, Chapel Hill, 1956.

Kaufman, Harold F., Willis A. Sutton, Jr., Frank D. Alexander, and Allen D. Edwards, *Toward a Delineation of Community Research*, Social Science Research Center, State College, Mississippi, 1954.

Marshall, Douglas G., "Hamlets and Villages in the United States: Their Place in the American Way of Life," *ASR*, 11:159–65, 1946.

Mercer, Blaine E., *The American Community*, Random House, New York, 1956.

Ministry of Community Development, Government of India, *A Guide to Community Development* (written by Douglas Ensminger), January, 1957.

Park, Robert E., *Human Communities: The City and Human Ecology*, the Free Press, Glencoe, Illinois, 1952.

Reiss, Albert J., Jr., *A Review and Evaluation of Research on Community*, Vanderbilt University, Nashville, Tennessee, 1954.

Sanders, Irwin T., *The Community*, The Ronald Press Company, New York, 1958. Rural ?

Sanderson, Dwight, *The Rural Community*, Ginn and Company, New York, 1932, Chapters 1 and 16.

Sanderson, Dwight, and Robert A. Polson, *Rural Community Organization*, John Wiley and Sons, Inc., New York, 1939, Chapters 1, 3, 5, and 14.

Vance, Rupert B., and Nicholas J. Demerath, *The Urban South*, University of North Carolina Press, Chapel Hill, 1955.

Vidich, Arthur J., and Joseph Bensman, *Small Town in Mass Society*, Princeton University Press, Princeton, New Jersey, 1958.

Frontiers of Community Research and Action: A Symposium, May 8, 1958, on the occasion of the retirement of John H. Kolb, Professor of Rural Sociology, University of Wisconsin, Madison.

CHAPTER 2

The Community in Its
Space Relations

The characteristic which distinguishes the community from other social structures is space. The discussion of the local area in Chapter 1 pointed out that of all social entities, only neighborhood, community, and society are primarily distinguished on the basis of space. The "local area" concept rests on the fact that some needs must be satisfied at places within a radius of easy traveling distance within a short time. One's work, his church, his grocery store, and so on, therefore, must be included within the local area. That this is a crucial feature of the community is verified by the fact that advances in transportation have brought about much change in community life, even in aspects of the community not directly contingent upon transportation. This results from the interrelationship of the various elements of the community. Consequently, the variation of space relations among communities the world over is important in understanding structure and change.

THE SMALL COMMUNITY

Most people live in small communities, both in the United States and in the world. Nearly three out of every five persons in the United States live in communities of fewer than 25,000 and nearly two out of every five live in communities with fewer than 2,500, even though the United States is one of the most highly urbanized countries in the world. The proportions are even greater in most other countries. If the number of communities were taken, rather than the number of persons, the importance of the small community would be even more emphatically revealed.

Throughout the world there are many variations in the design of the community layout and in the density of the population which occupies it. Urban communities are usually densely nucleated, with the population

33

pyramided vertically storey by storey. In rural communities throughout most of Asia and much of Europe residences are also grouped, although the population of any one aggregate is limited by the need to have easy access to farm lands in the neighboring fields. In the United States and Canada, and throughout most of South America, farm homes are built on the farms, thus giving rise to a pattern identified as *scattered settlement*. The location of the home on the farm common in North America poses a problem in the delineation of the community. Then, too, communication is much different in a scattered settlement than it is in a village or a city, and participation and group loyalties are affected. The present purpose is to examine the various patterns that have arisen in America.

The farm village is not absent from the American scene, since it occurs in the Rocky Mountain area settled by the Mormons, in the Southwest Spanish-American area, and in other isolated settlements of religious groups, notably the Hutterites in the Prairie Provinces of Canada and in Montana and South Dakota.

In a report prepared for the guidance of settlers in the Columbia Basin, Carl C. Taylor, Walter Goldschmidt, and Glen Taggart suggested the following four types of settlement: (1) Individual locations or scattered settlement; (2) crossroad settlement; (3) village settlement; and (4) line settlement.*

Scattered Settlements

Individual location or scattered settlement in isolated farmsteads can be said to be the most universal pattern prevailing in the United States. This pattern developed primarily out of occupational and work adaptations to a relatively extensive system of agriculture, but was influenced sharply by the quadrangle survey and the Homestead Act passed shortly after population began breaking away from the earlier Atlantic seaboard settlements, many of which were village types. When the great pioneering march of population across the continent began, land was so cheap and plentiful and squatter settlement so universally the rule that the individual isolated farmstead quickly developed into a settlement pattern. When the westward movement penetrated the area of the quadrangle survey the size and shape of farms followed survey lines. When the Homestead Law was passed the typical pattern of the half-mile, perfectly square 160-acre farm was thoroughly established. In earlier settled sections of the country there was a tendency for the farmstead to be located at approximately the center of the farm unit because such a location offered easy access to all fields and pastures. This was modified by such considerations as good drainage, scenic views and avail-

* From Carl C. Taylor, Walter Goldschmidt, and Glen Taggart, *Patterns of Rural Settlement*, Columbia Basin Joint Investigations Problem 10, United States Department of the Interior, Bureau of Reclamation, 1947.

ability of water or trees. In those areas where a complete road system on section lines was established there was an almost universal tendency to locate farmsteads on or near roads rather than in the interior of farms. Seldom were farmsteads located with the predominant purpose of being near to neighbors, but rather they were placed with reference to two predominant foci, convenience to fields and convenience to roads.

As time has gone on, roads have been improved and motor vehicles have replaced horse-drawn vehicles. In order to be near these better roads there has been a slow tendency in the direction of moving farmsteads nearer the edges of farms. This has only modified, not sharply changed, the general pattern of the scattered type of settlement which resulted from each farmstead being located on the individual farm unit and oriented primarily to the problems of farm operation and administration (Fig. 1).

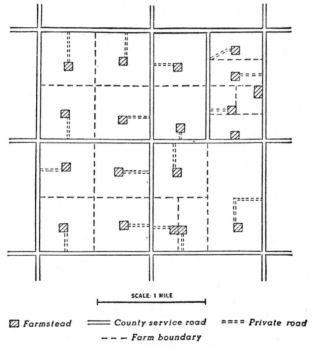

SCALE: 1 MILE

▨ Farmstead   ═══ County service road   ════ Private road

— — — Farm boundary

Fig. 1. Scattered Settlement Pattern

The scattered pattern of settlement is largely indigenous and can in a way be said to be an American creation. Yet it had to establish itself by overcoming the traditional influence of other types of settlement which were carried into the country by early colonists. It is true that many of the Dutch settlers in New York brought such a pattern, and this may have given precept to those who were moving westward. The existence of an immeasurable domain of unsettled lands was a constant invitation to the individuals seeking freedom and security to break away from the social advantages of closer settlement in order to gain the individual ownership of relatively extensive holdings. The typical American farmer in early homestead areas was separated from his nearest neighbor by an average of about one-half a mile in each direction. As succeeding homestead acts enlarged the size of homestead farms, the separation of farm houses became even greater. Such a form of settlement always has had many social disadvantages but today with modern means of transportation many of these disadvantages have been at least partially eliminated.

Crossroads Settlement

At no place in the United States has the crossroads nuclear pattern of settlement been systematically developed. Establishment of farmsteads in corners of holdings in such a way that several lie juxtaposed creates this pattern. It therefore appears sporadically in many places. The *reasons for its existence, however, is always to be found in the choices of individual families who first located the farmsteads and who did so for various and sundry reasons,* probably most often to be at the crossroads of a transportation system or to be near relatives or neighbors—reasons which never had importance to any but a small minority of settlers.

There are numerous instances in American rural life where farmsteads located on individual farms show some tendency to group themselves at crossroads. Although such groups were probably in all cases placed in these locations by design, they can scarcely be called planned settlements, because choice of location was always solely by the individual farm family and not by some overhead planning group. In its simplest and yet most complete form such nuclear settlements consist of four farmsteads at a crossroads. Often there are only two or three farmsteads in these groups and in no section of the country can this tendency in location be said to have established itself as modal (Fig. 2).

A number of theoretical patterns for small clustered settlements have been worked out in one or two cases definitely promoted. Such patterns have taken two

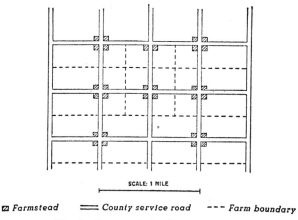

SCALE: 1 MILE

⊠ *Farmstead*   ══ *County service road*   --- *Farm boundary*

Fig. 2. Crossroads Settlement Pattern

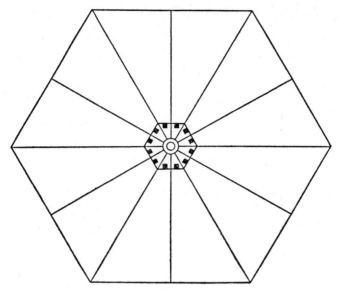

Fig. 3. A Type of Community and Farm Layout Which Is
Perfect Geometrically but Quite Unacceptable from the Standpoint
of Farm Management and Operation °

forms: (1) that which provides for triangular-shaped farms and radial roads with
the farmsteads to be grouped in a cluster at the acute angles of the farms, but
each house to be located upon an individual farm (Fig. 3); (2) the so-called
"F" pattern of settlement which groups eight farm houses (Fig. 4).

William Penn is said to have considered the hexagon form of settlement before
he decided upon the quadrangle pattern, and in one location in Nebraska during

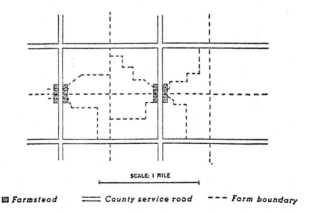

SCALE: 1 MILE

▨ Farmstead   ══ County service road   ⎯ ⎯ ⎯ Farm boundary

Fig. 4. Crossroads Settlement: "F" Pattern

° See Adams, T. "Rural Planning and Development," Ottawa: Canadian Commission
of Conservation, 1917. P. 62.

the 1890's the actual ground surveys for such a settlement were completed but the settlement itself never developed (Fig. 3).[1]

It should be quite apparent that farms of the shape necessitated by this pattern of settlement would be totally unacceptable to farmers, since practically every field and every crop row within a field would necessitate turning acute angles in planting and cultivating.

Figure 3 is presented purely for the purpose of showing how extreme and utopian, and thus impractical, planning can become when the day-by-day necessities of farming are not kept in mind.

Village Settlement

Farm village settlements, although not a common pattern in American rural life, do exist in a number of places. The pattern is quite prevalent in a number of European and Asiatic countries and was transplanted from Europe by early Dutch, English, French, and Spanish colonists.[2] The belief that it was the only form of early settlement is, however, in error. Early southern colonies, except when organized on a plantation basis did not follow the village type of settlement. The shift from this type of settlement began well before the Homestead Law was passed and gained momentum as population moved westward into new lands.

A farm village is created by placing the farmsteads in a compact unit and the number of farm families that can be brought together in a given village is theoretically limited. The size of a village is generally a compromise between the disadvantages of traveling considerable distances from village residences to the farm-operating units, on the one hand, and the social and institutional advantages which accrue from having a relatively large cluster of families per village.

Farmers living in such villages who strongly favor this type of settlement present the following arguments as proof of its advantages: (1) that the size, shape, and organization of the farm need in no way be conditioned by the location of the house and other farm buildings upon it, since it is purely a farm-operating unit and not a place of residence; that it is even possible for a given farm family to own a number of parcels of land, each adapted to a particular type of use but located separately and at considerable distance one from the other; (2) that there are great social and community advantages in the village type of settlement ranging from maintenance and support of such standard institutions as schools and churches to mere sociability.

The disadvantages most often named by families living in such settlements are: (1) The travel between the residence and the fields and pastures increases costs and jeopardizes immediate and constant supervision, especially of livestock enterprises; (2) the location of the livestock in the villages, especially during the

[1] See also T. Adams, *Rural Planning and Development,* Canadian Commission of Conservation, Ottawa, 1917, pp. 62 ff.

[2] H.B. Adams, *Village Communities of Cape Ann and Salem,* Johns Hopkins University Studies in Historical and Political Science, Series 1, Nos. 9–10, Baltimore, 1883; Erving Elton, *Dutch Village Communities on the Hudson,* Johns Hopkins University Studies in Historical and Political Science, Series 4, No. 1, Baltimore, 1886; and F.W. Blackmar, *Spanish Institutions of the Southwest,* Johns Hopkins Press, Baltimore, 1891.

winter months, creates problems of sanitation and makes necessary the hauling of animal manure a considerable distance from the village to farms.

Another disadvantage of the village pattern of farming is seen in the tendency toward fragmentation of holdings. Where the household is not on the land and there is no direct force holding the piece together, the farm tends to break up upon inheritance. This has taken place among the Russians and Hebrews, who developed legal restrictions to curb the trend, and among the early New Englanders.[3] The problem has arisen among the Mormons. Lowry Nelson [4] reports one case in which a farm operator had twelve pieces of land, no two of which were contiguous. This is a very real drawback which would require restrictive legislation of a kind difficult to impose in this country.

Figure 5 shows this pattern with a holding of eighty acres, each in a single lot.

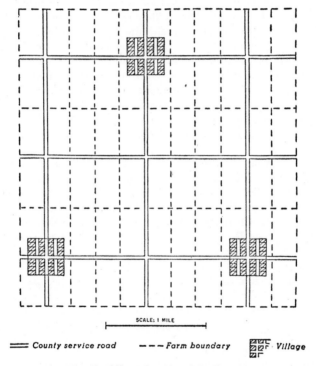

SCALE: 1 MILE

═══ County service road   ─ ─ ─ Farm boundary   ▨▨▛ Village

Fig. 5. Village Pattern of Settlement

In a number of the so-called "utopian communities" the settlement pattern was dictated by the desire to develop the greatest amount of cooperation possible among settlers. In some cases, the communities were completely cooperative. All these communities were established because of the inner unity, religious and

[3] T. Lynn Smith, *The Sociology of Rural Life*, Harper and Brothers, New York, 1940, p. 212.
[4] Lowry Nelson, *The Utah Farm Village of Ephraim*, Study No. 2, Brigham Young University, Provo, Utah, 1928, pp. 11–12.

ideological sanctions among their members. Generally they have been closed social groups. Because of this fact they have tended to disintegrate under the bombardment of various types of stimuli from the "outside world." Amish-Mennonite communities, best illustrated by those in Lancaster County, Pa., have, however, demonstrated considerable capacity to retain their inner unity through the church affiliation of their members even while living on scattered farms, often interstitial with non-Mennonite people.[5]

Line Settlement

There are many examples of line settlements in American rural life varying all the way from line villages or "string towns" to the general pattern which has developed out of the tendency of American farmers to locate their farmsteads on or near the main highways. The basic difference between an inadvertent form of line settlement, which has resulted purely from the establishment of main roads, and the tendency of farmers to locate their houses on these roads, and planned line villages is that in the latter the universal farm pattern is that of long, narrow farm holdings, with one of the narrow ends on an artery of transportation, i.e., fronting a street, a highway, or in some cases a river or a bayou. The farmsteads then line either one or both sides of the roadway or water front. In practically all instances where the line village type of settlement has developed, the average size of farms is small and the length of the farm is four or more times that of its width.[6]

The line village type of settlement in the United States came into existence chiefly under French influence, in Louisiana, and in a few places in the Mississippi Valley and the Lake States region which were settled early by French colonists. It also developed, however, to a considerable extent in southern New England, best illustrated in the Connecticut Valley. Here "the distribution of town lands was based on two considerations: each proprietor must have access to the river and each must also receive an equal share of the fertile meadow and the less productive but safer and hillier upland as the terrace was called." [7] This pattern, once established on river fronts, was carried inland and became an established pattern in a number of places. Roads and electric lines were constructed to accommodate and in turn serve to further develop this type of settlement. There

[5] Walter M. Kollmorgen, *Culture of a Contemporary Rural Community, the Old Order Amish of Lancaster County, Pennsylvania*, Rural Life Study No. 4, United States Department of Agriculture, Bureau of Agricultural Economics, Washington, D.C., September 1942. Also see L.E. Deets, "Data on Utopia," *Sociology*, Vol. III, No. 3, Hunter College, New York, 1940; L.E. Deets, *The Hutterites: a Study in Social Cohesion*, Hunter College, New York, 1939; and E.F. Row, *Communist and Cooperative Colonies*, Thomas Y. Crowell Co., New York, 1930.

[6] T. Lynn Smith, "An Analysis of Rural Social Organization Among the French-Speaking People of Southern Louisiana," *JFE*, 16:680–88, 1934; Horace Miner, *St. Denis, a French-Canadian Parish*, Chapter III, University of Chicago, Chicago, 1939; Edna Schofield, "The Origin of Settlement Patterns in Rural New England," *Geographical Review*, New York, October, 1938; and Martha Krug Genthe, "Valley Towns in Connecticut," *Bulletin of the American Geographical Society*, Chapter XXXIX, New York, 1937.

[7] Martha Krug Genthe, *op. cit.*

are areas in the Connecticut Valley where today farm houses are so closely spaced on main highways as to constitute an almost continuous line village. It is also quite prevalent in the French sections of Louisiana and the universal rule in certain parishes in the Province of Quebec in Canada.

This type of settlement can be easily visualized from the knowledge that a 40-acre farm, if four times as long as it is wide, is 220 yards wide and 880 yards long (see Fig. 6). Thus farm houses along one side of a road upon which farms

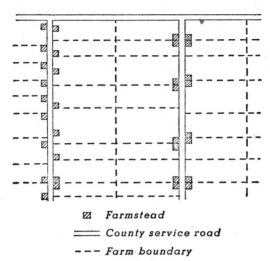

☑   Farmstead

══ County service road

─ ─ ─ Farm boundary

Fig. 6. Line Settlement Pattern:
Free and Clustered

of this shape and size are located average 220 yards apart. If houses are located on both sides of the road, they then average only 110 yards apart. Because the homes are so near each other, such an arrangement of farm residences literally constitutes a line village. In the case of some French-Canadian line villages, the farms are more than a mile long and only 400 feet wide.

There is practically no limit to the number of farm houses which may be located in this pattern of settlement. Where the pattern prevails, however, as in the Province of Quebec in Canada or in some of the sugar cane areas of Louisiana, a continuous settlement miles in length is organized into a number of adjoining line villages each with its own set of institutions and service agencies.

In the line settlement pattern, houses can be located on the individual farms according to the choice of each farm family. They can be evenly spaced with equal distance between them, grouped by two's or four's at the corners of the farms, be located exactly opposite each other or systematically staggered on the two sides of the road. It is even possible for an individual family to locate its farmstead elsewhere than on the road if it prefers to have the farmstead near the center of the farm. Figure 6 shows the various patterns of settlement which would result or be possible if all farms were 80 acres in size, four times as long as they are wide, and fronting both sides on the road.

Beyond providing an infallible system of land description and location, the rectangular survey had very important social consequences for that portion of the United States over which it was effective. The "quarter section" (160 acres) became the unit for individual settler acquisition. The township of the surveyor (i.e., 36 square miles) became the unit of local government in a number of states. In connection with the requirements for residence on the land, imposed particularly by the Pre-emption law of 1841 and the Homestead law of 1862, the rectangular survey made for scattered holdings instead of villages. The checker-board pattern increased physical isolation; in a time when distance was much more important than it is today, roads had to follow the section lines, cutting square corners instead of following the diagonal. In short, the invention of the rectangular survey affected practically all the generalizations that could be made about community organization in the past, with the exception of a few large urban communities. This influence is likely to remain for some time to come, for the institutions of government and (to a lesser extent) the schools are strongly conditioned by the system. Therefore, the relations between these institutions and other elements of the community are affected.

The Line Village in Louisiana

The only extensive areas in which the line village exists in North America are in Quebec, Canada, and in Louisiana, where "exiles" from French Canada settled. The line village occurs widely in France, and it is from the "motherland" that the North American patterns are derived. This form of settlement is clearly imbedded in French rural culture. In the selection to follow,* T. Lynn Smith discusses some advantages and disadvantages of the various forms of settlement and describes the forms which occur in Louisiana, including especially the line village. However, he points out the existence of several different types of aggregations of rural people occurring contemporaneously in that state. The various types exist in practically all parts of the world, with villages predominant in certain regions and dispersed farmsteads in others.

From a sociological point of view, the village community type of organization tends to attain a high degree of social integration and coordination at the expense of a low degree of economic integration. Ecologically, the village community is characterized by farmers' homes being grouped in close proximity to one another in village or hamlet and at a distance from the fields the farmers

---

* T. Lynn Smith, "Farm Trade Centers in Louisiana, 1901–1931," *Louisiana AES Bulletin No. 234,* 1933, pp. 1–5.

cultivate and the pastures their cattle feed upon. Daily trips to and from the fields to perform the acts of cultivation are necessary. Tools, machinery, seed, feed, etc., must also be transported between the village proper and the fields. Daily the livestock must be driven to the pastures and daily returned to the village. Under such a system the relationships between the households are close and intimate. Lines of cleavage of the special interest groups practically all coincide, resulting in a high degree of social solidarity. But the relationships between the family group and the land are more removed and intermittent.

The isolated farm system of organization contrasts very sharply with the village community. In it, a high degree of economic integration may be said to be obtained at the expense of a low degree of social integration. Ecologically, the dwellings of the farmers are scattered throughout the area of the community with little or no attention being given to placing them in close proximity to one another. Every man's dwelling is upon the plot of ground he cultivates. No daily trips from dwellings to fields are necessary. All the operations of agricultural production are carried on in the immediate neighborhood of the home. The relationships of the farm family to the land are constant and unbroken. Economic activities are highly integrated and coordinated, but social activities operate more haphazardly. Children may be sent in one direction to a school; the family may go in another on Sunday to gather at some church; lodge meetings may occasionally take part of the members of the family to another gathering place; and once or twice a week a village trading center is visited to dispose of produce or purchase supplies. Contacts with others, in this system of isolated farms, are less intimate and numerous, and more haphazard than in the village community. The lines of cleavage of the different interests fail to coincide. One's neighbors (those living nearest geographically) are less frequently members of the same kinship, religious, political, economic, fraternal, and recreational groups. In general, the pattern of social organization is much more complex, differentiated, and unintegrated.

The family living in a village community has the advantage of close and intimate contact with neighbors, with trading facilities, and with social institutions, organizations, and association. It has the disadvantage of making frequent trips to the fields, transporting bulky machinery and materials to and fro, and of constantly driving the livestock back and forth. The exceptional opportunities furnished for prying and gossiping are also probably to be listed as a disadvantage. The family on an isolated farm has the advantage of close, continuous contact with the agricultural processes and equipment. All the activities on the farm are carried on in the immediate vicinity of the home. But the opportunities to trade, to attend schools and churches, and to mingle with friends are curtailed.

The part played by the village center in these two types of organization is important. In the village community, the village center is primarily the seat of the homes of the farmers, and a center for the churches, schools, and other social institutions. Some shops for trading purposes are also present, but it is not primarily a trading center. In the isolated farm pattern of rural organization, however, the village is primarily a trading center. Few farmers dwell within its limits. It functions only secondarily as a center for schools and churches.

Forms of Rural Organization in Louisiana

Rural organization in Louisiana is primarily of the isolated farm type, although modified forms of the village community type and some intermediate types are also to be found. The presence of both the "family-size" and the "plantation" systems of farming complicates the pattern. Some of the variations will be indicated.

In a large portion of Louisiana the system of family-sized farms is similar to that prevailing in the United States in general. In the rolling or "hill" lands lying between the Mississippi and Red Rivers in Northern Louisiana, in the hill country south of the Red River, in the rice growing area of Southwestern Louisiana, and in the fruit and trucking section of the Florida parishes, such a system prevails. Lands are commonly divided according to the "checkerboard" system; each farmer lives on the plot of land he cultivates, the village is a trade center. At present schools are consolidated and usually located in a trade center, but occasionally they are to be found in the open country. Churches are located here and there in the open country to an extent characteristic of middle-western United States thirty years ago. Ecological similarities to the middle west, however, are much greater than the differences.

Parts of Southern Louisiana which were settled by French-speaking people exhibit an interesting variation growing out of the family-sized farm. Land was not divided according to the "checkerboard" system. Rather a river or bayou was selected as the point of departure and holdings plotted, measuring so many arpents along the river. The breadth was generally very small as compared with the length, which made the holdings a series of long narrow strips lying side by side. Rivers and bayous seldom run in a straight line for any great distance, and since they were the points of departure a somewhat confused picture has resulted. . . . Passing the land from one generation to another has further complicated the pattern. Whenever the land is subdivided, the division is invariably lengthwise, thus retaining the full length of the strips, all holdings continuing to front or head on the river or bayou. When roads are built they usually follow the bank of the stream. The significant thing for present purposes is that all dwellings are built at the end of the strip nearest the stream.[8] For miles and miles the river or bayou front presents the appearance of a long one-street village with all the houses on one side. Occasionally a school or church is found and here and there a small trading center. Plantations are interspersed among the small holdings in some localities. But the differentiation is not clear, fully developed, nor well defined. This form of organization contains elements of both the isolated farm and the village community types. This system is largely confined to Southeastern Louisiana, although in the rice area of Southwestern Louisiana it prevails along the stream fronts. It is interesting to note that in the rice area just back of these strips, large rice farms are laid out on the "checkerboard" system. The extent

[8] This system of land holding has been of great advantage from the point of view of road building. One road put through an area passes by the doors of everyone living in the region. The demand and necessity for putting an improved road around every square mile of land is absent.

to which other cultural factors coincide with the line of cleavage between these systems of land holding is remarkable.

The plantation system of farming has two main subdivisions. Cotton plantations are concentrated in the deltas of the Mississippi and Red Rivers, while cane plantations, interspersed with small holdings along the bayous and rivers, are found in Southeastern Louisiana. Cotton plantations present a variation of the isolated farm type of agriculture. The owner may live on the plantation or in a nearby town or village. But each family of tenants or croppers usually has its separate cabin located upon the plot of ground it cares for, so that cabins are scattered all about the plantation. In most cases the families are colored.[9] Social activities and ties are confined principally to the plantation and its immediate vicinity. As a rule both schools and churches are in close proximity to, if not upon, the plantation. And the owner of the plantation does most of the trading for the families upon his place, or frequently operates his own general store or commissary.

On the cane plantations in Southeastern Louisiana, a system of organization is present which more closely resembles the village community. As a rule cane is produced on plantations not by a group of croppers, but by an overseer and hired laborers. Dwellings of the laborers are grouped together in a small village, often beside a sugar house, and a short distance from the plantation homes of the owner and overseer. In this case a general store, at which the laborers are permitted to draw commodities up to a certain amount per week or month, is nearly always operated in connection with the plantation. Social activities are largely confined to the plantation and its immediate vicinity. Institutions are difficult to maintain, owing to the great mobility of the laboring population—the turnover among the laborers being very rapid.

THE LARGE COMMUNITY

The space relations of the large community differ from those of the smaller in at least two important ways. The "hinterland" of the business core, or "loop," is densely populated, not only within the juridical limits, but even beyond them, including the suburban fringe. The "hinterland" of the village, by contrast, is sparsely populated. Second, the urban loop dominates the social structure of the large community to a greater extent than is true of its counterpart (the village) in the small community. In the small community, also, the village center and the hinterland are more distinct in terms of their interests. Town-country relations may be of considerable importance in understainding the structure of the small community, but no comparable dichotomy exists in the large community.

An important similarity exists between the space relations of the large and small community. The zones, following roughly the pattern of con-

---

[9] In many of the delta cotton parishes over 70 per cent of the inhabitants are Negroes.

centric circles, represent differences in style of life in both the small and the large community. Figure 7 shows these zones for one city. The theory is that most cities follow this general pattern, although instead of the concentric rings, as in Chicago, they may be rectangular or star-patterned in other cities.

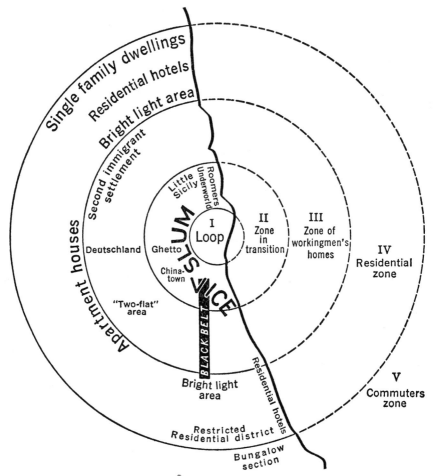

Fig. 7. Concentric Circle Pattern: Zones of Chicago [10]

The zones are produced by various historical factors. Cities grow outward from the business centers and therefore the center of most cities is the business hub. The necessities brought about by the economic structure re-

[10] R.E. Park and E.W. Burgess, *The City*, University of Chicago Press, Chicago, 1925, p. 55. Reproduced in William F. Ogburn and Meyer F. Nimkoff, *Sociology*, Houghton-Mifflin Company, Boston, 1950, p. 283.

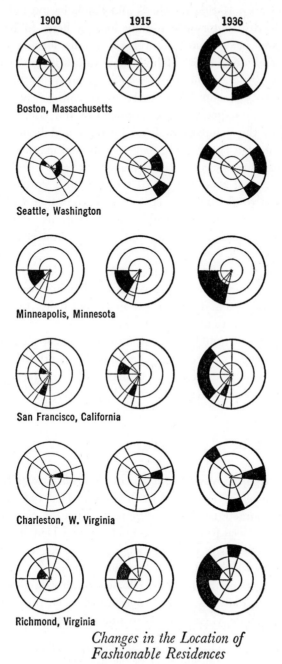

*Changes in the Location of
Fashionable Residences*

Fig. 8. Changes in the Location of
Fashionable Residences

quire that the transportation terminals and hotels be located in the central hub. Wholesale distributors are usually located here, to be close to the buyers. However, heavy manufacturing is usually located elsewhere, because of the combined factors of high land values in the central hub and because there is little advantage derived from proximity to other types of business. Initially, the central zone includes a wealthy residential area. The houses here are maintained through sentiment by the older families of name and wealth, but the competition from business and light manufacturing, with consequent high land values, makes continued maintenance extremely difficult. The usual result is a gradual movement to new residential areas.[11]

Outside the central zone is Zone II, which is in a state of deterioration. Formerly, it was residential, but it is now in transition with the business district expanding into it. The zone of transition is characterized by slums, high rates of delinquency, disease, and poverty. Minority groups of low status live in this zone.

Zone III is made up of the homes of skilled workers, interspersed with small shopping centers. Zone IV is made up of better residential areas including residential hotels. There is less apartment house living in this area. In Zone V, often in part outside the city, live the newly rich, the commuter, the white collar worker, and the truck farmer. A major pattern of variation from the zone theory is the growth along fast transportation lines, giving a star effect. The general patterns of growth and the effects of changes in residences of the wealthy may be seen in Figure 8.[12]

FUNCTIONS OF SPACE RELATIONS

Preliminary attention was given to the functions of proximity and distance in the discussion of the local area in Chapter 1. That the local area is the distinguishing characteristic of community structure as contrasted with society and other social forms was made clear at that point. More complete description is needed here of the functions which the local area fulfills to see the conditions which produce community structure.

The first function of the local area is accessibility of those institutional services furnishing daily needs. In a non-farm family, proximity to work is essential. Also essential is easy access to stores for the purchase of groceries

[11] See Homer Hoyt, *The Structure and Growth of Residential Neighborhoods in American Cities*, Federal Housing Administration, Washington, D.C., 1939.
[12] *Ibid.*

and certain other economic goods. The services of government and the economic institution, such as utilities, is often most effectively administered in a small local area. Travel to schools requires a small district even with modern transportation. Weekly attendance at church is likewise an activity within the local area.

The second function of the local area arises from the fact that all the institutional services of a village center or a city influence each other. They must necessarily agree upon their interrelations to avoid naked conflict when interests differ greatly. Further, they develop common beliefs, and some individuals and groups get higher prestige, more power, and so on. It may be seen, then, that the discussion in the first chapter showing that structure exists coterminously with the local area may be reversed to show that the nature of living in a local area sets up a condition making that structure necessary. The relations between the church, school, local government, businesses, and the rest are natural outgrowths of the problems of living in the local area. Common beliefs arise about these relations because they serve the same people. Status systems arise and communication exists essentially because of this common community living. Therefore, the local area is more than a defining criterion but is a causal condition producing a social structure with its dimensions and its elements.

Since the relations between institutions and the belief and status systems occur in the local area, it is obvious that many of the specific human relations within the area will be problematic. That is, just living together in a small area produces problems. This is another function, then, of the local area; it produces common problems for which adjustments must come in the community structure. The need of a stop sign at a given road, the need for better sewage disposal, the problem of delinquency, all these affect mainly those living in a given area and are problems because they live in this common area.

Still another function of the local area thus may be seen to result from the two facts just presented, namely, the community structure and the community problem. The problem requires some change in the structure if a solution is to be brought about. This is, by definition, social change. Therefore, the nature of local problems is a condition leading to social change. The ecological factor also produces another type of social change. It is that type brought about by changes in the physical environment itself. Since the local area is essentially an adjustment to the physical surroundings in relation to need, then changes in the relation between these surroundings and need will bring social change. There are numerous examples of changing economic demands "booming" and "busting" communities because of their resources in the physical environment. In one sense this change is brought about by the economic institution, but most properly it is a combination of economic and physical variables.

The pattern of settlement becomes a value in itself to the residents.[13] In the Blue Ridge Mountains the people live on small farms in scattered settlements. Because the land holdings are small the farm homes are not widely separated and dot the sides of the coves and hollows. When large sections of the Blue Ridge were incorporated into the Shenandoah National Park in the early thirties, the Federal Government established the Resettlement Administration to handle the problem of moving the mountain residents and re-establishing them on new farms in the valley and piedmont sections of Virginia.

Social planners in the Resettlement Administration designed and built model farm village communities with the houses, church, and school in the center and the farm land radiating out from this hub like spokes of a wheel. The facilities in this new community were far superior to the homes and farms which the people were forced to abandon, yet they would not remain long in the village settlement. Eventually the Government was forced to abandon and sell these model communities so that none remain intact today.

The farm-village pattern of settlement was unfamiliar and unacceptable to the mountain people who had lived in a scattered settlement pattern for generations. This attempt at resettlement of people from one pattern to another illustrates the difficulties inherent in any community development program that does not take into account the established living patterns of the people involved. It illustrates further the importance of the pattern of land settlement to the residents.

In analyzing the problem of the relationship between physical environment and structure it is important to see the relationship between the two, but it is also important to see where the relationship does not exist. Often a one-to-one relation is posited, as if the physical environment were the determining factor in the resulting community structure. The previous part of this chapter should show that the nature of the physical environment does influence the nature of the social structure. (See also Chapter 4.) But it also shows that given the same environment, different social structures appear, and given different environments, the same types of social structures appear. This oversimplification is closely associated with the single factor fallacy of economic determinism. (See the chapter on the economic institution.)

[13] Lura Beam, A Maine Hamlet, Wilfred Funk, Inc., New York, 1957.

Space relations, in addition to being a causal condition in producing community structure, also influence that structure in other ways. First, the community exists within a region and within a society and this will influence the structure considerably. For example, Southern communities, collectively, differ in many ways from Northern and Western communities because of the region in which they are located. Various ecological factors, including the regional economic history of agriculture, produced certain relations between laborers and farm owners, between Negroes and whites, and many other dimensions and elements of social structure unique to the Southern community. This is not to say that, for example, a lower status for Negroes is nonexistent in the Northern community, but it is of a considerably different order. Would the abolition movement have started had New England found cotton-growing profitable and used the same means of obtaining a labor supply?

Another aspect of this influence on social structure comes from within the structure rather than from without, as was the case with regions and society. Within any community, even very small ones, one form of segmentation is the neighborhood, also an area-based group. In the neighborhood, a social structure is based on one or two services and the need for "neighboring." It is one form of friendship grouping, larger than the family and clique group, but often nearly as intimate. This form of interaction is partly due to the fact that proximity is a necessary condition for intimate interaction. This is less true with modern transportation, but the change is really a matter of degree, since the non-family friendship grouping still must stay within a relatively small radius.

The Relation between Size and Structure

It is obvious that the number of people occupying a limited area is closely correlated with the degree of complexity of the community structure. The larger the community the greater the number of business units providing goods and services. The number of groupings of various types, informal as well as formal, increases with size. Face-to-face, intimate, interpersonal relations give way to more impersonal contacts and anonymity.[14] Otis D. Duncan and Albert J. Reiss, Jr. have shown that the median age of the population varies directly with size of place, as do also median cash income and proportions of the population single, widowed, and divorced. They found an inverse relationship between size and the following characteristics: mobility, percentage of native whites in the population, fertility ratio (children

[14] See Louis Wirth, "Urbanism as a Way of Life," *AJS*, 44:1–24, 1938.

under 5 per 1,000 women 20–44 years of age), proportion of population 65 and over, and the percentage married.[15]

Community Distribution Pattern

While size is important in determining the internal structure of the community, it in turn is a result of demographic and ecological forces. The ultimate source of population growth is the excess of births over deaths, but any given community in a society where persons are free to move about may not increase and may even decline, in spite of a high rate of natural increase. Why some communities grow and others do not, then, is due to the influence of migration. Because of a favorable location in regard to transportation, markets, natural resources, and the establishment of industry, a center may assume a position of dominance over a large area. The area immediately adjacent to such a center, say a county or several adjacent counties, is called a metropolitan area, while it may also be the dominant focus of activity representing a region composed of several states in whole or in part. Other centers in its area of influence will vary in size according to their relation to the major one. They form a sort of gradient from the comparatively large centers dominating the subareas and extending out to the small hamlet and the open country.

The result of the competition for survival and growth among communities in a given area is a configuration of service centers clearly related to distance. This spatial patterning according to size is of sufficient regularity that it has been found to fit rather neatly into a formula based upon size and distance. This phenomenon of spacing by size gives rise to a hierarchical arrangement of services and functions and hence to a corresponding variation in structure which is our concern in this book.[16]

PRINCIPLES

1. *The social phenomenon called community evolves out of the necessity of having human needs satisfied by institutions and other elements of the social system within a local area.*

[15] The variations in demographic features according to size are revealed in the elaborate statistical analysis of census data reported in Otis D. Duncan and Albert J. Reiss, Jr., *Social Characteristics of Urban and Rural Communities,* 1950, John Wiley and Sons, Inc., New York, 1956. See also Chauncy D. Harris and Edward L. Ullman, "The Nature of Cities," *The Annals,* 242:7–17, 1945.

[16] For further treatment of spatial distribution see Charles T. Stewart, "The Size and Spacing of Cities," *GR,* 48:223–45, 1958; Edward Ullman, "A Theory of Location of Cities," *AJS,* 46:853–64, 1941.

2. *The manner and extent to which these elements satisfy these needs is influenced by the geographic or ecological pattern of the utilization of space within the community.*

3. *The predominant pattern of rural communities in the United States is the scattered settlement, while in the world it is the village settlement.*

4. *In the scattered settlement the economic producer function of the family is carried on more easily, but the relations between the family and the community institutions, including social participation and economic exchange, is more difficult than in the village settlement.*

5. *It may be seen therefore that in the scattered settlement of farmsteads about a village center, the relation between the village and the surrounding farm area may represent potentially a divisive factor working against the feeling of community.*

6. *This may be true even though, in terms of support of the community institutions and dependence upon them, the farmer is a member of the community.*

7. *Yet the farmer exercises less influence over the course of action taken by many of those institutions than does the villager.*

SELECTED REFERENCES

Bell, Wendell, "The Social Areas of the San Francisco Bay Region," *ASR*, 18:39–47, 1953.

Brunner, Edmund deS., and Wilbur C. Hallenbeck, *American Society: Urban and Rural Patterns*, Harper and Brothers, New York, 1954.

Dewey, Richard, "The Neighborhood, Urban Ecology, and City Planners," *ASR*, 15:502–7, 1950.

Gilmore, H.W., "The Old New Orleans and the New: A Case for Ecology," *ASR*, 9:385–94, 1944.

Kligman, Miriam, "Human Ecology and the City Planning Movement," *Social Forces*, 24:89–95, 1945.

McMahan, C.A., *The People of Atlanta*, University of Georgia Press, Athens, 1950.

Mercer, Blaine E., *The American Community*, Random House, New York, 1956, Chapter 2.

Park, Robert E., *Human Communities: The City and Human Ecology*, the Free Press, Glencoe, Illinois, 1952.

Robinson, W.S., "Ecological Correlations and the Behavior of Individuals," *ASR*, 15:351–57, 1950.

Sanders, Irwin T., *The Community*, The Ronald Press Company, New York, 1958, Chapters 1 and 19.

Scaff, Alvin H., "The Effect of Commuting on Participation in Community Organization," *ASR*, 17:215–20, 1952.

Voss, J. Ellis, *Ocean City: An Ecological Analysis of a Satellite Community*, University of Pennsylvania Press, Philadelphia, 1941.

Zorbaugh, Harvey W., *The Gold Coast and the Slum*, University of Chicago Press, Chicago, 1929.

CHAPTER 3

Regional Variations in the Community

Variation in community structure is the fundamental problem in the study of the community. As mentioned in Chapter 1, this variation may be studied in terms of the social action taken by the community in defining and solving the problems. Variation in the community is found to correlate with various types of conditions: within community variables, elements and dimensions of the community, as well as pan-community factors. It has already been mentioned that throughout the book, societal influences on community variation will be analyzed and described. However, within the society, variations in structure are found by region, with Western communities differing in some respects more from Northern and Southern communities than they do from each other. The problem of this chapter is to show the ways in which the region influences community structure.

To speak of regions is to speak geographically. This is not to admit to any theory of geographic determinism, but merely to note the fact that regions are identified by geographic features. Thus we have the Great Plains, the Atlantic and Pacific coastal areas, the Gulf Coast, and so on. The relation of man to his physical environment is a problem of ancient concern. That there is a relation is quite obvious, but the nature of that relationship is not always so clear. The social structure of the community, particularly the economic system, is limited by the geographic factor, but as Robert S. Platt points out, there are always more alternatives than that chosen by the community. This raises two basic questions. What limitation does the geographic factor impose on the social structure of the community? The answer to this is found in a close look at the geographic environment itself. Among the social alternatives allowed by the environment, why the particular one chosen by the community? The answer to this is to be found only in factors other than the geographic environment. One of the most intelligent discussions of the relationship between the natural environment and structure is found in the following excerpt:

The Interrelationship of Man and Environment *

It is misleading to advance the hypothesis of an active influence of natural environment tending to shape human life in the natural and proper way and to look for coincidences between environment and life as evidence confirming this hypothesis. Increasing evidence shows that the hypothesis of a simple and direct relationship is not thus confirmed, that there is no proper natural way of shaping life but innumerable ways, not sorted out by nature but reduced by man's choices past and present. People live differently in similar environments and differently at different times in the same environment, without feeling any environmental pressure to lessen these differences.

In equatorial regions savage life is natural, but all the other forms of life there are natural also. There are not only jungle savages living in many different ways but also in the same region many people who are not savages and are under no inducement to become so. On the contrary, some of them are engaged in horticultural enterprises as highly developed as any in the world. In addition, there are innumerable untried possibilities for other ways of living, some of which would require thousands of years for full realization through the development of plant or animal resources. In any given type of regional environment, people have alternative ways of living, apparently many in some places and few in others. Probably everywhere the conceivable number of possibilities is far greater than people can imagine and far beyond the range of choice now open to them.

Actually, people are limited by things other than natural environment, though set within the confines of that environment. Particularly are they limited by habits they have learned and facilities available to them, accumulated through an unbroken series of choices and rejections in the entire course of their history—in other words, by the cultural heritage of the group to which they belong, by their culture defined in the broadest sense. The choices made in the past which now limit people in their activities have been impelled not by natural environment but by the play of history thereafter embodied in their culture.

For example, in the Great Lakes region farmers have been limited agriculturally to a certain range of possibilities, mainly involving cereals and livestock. But if some of our ancestors at the dawn of civilization had not chosen to domesticate certain grasses as cereals and certain four-footed animals as livestock but, instead, had chosen to develop fungus growths or edible insects as a basis of productive culture, our mode of life might be now utterly different in ways which the natural environment might support as well as it does our present agriculture, or conceivably better.

Likewise, in all history there are innumerable possibilities within the same natural environment. It was natural for Napoleon to have been defeated at Waterloo; but another outcome would have been no less in accord with nature. Napoleon might have won the battle, or there might have been no Battle of Waterloo, or no Napoleon, or no France, or no nations of the type which France represents. Simi-

* Robert S. Platt, "Environmentalism Versus Geography," AJS, 53:351–58, 1948. Reprinted by permission of the University of Chicago Press, Copyright 1948.

larly, the United States might not have dug the Panama Canal. Instead, in the same natural environment, the French might have finished the canal, or the United States might have dug a Nicaraguan canal or no canal at all, or there might have been no United States at all.

At the present moment in history we see a complex assortment of events which may lead to any one of numerous different possibilities in world order or disorder, depending on many circumstances other than natural environment, including individual decisions and inconspicuous incidents. But when the present period is observed from the perspective of some future generation, the trend of events in our time will seem to have been natural if not inevitable, no matter what alternative courses of action now seem open to us in the same natural environment.

So our relation to the natural environment is one of intricate and perpetual association historically, culturally, and biologically. In addition, our very conception of the natural environment is molded by our history and culture. The distinctions which we make between different areas of the natural environment are governed by our ideas of what differences in natural environment are significant for one or another sort of occupancy with which we happen to be familiar. The very word "environment" implies conditions surrounding something; specific-conditions surrounding certain people, in one case, or certain bacteria, in another case.

Therefore, the types of natural environment in physical science are actually expressions of social science in their dependence upon cultural criteria. We may describe a region of rolling plains or of dry subtropical climate in physical terms of altitude and annual rainfall; but our distinctions are made through human experience and for human occupancy under known forms of culture.[1] We may calculate the population capacity of the Amazon Basin or of Illinois; but apart from precise cultural specifications our figures are meaningless: the potential range on an absolute basis would be far beyond any possible calculation.

In this world all life, all history, all culture have developed and now continue under the circumstances of the natural environment of the planet on which we live. The regions of the world provide a setting of positive and negative potentialities so vast and intricate as to be totally unfathomable by us human beings except within the limited zone of our life and culture and in terms of our life and culture.

The natural environment is not to be understood as a causal factor but rather as an all-pervading and all-enveloping condition of human life. The history of the world with all its complexity and the culture of the world with all its constituent varieties belong only in the environment of this world and its regions—even as living things, including man, are biologically conditioned in all their parts by their natural environment.

To study the influence of natural environment on human life is like studying the influence of houses on housing or of farms on farming or of a tortoise shell on a tortoise.

It is not only environmentalism that should be discarded as a misleading approach to understanding but also the conventional concept of natural environment as a separate phenomenon clearly distinguished from cultural environment and

[1] Richard Hartshorne, *The Nature of Geography*, Association of American Geographers, Lancaster, Pa., 1939, pp. 299–305.

from human beings themselves. Our natural environment can be understood by us only in terms of our life, history, and culture; and, conversely, our life, history, and culture can be understood fully only in our natural environment. Separate studies of natural environment may have analytical value, but only as abstractions made in full view of the indivisible totality.

Thus the rejection of environmentalism is based not on a simple denial of relationship between natural environment and human life but on a complex denial of the implications and impressions that necessarily accompany the orthodox environmentalist approach. The rejection is of a particular line of thought, leading too often to faulty conclusions, and not of the meaningful relations of environment and life, seen better from another angle. Human life and environment are intimately interwoven in every aspect of their being, biologically and culturally, from the beginning of life on earth. The more obvious manifestations of this all-embracing relationship appear deceptively to spring from a direct influence of the environment and response of life. But actually these are not good evidences of direct and simple interaction but merely superficial symptoms of profound, complex, and indirect interrelationship. Therefore, we cannot rightly concentrate attention on these superficialities and thus misinterpret their meaning but must use other lines of approach, not through absolute principles of environmental influence, but through spatial correlations in a certain pattern of life.

Carle C. Zimmerman and Richard E. DuWors describe briefly the broad regional segments of continental United States. The influence of the region on social structure is marked by the fact that types of agriculture, industry, and other ways of making a living are useful in delineating regions. These activities are conditioned by climate, soil, and location with reference to bodies of water and to natural resources. Some of the ways in which regional physical characteristics influence community structure may be inferred from the following description of the relationship between region and social structure generally.*

Major Regions of the United States

America has its "provinces," its "localisms," and its provincial minds. But from the beginning of settlement early in the seventeenth century it began to regionalize itself into a *South*, an *Urban-Northeast*, and a backwoods general region known as the *Appalachian-Ozarkian*. In our Revolutionary War, after which we departed from European sovereignty, these were the three dominant regions. Samuel Adams was a character of the *Urban-Northeast*, but George Washington represented the planter class of the *South*. The soldiers of the backwoods, who, inspired by Tom Paine's revolutionary tracts, did so much to keep the war alive until victory, were *Appalachian-Ozark* types.

* *Graphic Regional Sociology*, Chapter 1, by Carle C. Zimmerman and Richard E. DuWors, Phillips Book Store, Cambridge, Mass., 1952. Used by permission of the senior author.

This same general organization of three dominant regions carried on in the new nation until after our Civil War, 1861–1865. We had our presidents at first almost alternately from the South and the Urban-Northeast until the Jacksonian movement in the eighteen twenties after which the *Appalachian-Ozarkian* group participated. Our Civil War was a struggle between the social systems of the Urban-Northeast and the South (slavery and states' rights) but it was fought largely *in* [the region of] and *by*, the *Appalachian-Ozarkian* people. All the campaigns until Sherman's march to the sea and Grant's move on Richmond, parts of the same encirclement, were in the *Appalachian-Ozarkian* border states.

After that war, our regionalism, well implanted in the East and incipient in the West, began to grow and expand. Very quickly we organized and put into being the *Cornbelt,* the *Wheatbelt,* the *Arid West,* and the *Pacific Mediterranean* regions. In our 1948 election campaign the two presidential candidates, Mr. Truman and Mr. Dewey, were from the Cornbelt and the Urban-Northeast. The two vice-presidential candidates, Mr. Barkley and Mr. Warren, were from the South and the Pacific-Mediterranean. In this campaign the combination of Cornbelt and South won over the Urban-Northeast and Pacific alliance.

Today, due to its regional organization, the United States is vastly different from any other nation and contains within itself the germs of a larger and world-embracing social organization. Each region is a specialist in one or several connected lines of production in which it excels. Each region also has its use of surplus and excess labor and resources applied to other things, oftentimes the main effort of other regions. But the surplus and excess activities of any particular region are used according to the extremely advanced methodology of that great region in which it is a specialized product. To illustrate, we may think of North Carolina as a southern tobacco and cotton state. But North Carolina grows hybrid corn, as in Iowa, and uses the Iowa techniques. By so doing it increased the per acre corn yield for the state 75 per cent (or from 20 to 35 bushels) in five years. Every American region is that combination of superior main effort or efforts and the use of superior borrowed techniques for its incidental subsidiary efforts.

The word "production" is used here in a very general sense. In the Cornbelt most of the products are organized about corn, which even accounts for the presence of soy beans and nitrogen-replacing legumes. The towns, the merchants, and the business enterprises stem largely from corn with its beef, hogs, and associated products. In the South we have cotton generally, with tobacco in the East and the oil industry in the West. The Wheatbelt functions almost entirely about its wheat and associated grains. The Arid West combines grazing in the uplands, wheat and cattle-feeding grains in the benchlands, and very intensively cultivated irrigated crops in the commercial oases. The Pacific region has its specialty crops and something not generally considered a commodity—a residential appeal. In its north, of course, is lumber, Alaska trade, and fisheries. The main production of the Appalachian-Ozarkian region has been timber and subsistence living, but this region will more and more focus on small manufactured items and leisure-time residences for people from the lower-lying Cornbelt and the South. The main efforts of the Urban-Northeast is manufactured goods, although its upper fringes from the Lake States Cutover to Northern New England are in great part a seasonal residential adjunct.

Secondary (as well as primary) aspects of production in these regions overlap very much. Examples are the rise of factory production in the Pacific region and the plastics industries around the petroleum wells in the western part of the South. With this rough sketch of American regional structure before us, two very important general sociology problems come up for analysis. The first concerns the psychosocial structural form of a country with such a regional organization; and the second analyzes those traits most inherently "Americanisms" in terms of their direct relation to regional organization. What is there about America as a totality that is different? What are the certain dominant American traits integrated with these differences?

Before we proceed, it must be pointed out that all traits discussed are found everywhere men live because they are inherent possibilities of the human species. What America possesses is in amount and ease of attainment, not in traits exclusive to it. For instance, freedom of a sort is found in all countries and all times but certainly not always in the amounts and ease of attainment as in America. Voluntarism is found in every social system but in America it is unusually great. To illustrate we may compare the changing of the agrarianism of Russia and the United States. In both countries the social aim was efficient farming with fewer commercial economic producers on the land. This aim required improving and standardizing seed and cultural practices. In Russia it concerned wheat because they are a bread country; and in America it concerned principally corn. In America wheat is *a* dish; in Russia wheat is *the* dish.

In Russia the modernization processes included a maximum of compulsion and a minimum of voluntarism. The process of changing to the . . . large communist farms with improved seed and standard practices began before the twenties and is not completed today. It has, even in the admissions of Stalin, been accomplished with large-scale bloody liquidation. In America we started the transfer from crossbred corn to hybrid in 1932. In ten years this was accomplished for the Cornbelt with almost 100 per cent efficiency without a single compulsory act. North Carolina, not a Cornbelt state, and one where the sophistication of the rural people is relatively narrow, achieved almost complete transition in five years, 1945–1950. The amount of voluntarism in the two social systems varies greatly.

In 1933, the United States planted 110 million acres in corn, only a tenth of one per cent of which was hybrid. In 1950 we raised a tremendously larger amount of corn on 85 million acres owing to the fact that 65 million acres were in hybrid seed. In the Cornbelt almost all corn is hybrid, and the rapid increases in its use now are in the non-Cornbelt states. Under a voluntaristic system, production practices were revolutionized on 70 million acres in 19 years, 1933–1951. From this corn change we fed ourselves better even with our rapidly increasing population, much of the remainder of the world, and put aside 25 million acres of cornfield for other products.

Psychosocial Structure and Regionalism

Regionalism in America consists of seven geosocial entities, each with its own peculiar social system, and each struggling for the maximation of its economic rewards within the same general system of values. Each region puts its unique commercial production into the same general fund and withdraws a part of the production of every region to round out its living. A breakfast table illustrates the typical scene. At it are assembled products from every other region as well as its own. As a matter of fact, the breakfast is surer to use the products of every other region more than it is the local product. Farmers in the Urban-Northwest oftentimes sell their dairy products and purchase margarine—cottonseed oil from the South or soybean oil from the Cornbelt. In California many persons purchase frozen citrus fruit juice from Florida rather than local fruits for breakfast.

Thus a first phase of the psychosocial structure under regionalism is an apparent unrelatedness between local production and local consumption based upon geosocial entities. This is far different from all other divisions of labor, including international exchange, and as such has different psychological influences.

Along with this geosocial division of labor within the same general system of values are certain related psychosocial structural forms. The first of these is the elevation of regional minds, mentalities, or personalities to informal governing or regulating bodies. These regional mentalities concern themselves with the major social problems of the regions such as race in the South; cultural and religious disparity in the Urban-Northeast; or provincialistic dispersion of the former subcultures among the various European communities now settled in the Corn and Wheat belts. In the Arid West it is water control and in the Pacific it is newness of the people to their physical and social environments. In the Appalachian-Ozarkian region the main social problem dealt with by the regional mind concerns the relations with the South. This is one in which the poor whites compete with the Bourbon class for control of the social system.

Americanism and Regionalism

There are a number of other elements of the psychosocial structure of America tied up closely with regionalism, but these two, economic production and a sustaining regional mentality which seeks to meliorate the major social strains, are most important and sufficient for illustration. Associated with these regional structural elements are certain "American" traits or emphases which are also causal-functionally regional. Among those which might be enumerated first are emphases upon freedom, upon organization of *world peace*, and the gospel of universalistic *technical progress toward plenty*.

The vastly increased emphasis upon freedom in the United States is inherently regional. America is in one sense a nation of seven nations, each a geosocial region with a firmly entrenched personality. Any attempt to "enslave" a particular segment of people must embrace the consent of seven regions in each of which that social class or group has a differential appeal to the political mind. To illustrate, the Negro is in one situation in the South, another in the Cornbelt, and still another in the Pacific region. The commercial farmer dominates our three interior regions, Cornbelt, Wheatbelt, and Arid West, but is only a minority in the other four. The industrial employee is dominant in the Urban-Northeast, but a minority in most other regions.

Out of this situation comes a powerful give-and-take, the net result of which is an elaboration of the older Western ideal of freedom. Thus American political leadership has to step warily among the regions because what is popular in one is not so in others. To illustrate, in one region it is popular to be a Dixiecrat; in others that is most unpopular. Out of this resultant compromise comes a gradually growing freedom.

This resultant system of gradual compromise among vast but different regions forces the thoughtful American to think in terms of larger cultural peace. If it can be worked in the "United States of America" why can it not also work in a "United States of Europe"? That is a common American question. It has been elevated in the past half century, along with the increase of communication, to an ideal of a "united world." Thus in American regionalism we see the *causal* forces which have made us come back again and again toward the ideal of a united world. Woodrow Wilson, Wendell Willkie, and Franklin Delano Roosevelt have most clearly grasped this ideal and used shibboleths based upon it as political platforms.

The final ideal of technical progress toward a world of plenty, which is now official American policy as seen in the Marshall plan, in the ECA, and in President Truman's "Point 4" for help to economically retarded areas, is also inherent in our regional organization. The older theory of submarginal lands and submarginal regions has disappeared in the United States. Rather we hold that every region has a large potential of hyper-marginal and valuable uses. If areas are classified at any given moment as submarginal that means that the proper use has not been found. Our tidewater strip around the coast of the South was once considered submarginal. Now we seek grasses, cattle, and other products peculiarly suited to it. When these are fully developed the area will reach its correct productivity. In the Urban-Northeast the upper hill towns or older New England have been considered submarginal for agriculture. Now we see that legume coverage putting nitrogen directly into animal food can be developed there, shortening the older costly process of first planting grain and then converting grain to animal food. This new idea inherent in our regional technical progress makes us impatient with other regions which give up in despair or muddle along customary paths when they have inherent advantages of proper use.

The two papers that follow describe two widely separated communities: Landaff, New Hampshire, and El Cerrito, New Mexico. These represent two of the regions designated in the previous paper by Zimmerman and Du-Wors. They are only intended to illustrate the way that communities may vary in different parts of the country. They are not necessarily to be regarded as "typical" of their respective regions, for they may or may not be. It can be argued convincingly that no community is typical of its region, for the simple reason that communities within a region vary greatly because of factors other than regional characteristics. Even so, each of these communities will possess many similarities with other settlements of their respective areas.

Changes in Landaff, New Hampshire *

Informal cooperation in the community at present is less marked than it was previously, but while great value is placed upon independence and self-reliance, certain practices of mutual aid persist. Patterns of cooperation are of a rather general character. If a neighbor is ill and cannot do his own work, others will try to do it for him. Women will bring food to his house and offer to help. However, if the sick man were a laborer or mill worker whose residence in the community had been short and whose interests in town affairs had been negligible, this neighborly assistance would probably not be given. The community sets standards for the assistance of the people who are its components, but not for outsiders who are not fully accepted.

It is still common for certain individuals to "change work" with others. In so doing they are complying with a rather definite pattern, but the actual arrangements have much to do with specific and varying personal relationships. Changing work implies a fair exchange; it is not a spontaneous thing whereby a man feels moved to go to his neighbor's aid. Arrangements are businesslike and satisfactory to both parties, and are often determined by the kind of skills or machinery the two participants possess. For instance, a man with a two-row corn planter went to work for another man and planted all of his corn in one day. Since the planting was late this saved the owner of the corn a lot of hard work and a delayed crop. In return, he went to work for the man who did his planting as a regular hand and put in two or three days doing more or less unskilled labor. On another occasion, a man went with two of his teams and two of his harrows and one hired man to work another man's land, while he, the happy possessor of a tractor with two-way hydraulic plows came to plow a difficult stretch of the farmer's land.

The loaning of machinery is related to cooperation. This is not a universal practice, but certain well-equipped operators have loaned their seeders or binders upon occasion. Such loans almost always occur among the old families whose members have known each other all their lives. Unlike the giving of time and work, these loans of machines are made without any definite expectation of a return loan, for they mean no loss of time or money to the lender.

Even in the days when several kinds of informal cooperation existed, the ability of the individual to operate independently of others was considered a virtue, as it still is. Cooperation was probably practiced because the people understood that along specified lines cooperation was convenient and valuable. Never did these customs become strong enough or extensive enough to permit the group to have any voice in deciding the way in which individual farms were operated. That is, cooperation always operated within the larger framework of individualistic enterprise.

A clearer picture of the present situation as compared with the past is brought out by the statements of some of the farmers. An old man, now retired, recalled:

* Kenneth MacLeish and Kimball Young, "Culture of a Contemporary Rural Community: Landaff, New Hampshire," United States Department of Agriculture, April, 1942, pp. 59–63.

"Things are all changed now from the way they used to be. When I was a boy, there'd be big gangs of men going around from farm to farm working on the harvest and they still had raising bees. You don't get that any more. Sometimes I think folks are less obliging, and then again I think it might be because work is worth a lot more money now. Nowadays, when nobody calls on the neighbors for that kind of work, folks wouldn't think much of a man that did. Nowadays you got to manage by yourself and hire work done."

At present, visiting is extraordinarily infrequent. Although roads are now passable in the winter (except those in the back country), there is still a seasonal quality which may be a hold-over from the past. Even in summer, the extent of such association is very limited. It would not be unusual for a farm wife to go a week or two without making or receiving calls, and in winter social calls might occur as infrequently as once a month.

There is now, and presumably there always has been, a marked difference between men and women in this relationship. It is often said that in the past women were the ones who suffered from the loneliness of back-country farms because they were kept busy at home whereas the men came into contact with other people in the course of their regular business. This is still true, but a genuine distinction is to be made between the past and present situation. It seems safe to assume that in the past a visit to the neighbors meant far more than it does now. The woman, who had seen no faces but those of her own family and had heard no voices but theirs for several days, would value conversation with her neighbor far more than would the present-day farm wife who may listen to her radio, [watch her TV] read her papers or magazines, and talk to her neighbors on the telephone.

The men make only occasional social calls. But they meet one another in connection with their daily routine far more than in the past. At the milk station, for instance, local news and gossip are discussed every day, summer and winter. There are always several farmers there at once, and brief conversations are carried on. The buying and selling of livestock means seeing and talking with other people, as does shopping in the village which is done by both men and women.

Actual visiting for non-business reasons is almost entirely confined to women, though husband and wife sometimes go together to the home of a neighbor for a game of cards or something of the sort. Invitations to meals are rarely given or expected, usually being limited to family members. It would not be unusual for an average farm family to live through a whole year without once having a meal in a neighbor's home.

The visiting, such as it is, is limited chiefly to the farm families in better circumstances. The small and usually impecunious farmers living away from the good roads have no telephones and some are without automobiles or trucks. Because it is difficult for them to take part in the social activities of the town they often lack interest in such things. Their isolation means that contacts with other people are limited, so that real friendships do not develop between them and the other farmers. Their very way of life, based upon occasional labor and subsistence farming, makes personal contacts rare. The nonfarm people, independent as they are of the community and being often newcomers, according to the local viewpoint, are no more likely to have friends within the town than beyond it and are frequently content to be left to their own devices.

It appears, then, that visiting is no longer particularly necessary to such people as the larger farmers—the milk shippers—and no longer available, except in small measure, to the little farmers. As the need for this means of relaxation and of overcoming isolation has grown less, the emphasis upon it as an actual obligation has almost ceased.

The telephone has become an increasingly important form of social interaction. To some extent the visiting pattern has been adapted to it. Telephone calls between farm women are frequent, detailed, and almost interminable. At present, however, only the larger farmers have telephones; only twenty-three homes are on the town's three telephone lines. These represent only about one-third of the total number of families, but they are the social elect—the backbone of the community. It is obvious that, as telephones are not used extensively for business, the families who spent considerable sums to have them installed are those who had a lively interest in communicating with their friends and neighbors and in preserving a sense of solidarity.

The Community of El Cerrito, New Mexico *

The physical structure of this community greatly facilitates cooperation and mutual aid. All houses in the village are within a stone's throw of one another. Through years of interdependence, the people are conditioned to call upon neighbors and relatives for many types of assistance and, in turn, are expected to reciprocate when the need arises. Any task that requires greater strength or physical effort than a single family has at hand is solved by calling in a neighbor. Such service is freely asked for and given. In case of sickness or similar misfortune the efforts and resources of the entire village may be utilized in order to bring the family through the crisis.

Informal visiting far exceeds any other mode of contact between the villagers. The latchstring is "always on the outside" for any neighbor or relative who may have the time and inclination to call. In a single afternoon fourteen different visitors were counted coming to one household, some of them returning as many as three or four times. This was not a peculiar case. Other homes in the village probably had as many. Such visits are expected. If a housewife fails to make a call in the afternoon it is taken for granted that she is ill or has company.

Although visiting is general in El Cerrito, the degree of blood relationship is the chief factor affecting their frequency. The house of the parents of several married sons and daughters is the nucleus for the different visiting groups. The wives and children of such families may come to the central house a dozen or more times in a day. They come to distribute a piece of news or to borrow a little something for the next meal. The children are continuously running into and out of each others'

* Olen E. Leonard and C.P. Loomis, "Culture of a Contemporary Rural Community: El Cerrito, New Mexico," United States Department of Agriculture, November, 1941, pp. 37–46.

houses. They are together so much that it is difficult to learn to which house they belong.

It is not difficult to understand what these informal visits mean to a woman in these villages. Tied to a drab routine of household duties and child care she is allowed few means of self-expression. Social censure prevents any activity outside the village or even in the organized social life within the village with the exception of attendance at church. Even conversation with the opposite sex, other than members of her immediate family, is denied her. Thus visiting among her own sex and status offers the most important means of expression open to her.

Although the visiting of the women far exceeds that of the men, each day affords them also a number of opportunities for conversation. After a day in the field is over they are likely to meet for a short time around the house or in going to and from the corrals. Also for the men there are other outlets, such as the field work, the local meetings, and the trips to town.

All the visiting done within the village is informal. It would be unusual for a visitor to announce his coming or even for the entire family to visit at one time. Only the most general invitations are given. A person is expected to feel welcome whenever he has the desire and the time to come.

The world over the taking of meals at the table of another's family signifies familiarity. This is true in El Cerrito. Those families which in the course of their visits stayed for meals at the visited family's home were in most cases closely related. Most meals were taken when visiting relationships were between parents and children or brothers and sisters. In fact, the families who took more than five meals together during the year and were of more distant kinship than father and child or brother and sister were negligible. Sharing food frequently at the same table during visits is an act which signifies close blood ties in El Cerrito, and the frequency of the act is positively correlated with the degree of consanguinity.

The coming and going of children of one family across the hearth of another is also almost a universal indication of close family ties, although it may be less so than the taking of meals during friendly visits. In large cities children may visit one another in homes where their respective parents have never been. In El Cerrito, the frequency with which the children and other separate individuals visit is directly proportional to the closeness of kinship. There is a great frequency of visits of children and separate individuals in the homes of the grandparents of children. Several of the grandparents have grandchildren, the sons and daughters of unfortunate parents, living with them. These grandchildren may return the visits of other grandchildren from other families. Some families are almost isolated; these are young childless families. If the high frequencies of visitation of children seem surprising, one should live with one of the families and attempt to learn which children belong to this family. Without asking or remaining for some time, it would be a real task. Nothing could be more informal than the visiting of the children but the frequency of the visitations are, for the most part, governed by kinship. However, geographical distance also plays a part. The children of cousins who live next door, other things being equal, will probably visit more frequently than the cousins whose families live 200 yards apart.

Little visiting is done outside the village. This is especially true of the women, who seldom see a woman from the outside. The majority do not leave their own village more than once or twice a year.

Visits outside the village are usually to the homes of relatives in Las Vegas. Such a trip to town serves three purposes: a chance to remain in town for a few days, a chance to make periodic purchases, and a visit with friends and relatives. This visit to Las Vegas may last for as much as a week. That these visits are seldom repaid does not matter. Such hospitality is accepted by both parties as a responsibility the town people owe to their country relatives.

Isolation from the city markets and stores has made it necessary for these families to resort to considerable borrowing and lending. This applies particularly to items of food. In case a family should use its supply of flour or lard before a ride to town can be arranged for, it is obliged to borrow. These loans are strictly, if informally, kept account of. Such courtesies could not be lightly regarded. They are repaid promptly after the first trip to town.

Borrowing and lending among the villagers is not limited to items of food. Farming tools and equipment are loaned freely. Brothers may buy tools together or they may buy different tools for the purpose of exchange. It is not uncommon for several distinct families to own jointly or severally only a single set of farm tools.

Resettlement of people from these villages where the land resources are too meager has been proposed. One family in El Cerrito is attempting to resettle itself, with great misgiving. It owns a ranch some thirty miles from the village, and the families of four sons are working and saving to restock the ranch so that the whole family can move.

For Governmental resettlement or rehabilitation schemes the fact must be borne in mind that it is the larger family of grandparents, children, the grandchildren with which the schemes should deal. To remove a single smaller family would frequently create hardships and in addition would increase expenditure for frequent visits back to the village. Smaller families than those which include the grandparents and the families of the sons should seldom be considered for resettlement in a new location. If the daughters' families, uncles, aunts, nephews, and nieces, and in some cases, cousins could be part of the group to be removed so much the better. In many cases the parental family would not even consider leaving the family of the daughter. Small familial rehabilitation cooperatives composed or several related families have been successful in their effort to rehabilitate in peace. Thus it is important that action agencies know the importance of familism in this culture.

Within as well as between these broad regions of the United States, there are recognizable differences in community life. It is a very common experience of everyone to hear a certain community referred to as a "good community" or a "bad community." These differences from place to place may be due to (1) differences in the way people make their living or (2) differences in standards or values. These factors—ways of making a living and value systems—are of course related to others, including cultural and ethnic background, race, and so on, but these need not be of concern to us here.

Ways of making a living are related to the physical environment; but as Professor Platt pointed out earlier, there may be wide differences in cultural responses within the same geographic area.

PRINCIPLES

1. *The regional environment sets limits on the economic system of the community, but there are always alternatives to the particular system developed.*

The implication of this principle is that geographic (or demographic) determinism as an explanation of community structure is insufficient. This is, of course, merely one example of the single factor fallacy in explaining community behavior.

2. *The limits set by the demographic factor are also limits for the course of social change where the economic element is involved.*

The alternatives in economic adjustment to the environment represent the choices open to a community in selecting the nature and direction of change.

3. *Other than the relationship in the second principle above, the demographic factor alone does not explain social change, since change is a variable of the social system and the demographic factor is a constant.*

4. *Types of industry and agriculture in the community area are the basis of regional delineation, but these are conditioned by climate, soil, natural resources, and proximity to waterways or other natural features.*

Once social organization is built up in a given region, some man-made variables, like roads and railroads, and existing industry, are likely to operate in much the same general way to shape the community structure as does the natural environment. However, these man-made factors are more subject to change and thus may operate more actively in changing the social system of the community.

SELECTED REFERENCES

Bell, Earl H., *Culture of a Contemporary Rural Community: Sublette, Kansas,* Bureau of Agricultural Economics, Washington, D.C., 1942.

Bell, Wendell, "The Social Areas of the San Francisco Bay Region," *ASR*, 18:39–47, 1953.

Hutton, Graham, *Midwest at Noon*, University of Chicago Press, Chicago, 1946.

Kollmorgen, Walter M., *Culture of a Contemporary Rural Community: The Old Order Amish of Lancaster County, Pennsylvania*, Bureau of Agricultural Economics, Washington, D.C., 1942.

Leonard, Olen, and C.P. Loomis, *Culture of a Contemporary Rural Community: El Cerrito, New Mexico*, Bureau of Agricultural Economics, Washington, D.C., 1941.

Lively, C.E., "Social Planning and the Sociology of Sub-Regions," *RS*, 2:288–98, 1937.

MacLeish, Kenneth, and Kimball Young, *Culture of a Contemporary Rural Community: Landaff, New Hampshire*, Bureau of Agricultural Economics, Washington, D.C., 1942.

Nelson, Lowry, *The Mormon Village*, University of Utah Press, Salt Lake City, 1952, Chapter 1.

Odum, Howard W., and Harry E. Moore, *Southern Regions of the United States*, University of North Carolina Press, Chapel Hill, 1936, pp. 163–73.

Smith, T. Lynn, *The Sociology of Rural Life*, Third Edition, Harper and Brothers, New York, 1953, Chapter 10.

Taylor, C.C., and others, *Rural Life in the United States*, Part iv, Alfred A. Knopf, New York, 1949.

Wynne, Waller, *Culture of a Contemporary Rural Community: Harmony, Georgia*, Bureau of Agricultural Economics, Washington, D.C., 1943.

CHAPTER 4

Demographic Factors
in the Community

Sociologists and community leaders alike often overlook the functional importance of demographic factors in community structure. This chapter will demonstrate some of the ways in which these factors operate to bring about and to solve community problems. From the point of view of community leaders and organizations, population phenomena are causally related to many of the problems which are their concern. From the point of view of sociology, if demographic factors bring about problems and can be used to ameliorate them, then these factors are functional in the social structure of the community. This in turn means that population is an important area of sociological theory.

Before moving to the analysis, an example may help to show the more obvious implication of population phenomena for community programs. Suppose a hospital or sewage system is a felt need in a community. Considering the costs involved and the necessity of assurance for long-range use, the population trends projected into the future would be indispensable to intelligent planning. In spite of the obvious nature of this point, it is often overlooked. Some of the more subtle effects of population phenomena are, of course, even more often overlooked.

Population phenomena are those aspects of society related to size of a social unit, a community, an organization, a county, an age category, and so on. Important aspects of population analysis include among others the change in size, birth and death rates, migration, long-range trends and distribution.

THE GENERAL INFLUENCE OF DEMOGRAPHIC FACTORS

The general relationship between community structure and change on the one hand and population size on the other may be described in terms of the following principles:

(a) *A social unit with a population base sufficiently large to support enough services to be classified as a community is too large to offer each person an opportunity to interact with everyone else.* This proposition has several very important implications. First, definitions of the community based on the concept of interaction of people have to be carefully qualified or they will be misleading. It is true that there will be more interaction among persons who are "members" of the community than between members and non-members. It is also true that, by the definition used in this book, there must be interaction between each member and the institutions of the community, that is, purchasing, participating, and interinfluence. But the qualification of interaction occurring among all members is important because of the second implication.

The second implication is that communities will not act as primary groups do since every person in the community area will not interact with every other person. This means that a large series of fairly well-established generalizations are lost in attempting to understand and predict community behavior. This of course does not mean that primary groups as such do not influence community behavior, but rather that communities are not themselves primary groups. Naturally, this is much more true of larger than smaller communities. It is doubtful, however, if any community is a primary group.

A third implication is that the sharing of ideals and common experiences is variable within the large community. Thus materialism may characterize one class and religious ideals be predominant in another.

(b) *There seems to be roughly an optimum size and density for communities, with too sparse a population causing low level of living and lack of human resources, and with too dense and large a population being associated with problems of low level of living and inadequate social control.*[1] There is no direct evidence for this proposition, but there is much indirect evidence. In the first place, the lack of human resources in the very small community probably sets up a condition where there is little incentive and little possibility of development. Many of the communities in the extreme northern part of the United States, where land and physical resources are poor, have further handicaps through extremely sparse population. While the poor land and physical resources represent a handicap, the consequent low level of living for the inhabitants is not necessary. For example, many

---

[1] For a discussion of the question of optimum size, see Otis Dudley Duncan, "Optimum Size of Cities" in *Reader in Urban Sociology*, ed. by Paul K. Hatt and Albert J. Reiss, Jr., the Free Press, Glencoe, Ill., 1951; and Otis Dudley Duncan and Albert J. Reiss, Jr., *Social Characteristics of Rural and Urban Communities*, 1950, John Wiley and Sons, New York, 1956, Chapter 2.

of these communities, through the development of their human resources, have become vacation lands or have developed some other specialty through which the local residents could realize their ambitions. However, with an extremely small population base this is more difficult. This point will be analyzed later in the chapter.

Many students of the community who have worked in underdeveloped countries have observed the sheer effort to eke out a living among peoples who have more food demands than food. Similarly, everyone in America is aware of the difficulties of social control—e.g., problems of delinquency, crime, adjustment, and so on in the larger urban centers. The "evils of the city" is an expression much overused and perhaps an exaggeration. However, the fact is that when a city reaches a size large enough to furnish anonymity to a person merely by traveling a few blocks, social control through gossip and informal pressure is much less effective. The secondary controls, such as the police force, can never have the hour-to-hour preventative effect brought about by having one's neighbor watching him.

The optimum population, then, is a very wide range of both size and density. It is unlikely that a very precise range can be given in terms of numbers. However, the optimum size concept relates to the community mainly in terms of the creation of problems.

(c) *An unplanned adjustment of numbers to opportunity for a higher level of living occurs continuously through migration.* When opportunities for decreasing the gap between the level of living and the standard of living (aspiration) diminish, the migration of people out of the community will partially ameliorate the problem. The reverse is also true; when a community has a sudden increase in jobs, such as the building of a dam, canal, or industrial plant, immigration will help the situation considerably without much planning. Migration has also been used in rural development (resettlement communities) as well as urban (slum clearance) as a deliberate action program against the problem of level of living. This point will be analyzed in more detail later in the chapter.

(d) *Migration may be selective of talent within a community, so that leaders leave in disproportionately high numbers.* The loss of leaders through migration from rural to urban communities has been of interest for a long time. A point of growing concern is whether the leaders who do migrate become leaders in the new community. These points also will be analyzed in some detail later in the chapter.

(e) *In summary, size, density, and shifts and trends in size and density bring about problems in community structure, condition the means of solution to these problems, and in turn are affected by the solutions.* For example, a small city may increase tremendously in size in a short period of time owing to, say, construction work, as happens often during war. The sewage plant and schools may be insufficient for the increase, and therefore a problem is created by size. If the community is very small originally, the needed expansion of facilities may be too costly—in which case further in-migration may be discouraged. If the original community was very large, the expansion will be made, thus encouraging further in-migration.

EFFECTS OF SIZE AND DENSITY

The general trend in the United States has been for urban communities to increase in size and influence more rapidly than rural. The effect of size on community organization has already been described in general, but there are several special aspects of size which are not obvious from mere population numbers. One such aspect is the relative size of the male population to the female population, and another is the relative size of farm to non-farm population. Several studies have shown the relationship between measures of size to the way in which the community functions in serving the needs of its people. One such study, conducted in Maryland, gives a general picture of this relationship.[2] The great increase in population occurred in centers of population over the years, while the open country and some of the smaller centers either remained relatively constant in size or lost population. The results were that institutional services which previously had been offered in the open country became village-centered. Rural churches closed, while village churches increased in number and in attendance. Rural schools were consolidated or centralized, and these usually were located in the population centers. Homemakers' Clubs had a larger proportion of village and non-farm women as members, and 4-H Clubs a correspondingly higher proportion of non-farm girls. The rural community then became increasingly village-centered. As a result of the influence of migration, numerous studies have shown that the opposite trend is occurring on the fringes of the large urban centers. Businesses, schools, and churches are decentralized to meet the local needs of the tremendous population growth around the fringe, as, for example, in the way a business or bank may have a "branch" in several fringe area business centers.

The changes with respect to size and distribution of the population thus clearly condition the organization of the community and affect its change.

[2] Adapted from S. Earl Grigsby and Harold Hoffsommer, "Rural Social Organization of Frederick County, Maryland," *University of Maryland AES Bulletin No. A 51*, 1949.

This is the normal pattern in the United States. It remains to demonstrate the effects of low density. A study in Montana illustrates the importance of a concept of optimum population density.

Population Sparsity as a Social Cost *

Montana has a sparse population and promises to have continued sparsity in the future. In 1950 there were 4.1 persons per square mile, while the average for the nation was about 50 persons. None of the mountain states had more than 13 persons per square mile. None of the states bordering on or located east of the Mississippi River had fewer than 25 persons per square mile. Maine had the least with a density of 29.4 persons, followed by Vermont with 40.7 persons. Rhode Island had the heaviest population, 748.4 persons per square mile, with Massachusetts next with 593.7 persons per square mile.

But the average low population density for the states in the mountain-plains region tells only part of the story. There are striking variations in population density within each state. Such variation, coupled with the overall sparsity for the state, creates certain very special problems. It adds to the cost of private and public services, organizational structure, and institutional programs. It means that some people live far removed from some of these services and that costs are much higher to them than to people closer by unless costs are offset by state aid. In that case, costs are higher to all involved.

Here, then, are illustrations of social costs that have their explanation in space. Space, in itself, is a cost that is not generally paid directly, but indirectly, by the public at large. To study this fact of variation in population density and the implications of social cost attached thereto, a special tabulation was undertaken for a limited sample area of Montana, using the census data for 1940 and 1930.

One area, the one having the denser population, might be called the Sutland. By definition, it included largely irrigated land and some immediately adjacent territory. This area was of equal size in 1930 and 1940.

The contrasting area, called the Yonland, consisted chiefly of nonirrigated land. It was of equal size in 1930 and 1940.

The Sutland contained 2,227.3 square miles of territory compared with 32,076.9 square miles for the Yonland. The latter was 14 times the size of the former. In 1930 the population of the Sutland was about 54,945 and that of the Yonland about 49,152. This is a density of 24.7 and 1.5 respectively. In the Yonland the population was predominantly rural, including almost 6 out of 7 persons. In the Sutland more than half the population was urban.

By 1940 a decrease in population for the Yonland of more than 12,000 persons resulted in a density of 1.2 persons per square mile. The Yonland urban popula-

---

* Carl F. Kraenzel and George Engstrom, "Montana's Population Changes, 1920 to 1950," *Montana AES Bulletin No. 520,* Bozeman, Montana, 1956. See also A.H. Anderson, "Space as a Social Cost: An Approach Toward Community Design in the Sparsely Populated Areas of the Great Plains," *JFE,* 32:411–30, 1950.

tion loss was all in the farm and village areas. For the Sutland the population had increased by more than 12,000 persons, with an addition to both the rural and urban areas.

Between 1930 and 1940, then, the difference in total population between the two areas had been increased from a total of 5,000 to more than 30,000. The density decreased from 1.5 to 1.2 in the Yonland, and increased from 24.7 to 30.1 in the Sutland.

To get an area with about 70,000 people in 1940 for the Sutland area required about 29,083 rural persons to be added to the urban. The size of the Yonland area was governed by the attempt to get, as nearly as possible, the same number of rural people as in the Sutland area in 1940. The total and the urban populations for the Yonland were the variable figures.

The figure 70,000 was selected because it corresponds roughly to that size of community which, perhaps, represents a minimum population necessary to support certain essential public services such as full-time public health units; a strong public library program; strong high school, grade school, and religious service opportunities; and a hospital and medical care service program of adequate volume and specialization to bring economy and quality to the community. It was assumed, in addition, that this would give adequate volume and variety of organization and service in such matters as church and religion, newspaper circulation, radio listening, service clubs and social organizations of all types, and a wide choice of economic services so that a community might be reasonably complete.

The selected Sutland area approximated this number of people and also the variety and quality of services indicated, modeled on a scale and number found in Billings, Montana. A guess is that these services—their quantity, quality, and variety—are available to Billings and immediate environs because Billings serves more than its immediate trade area, including the Yonland area and beyond. If this is not the case for retailing services, it is at least true for wholesaling functions. Thus, a good guess is that the 70,000 population figure is more nearly a minimum rather than a maximum figure for full community development. In this connection it should be recalled that in 1950 Billings itself had a population of 31,834, and Yellowstone County, of which it is the county seat, had 55,875 residents.

In addition to approximating the 70,000 figure, the Sutland population was reasonably well concentrated, with a 1940 density of 30.1 persons. Thus space would appear to be less of a social cost than if population were more sparse.

In contrast, in 1940 the Yonland had only a little more than half (37,012) the 70,000 population used as a standard and 30,000 less than the Sutland. To get this many people, the area of the Yonland was 14 times the size of the Sutland, and the total population density was only 1.2 persons per square mile. In addition, the trend between 1930 and 1940 was a decrease of 12,000 persons for the Yonland.

If the Sutland area had a minimum population for basic community organization, the population for the Yonland was considerably below this minimum. In all probability, then, space is much more of a cost in the Yonland than in the Sutland. Since it is true that some of the Yonland services are obtained in the

Sutland, especially in Billings, the travel between the Yonland and the Sutland involves a further space cost.

It is difficult to measure the cost of space in the Yonland as contrasted with the cost in the Sutland. That the Yonland is probably burdened with public service costs can be inferred from the fact that the population of that area (37,012 people) now supports the equivalent of at least 10 county governments and the related functions—public health, public welfare, unemployment compensation, road building, board of equalization, canvassing board, and school budget costs and supervision. This is in addition to the costs for carrying out the functions of law enforcement, taxation, election supervision, recording of public records, and other administrative obligations. On top of this there are the costs for the educational, religious, economic, and other social functions that need to be performed for people; and the administration of village, town, and city governments, plus a share of state and federal governmental costs.

The Sutland area included the equivalent of very few counties, though made up of parcels of eight. Together the two areas in 1940 involved 34,304.2 square miles and 104,069 persons for an over-all density of only 3.03 persons per square mile. This area is the equivalent of five states, namely: Rhode Island, Connecticut, Massachusetts, Vermont, and New Hampshire. The 1940 population for these states was 7,590,064.

The density for the Sutland counties, as a group, was 12.4 persons per square mile, ranging from 5 to 21.2. For the selected Yonland counties, as a group, the density was 0.7 persons, ranging from 0.5 to 1.3. There were 2.1 pupils per square mile in the Sutland and only 0.15 pupils per square mile in the Yonland.

The per capita grand total taxes in 1950 for all purposes in the county and in its minor civil divisions was $75 in the Sutland and $104 in the Yonland. This evidence supports the argument that distance or space is a social cost. By counties, this per capita cost varies from a high of $96 to a low of $64 in the Sutland. For Yonland counties this per capita cost varies from a high of $132 to a low of $87. Undoubtedly, in many instances the higher per capita cost in the Yonland counties does not carry with it as adequate service as in the Sutland. School services tend to approximate a more uniform standard, regardless of the location of the district in the Sutland or the Yonland. However, the school service in the Yonland does not equal that of the Sutland in terms of quality and variety. In this case, the per pupil cost for the Sutland was $188 compared to $217 for the Yonland. The range in the former was from $151 to $256, and for the latter it was from $177 to $250. This evidence would appear to support the argument that distance does represent a social cost. State and federal aid support the argument still further. For the Sutland this aid amounts to $68 per pupil compared with $132 for the Yonland. The total per pupil school cost averaged $256 for the Sutland and $349 for the Yonland. Put on a per capita (total population) basis, the figure was $42 for the Sutland and $65 for the Yonland.

It would appear, then, that space is a social cost in both the Yonland and the Sutland, compared with more densely populated parts of the nation. The extent and precise nature of these social costs are, however, difficult to demonstrate without further study. The purpose here is not to demonstrate their extent and nature but simply to call attention to their existence and their importance.

MIGRATION

Migration is the term which refers to changes in domicile of families of persons. Inasmuch as it may drain off the leaders or the more intelligent from one area, it influences the social structure. Similarly, because size is a factor in the nature of community structure, the areas experiencing heavy out-migration or in-migration are strongly affected.

One of the most dramatic changes in community results from the fringe or suburban migration. The area around cities is becoming densely populated and the open country near industrial employment is likewise becoming the place of residence of the urbanites employed in the city. This fringe migration not only has strongly affected community organization and problems but has actually created new communities.

After several intensive studies, W.A. Anderson [*] summarizes some of the many effects of this migration.

This Movement Is Creating a New Residential Class in Our Rural Society

Customarily we think of our population as being urban and rural. In this differentiation we not only think of urban and rural residents as living in the cities or the country but as finding their employment in each of these places as well. Our rural population was customarily subdivided into those persons who lived and worked on farms or "the farmers," and those who lived in the small villages and hamlets and who also had their work there. Beginning with the development of our paved highway systems and the use of the automobile, together with the extension of electricity, the movement of families into rural territory for residential purposes only while still retaining work in the cities began to grow apace. Now we have a vast population that is rural in residence but urban in occupation.

But the Flight to the Fringe Is also Attracting Business and Industry More and More

While our emphasis is upon the movement of people to the fringe and the open country, it must be added that the flight now includes business and industry also. No longer is it just families who move there for home building and residential purposes. While this is still the chief characteristic of the flight, the rural areas are becoming attractive to business enterprises also and so will increasingly

---

[*] W.A. Anderson, "The Flight to the Fringe: Opportunities for Extension Activities," *Cornell University AES Rural Sociology*, publication No. 46, 1956.

become places to work as well as to live, thus adding substantially to the urban population that lives there.

Shopping centers, new industrial plants, and retail service and distributing units are locating in rural areas. Data from the United States Department of Labor and Commerce show that, in 1954, 69 per cent of the building permits issued in the United States were for construction in suburban territory and only 31 per cent were for construction in central cities. More than 40 per cent of all store and mercantile establishments were built in the suburbs, and a substantial part of these were on the main highways in the open country.

New York State is having its part in this expansion. Congestion in urban centers, decentralization in business and industry, and the rapid growth of the rural and total population underlie these shifts, as well as those of the families.

When families and business enterprises locate in the fringe and open country, there are inevitably introduced many problems related to land use, sanitation, schools, roads, and other public requirements that demand coordination. Community and regional planning and zoning, therefore, becomes a major necessity.

The Rural Areas of the State Will Be Characterized Increasingly by Occupational Diversity and the Dominance of Nonfarmers

One of the attitudes that is common with us is that the rural areas are occupied predominantly by farmers and we tend to put all farmers in one occupational grouping. This view comes as a holdover from our experience of the past when it was true that rural areas were predominantly farming areas and a large proportion of the farmers were carrying on similar activities.

More than three in each four employed males fourteen years of age and over who lived in rural territory in New York in 1950 worked at another occupation than farming. Over one in each three employed males of these ages who lived on a farm was in some other occupation than farming; only two in each three farmed. Farming itself is becoming increasingly specialized so that within a community and certainly between communities the interests of the farmers are not the same; they are often competitive.

As this increase of non-farming people in rural areas continues and the number of farms and farmers themselves decreases owing to increased mechanization and the pull of other occupational opportunities, the proportions of non-farmers to farmers will continue to rise and occupational diversity will grow at an accelerating rate. This will result, already has in fact, in situations where the chief task in the rural community will be the integration of residents with many different interests and outlooks around the common community goals.

It is possible for people to reside *in* rural communities but not be *of* these communities. The changed conditions make it possible for the farm family as well as the non-farm family to stand aloof, just as many city families have no part in the organizational life that surrounds them. They can even be a divisive factor because of varying interests and values. On the other hand, they can improve local community relations through increased contacts and understanding of each other's problems. One of the challenges of this new social frontier is for agencies such as Extension to accept and add the responsibility for promoting community development programs to an already full program, so as to avoid internal conflicts and to create appreciation for the common concerns farm and non-farm residents in the rural areas have. One of the essential objectives must be to avoid sharp social stratifications that can be isolating and to promote working together to develop harmonious rural community life in this mixed class structure our rural society is developing and in which non-farmers will dominate. With the passing of open-country neighborhood schools and churches, farmers and open-country non-farm residents must increasingly become a part of larger community activities or a different type of isolation than the physical, namely a social, isolation can result.

The Educational Attainment Level of the Whole Rural Population of the Future Will Be Considerably Higher than that of Today

Not only will the rural population of the future be much more numerous and much more occupationally heterogeneous than in the past, it will also be better schooled. The average educational attainment level for the population of the State twenty-five years of age and older, increased by one whole year of schooling between 1940 and 1950. It increased almost that much for each class in the rural areas, so that although the average number of school grades completed by farm residents was slightly lower than that of urban residents in 1950, the schooling of the rural non-farm adults was slightly higher than that of urban adults. As farm and non-farm children increase their schooling and more non-farming people move to the rural environment, any important differences in schooling will disappear. The constituency that must be served in the rural areas is or will be as well schooled as that in any other areas.

What this means to Extension is that the population of our rural areas will expand their interests and activities. They will have higher standards for institutional operation, community development, and community organization. As they use increasingly the ideas suggested by our enlarging mass means of communication, their demands for programs that deal with community and public problems, with techniques of social organization, and others of public concern, will increase. This better-schooled population will expect its employed leadership to have training and interests in areas of knowledge such as government, economics, sociology, and the humanities, or it will not be challenged. Extension has an opportunity here to develop its services in institutional and community planning almost limitlessly. These challenges may require an expanded program of training for Extension Service personnel.

The Changes Will Have Important Effects on Rural Institutions

There are other characteristics that rural New York will have because of this flight to the fringe, such as greater economic security, longer life for its population, a considerable increase in its total economic well-being, an increased proportion of aged residents, and the dangers of creating an unnoticed low-income group. I will close, however, by emphasizing only one more important change: namely, some influences on the rural organizations and institutions. The mere fact of increased population in the rural areas means that local organizations will have larger clienteles with which to work. The presence of more people means more wealth so that the institutions will have better possibilities for adequate support. The farm and non-farm populations will demand that the facilities and services be on a par with those in other areas. Therefore, one may confidently predict considerable up-grading in these institutions and their programs. This is already evident so far as schools are concerned, for the centralization and enlargement of these is going on apace.

Because there may be increased support in wealth and numbers, these very things may simply add strength to each of the already operating units and intensify competition. This is a problem each community must deal with, but guidance is an essential need. More than ever, community councils become an important device for directing community planning and Extension can do much to help in their promotion.

As numbers of people with more and different interests increase in the rural areas, competition for their participation in the organizations already there will increase; and new organizations not now in the rural areas will enter. Therefore, any institution or organization already operating in the rural areas has a field for expansion. In some instances the activities of these organizations can be made a part of the already existing agencies. In most the new activities will divide the field, and may even, in some instances, supplant those already there. The meaning of this suggestion for Extension is that its program, both for youth and adults, for farmers and non-farmers, must be such as to claim loyalty in the face of increasing opportunity from other sources.

Anderson's summary defines the problem resulting from the fringe migration. Three of the most important aspects of involving the rural non-farmer in community programs are communication, participation and leadership. In another study in New York State, the effects of the flight to the fringe on these three aspects were observed. This study was concerned only with open country dwellers in a single county. By comparing farmers with the new non-farm resident, change in channels of communication, participation and leadership could be recognized.

With regard to changes in the use of channels of communication resulting from the fringe movement, some of the more important findings were as follows:

(a) *Farm and part-time farm families concentrate their listening to one radio station, while non-farm families diversify their listening to include several stations.* While most families changed radio stations to some extent during the day, most families tended to listen to one station predominantly through the weekday mornings. There was one station to which most farm families listened. The same station was predominantly listened to by part-time farmers. However, a change in this pattern was indicated by the fact that a nearly equal proportion of non-farm families listened to three different stations. This would mean that in fringe counties the utilization of only one radio station may serve to reach a large proportion of farmers, but it may not be an effective means of reaching the non-farmer.

(b) *The metropolitan daily which reaches the largest proportion of farm families is far exceeded in circulation by a second metropolitan daily in reaching part-time farmers and non-farmers.* The locally published metropolitan daily which had been used to reach the traditional resident of the open country was found to reach approximately one-half of the farmers. This circulation compared favorably with that of the competing metropolitan daily, which reached only one-third of the farmers. However, the situation was reversed in the case of the part-time farmers and the differences were even greater between farmers and non-farmers. The paper reaching the larger proportion of farmers reached only one-fourth of the non-farmers, while its competitor reached approximately three-fourths of the non-farmers.

(c) *Local weekly newspapers are much more effective in reaching farmers and part-time farmers than in reaching non-farmers.* The local weekly newspaper, published in most of the larger rural community centers, reached a fairly large proportion of the farmers nearby. However, the new non-farm resident subscribed to and read these weeklies far less frequently than did the farmers. In some communities the proportion of farmers reading local weeklies was as much as five times the proportion of non-farmers.

(d) *The more extensive communications, such as mimeographed material, circular letters, and "do-it-yourself" bulletins, are about equally effective in reaching the large proportions of the three open-country population groupings.* Often the type of communication necessary for the purpose of the rural organizational leader involves describing skills or items of knowledge which cannot be covered in the short space or time available in newspaper and radio channels. One solution has been to send a mimeographed sheet to each "Householder." When the subjects of the communications are of widespread interest, these communications are sometimes printed, such as those referred to popularly as the "do-it-yourself" bulletin.

If the subject was of general interest, all three occupational groupings would be reached through this channel of communication in about equal proportions. There was a slight tendency for farmers and part-time farmers to use the printed bulletin more than non-farmers, but this can be explained by the greater availability of such bulletins for farmers through the medium of Agricultural Extension bulletins.

(*e*) *Announcements given in two types of communications channels, such as metropolitan dailies and radio stations, or radio and television news programs, reach nearly all of the population.* Approximately nineteen out of every twenty persons listened either to radio news programs or television news programs or both. Similarly, eighteen out of every twenty persons listened to the radio or read a metropolitan daily newspaper or did both. Since approximately one out of twenty could not be reached through any of these channels, it would appear that an announcement placed in either of these sets of communications channels would reach anyone who could be reached by any means except personal contact.

(*f*) *The local weekly newspaper reaches the population around the community in which it is published.* The local weekly newspapers reach only a very small proportion of the total county population. However, insofar as announcements are concerned with the area around a given community, the picture is more encouraging. Approximately one-fourth to one-half of the open country population take the local country weekly in the community where it is published. Nearly all these residents may also be reached through one of the county-wide channels of communication described above. In a large majority of cases, both husband and wife read the country weekly if they subscribe.

Not only does the deliberate action program require effective use of the channels of communication, but the dissemination of knowledge about the program must be followed by a broad participation base and leadership responsibility. The study on the use of channels of communication cited above also included an analysis of the effect of the fringe movement on participation and leadership.

The social participation of the families was classified according to type of organization in which membership or attendance at meetings was regular. Under this classification, civic organizations include parent-teacher associations, volunteer fire departments, community chests, chambers of commerce, various boards such as hospital boards, and organizations of political parties. About one-third of each of the two groups studied (farmers and non-farmers) are active members of these civic organizations, and more so in the local community than in the urban center. This means that, proportionately, the new fringe migrants are accepting their share of responsibility in solving local civic problems.

Very close to the organizations classified as civic are those such as lodges and veterans' associations. While the primary purpose of these organizations is fraternal, a secondary purpose is nearly always civic. It was found in this study that the amount of participation in such organizations is equally small in both the farm and the non-farm groups. Also, the proportion of non-farmers who belong to city fraternal organizations is only slightly greater than that of farmers.

Recreational organizations include athletic clubs and leagues of various kinds, as well as specialized associations based on individual sports. Participation in these was found to be almost identical with that in fraternal associations, for both farmers and non-farmers.

Another aspect of fringe migration is that the rural community now has more types of organizations as a result of special-interest groups among the non-farm migrants. The new formal organizations represent new interests, which, paradoxically, create new civic problems and at the same time provide resources for meeting them that were not previously available to the rural community. Many open-country residents are leaders of the new organizations, even though the meeting place may be in the city. The non-farm residents seem to have as much propensity for leadership as do the farmers.

Of equal importance is the fact that the new open-country residents are leaders more in local community organizations than in urban ones. It appears from this that these new residents are matching the farmers in accepting leadership responsibility in the rural community. This is particularly true of civic and recreational organizations.

In summary it may be said that the non-farm resident of the open country is shifting his organizational ties from the urban to his local community. His participation and leadership activities indicate that he may be depended upon to take an active part in solving the problems created by his migration from the city to the rural community. The resulting organizations are neither traditional rural nor urban in nature, but a fusion of the two into a uniquely "fringe" structure and function.

In addition to the fringe migration described above, there are other aspects of migration which affect the community. As was mentioned earlier in the chapter, migration may be a way of solving family problems, as is illustrated by a deliberate action program involving the resettlement of persons from communities with a low level of living to others where they may have a better opportunity to realize their goals in material comfort. Much resettlement was accomplished during the 1930's. A study in Minnesota indicates the general effects of such resettlement programs.[*]

* R.W. Murchie and C.R. Wasson, "Beltrami Island Resettlement Project," *Minnesota AES Bulletin No. 334*, 1937.

Resettlement of Families From Submarginal Land

The first of the demonstration resettlement projects to get under way under the land retirement program of the United States Government was the Beltrami Island Settler Relocation Project in the northern Minnesota cut-over region.

In this typical cut-over area, the forest cover which was responsible for its original settlement was gone, and the soil, when put to agricultural use, was too poor and unproductive to give the population an adequate income. An area of better soils nearby was available for the resettlement of the families removed from the evacuation area.

Contrary to popular impression, living off the country supplied the minimum physical needs of these people for food, clothing, and shelter. Their distress was due to the lack of sufficient cash income to pay for their public services. Tax delinquency was so high that schools and roads were almost entirely paid for by the state and the people on the better land outside the area. Children were practically denied education beyond the grade school level. Medical service was distant and often not available because of road conditions. Churches also suffered from lack of adequate support. The public had a very definite interest in the evacuation of this area because the 300 families in the area absorbed $20,000 to $30,000 per year above what they paid in taxes for the support of schools, roads, and relief, and because the settlers were often responsible for high forest fire losses.

Beltrami Island was chosen in 1934 by the Land Policy Section of the Agricultural Adjustment Administration for experiment in settler relocation within the cut-over area because the need for evacuation was obvious and the nearness of an area of better soils would make possible the minimum of social readjustment involved in any move.

A plan for purchase and resettlement was evolved by persons thoroughly familiar with the region and its people. This plan involved (1) a system of appraisal according to the public benefit of evacuation of the area, (2) debt adjustment, (3) resettlement with the lightest debt load possible, (4) a grubstake, and (5) the maximum of choice for the client in planning and farm development.

Work started in August, 1934, but it was the end of 1936 before the bulk of the settlers were moved. The people have been placed on demonstrably better soil, their financial position has been definitely improved, and they can now obtain the public services which they could not afford previously. From the public standpoint, the financial condition of the county has improved and the promised savings in costs to the public have materialized. It is, of course, too early to make a final judgement of the results.

The evacuation area is being developed as a forest and wild life reserve.

Results of the Move

Tax delinquency and governmental aids in the cut-over area of northern Minnesota furnish adequate reason for experimentation in settler relocation, but a raised standard of living for those affected can be the only social justification of the particular methods followed. Available evidence indicates that the economic and social position of the settlers has been improved.

One of the main reasons for the impoverished condition of the settlers was the poor quality of the soil in their farms. The soil on the new farms is much better. The 65 old farms had an average soil rating of 44; and the 65 new ones, an average of 76.

The economic condition of the settlers, so far as it can be measured by net worth, has definitely improved. Statistics summarizing this result for all cases moved are not available, but those for a typical case can be cited:

A———— had prior to 1934 lost title to his property by failing to make the necessary payments; therefore, he had no equity in land or buildings. He was a "squatter." His chattels were mortgaged for $145 and his net worth was about $440. The Rehabilitation Corporation approved a loan of $1,750. This included 160 acres of land for $653, building material, and grubstake to the value of 60 per cent of the improvement work. The Corporation also took over the chattel mortgage and up to December, 1936, had advanced $1,522. His inventory at a conservative appraisal made by Resettlement Administration officers totaled $3,480, his liabilities $1,522, and his net worth was now $1,958.

Some credit for such gains in net worth is due to the skill of the project staff in advising the client on land purchase and farm set-up. But a very large portion of the gains in net worth must be accredited to the opportunity accorded the settler to capitalize his own labor. To those not familiar with building costs and conditions in such an area, it might be thought that an average loan of $1,700 would be too small to allow for good housing. That flexibility of architecture to permit fullest utilization of local low-cost materials and whatever skill and labor is available to the settler can result in desirable housing is illustrated by the following case:

A resettlement client who was a renter in the forest area and hence had no property to sell, moved out and selected 160 acres of land six miles from Baudette. He was fairly well equipped with livestock and machinery. He bought his entirely unimproved land at $7.50 per acre, for $1,200. He had no buildings to move and was too conservative to assume a large amount of debt. He had a small amount of lumber and planned to build a cheap, temporary house. The building supervisor urged him to begin a house that would have some permanent value and could later be added to or completed. They went to see several buildings under construction. Then he and his wife and the building supervisor worked over plans that seemed best to meet their requirements and decided upon a house 24 x 28 x 12 feet. The client, because of lack of funds, expected to build without a foundation. The supervisor showed him that he and his sons by doing their own work could get a foundation and full cement-wall basement for about $75 in actual cash outlay. With the plans furnished and a little help from a son-in-law who is a mechanic, also a client, they built a house. The house as it stands, ready to live in, with full cement basement and shingle roof, had cost $325.37 in actual cash outlay. During the following winter the owner spent stormy days in insulating the house thoroughly, fastening building felt and other materials between studdings and rafters, built a chimney, and then put on lath.

The following summer he planned to stucco the outside and plaster the inside, and then he would have a really comfortable and attractive farm house. It is expected that in two or three years this family will have a home that even in this region of low building costs will be worth $1,200 to $1,500 for a cash outlay of less than half that amount.

Another result of the moving has been the possibility of better school facilities and better roads. Since the area into which they are moving is already well settled, schools are larger and more stable. Some are consolidated.

The settlement has been made more compact in the resettlement area. This relocation area has thus also benefited. School district population and tax base both have been increased, permitting better facilities. It has been necessary to build only two additional schools. The more compact nature of settlement has also lightened the road tax burden for those already in the area.

The main reason for the project from the public point of view was the state of the county finances. These have also been directly improved.

One important saving in the future will be on road construction and maintenance. During the period 1923–1935, inclusive, Lake of the Woods County spent for construction and maintenance of roads within the evacuation area a total of $18,964, an average of $1,458.77 per year. During the period 1923–1935, inclusive, the state spent a total of $60,630 on roads within the area, an annual average of $4,663.85.

School District No. 119 also will be an important beneficiary of the program. Five schools were operated in the evacuation area in 1934, the last year before the residents began moving out under the resettlement program. The average cost of operating each school in that year was about $1,200, and the total for the five schools was slightly in excess of $6,000. The amount of state aid expended on these five schools in 1934 was approximately $4,900, and the amount paid by District 119 was $1,100.

Therefore, the closing of these schools will effect a saving to District 119 of $1,100. This, however, is offset by the fact that two other schools have been opened in the district to provide for children of clients who have moved. Since the cost to the district of maintaining each school is approximately $200 a year, the saving will be made on but three schools and will amount to about $600 a year for the school district.

In addition to the above, it is expected that marked savings will be made to the Department of Conservation in the evacuation area. The settlers were continually setting fires for purposes of land clearing, and their fires often spread to the forests with resultant great expense to the state for fighting them.

Such studies as this one done during the depression of the 1930's have been repeated many times to establish the relationship between resettlement and level of living. In a more recent one, Strauss and Parrish found that families who had resettled in the Columbia River Basin had increased their level of living considerably.[3] However, this relationship is neither auto-

[3] Murray Strauss and Bernard D. Parrish, "The Columbia Basin Settler: A Study of Social and Economic Resources in New Land Settlement," *Washington AES Bulletin* 556, 1956.

matic nor simple in the case of farmers. It has been found generally that at first the resettled farm family faces the problem of deciding the extent to which income should be reinvested in the farm or devoted to consumer expenditures. Thus, in the case of farmers, the immediate effect of resettlement on level of living may run counter to long-term results.

The use of migration or resettlement in solving problems associated with levels of living in large urban places is also neither automatic nor simple. Often the values attached to separate residences by people deter them from occupying apartments and result in vacancies in new housing projects. In general, lower middle class families living in separate residences will move into housing projects and their vacated houses will be taken over by tenement residents, resulting in a relocation of the slum area within the community. Thus, migration or resettlement as a means of changing levels of living may be influenced by the social status of the migrant, his system of values, and his educational aspirations.[4]

PRINCIPLES

1. *Population size and density will influence both the creation and the solution of community problems. Extremes either way will tend to accentuate problems.*

2. *The numbers of people to be served condition community organization and influence the over-all community structure.*

3. *Changes in the size, density, or composition of the population necessitates changes in the individual service elements and within the community as a whole.*

4. *Changes in population may introduce unplanned changes in community structure.*

5. *The optimum size and density for communities is not yet determined.*

6. *Community development programs must be sensitive to changes in the composition of the population and must anticipate changes that may result from economic or social forces.*

[4] For the demographic characteristics by size of place, see Duncan and Reiss, *op. cit.;* also the summary in Chapter 2 of this work.

SELECTED REFERENCES

Blizzard, S.W., "Research on the Rural-Urban Fringe: A Case Study," *Sociology and Social Research*, 38:143–50, 1954.

Duncan, Otis Dudley, and Albert J. Reiss, Jr., *Social Characteristics of Urban and Rural Communities, 1950*, John Wiley and Sons, New York, 1956.

Goldstein, Sidney, "Repeated Migration as a Factor in High Mobility Rates," *ASR*, 19:536–41, 1954.

Hagood, Margaret J., "Rural Population Characteristics," in Carl C. Taylor and others, *Rural Life in the United States*, Alfred A. Knopf, New York, 1949, Chapter 12.

Landis, Paul H., and Paul K. Hatt, *Populations Problems: a Cultural Interpretation*, American Book Company, New York, 1954, Chapters 5 and 8.

Lively, Charles E., Stuart A. Queen, David B. Carpenter, Walter C. McKain, Robert G. Burnight, Paul K. Hatt, Samuel W. Blizzard, and Robert C. Angell, "The Sociological Significance of the Rural-Urban Fringe," *RS*, 18:101–21, 1953.

Martin, Walter T., "Some Socio-psychological Aspects of Adjustment to Residence Location in the Rural-Urban Fringe," *ASR*, 18:248–53, 1953.

Nelson, Lowry, *American Farm Life in the Twentieth Century*, Harvard University Press, Cambridge, Mass., 1954, Chapter 3.

Scaff, Alvin H., "The Effect of Commuting on Participation in Community Organizations," *ASR*, 17:215–20, 1952.

Smith, T. Lynn, *Population Analysis*, McGraw-Hill Book Company, Inc., New York, 1948.

Spengler, Joseph J., and Otis Dudley Duncan, *Population Theory and Policy*, the Free Press, Glencoe, Illinois, 1956.

Stone, Gregory P., "City Shoppers and Urban Identification: Observations on the Social Psychology of City Life," *AJS*, 60:36–45, 1954.

PART TWO

Dimensions of
the Community

The courses of action taken by a community are influenced by factors at three levels of analysis: the pan-community or mass society level, such as the influence upon the local unit that is exerted by national economic conditions; the local community level, such as the conflict which exists within the community itself; and the level of the component dimensions within the community which provide it with form and structure. In this section some of the influencing factors may be seen at all three levels, although somewhat more attention is given to the internal structure of the community.

These causal conditions were described in terms of two types, those which are manifested in nearly all situations involving interrelations of persons, groups, organizations, and institutions. These are called dimensions. Other aspects of structure may also influence the entire community, but usually do not. These are called elements. Examples of dimensions may be seen in the succeeding paragraphs and in the next six chapters. Examples of elements will be given in the introduction to Part III and in Chapters 11 through 18.

One of the most important distinctions between man and animal is that man has beliefs. Some beliefs merely rationalize that which exists, while others initiate new action. These beliefs are organized so as to be consistent, although inconsistencies appear and consequently create problems. These consistent bodies of beliefs are referred to as value systems. The nature of the value system is described in Chapter 5, and its functions analyzed in Chapter 6. The value system is important in all human relationships, because it guides action. Values are dimensions of community structure because they permeate all types of community action. For example, if tradition is an important criterion of decision-making, it is likely that all types of community action will be influenced by this value. Further, if changes occur, such as rapidly increasing dependence upon science as a thoughtway, this change will be felt throughout the community structure.

Likewise, any relationships among persons, groups, and institutions that are of relevance to the community hinge upon communication. Indeed, communication has often been used synonymously with the social process. Thus, another dimension of community is the generalized function of communications, both formal and informal. Various aspects of the communication system, its formal channels, public opinion, and stereotypes are discussed as dimensions of community in Chapter 7.

The stratification system, referring to the organized system of inequalities seen in all communities the world over, is expressed throughout the social structure. If women are given very low status, they will be given low status throughout the system of human interaction. If exceptions are made, these will be made explicit and rationalized as morally right. The executive of a large corporation, wielding much authority in his own corporation, will also be given power in his church and the school system, and the mayor is likely to listen to his complaints or encouragement. Thus, stratification, including prestige, power, leadership, and the like, is a dimension of community structure because it permeates all community relations. This system will be described in Chapters 8 and 9.

Age differences which are large enough to be socially meaningful (child, adolescent, elder, and so on) also condition all other aspects of the community. Some of the subtler aspects of this factor are considered in Chapter 10, along with the usual age-related problems included in social analysis.

Not all of the important dimensions are included in Part II, but all of those which are discussed are of utmost importance in understanding community structure.

CHAPTER 5

The Value System

The community, like any other social structure, involves people acting together to attain certain ends they hold in common. The attainment of these ends must be made through means acceptable to the people in the community. The ends people seek and the means they permit themselves to use in seeking those ends vary greatly from one social structure to another. The greatest variation is found from one culture to another, such as the differences between the Chinese culture and the United States. Variation within a culture is also found to occur, such as that between the North and the South or between different socioeconomic classes. As will be shown later, communities in a single county with a relatively homogeneous population may differ in ways which are significant in their effects on community structure and change.

The importance of variation in ends and means can hardly be overestimated. What people regard as morally right and wrong influences their behavior as profoundly as any other factor. The value system is expressed by and governs behavior, and therefore values and behavior can only be fully understood when considered together. For this reason, the discussion in subsequent chapters involves both behavior and values. It is helpful to view the value system as a separate entity for pedagogical purposes.

THE NATURE OF THE VALUE SYSTEM

The value system is the organization of, or interrelation among, codes of conduct, including means and goals. Thus the value system includes four essential aspects: prescribed goals toward which people should strive, prescribed means of achieving these goals, sanctions enforcing conformity, and the organization of these prescriptions so that there is no contradiction or conflict among them. The codes of conduct, as they are expressed in behavior, are not clear-cut, since the relationship between goals and means is often unclear and sometimes contradictory. However, the division of values

93

into goals and means is convenient for purposes of analysis. The deviation of real life situations from this model will be discussed in detail later in the section on value orientations.

Many theories of human behavior posit inborn needs and instincts to explain the nature of human goals and the means of attaining them. The evidence does not support such a proposition, nor does this point of view explain changes in time and differences between cultures in space. A person of one nationality or race reared in another country pursues the goals of the culture in which he is reared, not those of his nationality or race. Further, the same person who moves from one culture to another or from one social class to another adjusts his goals and means accordingly to fit the new situation. This assumes that he has not reached an age where he cannot easily acquire new values. Similarly, the instinct theory does not explain social change, for instinct is constant or relatively so, while social change is, by definition, variable. The difficulty of explaining differences between cultures or value systems with the instinct construct follows from these two criticisms.[1] It is fortunate for action programs that the instinct theory is fallacious, since little change could be expected if one holds explanation of human differences in goal-seeking behavior.

Goals

Goals vary in the level of abstraction at which they are viewed by persons living under the value system. Some goals are quite specific and concrete, such as the goal of a high income in American society. While income may be viewed as a means to other goals, it operates as a goal in many situations, as, for example, in changing occupations.

Other goals are so general that they may best be represented by the term "situation" or "state of affairs," for example, happiness or job satisfaction. The general goals may find expression in specific goals, as in the case of a community development program aimed specifically at sewage disposal but generally toward health. It is also important to note that specific goals are more often viewed as issues than are general goals. There is little discussion of the need for health but there may be much disagreement on the wisdom of a sewage disposal system.

The most important principle of all is that in any given value system, some goals are obligatory, some are preferred, some permissible, and some

[1] For the classical statement of instinct theory see William McDougall, *Introduction to Social Psychology*, Methuen, Ltd., London, 1908. For a critique of this position see L.L. Bernard, *Instinct: A Study in Social Psychology*, Henry Holt and Company, New York, 1924.

are taboo.[2] For example, health of children in American society is an obligatory goal for parents, a high level of living is preferred, and aspiration to college is permissible. Codes of conduct which are taboo are obligatory, but are "don't" rather than "do" rules.

The Hierarchy of Values

The pursuit of goals follows a course wherein choices must be made such as those between honor and life, success and integrity, money and leisure. It should not be inferred from this that these examples are always, or even usually, mutually exclusive. However, no one can pursue one of these pairs of goals for long without being forced to make a choice between them, at least temporarily. The concept is most easily understood at the individual level, where a secondary occupation may bring more money but conflicts with the desire for leisure time. The important characteristic of the hierarchy of values is its variability from situation to situation. Thus, a marginal farmer may become a part-time farmer, sacrificing leisure, until he is "on his feet," at which time he may leave the non-farm job, or perhaps discontinue farming entirely.

At the broad cultural level, the hierarchy of values varies not only with the situation, as in the case of the individual, but between value systems. For example, among certain classes in Japan, honor was chosen over life, with suicide defined as honorable death, while in American society, suicide is never honorable. This example also shows situational variation within a culture, where a "suicide mission" in wartime is honorable in the American value system, and is sometimes chosen over life. The hierarchy of values may bring about very noticeable differences in types of problems faced by communities and in the way communities set about to solve these problems.

Explicit and Implicit Values

Both goals and means are observed at two different levels, one the ideal or explicit and the other at the implicit cultural level. Lynd [3] cites several cases of the explicit versus the implicit culture in America. Some examples of Lynd's dualistic value statements will indicate the nature of the difference between the implicit and explicit culture.

[2] An excellent discussion of the value system is given in Robin Williams, *American Society*, Alfred A. Knopf, New York, 1952. See especially Chapter 3.
[3] For a more complete listing of this dualism, see Robert S. Lynd, *Middletown in Transition*, Harcourt, Brace, and Company, New York, 1937.

1. Democracy, as discovered and perfected by the American people, is the ultimate form of living together. All men are created free and equal, and the United States has made this fact a living reality.

But: You would never get anywhere, of course, if you constantly left things to popular vote. No business could be run that way and, of course, no businessman would tolerate it.

2. Everyone should try to be successful.

But: The kind of person you are is more important than how successful you are.

3. Life would not be tolerable if we did not believe in progress and know that things are getting better. We should, therefore, welcome new things.

But: The old tried fundamentals are best and it is a mistake for busybodies to try to change things too fast or try to upset the fundamentals.

4. Honesty is the best policy.

But: Business is business and a businessman would be a fool if he did not cover his hand.

5. Education is a fine thing.

But: It is the practical man who gets things done.

6. Science is a fine thing in its place and our future depends upon it.

But: Science has no right to interfere with such things as our fundamental institutions. The thing to do is to use science but not let it upset things.

7. No man deserves to have what he hasn't worked for and it demoralizes him to do so.

But: You can't let people starve.

On the one hand, this dualism in values may indicate culture change. The explicit or ideal culture may be the vestige of traditional culture, while the "but" statement may represent the beginning of a new value. On the other hand, it may be that these are merely rationalizations for the violation of culture traits or codes of conduct. It is by the nature of values that they include their sanctions, or reward and punishment for conformity and violation. Thus, a rationalization such as this cultural dualism may be needed in order to avoid guilt feelings for the violation of a code of conduct.

This dualism in beliefs is also important in understanding other cultures and subcultures which are relatively strange to the student. The ideal or explicit culture patterns are those which will be apparent first to the stranger. The implication of this is clear: the student of the community must look beneath the surface for the total understanding of the total value system in the community. It also implies that the nature of the value system may be a subject of disagreement among the members of the community themselves. For example, the more naive person may accept the explicit codes as fundamental and not only feel guilty at their violation but also avoid any type of community change which violates these explicit codes. Usually the top power figures in the community will be the most likely to recognize the discrepancies between explicit and implicit culture. The explicit values will more likely operate as codes of conduct for less powerful figures while the implicit value codes will operate for those higher in the power structure.[4]

Means

The means through which an individual, family, community, or society may pursue ends will vary in important ways. A completely rational means-ends schema would entail any means which effectively brought achievement of the goal.[5] But a hungry people may prefer to remain hungry rather than eat a type of food which another people relish. The Indian taboo on beef and the Jewish taboo on pork are cases in point. There is a level of hunger at which this taboo becomes problematic, but these are extreme cases and the triumph of the physiological need over the taboo is not universal.

Another interesting relationship between means and ends is that the demonstration of relative effectiveness is often not sufficient to bring about change. Codes of conduct as they refer to means of pursuing ends also include sanctions. Money is a goal which may be obtained easily by burglary, but such a means is taboo. At a more subtle level, the alternative means to any given goal are much more limited than is generally recognized. For example, in a bureaucracy, which is defined in terms of written rules, the high level decisions are made informally and outside of the rules. Likewise in a social system which appears to have a minimum of written rules, and operates with a great deal of freedom and informality, there may be informal precedents or traditions which limit alternatives. It is in the latter situation in which communities will ordinarily operate. The legal basis of the community is not usually well established, except in village centers which are coterminous with legal units. Thus, resistance to a more rational means of reaching a goal may be found even when the relationship between the means and the end is quite clear. It is only with an understanding of the value system that the resistance to this change in means can be understood.[6]

VALUE ORIENTATIONS

Two principles that have been suggested imply that the means-goal model is not the only or perhaps always the best theory for describing a

[4] Floyd W. Hunter, *Community Power Structure: A Study of Decision Makers*, University of North Carolina Press, Chapel Hill, 1953.
[5] For differing positions on this see Edwin A. Burtt, *Right Thinking*, Harper and Brothers, New York, 1946, Part IV, and John Dewey, *Theory of Valuation*, University of Chicago Press, Chicago, Illinois, 1939.
[6] Edward H. Spicer, *Human Problems in Technological Change: A Case Book*, Russell Sage Foundation, New York, 1952.

value system. These principles are: (1) a given value may be a means in some situations but a goal in others; and (2) the most rational or effective means to a goal may be taboo. For this reason it may be better to describe a value system in terms of orientations. These orientations may be classified according to (1) the emphasis given some institution, such as the family or economic institution; (2) the interest in some segment of the population, such as youth or the aged; or (3) the general criteria of decision-making, such as belief in science or tradition.

Rationality

The simplest scheme of value orientations is the dichotomy of traditionalism and rationality.[7] These two orientations are opposite types similar in many ways to the types of societies to be discussed later in this book, including the section on social change and the value system. They also bear directly upon the work of community organizers, since they are often plagued by two difficulties involving traditionalism and rationality. First, the professional sometimes comes from a value system different from that in which he is working. At worst, this involves a resource person from a completely different system, as in the case of a scientist in a technical field in the United States working with lay people in Southeast Asia. At best it often involves merely the differences between scientist and layman. A scientist is usually not scientific in problems outside his own discipline. Even within a scientist's own discipline, complete rationality is never known, since the fictions and fallacies are only slowly dispersed in any area.

In discussing the meaning of traditionalism and rationality it is important again first to separate means from ends. It is perhaps easiest to learn the meaning of these two concepts by taking rationality first, although in terms of frequency and intensity in decision-making this is a reversal. Traditionalism is by far the master of the situation.

Most theories of human behavior assume man to be goal-directed. For purposes of describing the rational decision, suppose money is taken as a goal or end. The means-end scheme holds that one goal is in mind, in this case money. There are several means which would achieve the end. For a farmer, money might come through hard work, adopting farm practices recommended by the agricultural extension service, and robbing a bank. Within the means-end scheme, to be completely rational, he would select

---

[7] See Howard Becker, *Through Values to Social Interpretation*, Duke University Press, Durham, North Carolina, 1950, and Hans H. Gerth and C. Wright Mills, *From Max Weber: Essays in Sociology*, Oxford University Press, New York, 1946.

robbery or burglary, since it would attain the end quickly, easily, and neatly. However, the means in this case are not judged in terms of the end, but rather in terms of another consequence, namely imprisonment. Indeed, this second consequence is placed higher in the hierarchy of values than the original one, which was the goal of making money.

A more completely descriptive theory of rational thought is presented by Dewey's theory of valuation.[8] Any problem arises not as an end but as a situation in which there are feelings of discomfort. Through an analysis of this situation certain alternatives appear feasible. These alternatives, which are means in the theory previously described, are courses of action which are judged in relation to their many consequences. Robbing a bank would not often be seriously considered as an alternative because the consequences of imprisonment, loss of civil rights, loss of prestige and respect and so on are too severe. The other two alternatives, namely of hard work and adopting practices, would be judged in terms of the risk involved in spending money for practices, the respect hard work brings, and the profit to the farmer. It should also be noted that the two alternatives used in this illustration are not mutually exclusive, that is, the farmer may both work hard and adopt practices. However, this is not always the case.

The value orientation toward rationality may be defined as the uncritical adoption of consequences as the criterion of choosing a course of action. This means that among the various alternatives the choice is made which the person or group believes will bring the best consequences and avoid the worst ones. The implication is clear that the relationships between alternatives and consequences need not be accurate; indeed they are often cultural fictions. It may be that hard work is not really a means to making money in American society, but to the best information of the person making the decision this is a fact. If he makes the judgment on this criterion it is rationality, regardless of the accuracy of the relationship assumed between alternatives and consequences.

Rationality is the practical side of science, then, and as such it is obvious that science itself is a faith. While any given scientific study is accepted on explicit criteria, the criteria themselves are values held by the body of scientists. Problems are selected on nonscientific grounds more often than not; whether the projected experiment, case study, or survey method is to be used is determined on nonscientific grounds; and many decisions during the research process are made because of time, money, personnel, and so on, all of which are nonscientific factors.

[8] Dewey, *op. cit.*

Traditionalism

If in rationality the consequences or ends hold high priority with means relegated to the low prestige of selection in terms of the consequences, then traditionalism is quite the opposite. Traditionalism is the uncritical adoption of precedents as the criterion of choosing a course of action. The phrases "what you have been used to" and "what has been done before" describe this perfectly. In traditionalism, means are raised to the level of ends, alternatives to the level of consequences. For example, extremely hard work in farming was a necessity in pioneer society. It is right and proper, then, for a man to work hard. While he gains respect and perhaps even more money through hard work, the important thing is that hard work itself is right. Robbery is not an alternative, not because of imprisonment, but rather because it is morally wrong. Means, then, are judged as right and wrong in and of themselves, although they may have been rationally thought out in the beginning. They may still achieve their assumed goals. However, the criterion of selection is not relationship to ends and consequences, but moral rightness and wrongness in and of themselves.

In any given decision, rationality is never completely realized. It seldom exceeds traditionalism in importance in any decision. Since, in the individual, traditional patterns often become habits, everyone takes some courses of action which are entirely based on tradition.

Actually, one cannot consider rationally every course of action that one must take in a day because there are too many decisions to be made and too much knowledge would be required to make them rationally. Furthermore, since values are in systems, so that changes in one aspect of the system bring change in other aspects, traditional values reinforce each other. It is small wonder that communities resist changes even though the proposed changes may appear to be a better way to the goals set by the community itself. Many proposed changes require more rationality than most of us can muster and may involve changes in other parts of the system not anticipated in the narrow problem of immediate concern.

External Conformity

External conformity appears in many ways to coincide with traditionalism in American communities. This value orientation has been treated by various theorists, including Alexis de Tocqueville over 100 years ago and, more recently, by Williams and William H. Whyte.[9]

[9] Alexis de Tocqueville, *Democracy in America*, Sever and Francis, Cambridge, 1862;

An orientation toward conformity is the uncritical adoption of group patterns as a criterion in choosing courses of action. It may be that in a given situation a person may independently reach a decision identical with that arrived at by his fellows; however, this is not external conformity unless he arrived at his decision only because it was in agreement with that of his fellows. There is much external conformity in American communities by individuals and substructures within the community. For example, landscaping and type of house may be homogeneous within a neighborhood area. Time is also a factor in producing such conformity owing to the influence of fads such as the "Cape Cod" or the "rancher." Inside these houses, there may be many decisions reached by the family because of the pressure for external conformity, such as seeing the right movies, belonging to the right clubs, drinking intoxicating beverages, shoveling the snow or mowing the grass, and buying a prestige car. In the area of ideas, there are limits beyond which the solid citizen does not go in proposing a community action or a program for a formal organization. Actually, in comparison with all the alternatives open to communities and organizations, these limits are surprisingly small.

External conformity and traditionalism are value orientations which bring social control of the individual. The codes of conduct set in the past or by the group allow less room for the unique and the peculiar. In fact, the change in the usage of the word "peculiar" reflects this nicely. The word was defined as "different from the usual," "not common," "belonging only to one individual," in the original usage of the term. It has come to mean eccentric or queer, and is seldom used without connotations of "bad." A "peculiarity" is almost a mental disease rather than a distinctive trait, as it was once considered. This merely reflects, in a very small way, the tremendous effect the value orientation toward external conformity has had in American life. Whyte calls this the "social ethic." [10] He says in essence that the philosophy that man is a product of his society and groups (a position to be taken later in this book) and the assumptions (1) that man's basic need is "belonging" and (2) that the group is the main source of creativity, have all led to a value orientation that man and society are not in conflict. Apparent conflicts are rather results of lack of communication.

As Whyte points out, and as is obvious from any objective or disinterested view of society, external conformity has been a value code throughout history. Feudalism, to mention only one form of society, demanded conformity of the man-in-the-field. Communist Russia, Nazi Germany, and Fas-

Williams, *op. cit.* Chapter 11; and William H. Whyte, Jr., *The Organization Man,* Doubleday and Company, Garden City, New York, 1957.

[10] Whyte, *op. cit.,* pp. 7–8.

cist Italy, as well as democratic-capitalist America and England, demand and/or demanded external conformity. Any change in the governmental structure is likely to loosen the ties but little.

Achievement

As a value, achievement is a state of satisfaction based upon a choice of alternatives which results in a high position in the social structure (income, prestige, education, level of living) that brings self-respect (and often envy from others). As it appears on the American scene, this value is not "uncritical adoption," as was the case of value orientations previously discussed. Traditionalism is usually adopted completely and uncritically. In the case of external conformity, trust is placed in the proposition that "forty million Frenchmen can't be wrong" to take care of the effects of a particular conformity to the remainder of the value system. Williams points out, however, that there is not much evidence as to the relative importance of achievement (valued accomplishments) and success (rewards).[11] He says that this issue is crucial, since success orientations are more independent of the remainder of the moral system, and therefore allow room for a "corrosion of regulative norms." The business heroes of the past have not been better morally than the common man, and perhaps worse in situations relevant to their achievement. Their image, however, emphasizes their "good points" consistently with other codes of conduct. The gossip magazines, so popular in the middle 1950's, are also a case in point. Common gossip on the immorality of Hollywood stars has been passed about and joked about for years. But specific concrete cases, whether reported truthfully or not and printed with the risk of libel suits, were too much for the American people and some film careers were at least temporarily ruined. The injury to these careers included nothing of acting ability, the real criterion of achievement, but rather involved other values. If the value orientation had been shifted from achievement to success, as Williams distinguishes the two, this damage would not have happened. On the other hand, not all persons about whom these magazines printed stories of violations of the codes of conduct suffered ruination. This may indicate a trend toward success rewards divorced from other value orientations in greater measure than most Americans would care to admit.

Insofar as achievement is the core of the value orientation under consideration, it operates toward accomplishment at the community level. Thus

[11] Williams, *op. cit.*, p. 392.

a person's talents may be directed at altruistic ends, even though his motives are essentially selfish. The community leadership may often take the form of a channel through which personal achievement may be realized.

Williams again points out an interesting aspect of the value orientation on achievement which bears not only upon community structure but upon the situations which communities define as problematic. This is the value of "bigness." Growth in population, the number of people who "turn out at a meeting," and the amount of money donated to a cause are all implicitly valued in the American community. On this Williams points out that "things are good not so much because they are big, but because goodness is assumed and bigness, therefore, means more of something already considered valuable." [12]

Individualism

Individualism may be defined as the conviction that the best state of affairs is one in which self-reliant and independent men assume the responsibility for their own decisions. It is the freedom to avoid concern for the rigid norms of a closed value system with no compulsion from an external power structure. The question was raised whether there was any room for individualism in a social world in which traditionalism and external conformity are so strong. It was suggested that achievement may represent one channel for individual expression. This possibility rests on the proposition that there are alternative, socially approved, goals toward which the individual may strive. However, many types of achievement produce conformity and operate as a social control. One theory of social mobility places conformity as an important aspect of raising ones status: [13]

(1) The goals and means are somewhat different, according to the position one holds. For example, the leader must act differently from the member, the minister differently from the layman.

(2) The different codes of conduct are agreed upon by everyone, for their own position as well as for others. For example, the codes appropriate only for the leader are believed to be morally right by leader and member alike. The codes assigned to the minister are assigned by both minister and laymen.

(3) Violations of the codes appropriate to any given position bring moral indignation from others and guilt feelings for the violator.

[12] *Ibid.*, p. 394.
[13] Talcott Parsons, "An Analytical Approach to the Theory of Social Stratification," *AJS*, 45:841–62, 1940.

(4) As persons or groupings move upward through the status system, they gradually adopt those codes which are fitting for those just above them, insofar as possible. For example, if one wishes to be a vice-president, he must convince others he can act as a vice-president is supposed to act.

(5) The one who aspired to achieve must then act within a narrow range of alternatives, insofar as his achievement depends upon others.

The problem of free will versus cultural determinism is involved in the definition of individualism. Is it really possible for a man to ignore the value system, since it has been ingrained in him from childhood? [14] Is it not true that conscience is really a product of unique combinations of value training? This issue is perhaps best stated and left untreated here, since the intent of the definition involves merely the right to disagree at a given time, and what is perhaps as important, to disagree frequently and on important issues. Disagreement may be merely the introduction of different learned values into the decision-making situation from those brought in by the group. On the other hand, it may be that this is the result of free will. Whatever it results from, the value placed on individualism is most often expressed in relation to the symbol "individualism" but regarded as disruptive in actual operation.

One of the authors attended a meeting of a Parent-Teachers Association where three issues arose, the purchase of a coffee urn for use in PTA meetings, the signing of a petition for a school to be built in a certain location, and a program for a subsequent meeting. Committees had been appointed to make proposals in all three cases. One mother raised an issue as to whether the purchase of the coffee urn might not be less functional than contribution of the money toward fluorescent lights in the school. The same mother raised a question on the petition. It seems that several persons in another part of the large city had signed a petition against building the school in the location named. No reason was given. The petition in the meeting was in favor of building the school. The assumption was that business interests had promoted the first petition against building the school and the assumption was implicit in the discussion that these interests were "anti-education." The mother previously referred to arose and suggested that it had not been determined why the first petition had been signed. She suggested that perhaps the location was not central to the school district. On the third issue she again stood for recognition, and among groans from the 200 or more people in attendance, made her criticism of the proposed program. It was interesting that in all three cases her points were logical,

[14] Leslie A. White, *Science and Culture: A Study of Man and Civilization*, Farrar and Straus, New York, 1949.

and that in the case of the petition, she was successful in delaying a hasty vote in ignorance of the situation. It was also interesting that the same person, and only one person, raised questions on all three issues. It is significant for the study of the community that, if that particular organization follows the pattern described by previous research on the roles of leadership and "idea men," she will never be elected president of the local organization.[15]

Democracy

The value orientation toward democracy is certainly more toward the symbol or the word than toward the application of the concept to everyday life. Democratic process, as a term, begets favor and any direct evidence of its violation gets either moral indignation (the test of a value) or rationalization.

Democracy in the American value scheme has been closely associated with equality and freedom, although the three orientations are not the same. Since these three concepts are discussed elsewhere, it is important here to show only what democracy is and what it is not in the American value system, and to give some indication of its relevance to community structure. Through its association with freedom and equality, the value on democracy is an ill-defined concept. It is often confused with *laissez faire* philosophies which are analogous to anarchy in the political institution. The term, as it applies to social relations, is borrowed from economic theory, where it means free competition. In the social structure, *laissez faire* means that each person or grouping pursues its own ends, compromising only when it is instrumental to those ends to do so. It is probably most closely associated with the idea of freedom, but not with the practice of freedom. The more powerful persons and groups are likely to win freedom for themselves at the expense of the weaker unless some control is exercised by an external force. The idea itself is acceptable within the value orientation on democracy, but the consequence of might making right is not. Therefore, it can be concluded that when the issue is real, *laissez faire* is not essentially what is meant in the value orientation on democracy.

A second qualification is that the moral "rightness" of democracy is probably limited to two kinds of substructures, the political structure and formal organizations. In both of these situations, moral indignation is felt when it is recognized that undemocratic procedures are in operation. Democracy

[15] Helen H. Jennings, *Leadership and Isolation,* Longmans, Green, and Company, New York, 1950.

in the work world is almost unknown, and it is found only somewhat more frequently in the family, the religious institution, and the educational institution.

While a formal definition of democracy is difficult, it does help to avoid one further fallacy which often serves as a channel through which the value may be circumvented. The democratic process may often end in a vote, but voting does not constitute democracy. Rather, democracy is the process of discussion and compromise whereby individuals or social units make a unitary decision which is binding where the majority position is modified to satisfy the minorities. This is found in Rousseau's concept of the "general will" or more familiarly in the Quaker "sense of the meeting." Thus, in a genuinely democratic situation, agreement is achieved on terms universally acceptable to the group.

Material Comfort

Another set of value orientations, less associated with social control than those previously discussed, reflects the major orientation toward the economic institution. These are material comfort, progress, efficiency, and security. Further, these values are probably more nearly goals than a coalescence of means and goals, as is the case with those values previously discussed.

Material comfort, and its cohort income, is probably the most famous value orientation attributed to the American system.[16] There is no doubt that material comfort is extremely important in the American scheme of things, and much of the foreign aid program carried on by the United States assumes the inherent worth of this value. While the contention that material comfort is inherently and universally good cannot be proved, the near-universality of the orientation among the power groups of other nations does seem to hold up. Few governments will reject gifts and loans which will raise the level of living of their people. If this is more than altruism on their part, extending to a realistic appraisal of the means of maintaining power, then it must be that the value on material comfort is either universal or easily aroused.

Progress

Another value orientation is that toward progress. The best is yet to come, socially acceptable trends are all good, and mass optimism are expressions

[16] Williams, op. cit., pp. 406–9.

of this orientation. Some of the scholars who have considered the nature of historical trends believe that human organization moves in cycles and/or on a relatively straight line toward a better world. The straight-line theory has been characteristic of the American value on progress. As one author says it, "Progress was not [to an American] a mere philosophical ideal but a commonplace of experience." [17] Indeed, the American experience in striving toward the more discernible goals, particularly material comfort, has been evidence of this linear relationship. In fact, if there has been any deviation from the straight line of progress in the material sphere, it has been a rising rate of increase rather than a "tapering off." By defining new problems as "new" rather than as having been created by social trends or by solution to previous problems, this concept of progress has been extended to include other aspects of community life in addition to the economic. There are many facts in the history of the United States which allow such a philosophy. One is the fact that the nation has never lost a war, and secondly, that in international relations the United States has moved rapidly to a position of world leadership. Also, crises, such as the great depression of the 1930's, have been solved with but little apparent change in "our way of life," at least in major features of our social structure. The great man theory of history, a philosophy that holds that change is brought about by the great leader rather than an adjustment in the total social structure, has fostered this confidence and mass optimism. Some goals which have been unattainable have been replaced by substitutes. This also operates to instill confidence, and seemingly, from a point of view of rationality, warrants confidence. That is to say, if the social structure is such that adjustments can be made in the value goals, human happiness will have increased its opportunity to be realized.

Efficiency and Practicality

A similar concept in some ways is that of orientation toward efficiency and practicality. There is no better example of a means becoming an end than in this value orientation. Efficiency probably began as a means toward arriving at an objective with the least time and effort and with the least waste. Both in the white collar world (bureaucracy) and in the blue collar world (the assembly line) the concept has become so pervasive that it is difficult to relegate it to the order of means. The point was made earlier in the chapter that, in general, means and ends are often indistinguishable,

[17] Henry Steele Commager, Editor, *America in Perspective*, Random House, New York, 1947, pp. 11 and 14.

and this is one example. This orientation has also promoted the warranted reputation of mastery in "technique-ways" which the American people have gained throughout the world. The reputation of American intellectual effort is the application of concepts rather than the isolation of new phenomena; that is, engineering rather than fundamental science. Even in the field of human relations, this value orientation is reflected; community development is a case in point. Workable "gimmicks" in salesmanship and leadership are often preferred to fundamental thinking about goals, means, and human relations. Usually these techniques work because they were developed by the application of fundamentals, but the teaching and application are often limited to the techniques rather than the rationale behind them. Williams states that the theme of practicality "points to a dissipation of 'ultimate' values in favor of immediate adaptability to immediate interests and satisfactions." [18]

Security

The security orientation in some ways seems the opposite of individualism and progress. Logically, a complete belief in progress would make the security orientation unnecessary, since "holding the line" is not necessary if the best is yet to come. Likewise, individualism is in a sense taking a risk and accepting the consequences. Some authors have shown a "strain toward consistency" in values, but it is also true that the value system is essentially nonrational, rather than rational or irrational. Nonrationality means that logic is irrelevant, rather than relevant but violated, as in the case of irrational behavior. The concept of a hierarchy of values allows opposites to coincide. This is to say that in a given situation the orientation toward progress will assume high acceptance and allow risk-taking, but in other situations security becomes of prime importance. In such a case it is not that progress is not trusted but rather that it is itself irrelevant as the situation is defined.

The orientation toward security is probably less often involved in economic considerations than in other realms of human activity in American society. The willingness of the American people to invest in "securities" is widespread, even though the depression was personally experienced by many of them. Investment is another evidence of this. However, in other types of social relations, risk-taking and drastic or rapid change of the status quo comes seldom. In solutions of problems like divorce, juvenile delinquency, teaching the young, belief in God, military organization, and po-

[18] Williams, *op. cit.*, p. 404.

litical activity, to mention only a few examples from other institutions than the economic, the status quo is held to. This orientation is similar to traditionalism, but differs in the criterion of decision-making. If it can be shown that change is a solution with little risk, then the security-oriented person or grouping will change; while if traditionalism is the criterion of the decision, such proof is not effective.

The advertising approach of two large competitors in the field of electrical appliances indicates the interesting relation between progress and security. One company approaches the field by saying, "Progress is our most important product." The remainder of the advertisement then is proof of progress in material comfort due to electrical appliances. The competitor approaches from the standpoint of security: "You can be sure if it's made by [our company]." That both of the companies remain on top in sales in the field of electrical appliances indicates that, insofar as advertising is an important factor in sales, quite different value appeals work.

Hard Work

The value orientation toward hard work, referred to as the Protestant Ethic, is essentially bound up with such concepts as frugality, thrift, individualism, and individual achievement. It is the idea that the individual determines his own destiny by mobilizing his efforts toward his goal. Initiative and hard work are the means of achievement, and initiative and hard work are defined as individual traits. Earlier, this concept usually meant physical work, and in this sense it is declining as a value. But it has been shifted to the professional and managerial worlds where night work and long hours are common. With appliances taking over some of the household duties of the housewife of higher than median status, work in voluntary organizations among these persons may result from the value orientation toward hard work.

Ethnocentrism

Ethnocentrism is a concept easy to understand but difficult for the scientist and applied community worker to keep from interfering with his work of analyzing, conceptualizing, and applying. This is so because the scientist and applied community worker are people, and therefore they behave in conformity with the generalizations drawn so far in this chapter. Ethnocentrism is the conviction that one's own value system is absolutely and morally right and that all others are absolutely and morally wrong. Moral indignation and scorn are results of seeing others hold to different codes of conduct. This attribute of human nature is probably the source of as much conflict as any variable with the possible exception of conflict in interests. Even the conflict of interest bears upon ethnocentrism insofar as it is a result of defining the goals toward which others are striving as being morally wrong rather than as expressions of "self-interest."

Ethnocentrism results in an interesting dichotomy defined by the people. The in-group and the out-group, while varying from time to time, prescribe the relations among groupings and persons in most cases where a value difference is observed. The enemy in wartime, the higher social class, the persons in another occupation, and perhaps the professional persons in a community development program are all examples of out-groups at times. That these groups vary and are not absolute is indicated by the fact that Brooklyn and Texas are the same in-group in wartime but in another situation may define each other as out-groups. Unity in wartime or in other crises is basically a feeling that the entire community, nation or state, is a single in-group. It is for this reason that the generalization can be drawn that in the face of external threat, inner unity is highest. This is because the new out-group is even more different, and therefore small internal differences, relatively speaking, can be overlooked.[19]

PRINCIPLES

1. *An important dimension of the structure of the community is the codes of conduct which prescribe what ends are right and wrong for people to seek, and also by what means they may strive for these goals.*

In any particular situation it is usually possible to isolate goals, possible means, and taboos. At the intermediate level of generalization, it is often difficult to separate means from goals. For example, in the work world, people conform to patterns of behavior which may be directed at the immediate goal of making more money. Yet money may be viewed as a means to material comfort. At a still higher level of abstraction it is again possible to separate means from goals. One well-known attempt to describe almost universal goals is that of W.I. Thomas.[20] He calls these the four wishes: recognition, security, new experience, and affectional response. At various times in the practical work with, or analysis of, the community, all three levels of

---

[19] William G. Sumner, *Folkways*, Ginn and Company, New York, 1906. Chapter I.
[20] W.I. Thomas, *The Unadjusted Girl*, Little, Brown, and Company, Boston, 1923.

analysis are helpful; the immediate situation, the generalization to a particular set of communities at a particular time, and the universal principles.

2. *Codes of conduct, whether they apply to goals or to means, include the prescription of penalties for violation. These are called sanctions.*

Sometimes these are formal, as in the case of written laws; or informal, as in the case of the mores and folkways. In the latter case, gossip and loss of respect and self-respect are often employed as sanctions.

3. *Codes of conduct vary in the intensity with which they are held.*

Codes which bear upon the survival of the group are called mores, and are the most deep-seated. Folkways are those codes which are important but not basic to group survival. Mores forbid murder and treason, while folkways forbid infidelity, robbery, and other types of serious violations. Customs are still less important, but violations, say, with regard to clothing, are inhibited by ridicule.

4. *Since values may conflict with each other, a hierarchy of values is set up where one value orientation is given precedence over another provided they are mutually exclusive. This hierarchy changes from time to time, so that in one situation material comfort may be dominant while in another it may yield top position to another goal.*

5. *Qualifications are imposed upon value codes which allow a patterned evasion of a code by an explicit rationalization that the code will not work in certain situations.*

The examples cited from Lynd's study of Middletown are a case in point.

6. *At the intermediate level of analysis, values are described as orientations which, in the American community, are as follows:*

Traditionalism: the uncritical adoption of precedents as the criterion of decision-making.

Rationality: the uncritical adoption of consequences as the criterion of decision-making.

External conformity: the uncritical adoption of group patterns as a criterion of decision-making.

Achievement: a state of satisfaction based upon a choice among alternatives which results in a high position in the social structure for the person, and which brings self-respect along with respect and often envy from others.

Individualism: acceptance of decision-making based upon the conviction that the best state of affairs is one in which self-reliant and independent men personally assume the responsibility for their own decisions without com-pulsion from external powers.

Democracy: the process of discussion and compromise whereby individuals or social units make a unitary decision which is binding upon all but where the majority position is modified to satisfy the minorities.

Material comfort: satisfaction in the possession of material items of the culture.

Progress: belief that socially acceptable trends are good.

Efficiency and practicality: selection of courses of action in terms of the least waste of time and effort.

Security: selection of alternative courses of action which involve the least risk of changing the status quo.

Hard work or *Protestant ethic:* the conviction that the individual is the master of his destiny through quantity of work performed and the practice of frugality.

7. *Whatever value codes are held as morally right, people believe their own orientations to be absolutely and ultimately right and all others to be absolutely and ultimately wrong.*

Moral indignation and denial of respect, as well as ridicule and sometimes conflict and hate, result from the observation of codes of conduct of other groups. This phenomenon is referred to as ethnocentrism.

8. *Ethnocentrism results in the division of all people and human groupings into the in-group and the out-group.*

While an out-group at a given time may be included as an in-group at another, because of a common threat, ethnocentrism always exists and its variations are produced by the amount of difference in values observed.

SELECTED REFERENCES

Becker, Howard, *Through Values to Social Interpretation*, Duke University Press, Durham, North Carolina, 1950.

Burtt, Edwin A., *Right Thinking*, Harper and Brothers, New York, 1946, Part 4.

Dewey, John, *The Quest for Certainty*, Minton, Balch and Company, New York, 1929.

———, "Theory of Valuation," in *International Encyclopedia of Unified Science*, Vol. II, No. 4, 1939.

Huxley, Aldous, *Ends and Means*, Harper and Brothers, New York, 1937.

Linton, Ralph, *The Cultural Background of Personality*, D. Appleton-Century Company, New York, 1945, Chapters 2 and 3.

Mercer, Blaine E., *The American Community*, Random House, New York, 1956, Chapter 4.

Reiss, Albert J. Jr., *A Review and Evaluation of Research on Community*, Vanderbilt University, Nashville, Tennessee, 1954, Chapters 4 and 6.

Sanders, Irwin T., *The Community*, The Ronald Press Company, New York, 1958, Chapter 5.

Spicer, Edward H., *Human Problems in Technological Change: A Case Book*, Russell Sage Foundation, New York, 1952.

Wasserman, Paul, and Fred S. Silander, *Decision-Making: An Annotated Bibliography*, Cornell University Press, Ithaca, New York, 1958.

Williams, Robin, *American Society*, Alfred A. Knopf, New York, 1952.

CHAPTER 6

The Functions of the Value System

VALUES AND UNIFORMITY OF BEHAVIOR

If by structure we mean uniformity and patterned behavior, then it is doubtful that any single force making for structure supersedes the importance of values. In American society there is a high value placed upon monogamy, and the uniformity produced by this value is so great that one may truly characterize the American family as monogamous. There is also a value placed upon education. One may describe American society as having a great deal of energy and resources employed in the educational institution, as compared with other societies in which the value is less important. This list of uniformities produced by values is indeed so long that it could not be contained within a single treatise.[1]

Very close to the first function of producing uniformity in behavior is the system of sanctions which extends far beyond the codes of conduct to which the sanctions were originally intended to produce conformity. A penalty and a reward system which characterizes so much of the community structure is produced by the necessity of rewarding conformity and penalizing nonconformity. Thus, the entire penal system and much of the stratification system are in this sense products of the value system.

VALUES AND PROBLEMS

A third function of values concerns their relationship to the kinds of problems to which people in communities and communities address themselves. Problem orientations are closely related to social change which will

---

[1] For a discussion of many of the value uniformities in American society, see Robin Williams, *American Society*, Alfred A. Knopf, New York, 1951. For uniformities throughout the world see George P. Murdock, *Social Structure*, The Macmillan Company, New York, 1949.

be discussed later, but it is important here to show the mechanism through which the value system may attract attention to certain types of problems and even in certain ways produce these problems.

One set of social problems comes from the nature of values themselves. In the first place, there may be goals which are beyond the resources available. Thus, the differential between goals and what can be achieved is a problem of great difficulty in many communities. The frequent concern over a low level of living is an example. But it should be pointed out that this difference in aspiration and achievement must be held by the people in the community rather than by some person from another culture who is helping the community.

The second type of problem inherent in the nature of values is the existence of a goal for which all of the effective means of achievement are tabooed, as in the case of hunger when most of the available food is tabooed.

A third type of problem resulting from the nature of values, particularly in the case of unwritten codes of conduct, is that sanctions are often unclear and the penalty appropriate to an offense is difficult to establish. One of the situations involving vagueness is in the conflicting codes of conduct for adolescents. "Boys will be boys," but there is much concern over the rise in juvenile delinquency. Sometimes this lack of clarity in sanctions results in failure to enforce a goal. Often, too, the penalty for disobedience or nonconformity is more severe than the importance of the value would justify, as, for example, in the early days of cattle ranching in the west, when law had not yet entered the society and the penalty for stealing cattle or horses was death.

Another set of problems arises from the relationship between the value system and the social and physical situation. Codes of conduct are hard to enforce because it is difficult to identify the persons or groups violating the code. Individuals in a large urban center where there is anonymity may escape detection for a violation, as may also industries where the spirit if not the letter of laws may be broken through clever but antisocial juggling of bookkeeping.

Another type of problem resulting from the relationship between the value system and the situation occurs when there are conflicts in values. One subgroup in a community may hold to a particular value which may be in direct conflict with the major value system of the community. Such conflicts in values result in behavior which is morally right for the subgroup, yet viewed as morally wrong by the majority group. Since the contradictory values may be held as deeply by the subgroup as the dominant community value by the majority, this presents a problem that is difficult to solve.

In the ever-increasing size and complexity of American communities, clearly defined dominant value systems are giving way to a constellation of subgroup value systems. Thus, law and social sanctions are weakened as means of enforcing conformity, since there is no single system to which conformity can be demanded. This is particularly true in the nature of social change in time. Adolescents develop subgroup value systems in conflict with the values held by older generations, thus fashioning a culture peculiar to their generation that is, in fact, building changes into the society, yet producing conflicts between value systems at any given point in time. This is seen not only in the family, but in the school and in the leisure-time activities in the community. It increases in those areas where the family occupation no longer includes work for the adolescent, as in the case of farming families.

Still another type of problem defined by the value system is the code of conduct subject to numerous violations. Many students of social disorganization emphasize this type of problem. They are primarily concerned with major areas of social problems, such as crime, sex offenses, prostitution, mental disorder, and suicide. While all these problems have elements of the other types of value problems, they are predominantly a matter of nonconformity to existing codes of conduct.

VALUES AND STRUCTURE

The relationship between the value system and social problems is a complex one. One of the best studies that developed hypotheses as to the relationship between the value system and social problems and structure was that conducted in Alabama by Irwin Sanders and Douglas Ensminger. They approached the definition of particular value orientations somewhat differently from that presented in the previous chapter. They analyzed the relative importance of institutions in the different communities studied. From this study one sees not only the relationship between the value system and the social structure and problems, but also feels a certain sensitivity for the importance of the value system which cannot be gained easily otherwise. Since values are in reality abstractions that are difficult to define and to analyze, this case study will augment our earlier discussions by illustrating the varying perceptions within communities of those things we call values.

Case Studies *

Clanton

Clanton is an adolescent business town of 4,000 people; it is adolescent in its optimism and energy, as well as in its rapid growth. It is primarily a trade center where people come from miles around to push through crowded streets and wait in line to enter a popular "Five and Ten."

The aristocratic principle, which governs life in Verbena, finds little acceptance in Clanton where the old families have been overwhelmingly outnumbered by the incoming business people. One family has lived in Clanton for a century and in a few other families sons have succeeded their fathers in businesses established half a century ago, but these are decidedly in the minority today. The reason given for Clanton's rapid rise as a commercial center is the opening up of the rich farm land in the region after the lumber mills moved away. Today Clanton has an unusually varied group of business enterprises, an airport, as well as two newspapers, Democratic and Republican, whose editors get along amicably in spite of bitter editorial combat at election time.

Like the Maplesville of today, Clanton was a highly individualistic community until the formation of the Kiwanis Club in 1928. By endorsing needed civic projects and by bringing about friendship between business rivals, this club has assumed such a place of prominence that it was named second only to the church as an agency influencing public opinion. As a source of community leadership it was named first nineteen times, far outstripping the second-place organization which had been named only twice. One man phrased the situation this way: "Twenty years ago it was every man for himself and plenty of hard feeling. The Kiwanis Club was organized and they have made it hard for the unconcerned, selfish fellow." The Kiwanis Club cooperates willingly with other more recently organized civic groups.

The adolescence of Clanton is shown in still another way than that mentioned in the opening paragraph; it is undeveloped and even gawky in spots. It has not yet worked out a well-rounded civic program; that would be expecting too much for its span of life. The development of phases other than business has been neglected. One citizen commented: "Clanton has as yet very little community pride. The attempts to promote libraries have failed through public apathy. People of the town are mostly from the farms and have very little civic conscious-ness." There are no supervised playgrounds for children, few recreational facilities for young people other than three pool halls and the movies. With increasing maturity Clanton will meet these problems if the mayor, to whom credit is given on all sides for much of Clanton's progress, can have his way. The chief community needs as cited by persons interviewed were a library (mentioned twenty times), recreational center (seventeen times), swimming pools (eleven

* Irwin T. Sanders and Douglas Ensminger, "Alabama Rural Communities: A Study of Chilton County," *Alabama College Bulletin No. 136,* Montevallo, Alabama, 1940.

times), park (seven times), more industries (seven times), cemetery (six times). To achieve most of these, civic cooperation will be necessary.

The dominant tradition underlying the social organization of the Clanton community is "if it's good for business it's good for Clanton." This seems to explain why, in the past, little interest has been shown in a library. The answer to the question: "How can a library help business?" has not been found. But being thoughtful of others, whether one is tourist, salesman, or farmer, does help business. The merchants of Clanton have learned that cooperation and friendliness, like honesty, are the best policy. This makes Clanton a pleasant place in which to live. One man put it this way: "Few people ever move away from Clanton. If you live here a while you like it and want to stay."

There is a difference of opinion among Clanton leaders as to farm-village relationships, though the consensus is that the situation is not yet what it should be but is steadily growing better. The reasons most often given for the more friendly contacts are twofold: first, the county is evenly divided between two political parties, thus making it necessary for politicians really to go out of town and "shake hands for votes"; and secondly, the work of the Kiwanis Club. This organization, mentioned in the description of Clanton, takes from 50 to 300 farmers to Auburn every year to visit the State College of Agriculture, it holds meetings out in the various neighborhoods where each Kiwanian invites a farmer as guest and pays for two dinners, the money going to the cause supported by the local women serving the lunch. The County Fair held each year at the Clanton Airport attracts 12,000 paid admissions. The mayor of Clanton insists in all of his talks of dedication and welcome that "Clanton needs the country people and the country people need Clanton; that the larger Clanton gets the more taxes they will have to build roads and schools in the country." He says that he has always seen to it that at least half the WPA workers on any job in Clanton were rural people.

Jemison

Young people call Jemison dead. True enough, there are few recreational or economic opportunities for them there. Adults who have once lived in other communities upon becoming acquainted with Jemison people accuse them of being "set in their ways" because Jemison does not support many civic projects. There is, however, a consistency about the community organization of Jemison which, if understood, explains why the community behaves as it does. It is simply that the Jemison business men pursue an active policy of being out-of-date, of keeping behind the times. Perhaps they were left behind in the rush of business years ago, but they certainly are making no effort to catch up nowadays. But they have a reason for this.

Their explanation would run something like this: "Our trade is rural. The more countrified we are, the more trade we'll draw in." The leading hardware merchant calls himself the "farmers' friend." This business creed sets the tone of life in Jemison. The creed may be based on fact or fancy; it may increase or it may decrease business now or in years to come. But it does exist and must be taken into account in any sociological interpretation.

Some of the professional men of the community and a number of the wives of the business men do not share this philosophy and are bent on civic improvement. They want to make Jemison an attractive village so that outsiders will come in to establish residence and perhaps bring some industry with an added payroll. But the local merchants are not interested in the talk of a payroll; in fact, they would fight the establishment of any industry or even the dressing up of the community if they thought farm people would feel any less at home. There are concessions which the business men have made, however.

Between the row of stores and the railroad track, the road was full of ruts in 1936. The women could not get the men to do anything about it so they took rakes and hoes and went down to clean up the place themselves. One by one the men hanging around the stores felt ashamed and came to take over a rake or a hoe. The result was the creation of a little park which was planted in trees and shrubs according to a plan worked out by horticulturists in Auburn. The city now pays $1 a month for the upkeep of the park.

Two years ago a young woman who taught in Auburn during the school term was spending the summer at her home in Jemison. She organized a community playground with the help of some of the young people and financial assistance from the Town Council. Everyone seemed satisfied. There was consternation in the community, however, when some of the girls began to play tennis in shorts. The opposition to such attire did not arise from the women of the community but from the business men who again were consistent with their conservative philosophy.

As would be expected, social control is still very rigid in Jemison. The community is not gossipy but kindly. However, one who does not conform is ostracized. There is considerable opposition to women teachers smoking or to any teacher playing bridge. If the moral code is broken the community generally accepts the individual provided the family forgives everything.

The merchants thoroughly approve of the local school which has done more than anything else to break down farm-village differences. One merchant is impressed by the fact that it is impossible to tell the difference between a country girl and a city girl since their wearing apparel and conduct are the same. He says the consolidated school is responsible for that. But what really makes the school the chief point of organization in the community is its rich program of vocational home economics and vocational agriculture. The Future Farmers of America are active and receive the support of the business men where other extracurricular activities would go begging. Indeed, one informant, when asked: "What holds the community together?" said "Farming." The school does not overlook this factor. Some of the older families not closely identified with the business men dislike the invasion of bus children into Jemison but usually maintain a discreet silence on this score. These families staunchly support the local churches where they count upon the active cooperation of teachers.

Since the school is the only agency supported by all people in the village as well as around Jemison, it is often thought of as a school community, with the implication that the school rather than the business center keeps the larger community together. This would be denied by most business men.

Of course, the merchants are only a part of the population. They have been given such a prominent place in this analysis because their way of looking at things makes Jemison what it is today. They do not worry much about the future and take comfort in the fact that an unusually large number of people ask to be brought back to Jemison for burial when they die.

Maplesville

Life in Maplesville for many years has been based on an individualistic or "live and let live" principle. One very discriminating woman from an old family said: "I like to live in Maplesville because people leave you alone. You don't have to spend all your time going to things and burdening yourself with civic responsibilities." Another informant said: "Women in Maplesville don't average twelve social calls a year." Here then is a place where individualism rather than community service is a traditional virtue. To what sort of social organization does such a value lead?

For one thing, it develops strong personalities. Maplesville is full of "characters" —people who have followed their own inclinations to such an extent that they differ in marked degree from those about them. Public opinion has not forced them to conform to any set pattern of behavior. In one day in Maplesville one could collect more colorful anecdotes about local people than during a much longer residence in many other communities.

But these strong personalities often clash and rip the community wide open with conflict. There are leaders of factions not on speaking terms; what one leader starts the other may tear down. In interpreting the social scene everybody has his own explanations; that is, there is no common reason given for the source of conflict between the prominent individuals. Some say that the trouble arises out of personal grudges; others say that it is economic competition. Political divisions have played their part, since Maplesville had always been Republican until the Roosevelt administration. Most of the people interviewed do say, however, that much of the present difficulty dates back to 1901 when Maplesville was incorporated for a few months. There were those in the village who objected to this incorporation and fought tooth and nail to dissolve it. Finally, they succeeded. Since then, it has been impossible for people to get together on any civic enterprise. Other communities which are incorporated get government projects; but Maplesville receives no such help; county officials surface roads throughout the county but disregard Maplesville's demand that the Montgomery-Tuscaloosa highway be hurried to completion through Chilton county; other communities unite to invite industry but Maplesville, in spite of its excellent highway and railroad connections, loses its lumber mills at periodic intervals and no other industries come in to take their places. One former Maplesville resident said: "It is truly a village of the 'four hundred.' It never will be any larger than four hundred inhabitants because it can't keep any industry." Those who deplore Maplesville's failure to get its share, blame the conflict within the community; some prominent people in Maplesville, however, remain content with things as they are—especially if a new state of affairs should call for increased taxation.

This individualistic strain accompanies the agrarian interest of the inhabitants. Six out of the eight most-named leaders farm as an investment or as a side-line.

Even the school principal farms. Maplesville, therefore, is much more closely linked with the agricultural than with the urban viewpoint. This should explain in part the individualism, assuming the validity of the commonly held belief that farmers tend to be individualists.

In spite of their disagreements the people of Maplesville rally to the aid of any local citizen in trouble. The mutual aid is spontaneous and genuine. No matter how many critical things are said in the intimate gossiping groups these remarks are forgotten when there is need. Furthermore, the people of Maplesville may criticize each other freely among themselves but are quick to defend their neighbors in the presence of outsiders. Such behavior is quite in keeping with the individualistic philosophy, for the aid rendered is voluntary and traditional; then, too, it is good policy, for one never knows when one will be in a tight place oneself.

A Maplesville resident pointed out that a state-wide survey showed that they sent more young people to college than did any other locality of similar size in the State. This was a fact difficult to accept when it was discovered that the people generally did not support their school as loyally as many other communities do. They all greatly admire the school principal and a score show interest in the PTA. Some of the children do not go to school because their parents cannot see that schooling is necessary. Apparently the school is not generally viewed as an institution to make a better community but more in accordance with the older belief that schooling existed to make a better man. Here again the emphasis is individualistic. Parents send their children off to college for individual prestige and advancement; a local school is a necessary step in the ladder of success.

Young people sent off to college do not want to return to Maplesville to live. This is confusing to many parents and is beginning to make them think more analytically of their village. A characteristic remark along this line is that made by a Maplesville native now living in Birmingham who says: "I'm going down to Maplesville to rock awhile." When asked to explain what he meant he said: "First, you go in and shake hands with everyone and then sit down on the front porch and rock with them; then they bring you in something to drink and you rock some more; afterwards you eat a big meal and then rock until bedtime." Some of the business and professional men, conscious of the present state of affairs, have embarked upon a crusade to create more civic pride and community cooperation. They are encountering the inherited individualism which has so long been characteristic of Maplesville. In the past, conflict may have centered around personality, political, or business differences; now the conflict situation has been redefined as a difference of opinion between those who want to keep the status quo and its accompanying individualism or surrender it in order to achieve growth in community living.

Thorsby

"Thorsby is the biggest little town in the State." Well does one realize this in visiting the mayor who lives a mile and a half from the village in as rural a setting as one could picture. Yet he is still in the city limits of the 1901 incorporation. "Why," we asked, "does Thorsby, numbering less than one thousand inhabitants, cover as much space on a map as does Clanton, the county seat?" The explanation proved simple but carried us back again to those founding fathers who were so intent on having enough land for school taxes that they embraced many farms in their city limits. The result was that the first nine-months high school to be established between Birmingham and Montgomery was at Thorsby, so the citizens claim. Even their elementary school held classes nine months each year until the county took it over. Out of this high school grew Thorsby Institute, a secondary school of strictest academic and disciplinary standards, of which Thorsby people are very proud. This also gave rise to the saying still current in the village: "Thorsby is a church and a school town." The churches do their part. The Norwegian Lutherans sold their building to the active Congregationalists; the Baptists are strong, though with the disappearance of the Swedes, the Swedish Lutheran Church is passing out of the picture. The town clerk estimated that only 5 per cent of the population is now descended from Scandinavian stock. In spite of this, many people even in Chilton County speak of Thorsby as being a settlement of foreigners. Perhaps what is foreign is the manner of life in Thorsby.

Thorsby, as every community does, attracts to itself the type of people fitted into its life. Over a period of years it has appealed to those recognizing the value of cooperation, civic responsibility, and hard work. Only ten of the one hundred and fifty local families have domestic help. Negroes are scarce because people do their own work, with the exception of the washing done weekly by members of the neighboring Negro community. There is not a single vacant house in Thorsby. One person who recently moved in said that he came so his children could have the educational advantages of Thorsby. He told of one other family looking for a home. A sewage system is being installed with government help. Protests against it were few in spite of the great expense falling upon many people in the sparsely settled parts of the town.

Verbena

A great source of pride to Verbena residents is their imported Black Belt heritage. When Clanton put up a sign "Drive Careful" it would be a Verbena resident who, by letters to the papers throughout the state, corrected the adverb. The early landowners of Verbena were well educated and kept up their social connections in Montgomery. They founded Verbena Academy, the predecessor of the present high school which Verbena people claim was the first consolidated school in the county. The descendants of these first settlers now own most of the land around Verbena. Throughout Chilton County people attribute the stability of Verbena's life to the fact that its landowners will not sell their land because they want to see Verbena kept as it is. However, these Verbena landowners are quick to reply: "There is plenty of land for sale if one will pay a reasonable price. Only one man is unwilling to sell." This one man, by far the largest landowner, readily says: "Of course, I won't sell. I don't want any convict camps or broom factories in Verbena."

Preservation of traditions therefore parallels the ownership of land by those born into these traditions. Those who have connections elsewhere and are financially able, go outside the village for their cultural and recreational life; those who have to remain at home feel that more should be done locally to organize lecture courses and recreational groups, but are not in a position to make a success of such ventures without the help of the more influential group.

Landowners and tenants alike are loyal to Verbena if they have resided there for any length of time. One housewife, living in a rented house, told of the Homecoming Day held under the auspices of the Parent-Teachers' Association at the high school last year, emphasizing how glad people were to return. She added, "We have a little saying, 'If once you've dipped your foot in Chestnut Creek you always want to return.'" Further indication of the satisfaction people feel with Verbena is shown by the following remarks of a woman who moved in from Birmingham. "I love Verbena. This is the only place I've ever lived in where I want to spend the rest of my life and be buried."

While there are many other studies which show the intricate relationship between values and community behavior, the Alabama study is sufficient to show the importance of each to the other.[2] Values are slow to change, and the type of community resulting from a particular value orientation may develop problems illustrated by the failure of children to return to Maplesville once they have gone off to college. This is a loss of leadership and trained professional talent to the community. While the local values may create the problem, it is equally important to recognize that those same values may prevent any deliberate action to solve it. In Maplesville, individualism would prevent the cooperative action necessary to provide occupational and leisure time opportunities that are necessary to draw the young people back to the community.

It is frequently the case, however, that a misconception occurs concerning values. Values have been developed as workable and agreeable solutions to persistent problems. After generations of acceptance as solutions, they become moral values. It is for this reason that they are slow to change, and therefore one should avoid inventing quick solutions and quick criticisms of others' values.

One generalization that may be drawn from the functions briefly described above is that the value system is an important factor in structuring human relations. By structure, again, is meant the patterning of human relationships into recurrent, dependable, predictable channels. This structure may be well organized, so that an element or dimension does not produce problems in other elements or dimensions. Or the structure may be

---

[2] For example, see: Richard DuWors, "Persistence and Change in Local Values of Two New England Communities," RS, 17:207–17, 1952; Peter A. Munch, "Social Adjustment among Wisconsin Norwegians," ASR, 14:780–87, 1949; Evon Z. Vogt and Thomas F. O'Dea, "Comparative Study of the Role of Values in Social Action in Two Southwestern Communities," ASR, 18:645–54, 1953; Carle C. Zimmerman, The Changing Community, Harper and Brothers, New York, 1938.

full of patterned, dependable behaviors which are dysfunctional or disorganized. In either case, the value system produces much of the repetitive nature of community-related behavior.

VALUES AND CHANGE

If it is a general and important function of the value system to produce structure, then it is obviously an important function of the value system to produce or prevent changes in that structure.

The relationship between the value system and social change is a response to the relationship between the value system and social problems, previously described. Much of the change in the value system as well as in social structure is a response to social problems. As Martindale and Monachesi describe this relationship, "A problem situation rests upon the involvement of tension that motivates men to take stock of the situation and to attempt to so manipulate the essential phases of the situation as to reduce the tension. Change is the primary object of the problem-solving process. The existence of obstacles to a desired end may and often does produce change. Thus, one aspect of the relation of problems to change is noted. Change follows a situation which the individual or group of individuals cannot control or manipulate by the utilization of already established patterns of action. Situations that cannot be coped with successfully by traditional methods produce tensions which stimulate individuals to create novel methods and thus serve as initiators of change in culture and social relations." [3]

The relationship between problem and change, however, varies with the nature of the particular value system itself. Some value orientations allow change much more easily than do others. Becker has built a theoretical scheme classifying value systems according to their permissiveness with respect to change. While this scheme was built around societies, it also applies to communities, even within a single society.

Sacred and Secular

To describe value systems which are oriented toward change, Becker uses the term "secular," and for those oriented away from change he uses the word "sacred." These terms do not mean necessarily profane and Godly, but mean rather that whatever values are held may be viewed *rationally*,

[3] Don Martindale and Elio D. Monachesi, *Elements of Sociology*, Harper and Brothers, New York, 1951, p. 609.

changing if they fail to work, or *traditionally*, that is, held for their own sake.[4]

The sacred community is one in which the value system "elicits from or imparts to its members . . . unwillingness and/or inability to respond to the culturally new . . ." "The secular community is one that elicits from or imparts to its members . . . willingness and ability to respond to the culturally new . . . Stated in another way, a network of sociation . . . develops [which allows or promotes] a high degree of readiness and capacity to change."[5]

There are several types of communities with regard to this system of classification. The two general types, secular and sacred, resemble the two major value orientations described in the previous chapter, rationality and traditionalism. However, the value orientations are only one aspect of these types. The types encompass also social relations which bring about variations in both sacred and secular communities.

The first type of sacred, or nonchanging, community is the *folk* type. Folk communities are nonchanging because of traditionalism and therefore the enforcement of the codes of conduct is brought about by the people themselves. That is, no authority vested in an enforcement agency is required, since traditional values are internalized by each person, and conformity is enforced through the desire for self-respect and the respect of others. The folk community is isolated, either through a lack of contact with other communities or ways of life or through what Becker calls mental isolation. Mental isolation involves a lack of communication by refusal to respond to a stimulus. One example of this is the failure to understand the other. An example of a folk-sacred society will be given in an excerpt later from a description of a community in the United States.

The word "prescribed" has been used heretofore to indicate that all codes of conduct delimit and produce behavior patterns. Becker uses it in a much more technical and narrow meaning to indicate the second type of sacred community. The prescribed-sacred community then is a community in which a "definite body of dogma calls forth, sets up, or maintains a totalitarian kind of social structure."[6] The conformity to the status quo here does not come from the fact that everyone has internalized the value system, but rather it is enforced through an authority structure. Certain positions are designated to watch for and punish violations.

Secular systems are also divided into two types. The first is the principled. Change is valued in the principled-secular community, but not for

[4] Howard Becker, *Through Values to Social Interpretation*, Duke University Press, Durham, North Carolina, 1950, Chapter 5.
[5] *Ibid.*, pp. 252–3.
[6] *Ibid.*, p. 254.

its own sake. It is a willingness to change when the present value system or social structure is not producing smoothly operating human relations. Change, even when needed (as defined by the value system itself), may not occur in the principled-secular community, and the barrier is usually some principle or code of conduct. Thus change, with attention to means as well as ends as morally right and wrong, is of utmost importance.

In the normless-secular society or community, attention is given only to ends, and any means is used to achieve the end. In these communities, change is likely to be rampant. Revolutions are always indications of normlessness, provided the new regime actually changes the social structure. In some revolutions, the social structure is maintained with new people filling old positions.

The actual existence of pure types of communities or societies in this scheme is questionable, since the typology is intended as a logical scheme for analytical purposes. Nevertheless, there are many communities the world over which are strongly oriented in one direction or another. In modern United States the student who reaches college probably will have some difficulty in believing in the actual existence of folk-sacred and normless-secular communities. Most dimensions in the life of the college student and in the professional world are either prescribed-sacred or principled-secular. That the other types are present in large degree in some communities, however, is true. The following excerpt from *Hollow Folk* describes a situation in the recent past in which the folk-sacred was found to exist within easy commuting distance from the principled-secular community.

Hollow Folk *

The dark interior valleys of the Blue Ridge Mountains are realms of enchantment. Here, hidden in deep mountain pockets, dwell families of unlettered folk, of almost pure Anglo-Saxon stock, sheltered in tiny, mud-plastered log cabins, and supported by a primitive agriculture. One of these settlements, Colvin Hollow, has no community government, no organized religion, little social organization wider than that of the family and clan, and only traces of organized industry. The ragged children, until 1928, never had seen the flag or heard of the Lord's Prayer. They speak a peculiar language which retains many Elizabethan expressions.

Colvin Hollow is close to a center of American civilization, less than one hundred miles from the national capital. It is less than eight miles from a hard-surfaced road. Automobiles have been driven within three miles of it. Airplanes roar across it. Vacationists tramp through it. Yet the community is almost

* Mandel Sherman and Thomas R. Henry, *Hollow Folk*, Thomas Y. Crowell Company, New York, 1933, Chapter 1.

completely cut off from the current of American life. It is not of the twentieth century. Both in time and space it seems to be isolated and self-sufficient.

Scattered about through the mountains, the scientists discovered, were other hollows in various degrees of isolation from the outside world and, as it afterwards developed, approximately corresponding culture levels. The investigators selected five of these communities for study: one, a hollow of scattered families subsisting off the grudging, unaided bounty of nature; another, a community of primitive agriculturalists; another, one of small farmers; still another one in which were found in crude forms nearly all the institutions of modern society; and finally, a small town at the foot of the mountains. Thus, within a radius of twenty miles they were able to keep company with the human race on its long journey from primitive ways of living to a modern social order.

At the lowest level of social development in this region is Colvin Hollow. The inhabitants live in scattered, mud-plastered, log huts. No one in the Hollow proper can read or write. There are no cattle or poultry in the Hollow proper. One family owns a pig and another a horse. Near each cabin is a small patch of maize and cabbage, the largest of which is about two acres. There is no general system of communication between the cabins. There is no road to the outside world. In every direction the perspective is closed by mountainsides covered with ghostly trunks of dead chestnuts. One building, closed for many years, is called a school. Otherwise there is no common meeting place. Neither is there a church nor any local government. Actually there is very little governmental influence, since the mountaineers, especially the squatters, are generally ignored by political headquarters. There is no evidence of any organized group life beyond the immediate family, itself loosely organized. Nearly all the inhabitants are blood relatives, and their social organization is in some ways below the level of the clan.

Next in the scale of social organization in this region is Needles Hollow, at the head of a rocky mountain trail which connects with the county road. Here a few men are literate. The community has a combined church-school where occasional religious meetings are conducted. The cultivated ground approaches the status of farms—approximately five acres in area, although many of the farmers say they have twenty or thirty acres. Nearly every family has a pig and chickens. There is no local government or definite social organization, but the cabins are easier of access to each other and there is more recognition of kinship and friendship between the related families.

Oakton Hollow, at the head of a mountain road up which an automobile can be driven with difficulty by a skillful driver, presents the third step upward in the scale. Agriculture here is organized as contrasted with the haphazard tillage of the soil for immediate needs, which is the situation in Colvin Hollow. The chief crops are apples and corn. There is a beginning of industry in the paring and drying of apples, as well as the shipment of fresh apples for markets in the lowland. The church-school is in fairly frequent use both for worship and education. There are two religious sects—Plymouth Brethren and Primitive Baptists. Most families have pigs, chickens, cows, and horses. Some of the cabins have three or four rooms, and there are slight intentional variations in their architecture. Nearly every home has a mail-order catalog, and much of the buying is done by mail. The community also has a general store which contains the post office.

Next comes Rigby Hollow. It is a more compact, socialized community near the foot of the mountains, connected by a fair country road with a lowland village. Mail can be received daily. Driftwood of politics, crime, industry, science, literature, music, and all other craft which mankind has launched on the stormy ocean of culture is thrown by the tide on this high beach.

The people of Rigby Hollow are physically cleaner and better dressed than in the three other communities, Colvin, Needles, and Oakton. The cabins are more substantial and much better furnished. The farm patches are larger and better cultivated. There is more money in circulation. The men and women are more friendly to each other and to strangers, and express their thoughts in more meaningful language. The children have a better home life. Food is more varied and tasty. Sanitation is better, however far it may range from the ideal for a rural community.

School is in session approximately seven months each year. About 75 per cent of the people are literate. They can read and understand the newspapers. They can order materials from the catalogs of the mail-order houses. They can read the Bible, however uncritically, both individually and in unison. Social gradations are established. Those people whose cabins are scattered along the road to the village are striving to "pass over" from mountaineers to lowlanders. Some families are "better" than others.

The final stage in this scale is reached in a small farm and sawmill town, Briarsville, in the valley at the edge of the mountains. Through it runs a hard-surfaced road which connects with several larger towns and eventually with cities. Here is found a progressive school in a modern building. Church services are conducted regularly with very good attendance. Newspapers are received every day, and the automobile and radio are familiar to every one. Although many of the people are originally from the mountains, they do not wish to be thought of as mountaineers whom they generally dislike. Regular working hours are maintained. All the common American games are played and there is a systematic knowledge of national politics.

These five communities present five stages of culture, Colvin Hollow representing the lowest level and Briarsville the highest. Colvin Hollow started a century ago on a level comparable with the others but it appears to have deteriorated socially. As one goes into the mountain even by stages of only a few miles, communication with the outside world becomes more and more difficult. Contacts are less and less frequent and people living only a few miles apart have difficulties of communication which cannot be stated in terms of so many miles. Perhaps four or five rocky miles are as significant a barrier as that which ethnologists accord to oceans and mountain ranges. Only a few hours brings one from Colvin to the main street of a small Virginia town lined with parked automobiles. Yet the journey, short and matter-of-fact as it is to scientific expeditions, presents forebodings of great problems to people within the hollows.

. . . .

The nature of the mountaineer's personality is difficult to define. If we accept the theory of the modern psychologist that personality depends upon training and upon the environment in which the child grows up, we have good material to test this theory. As a whole, these mountain hollows offer an excellent laboratory control from the standpoint of heredity. Although the hereditary influences do vary in these mountains, the variation is but slight compared to that in other situations. As we have seen, the people came from Scotch-Irish and English stock and there has been only occasional mingling with people of other extractions.

Considering personality from the standpoint of intelligence it may be assumed that the average child in the mountains develops an intelligence sufficient for an adequate adjustment to the demands of his environment. The Needles Hollow environment demands a higher intelligence for adjustment than Colvin Hollow. This does not mean, as we have seen, that the inherent capacity of the children of the different hollows necessarily differs. Indeed, it would be erroneous to conclude, without further experimental evidence, that the inherent capacity of the children of these mountain hollows differs even from that of children in an ordinary environment. But inherent capacity requires stimulation before children can develop those characteristics which we are accustomed to call intelligence. A child of twelve in Colvin Hollow does not need greater intelligence for successful adjustment than the child of eight or nine. Indeed, psychological tests show that at seven he begins to make a progressively poorer rating on intelligence tests. This is not interpreted as true deterioration but as a leveling out due to the relatively decreasing demands which the environment makes upon his intelligence. When we compare the very young children of these four hollows we see little difference between them. A comparison of the ten-, twelve-, and fourteen-year-olds, however, shows great differences, the children of the communities lowest in social organization rating far lower than the children of the communities highest in social organization.

The measure of the intelligence of the young child ordinarily gives a truer picture of inherent capacity than measurements taken of an older child. The young child is relatively free from complicating influences of the environment, and the demands of his surroundings are but simple compared to the environmental requirements made on the older child.

The differences in the personalities of the mountain children probably can be explained in the same way as the differences in their intelligence. Personality generally is defined by the social behavior of the individual. The adjustment necessary for the child under four years differs but little in different situations. The child below four reacts on a motor and sensory basis and his social and play adjustments are very simple. The training of the child less than two or three years old is generally perfunctory and varies but little under most conditions. When he develops a comprehension of language, however, his environment begins to have a direct and noticeable influence upon him. In the mountains we begin to see changes in the children above four or five. Whereas the personalities of the children below this age are difficult to differentiate, those above five begin to differ. These differences, however, are obvious only when we compare children of different communities.

In Colvin and Needles Hollows the personalities of children of the same age differ so slightly that it is difficult to differentiate them by customary tests. There is no great diversity of interest among the ten-year-olds, for example. Indeed, there is no great difference between the interest of the eight- and twelve-year-olds. They all are interested in their immediate welfare. If they have enough to eat and are not called upon to do a great amount of work they appear to be satisfied. Compared to children living in a competitive environment these children have few ambitions and few desires. Their personalities are not disturbed by concerns over the future. There are few children with feelings of insecurity compared to the number in a normal environment.

Psychiatric investigation of the children of Colvin Hollow discloses that they are remarkably free from conflicts, considering a conflict as an unpleasant emotional attitude toward personal failure. As we have seen, there are few rigid standards for these children to achieve. Therefore they do not develop conflicts as a result of lack of achievement. There are few frustrations because most of them have the attitude that nature takes care of their needs and if nature fails to provide them with necessities there is little one can do about it. Probably many of our conflicts arise from the realization that man's duty is to change nature and to alter its ways. In progressive civilizations nature's failures are considered personal failures, whereas the people of Colvin Hollow consider nature a part of themselves which no one can hope to alter to a considerable extent. To these people death, for example, is a natural phenomenon no matter at what time of life it occurs. Birth, sickness, crop failures all are considered as the inexorable workings of nature which are far above the futile efforts of man to change.

The children learn from the earliest age to accept their conditions and are loath to attempt change. For some mental hygienists this would appear to be a good sign of mental health. And indeed it is, but progress often is attained only at the price of mental disorganization. If good mental health means few conflicts and few worries, then the children of Colvin Hollow are in perfect mental health. But if progress includes the continual development of conflicts in the attempt to alter one's conditions, and the ability to solve conflicts by rational methods, then the children of Colvin Hollow must be considered as backward and undeveloped according to the standards of modern societies. The unavoidable price of modern progress in the form of social and mental disorganization of some of the people is not paid by the inhabitants of Colvin and Needles Hollows.

There are few neurotic people in Colvin and Needles Hollows. Among a similar number of people almost anywhere, but especially in urban populations, we would expect to find not a few neurotic individuals. Careful study of the young children of Colvin and Needles Hollows disclosed only two who had nervous habits, fingernail biting and excessive blinking of the eyelids.

The scarcity of neurotic symptoms among these mountaineers may be due to the simplicity of their environment, or perhaps to the simplicity of their attitudes toward their environment. It is a well-known fact that some people bear their hardships without resort to neurotic escapes, whereas others shrink from the least hardship and escape their difficulties and frustrations through a neurotic illness. If neurotic symptoms are escapes from the expectations of defeat and follow a period of insecurity and anxiety it can readily be understood why the people of Colvin Hollow have few of these symptoms; not only are they without the sense of insecurity so common among people in other situations but most of them seem to have no wish to escape from reality.

The personalities of the Oakton and Rigby Hollow children and adults are quite different from what is found in Colvin and Needles Hollows. In Oakton and Rigby Hollows there are some neurotic women and men. When the children of Oakton Hollow were examined physically a number of men and women asked for help for their ailments. Five of them were considered neurotic, for their symptoms did not coincide with their physical condition. Adults of Oakton Hollow frequently complain of their hardships and poverty. They often express anxiety about the future. Increased ambition and energy have brought anxiety and doubt. A number of the children suffered from conflicts of insecurity and inferiority.

Whereas the personalities of the children of Colvin Hollow, and to a lesser extent the children of Needles Hollow, could not be readily classified into different types, the personalities of the Oakton Hollow children differed in some cases as much as those of children in any ordinary environment. The relative complexity of their surroundings compared to Colvin and Needles Hollows modified their personalities by demands upon their social adaptability.

PRINCIPLES

1. *The first function of the value system is to produce common, predictable patterns of behavior among persons and groupings in the community.* Obviously people do not all act alike. Rather, certain goals and means are prescribed by the entire community as appropriate only to some members, positions or groupings in the community. For example, only physicians are permitted to prescribe medicine and they are obligated to do so. But recognition of the rightness of this is shared by everyone. Similarly, alternative courses of action are permitted by the value system for a given situation, but not just any alternatives. Internalization of the value system by individuals produces conformity even when a violation might be hidden from public view.

2. *The second function of the value system is to prescribe rewards and penalties for violation. Thus there is little difficulty in solving the problem of what to do when violation is observed.*

3. *A third function of the value system is the recognition and definition of problems of common concern in the community.* These are of four types. The first is that goals may exist for which there are inadequate means. Either the goal may be generally unattainable, or all means which could reach the goal may be taboo. Another type of problem exists when the sanctions are unclear. For example, juvenile delinquency is an obvious violation of codes of conduct, but the sanctions imposed upon adults for the same violation is not defined as appropriate in the case of a juvenile. Still another type of problem is the conflict in values, as in the case of a minority group which holds to a value in contradiction

to the majority value system. This occurs also as new generations take on different codes resulting from changing social conditions. Thus parental-youth conflict is produced. Another type of problem resulting from the value system is the extensive violation of a code, such as prostitution, homo-sexuality, or success orientation.

4. *The value system also promotes or deters social change, either through a value for or against social change itself or through the number of alternatives allowed in solving common problems.*

Thus sacred societies are opposed to social change itself and secular societies or communities either promote it or allow it. In societies made up of many specialized positions, all people share in codes of conduct specific to the position. These communities likewise are likely to allow a greater number of alternatives in solving a given problem. Thus as the frequency of choice moves from an old alternative to a new socially approved alternative, change is likely to occur.[7]

[7] See selected references listed at the end of the succeeding chapter.

CHAPTER 7

Communication and
Public Opinion

Community action occurs through communication among individuals, groups, organizations, and institutions. This communication occurs constantly, and without it, there is no structure. While we take it for granted, this process is difficult to understand thoroughly. Its many nuances have much to do with community structure, through misunderstandings, the anticipation of reactions from others, and commonly held notions of others which people live by. This communication process involves not only the informal discussion and formal means of "one-way" communication in propaganda, but also the development of a public opinion on issues. All these facets of the process will be described in the present chapter.

THE NATURE OF COMMUNICATION

In human thought processes the entire external world becomes a system of symbols. A tree which is observed in the external world becomes merely the word "tree" or a mental picture of a tree, or a series of connotations about trees. These symbols have variously been called signs or significant symbols. When they are made public by a person, and the same symbol has the same meaning to another, then communication has occurred. The significant symbols which are made public may be items of knowledge, skills or attitudes, and values. Communication refers to the exchange of knowledge, skills, and attitudes among persons or among social groupings. It is small wonder that some writers equate communication with the social process.[1] The major purpose of communication in this sense is the achievement of understanding between persons or groups, but whenever one person

---

[1] Charles H. Cooley, *Social Organization*, Charles Scribner's Sons, New York, 1909, Chapter 6, esp. pp. 61–62. See also Arnold Rose, *Sociology: The Study of Human Relations*, Alfred A. Knopf, New York, 1956.

133

or group desires to be understood by another person or group, the entire social process is involved. All generalizations elsewhere in this book contribute directly or indirectly to knowledge about the structure of communications. In this chapter two particular aspects of communication are singled out for separate treatment, namely, methods and structure. Method includes education and propaganda, while structure is described in terms of the channels through which communication is achieved. In addition to the mass media, the structure of communication includes informal groups, formal organizations, institutions, and the stratification system.

In some ways the communication process is identical with learning, but it is more inclusive. For example, when one person says "good morning" to another, communication has occurred, although no learning has occurred unless the recipient of the greeting is particularly interested in the "mood" of the person who greeted him. Another difference between communication and learning is that the latter, as treated by social scientists, is that particular aspect of communication which has become formal and institutionalized under the general heading of education.

Values are important to the communication process. Insofar as the purpose of communications is mutual understanding, the goals which people cherish are of utmost importance in determining success or failure in communicating an attitude. Similarly, research has shown that knowledge and skills can be transmitted only if they fit into the value system or interests of the recipient.

Communication and Diffusion

Communication is also closely identified with diffusion, a term which refers to that aspect of social and cultural change involving acceptance or adoption of an invention either in the material world or in the world of ideas by a progressively larger and larger number of people.[2] Not only are communication and diffusion causally connected, but they are in some ways overlapping in nature. For example, some communication cannot be complete until the acceptance of the idea has occurred. A person may understand an idea communicated, store it in his mind without agreement, but

[2] For a summary of literature see Rural Sociological Society, Subcommittee on Diffusion and Adoption of New Farm Practices, *Sociological Research on the Diffusion and Adoption of New Farm Practices*, Kentucky AES Rural Sociology Bulletin 2, Lexington, Kentucky, June, 1952. In another comprehensive survey of literature, the diffusion process is defined largely in terms of the communication of information; see North Central Rural Sociology Committee, Subcommittee for the Study of the Diffusion of Farm Practices, *How Farm People Accept New Ideas*, Special Report No. 15, Agricultural Extension Service, Iowa State College, Ames, Iowa, November, 1955.

insofar as attitudes are communicated the diffusion has occurred only when the idea is accepted. Further, the diffusion of knowledge and skills themselves represents communication, so that in this sense, diffusion and communication are identical.

FUNCTIONS OF COMMUNICATION

As mentioned previously, a major function of communication is mutual understanding. For example, when a person wishes to have his position on an issue understood, or when he wishes to have an item of knowledge or a skill become known by others, he employs communication. Teaching is an excellent example of communication performing this function. The school itself may be said to be an organization primarily directed at this type of communication.

An item which might otherwise be repulsive to the recipient by virtue of his value system may be communicated in such a way that it becomes acceptable. Or, as in the case of certain political concepts such as "creeping socialism" or "communism," they may be invested with unpleasant connotations that make them abhorrent to the recipient. This results from the fact that words may have not only denotative definitions but also connotations of good or bad that are subtle and influential.[3]

A third function is that communication helps to perpetuate the culture. Thus, traditions, mores, and values are handed down from generation to generation through communication. In preliterate society, this must depend upon oral communication and suffers from the fallibility of memory. Since preliterate cultures are probably more traditional and less changing than other cultures this is an indication that this type of communication is effective in spite of the fallibility of memory. In literate societies, much of the culture is transmitted through the written word. Thus, the Constitution of the United States and subsequent Supreme Court decisions are preserved intact because they can be referred to long after their specific provisions are forgotten, merely by searching through the literature to find the precedents. Even the written word is open to interpretation, as is indicated by the fact that much of the supreme law of American society is based on court interpretations of the original Constitution.

Communication performs other functions important to the understanding of community structure and change, particularly when the mass media are involved. Thus the swiftness with which communication is transmitted from

[3] See the section on stereotypes.

all parts of the world changes the structure of world society. In another instance, the access to all classes of persons influences relationships within the community.[4]

Communication and Social Relations

The function of communication in social relations hinges mainly on the achievement of understanding. Perhaps the most important principle here is that conflict often develops merely because of misunderstanding which develops in turn because of a lack of communication. Two illustrations may show the application of this principle.

The first illustration may be taken from the misunderstanding derived from the purposes of an organization. Ordinarily, any organization which has a large membership should be acceptable to non-members of the same community. Yet, a critical attitude toward it may often exist because of the failure of the organization to make clear to non-members its purposes and its functions in the community. Thus, lower and lower middle class people may have a critical view of the upper-class country club, while actually the purpose of the country club is merely for recreational purposes and may have no negative effects upon the realization of goals by others. Of course, there are organizations in many communities with relatively wide membership which do contradict the values of the community, as would be the case of a communist underground cell. The point here, rather, is that conflict sometimes but not always results from lack of communication.

Within a single organization a person of subordinate position may be given a directive from a person in a superordinate position. The subordinate may not understand all the consequences of the decision and all the difficulties involved in arriving at the solution to some problem. He therefore may, in terms of his own narrow work world, take a negative attitude toward the decision, while if the involved nature of the problem were explained to him, he might see that the decision was, after all, the best one that could be made under the circumstances. One of the best illustrations of this is the conflict between the Field General and the Pentagon General in the American Armed Forces. Thus, a decision by a Pentagon General which involves international relations and foreign policy may actually work to the detriment of the immediate situation in the field. This can be seen in nearly any bureaucratic situation where there are supervising positions.

Another important aspect of communication and its function in social

---

[4] Cooley, *op. cit.*, 1909, p. 80.

relations is that of the duplication of effort by organizations in the community. Thus, in problems such as delinquency, education of the child, and financing community projects, there may be a duplication of effort which is merely waste rather than reinforcement. If organizations had better channels of communication with each other, wasteful duplication of effort could be eliminated. It is often difficult to determine whether the same function performed by two organizations is complementary or wasteful. In the community problem of delinquency there may be many agencies such as the school and the family that are taking their own approach to delinquency but which may be actually contradictory and based on quite different philosophies. In some institutional structures such as the economic institution, the duplication of function is defined as desirable in American culture in order to keep monopolies from existing. Competition is evidence of this and much communication has been defined legally and morally in American society as undesirable where agreements between two competing industries on the price level has been found to exist.

Persuasion

The principal difference between education and propaganda rests on the one-sided nature of propaganda.[5] Propaganda is the use of persuasion to influence a person to one course of action in preference to others. Education is the presentation of the alternatives with, ideally, all the consequences, both culturally good and bad, of each alternative. Many of the principles and techniques of propaganda are also applicable to education, but they must be used with caution. One of the more important principles related to the formation of attitudes or the acceptance of knowledge is that persuasion is more effective with people whose basic predispositions are already in line with that for which persuasion is employed. This means that communication directed at increasing participation will be more effective with those who are inclined in that direction to begin with. Still further, it means that in any particular organization, participation is more likely to be brought about by communication if the people are originally interested in the problem which is the focus of the attention of the organization. Thus, communication can bring about participation in parent-teachers' associations much better among

---

[5] For an annotated bibliography of research in this area see Bruce L. Smith, Harold D. Lasswell, and Ralph D. Casey, *Propaganda, Communication, and Public Opinion,* Princeton University Press, Princeton, 1946. For more recent developments see various issues of the *Public Opinion Quarterly.*

people who have an interest in their children's relations in school than among parents who are more apathetic toward child-school relations.

Another important principle of persuasion is repetition which is used extensively by advertising agencies. In the application of this principle a favorable attitude is not essential, for it involves keeping the product at the level of awareness so that the particular brand being advertised will come first to the mind of the person purchasing the item. This will work also in other areas, as in memorizing the multiplication tables, which comes through repetition.

Another technique used in persuasion might be termed the "old shoe." This means simply that any item to be communicated is cast in the light of tradition and associated with older people or what has been done in the "golden past." The glittering generalization or slogan is another useful technique. In this case an idea or event is described in words which are acceptable, usually more so than the event itself. This may operate in reverse, where an event may be cast in more unfavorable light by using emotionally charged words which have bad connotations.

"Stacking the cards" is telling half-truths or telling only those facts which are favorable to the attitude desired by the propagandists. This contradicts the fundamental principle of education, although at certain points, the educational institution in American society employs this technique in teaching, as when it omits or glosses over certain unfavorable facts in American history. Another technique, quite often called the "bandwagon effect," is the testimonial. This is found frequently in political campaigns to indicate that everyone is voting in a particular way, and capitalizes on the value of external conformity. The counterpoint of this is the "underdog" technique which operates very well in American society. It is believed that the underdog technique brought some extra votes to ex-President Harry S. Truman in 1948, but most advertisers and propagandists choose the bandwagon effect rather than the underdog technique. The testimonial or similar techniques may employ the hero or the authority, so that the prestige of certain persons or positions is associated with the theme of a persuasion program. This is used both in advertising and in persuasion, as, for example, when movie stars are asked to testify to the smoothness of a cigarette, or the President supports some kind of philanthropic program such as CARE or the Red Cross.[6]

Another technique is that of demonstration, which may vary from accuracy as in the case of the Agricultural Extension Service to complete

[6] See Alfred McClung Lee and Elizabeth Brian Lee, *The Fine Art of Propaganda,* Harcourt, Brace and Company and the Institute for Propaganda Analysis, New York, 1939.

falsehood, where an experiment appears to show the miraculous advantages of some medicine or other product.

Another principle which aims to achieve long-lasting effects is that persuasion should be aimed at children. Thus, as they grow up it is assumed that they will become more favorable to the theme of the program as a result of the carry-over from their childhood.

There are many minor techniques used by various mass media such as the balance between space and print in an advertisement, or the use of black letters on a white background or white letters on black. These principles have been well established and are just as useful in educational programs as they are for propaganda purposes. They are aimed primarily at attracting attention and interest rather than disseminating knowledge or skills.

Another factor in public opinion formation is that it moves by spurts. This is especially so when particularly vocal people can create the illusion or fact that the whole community is "for their program." Continued advocacy also gives the same impression. If a previously apathetic person must take a stand he will side with the community as community loyalty takes over.

That these techniques are much used in American society is not to be denied. That they also influence community structure and change is likewise obvious. Whether they are to be used as techniques in deliberate action programs to change the community is of course up to the leadership involved. This again rests upon the value system of the individuals concerned, and in the value system in the organization promoting the program. Quite often people who ordinarily oppose propaganda techniques may employ them without being aware of them, particularly in using half-truths in an argument or stacking the cards. A good test to use to detect propaganda techniques is to support the opposite point of view to see if the statements supporting that position are acceptable as facts and then to determine if they have been presented adequately in the initial argument. In most social intercourse, propaganda occurs frequently at the individual level with facts or quasi-facts presented in support of one argument as opposed to another. Since teachers are human beings, it can be expected that teaching is not entirely free from the use of propaganda techniques.

CHANNELS OF COMMUNICATION

There are several channels of communication, the functions of which differ, depending upon several factors, especially (1) the purpose of the communication itself and (2) the degree to which the recipient of the communication is at present predisposed toward acceptance.

From the standpoint of the purposes of the person or organization initiating the communication item, there are four objectives which may influence the choice of channels. In brief summary, these are presented below, with some idea of what channel of communication may be found to be most effective.

(a) *To make announcements of meetings, exhibits, and educational activities and to attract attention to organizational programs and resources.* This objective requires that as many people as possible be reached. Even though the announcement of a meeting may be important only for families living in one geographical area or one social segment of the community, the need to attract general attention to the activity requires a larger public. Announcements are the simplest type of communication used by organizational leaders. However, the purposes in this type of communication extend beyond mere announcement. Even though it is directed at specific persons or one segment of the community, it may, by attracting the attention of a much wider audience, inform them of the organization's purposes and resources, and it may even call attention to the problem itself among those persons previously unaware of its existence. This is often referred to as the development of a felt need. It is to be distinguished from needs which are present but not at the level of awareness. These announcements are news and usually disseminated through the channels of radio, television, and newspapers, usually at no cost to the organization.

A study of rural urban fringe communities in New York State [7] found that announcements made through two types of communication channels, such as newspapers and radio, or radio and television, reached over 90 per cent of the population. This would suggest, as it has been verified in other studies, that concentration on one type of mass media is less effective for this objective than placing the announcement in more than one channel of communication.

(b) *To disseminate information and to teach skills to persons already interested.* This type of communication would include detailed information about tax issues, bond issues for schools, or instructions on how to operate a voting machine. Under this objective the organizational leader wishes to contact those already interested rather than the whole population, as in the case of a safety practice for children which may be of interest primarily

[7] C.E. Ramsey and R.A. Danley, "Some Effects of the Fringe Migration on Channels of Communication," *Cornell University Rural Sociology Bulletin No. 51,* April, 1957, pp. 11–12.

to parents, or a tax issue of interest only to taxpayers. These particular segments of the population are referred to as special interest groupings or publics. This objective follows from the principle previously stated under persuasion, namely, that persons and organizations will adopt a practice recommended through a communication channel if they are already predisposed toward the theme of the recommendation.

(c) *To promote acceptance or adoption of practices being recommended for individuals and families.* This objective is similar to (b), except that rather than being directed at giving information, it is directed at obtaining action. Again, only particular segments of the population, that is, the special interest groupings, are the objective of the communication. This means that certain channels, which are more extensively used by those particular segments, will be utilized by the communicator. Certain channels are more used by, say, upper status groups, or older persons, or children than by the remainder of the community. A careful analysis in each community is necessary for most effective use of channels of communication under this objective.

Usually both objectives (b) and (c) require a longer type of communication than objective (a), where the purpose is merely to attract attention and make an announcement. Quite often, in addition to newspapers, radio, and television, the mimeographed or printed bulletin explaining a procedure or a position on an issue is used in this case. While television is particularly effective because it appeals both to the auditory and the visual faculties, it is not often used for this type of communication. The reason, perhaps, is the expense involved. The radio is presently used, probably more for educational purposes than is television, but newspapers and printed matter, such as bulletins from the extension services, are perhaps the most extensively used at present.

(d) *To promote acceptance and adoption of ideas by organizations as such.* Quite often one organization in a community will desire the approval or active cooperation of other organizations. While communication with individual members through the various channels previously mentioned is effective in this situation, communication follows the channel of personal contact more often in this case. The most effective type of personal contact is with leaders, since this means reaching more people with fewer contacts. If the organization which is the objective of the communication is a formal organization, its leadership is more easily identified. In informal groups leaders are more difficult to identify.

In the foregoing discussion, channels of communication are considered from the point of view of the person initiating the communication item.

However, it is also important to note their effect on the person or organization that is the object of the communication. In a summary of various studies of the adoption of farm practices, the relative effectiveness of various channels of communication was included. The recipients of the communication items were classified into stages according to their adoption of social change. These stages were identified as follows: (1) the stage of awareness, in which a person got information merely that a particular farm practice was available; (2) the stage of interest, where the awareness had developed into a definite tendency to seek more information about the practice; (3) the evaluation stage, where the person mentally anticipated how the practice would fit into his own situation; (4) the trial stage, where the person actually tried the practice on his own farm to see if it would work; and (5) the acceptance stage, which included adoption of the practice if it had worked during the trial stage.[8] The communication items differed depending upon the level in the diffusion stage at which the recipient of the communication found himself with regard to a particular practice. Generally, during the awareness and interest stages, mass media were most important, with agricultural agencies second, neighbors and friends third, and agricultural salesmen fourth. During the trial and evaluation stage neighbors and friends were most important, agricultural agencies next, mass media third, and agricultural salesmen fourth. During the adoption stage, those communications channels through which the farmer could get definite information about the practice became more important.[9]

In many studies the audience has also been classified according to education, occupation or in terms of other characteristics which may correspond to special interest groupings.[10] In summarizing such research, Lazarsfeld concluded that those social characteristics which he calls primary characteristics, such as sex, age, education, and status, make a considerable difference not only in channels of communication used, but in the particular programs and newspaper items watched, listened to, or read. This suggests that the effiectiveness of a particular communication channel relative to alternative channels depends on the audience as well as upon the type of communication or the purpose of the communicator.

[8] North Central Rural Sociology Committee, Subcommittee for the Study of New Farm Practices, op. cit.
[9] Ibid. Also see James H. Copp, Maurice L. Sill, and Emory J. Brown, "The Function of Information Sources in the Farm Practice Adoption Process," RS, 23:146–57, 1958.
[10] P.F. Lazarsfeld, "Audience Research," in Bernard Berelson and Morris Janowitz, Reader in Public Opinion and Communication, the Free Press, Glencoe, Illinois, 1950, pp. 337–46. Also see the bibliography contained therein.

THE NATURE OF PUBLIC OPINION

The end product of much communication is public opinion. Likewise, public opinion cannot exist without communication. However, there may be communication directed at ends other than public opinion and there are many factors important in shaping public opinion besides communication.

There are two basic concepts about the nature of public opinion.[11] The first is defined in terms of the percentages of the majority and minority, respectively, on any issue, with every person considered to be of equal weight. The second concept involves weighting each person or group according to their power to see their opinion prevail or realized in action. Thus, the second concept of public opinion is intimately bound up with the principles of power and leadership discussed elsewhere.

Regardless of the concept employed, public opinion is more than a mere collection of individual opinions. In terms of its most important consequences, public opinion is a single entity including within it majority and minority opinions. It may be based upon observations of individuals, but this is a heuristic device. Most public opinion research has concentrated on the first concept, where each person's opinion is weighted equally in arriving at a description of the total opinion.

Public opinion may also be identified with many of the value orientations described earlier. However, while values change very slowly insofar as they represent mores and folkways, public opinion may change quite rapidly. Proof of this was offered in a study in Pullman, Washington, conducted by Marvin Taves. Taves had conducted a study of attitudes toward community services and institutions a few days before Easter Sunday. On Easter Sunday a citizen who had been handled with unnecessary discourtesy, killed several police officers in full sight of a large gathering of citizens who were holding an Easter picnic on a hill just outside of town. Because of the small size of the community, this fact was fairly well known to everyone and the efficiency of both the police force and the town government was doubted by some. Taves immediately went back into the field with the same questions to measure the change in the attitudes toward the institutions of the community and found, as could be expected, notable

[11] Herbert Blumer, "Public Opinion and Public Opinion Polling," *ASR*, 13:542–49, 1948, and immediately succeeding discussions by Theodore Newcomb and Julian Woodward, pp. 549–54.

changes, particularly in regard to those institutions and agencies which were close to the police force in functions. For example, there was a tremendous decline in opinion favorable to the police force as such, but very little change in attitude toward the library. Taves concluded that the change in attitude toward an institution was directly proportional to how closely it was related to the police force.[12]

Taves' study used the concept of public opinion as percentages of majority and minority, giving equal weight to each person, but there is little doubt that many situations, if not most, make the second concept more appropriate. The reasons for giving unequal weight to individuals and organizations rest upon the ability of one person to influence many others. This is the very basis of representative democracy or republicanism. There are also many instances where evidence of the greater predictive power of the second concept is evident. In American history the vote of Congress has often contradicted known public opinion measured by the equal weighting of individuals, as illustrated in the case of attitudes toward lifting price controls after World War II. This is acceptable in the American value system, where leaders are supposed to have more information and to be more far-sighted. If they disagree with public opinion, therefore, it is their responsibility both to make a contrary judgment and to accept the consequences of that judgment. Thus, Franklin D. Roosevelt has recently been criticized for his handling of agreements with Soviet Russia late in World War II, even though public opinion at that time was highly in favor of making concessions to get Russia into the war against Japan.

At the community level there is little doubt that both concepts of public opinion are important. It is for this reason that the situation should be scrutinized carefully before a statement is made about public opinion on any issue of social change. In some situations the fact of equally weighted percentages of majority and minority opinions is of great importance, for example, in the prediction of a vote. In predicting a course of action in a community where a single decision is to be made by discussion, individuals and groups should be weighted according to power and influence.

The discussion so far has been an attempt to point out that there are two concepts of public opinion which are relevant to particular situations. The point to be added to this nearly always includes both majority and minority opinions. Even in the individual there are contradictory criteria in any given decision. One may weigh advantages and disadvantages in

[12] Marvin J. Taves, "A Study in the Dynamics of Small Town Social Attitudes," *Scientific Paper No. 932*, Washington AES, Pullman, 1949.

taking a particular course of action. In the case of public opinion the situation is analogous. It is particularly important in a representative democracy to be sure that the minority opinion compromises the majority opinion. This has been the history of federal action in the United States, where the majority opinion prevails for the most part, but is always compromised in the direction of the minority opinion. In a given community where there is little precedent for compromise, this minority opinion may not often affect majority opinion.

The crux of public opinion does not rest upon agreement as much as it does on organization. An opinion is public when there is communication among people so that they may express their thoughts about matters and may know what others think.

THE FUNCTIONS OF PUBLIC OPINION
IN COMMUNITY RELATIONS

Public opinion in a democracy, whether this be represented by a community, a state, a nation, or even a larger unit such as the United Nations, is always limited in its ability to be realized in action because of the representative nature of democracy in units larger than a small group. Nevertheless, since representatives are chosen by those represented, public opinion, if sufficiently dissatisfied, functions to control the representative. While he may not conform on each issue, the representative will have to conform on a sufficient number of important issues to avoid severe negative public opinion. In any situation, whether a democracy, autocracy, or some other form of social control, public opinion is a necessary basis for overthrow of any controlling group. In the case of revolutions or civil wars, public opinion must be strongly dissatisfied before such organization as is necessary to conduct and overthrow can occur.

A very important aspect of public opinion in terms of community behavior is its function in developing loyalty to the community. Research on such loyalty is more commonly known as identification, and by this is meant that a person acts as if he were the community, or reacts to criticisms of the community as if they were criticisms of him personally. However, the broader aspect of this is loyalty to community goals and the accepted means of achieving those goals. This is believed to result in a greater activity on the part of the person in solving community problems.

It has been mentioned previously that the technical specialist may try to "help" the community, and may fail because of nonacceptance by the community. This, again, is a negative function of public opinion. For example, a well was dug in a village in Latin America which was never accepted or used by the people of that village. The reason for this may have been a failure to elicit favorable public opinion regarding the well. There was a public opinion which, erroneous though it may have been, prevented full acceptance and use of the well, causing the project to fail.[13] While this particular example is taken from a deliberate action program, the same will be true of other types of changes in a mass society. The increased breadth of communication exposes people of one community to what others are doing, thus doubtless increasing the rate of change in that community, since it forms a public opinion favorable to the change.

Stereotypes

There are many aspects of public opinion which are important to analyze if the most effective job is to be done in communication. One of the most important of these is that of the nature of human thought in relation to the formation of opinion. Stereotypes, introduced into the terminology of social psychology by Walter Lippman,[14] are symbols or concepts which classify or connote persons or groups. The experience of any given person is very narrow compared to the amount of information and quasi-information he must have to make decisions. He knows few of the facts he should know to live wisely. Furthermore, even within his own experience, a person does not see events, such as another man or a sunset, so much as he notes that "the thing is man or sunset, and he see[s] chiefly what [his] mind is already full of on those subjects." [15] Thus the common beliefs about a person, an object, or a situation are interchanged among people, and the reaction a person may give to a stimulus is influenced more by his definition of that stimulus than by the nature of the stimulus itself. Indeed, as far as man is concerned, one may say that the very nature of a stimulus is the definition placed on it.

Hardly too much emphasis can be placed on this concept. Extreme deviant behavior as well as normal behavior can be understood in terms of stereotypes.[16] Thus, a person whose mental illness takes the form of

[13] Allan R. Holmberg, "The Well that Failed," in Edward H. Spicer, editor, *Human Problems in Technological Change,* Russell Sage Foundation, New York, 1952.

[14] Walter Lippmann, *Public Opinion,* The Macmillan Company, New York, 1949, Part III.

[15] *Ibid.,* p. 88.

[16] Two closely related concepts are (1) the "definition of the situation" (see W.I. Thomas, *Social Behavior and Personality,* Social Science Research Council, New York, 1951, Chapter 13) and (2) the "self-fulfilling prophecy" (see Robert K. Merton, *Social Theory and Social Structure,* the Free Press, Glencoe, Illinois, 1949, Chapter 7.

suspicion that others are persecuting him will react as if they are persecuting him. The principle involved here is that when a situation is defined in
a given way, the consequences are the same regardless of the accuracy of
that definition. The classic example of this is the definition of the world
as being flat during the Middle Ages.

Cosmas of Alexandria, a convert who flourished in the sixth century,
wrote a book entitled *Topographia Christiana* (*circa*. 548 A.D.) in which
he introduced the idea that the world is flat to refute the pagan and heathen
doctrines then current that had been proposed somewhat earlier by Ptolemy
and Strabo (B.C.) that the world is round. Cosmas claimed to get his information from the writings of Paul, who said that the first tabernacle was
a pattern of the world. This concept passed out of fashion in the early
fifteenth century and we returned to the pre-Cosmas concept. The consequences of the Cosmas concept were that no one approached the edge
of the earth. A second principle is found here, namely, that the definition of
the situation is self-fulfilling, that is, no test of the flatness of the earth
was made until someone refused to accept the definition.

The interactions among people and the relationships between elements
of the community system and among communities are shaped by stereotypes.
Likewise, the manner in which problems are defined and solved rest upon
stereotypic thinking.

To fully understand the implications of these principles it is helpful to
see why and how these stereotypes arise. The desirability of having an
answer to any questions in a given situation in order to make a decision requires much more effort, time, and experience than any person or group
can possibly have. Thus, in a given day, a single person may have to vote
on fifteen candidates, none of whom he knows personally, with each one's
policies differing from the remaining fourteen opponents. The voter can
hardly understand all that is involved in each of the many issues upon
which these policies bear. The same day he may have to ask for a raise
in salary, without intimate knowledge of his employer's values and psychological make-up, much less the peculiar circumstances that will influence him on that given day. The person may also have to meet fifteen
customers each of whom he must "sell" with no knowledge whatever of
the persons' motives, needs, and circumstances. He must order lunch from
a waitress whom he identifies only by a uniform and an order book. When
he goes to the theater that evening to relax from this day of interacting
on guesswork, he can hardly decide to whom he should give his ticket
on other than the most superficial grounds, namely, sight of the man standing at the door in a blue uniform.

It should be obvious that stereotypes not only are necessary to interact in the situations in which a person may find himself on a given day, but also that they "work" for the most part. If they suffice in most situations, then it follows that people will use them to make decisions whenever they do not have time for investigation. This means that stereotypes may be, and often are, transferred from known to unknown situations.

Stereotypes are based in the main on three factors: (1) extreme cases, (2) very little and nonrepresentative experience, and (3) stereotypes held by one's associates. The first two bases of stereotypes produce inaccuracy. The third basis of the stereotype produces public opinion. It is in this sense, the exchange of stereotypes, that public opinion may form long before any satisfactory amount of information about a situation is communicated to the public. It is also in this sense that the relationship between communication and public opinion may be seen most closely. This relationship exists in three ways: (1) in the absence of information, stereotypes are exchanged through informal communication means and public opinion is formed; (2) if information which is not available to private citizens is to become the basis of public opinion, it must be disseminated through the communication channels before the stereotypes become well defined through informal means; and (3) misinformation and propaganda can foster the transfer of certain stereotypes from other situations to produce a favorable or unfavorable public opinion.

Stereotypes are also important for cross-cultural contact as they are essential parts of the value system. Thus community work, for example, involving activity of persons from one culture in the communities of another, is likely to produce some misunderstanding, frustration, and failure where the stereotypes are different.

PRINCIPLES

1. *Communication is the exchange of knowledge, skills, and attitudes among persons or social groupings. One major aspect of communication is education, while another is propaganda.*

2. *The major functions of communication are understanding, changing of ideas, communication through the use of connotation, fostering diffusion or broadening the acceptance of change, increasing the accessibility of knowledge through time, space, and the social structure.*

Secondary functions of communication change the style of life of families in the work world, in recreational life, in informal group relations, and probably in formal participation in community affairs.

3. *Persuasion, as a major aspect of communication, involves numerous subtle techniques, many of which are appropriate only to propaganda but some of which are appropriate both to education and propaganda.*

Some of these techniques are demonstration, repetition, testimonials, half-truths, glittering generalization, and associating an idea with a public hero or with tradition.

4. *Formal channels of communication, including newspapers, radio, television, magazines, and printed or mimeographed publications, on special topics are effective in a total context of the communication system, including influence from informal communications and characteristics of the public.*

5. *Public opinion as the major end product of communication may be the relative percentages of majority and minority opinion with each person given equal weight or it may be defined as a single entity, weighting persons or groups relatively to their power to influence others or to make a decision for which public opinion is a predictor.*

6. *Both communication and public opinion are influenced by elements of human judgment. One of the most important elements of judgment is the stereotype or mental picture that people bring to an issue. Thus judgments are often made less in terms of the issue than they are in terms of prior generalizations of good and bad that people bring with them from similar situations.*

SELECTED REFERENCES

Berelson, Bernard, and Morris Janowitz, *Reader in Public Opinion and Communication*, the Free Press, Glencoe, Illinois, 1950.

Cooley, Charles H., *Social Organization*, Charles Scribner's Sons, New York, 1927, Part ii.

Lippmann, Walter, *Public Opinion*, The Macmillan Company, New York, 1949.

Merton, Robert K., *Social Theory and Social Structure*, the Free Press, Glencoe, Illinois, 1949, Part iii.

Newcomb, Theodore M., Eugene L. Hartley, and others, *Readings in Social Psychology*, Henry Holt and Company, New York, 1947, Part viii.

Rose, Arnold, *Sociology: The Study of Human Relations*, Alfred A. Knopf, New York, 1956.

Sanders, Irwin T., *The Community*, The Ronald Press Company, New York, 1958, Chapter 4.

Schuler, Edgar A., Duane L. Gibson, Maude L. Fiero, and Wilbur B. Brookover, *Outside Readings in Sociology*, Thomas Y. Crowell Company, New York, 1952, Part ix.

Smith, Bruce Lannes, Harold D. Lasswell, and Ralph D. Casey, *Propaganda, Communication, and Public Opinion: A Comprehensive Reference Guide*, Princeton University Press, Princeton, 1946.

CHAPTER 8

Social Stratification
of the Community

THE NATURE OF STRATIFICATION

Social stratification refers to the study of inequalities among people. These inequalities include mainly the variation in ability of people to realize goals and to avoid misfortunes defined by their value system. The concept of varying ability is called *life chances*.[1]

There are several bases which make for a greater or lesser ability in life chances. Some theorists, such as Marx, hold that tenure with respect to the means of industrial production or land is the sole or at least major determinant in life chances. Other theorists add such bases as social honor or prestige, social power, authority, occupation, income, and so on. In most American communities all these bases operate to bring about differences in life chances. Likewise, there are probably many others in some communities, for example, religious conformity in a religious community, family name in a history-oriented community, and race in a biracial community.

While the nature of stratification is no more difficult to grasp than the nature of most of the other dimensions of social structure, the continual argument concerning classless societies makes it necessary to give a more complete description of the nature of stratification than has been done in the case of the other dimensions of the social structure. The Army is an easy structure in which to see the various aspects of stratification. However, all the variables which are in the Army are also in the community, but there are more variables in the community than one would expect to find in the usual Army situation.

One of the most obvious features of stratification in the Army even to the casual observer is the fact that enlisted men salute officers and address them as "sir." Further, lower-ranking officers treat higher-ranking officers with

[1] Hans H. Gerth and C. Wright Mills, editors and translators, *From Max Weber: Essays in Sociology*, Oxford University Press, New York, 1946, Chapter 7.

151

similar deference. To such behavior sociologists apply the term *prestige*,[2] which is expressed through deference, honor, and title. This feature of stratification, both as it applies to the individual and to positions in the community, has received much attention in research. It is important to point out that prestige may accompany either the person or the office. While the first point is common to American thought, association of prestige with position or office is sometimes overlooked when we analyze less formal social structures than the Army or government. No matter how much disrepute a general or the President of the United States may have, deference to his title still follows him as long as he holds office. It is obvious, then, that his personality does not completely explain his prestige.

A second feature of stratification in the Army which is characteristic of all communities is inequality in power. "Insubordination" is a serious offense in the Army, in government, in business, and often even in informal relations between individuals after a routine of recognized inequalities has come about. The ability to get other people to do as we wish, even against their own wishes, is referred to by sociologists as *power*.[3] When power is formally structured, as in the case of the Army and other bureaucracies, such as business and the government or a university, it is called *authority*.[4] Thus authority may be defined as institutionalized power—that is, an explicit code of conduct with formal sanctions to reinforce conformity. However, even in bureaucracy, and always in informal relations, some individuals are more persuasive than others and wield more influence, whether through persuasion or threat. Thus a general may exceed his authority, yet not be disciplined because of informal power. It is already obvious that prestige usually follows power, especially authority. Likewise, prestige may lend informal power beyond that authorized by the formal structure.

It is also noticeable in the Army that those persons who hold positions of high prestige and power do not serve on KP, indeed, may not even shine their own shoes. They have a higher material level of living and a more comfortable form of life that may not require certain hours of work, may allow more freedom, and may even include afternoon golf as part of the job. Thus, associated with their high prestige and high authority and power

[2] Harold Kaufman, "Prestige Classes in a New York Rural Community," *Cornell Agricultural Experiment Station Memoir 260*, March, 1944; W. Lloyd Warner and Paul S. Lunt, *The Social Life of a Modern Community*, Yale University Press, New Haven, 1941; A.B. Hollingshead, *Elmtown's Youth*, John Wiley and Sons, New York, 1950.

[3] See Reinhard Bendix and Seymour Lipset, editors, *Class, Status and Power*, the Free Press, Glencoe, Illinois, 1953, Part II and bibliography contained therein; C. Wright Mills, *The Power Elite*, Oxford University Press, New York, 1946.

[4] Robert K. Merton, Ailsa P. Gray, Barbara Hockey, and Hanan C. Selvin, editors, *Reader in Bureaucracy*, the Free Press, Glencoe, Illinois, 1952.

may come a *style of life* [5] much more desirable in the culture or subculture in which they live—both in material and non-material things.

While power, prestige, and style of life may be the means of reaching some other desired goal, many find that they are ends in themselves. Thus, it is more pleasant to be respected than disrespected; it is desirable to many to give orders rather than to take them, to have their own way; and it is a goal worth striving for to enjoy the freedom of keeping one's own time in work and to be free to attend recreational events whenever they may come. These features of stratification are, therefore, both life chances and means of increasing other life chances.

In addition to the three concepts above it is obvious that some of the variables which are more often thought of in common-sense language, such as income, occupation, and family name are also bases for life chances.[6] All these variables are ranked according to some value orientation placed upon them. Perhaps the most difficult to rank is occupation. Occupation is not naturally a ranked variable, except as other dimensions run through any classification. One of the most useful classifications of occupations is that developed by Alba M. Edwards and used with variations in the Census.[7] The dimensions on which the occupations are ranked are three: income, the amount of skill required, and the amount of educational attainment held by members of each occupation. This classification is as follows: the professional is the top category, followed by proprietary, managerial, and official positions. Clerical and kindred workers then complete the white collar class. Next comes the blue collar class, subdivided into skilled, semiskilled, and unskilled workers. Variations on this scheme, depending upon the purpose of any particular study or theory, sometimes include semiprofessional workers just under the professional and service workers just below the unskilled. This classification of occupations has been shown to be functional in society in the sense that nearly any life chance varies with the occupational classes. Of course, no classification is perfect, and this one suffers from two main difficulties. The first is that there is an overlap between any two categories on the dimensions of status which run through the scheme. The classification of a school teacher in the professional group above a manager of a large company like General Motors in the proprietary, managerial, and

[5] Bendix and Lipset, *op. cit.*, Part III; Thorstein Veblen, *The Theory of the Leisure Class,* The Macmillan Company, New York, 1912; and Nancy Shea, *The Army Wife,* Harper and Brothers, New York, 1942.

[6] Harold F. Kaufman, Otis D. Duncan, Neal Gross, and William H. Sewell, "Problems of Theory and Method in the Study of Social Stratification in Rural Society," *RS,* 18:12–24, 1953.

[7] Alba M. Edwards, *A Social-Economic Grouping of the Gainful Workers of the United States,* 1930, Bureau of the Census, Washington, D.C., 1938.

official group is an error. The second major weakness is the inability to place farming accurately in the scheme of occupations. This is of particular importance in some societies where this class of occupations is of major significance. In spite of these major weaknesses, the Edwards scale has been shown to be highly related to most life chances and may be taken in lieu of a more precise and more complex classification as a satisfactory description of occupational stratification.

FUNCTIONS OF STRATIFICATION

The main subject of this chapter is the way in which stratification functions in the community. This may in part be accomplished by presenting detailed evidence to show the extent to which stratification affects nearly every element of the social system. Table 1 presents some sample material established by sociological research on the functions of stratification and on psychological characteristics of family members, on the institution of the family, and on the religious institution. Generally, the findings are that the average intelligence of sons declines as the occupational status of the parents decreases. The same is true of the intelligence of wives. The percentage of children planning to attend college is consistently lower as one moves down the occupational status scale. The proneness to divorce and desertion is consistently higher in the low status groupings. The interest in religion is not a straight-line relationship and the differences are significant as among the various occupational categories. Some of the occupational categories are omitted in some studies, but generally all studies in the United States show the same relationship.

The studies presented in Table 1 have, for the most part, been replicated several times, particularly those regarding intelligence, college attendance, and divorce. Other findings which are not presented but which have been indicated by other studies are relevant to all aspects of the social structure. For example, voting behavior is related to occupational status, with white collar workers more often voting Republican than blue collar workers. With regard to the economic institution, consumer purchases are higher among the white collar groups and their income is higher. The choice of an occupation by boys usually follows that of the father. This is more often true of the white collar grouping than of the blue collar. Satisfaction with work is also related to occupational status, although the relationship is not linear. Further, upper status groups tend not to reproduce themselves and therefore have smaller families. However, more of their children survive birth

TABLE I

Factors Related to Occupational Status

Occupational Status	a Mean I.Q. of Sons	b % of Children Planning to Attend College	c % of Wives in Upper Third in Intelligence	d Index of Proneness to Divorce	e % Interested "Much" in Religion Since Marriage	f % of Adolescents Who are "Very Individualistic"	g % Saying College Education is Needed Today	h % of Sons Entering the Professions
Professional	118	85	55*	68	39	32	74	21
Proprietary	***	***	35	68	33	26	62	7
Clerical	111	70	28	72	27	19	65	6
Skilled	110	45	31	87	33	19	53	2
Semiskilled	109	42	28**	94	28	14	49	2
Unskilled	107	37	***	Much Higher	34	7	35	1

* Excludes teachers.
** Semiskilled and unskilled combined.
*** Data not presented.

a. Unpublished data from statewide sample of high school seniors in Wisconsin, 1948.
b. Unpublished data from statewide sample of high school seniors in Wisconsin, 1948.
c. C.T. Pihlblad and C.L. Gregory, "Occupational Selection and Intelligence in Rural Communities and Small Towns in Missouri," ASR, Vol. 21, 1956, p. 69.
d. Wm. J. Goode, "Economic Factors and Marital Stability," ASR, Vol. 16, 1951, p. 805. The index is a result of dividing the number of cases of "Other than single or married" by the number of cases "Married, wife present." The interpretation of the index is that the higher the index number the more proneness to divorce.
e. Gerhard E. Lenski, "Social Correlates of Religious Interest," ASR, Vol. 18, 1953, p. 537.
f. Richard Centers, "Children of the New Deal: Social Stratification and Adolescent Attitudes," in Bendix and Lipset, op. cit., p. 361.
g. Herbert H. Hyman, "The Value Systems of Different Classes: A Social-Psychological Contribution to the Analysis of Stratification," in Bendix and Lipset, op. cit., p. 430.
h. Natalie Rogoff, "Recent Trends in Urban Occupational Mobility," in Bendix and Lipset, op. cit., p. 445.

and they tend to live longer as adults. Health and use of health facilities is also related to occupations, with the upper status groupings using health facilities more and having better health. Delinquency is lower and participation higher in the white collar occupations.[8]

The major point is not so much that occupation itself is crucial in understanding the community, but that any status variable is the *sine qua non* of proper understanding and prediction of community behavior.

Are There Social Classes?

At various places in this book, the terms "upper middle class," "lower class," and so on have been used. Furthermore, these terms are often used in lay literature and conversation to denote certain groups of people who seem to have higher or lower life chances based on one or more characteristics. There is an economy in explaining stratification in a community by using the term "class" to denote a group of people who have several characteristics in common and are different from other classes. However, it is very important to distinguish a social class as a social entity from a mere statistical class. This is important because a social class will be recognized by people in the community and their behavior will be affected.

A social class is a distinguishable grouping of people, which is distinct or completely separated from adjacent groupings in a continuum. The line of separation is not arbitrarily drawn by a statistician but determined by the social structure itself. Differences must be observed in the defining characteristics such as power, race, tenure, and so on, as well as correlates, such as income, prestige, and other life chances. For example, in some communities in the United States, Negroes are completely distinguishable from whites on several status variables. The defining criterion, then, is the Negro, since some value is placed in American culture on being white. This does not imply that the defining criterion of any class must be any biological or other immediately distinguishable characteristic. For the Negroes to be a social class, however, they must not only be completely distinguishable on the defining criterion, but also on the correlates of the defining criterion. In some communities the highest Negro incomes are not as high as the lowest among the whites. Furthermore, they do not reach a point as high in the occupational structure as the whites. In some communities one may find that

[8] For an extensive bibliography of stratification literature see Harold W. Pfautz, "The Current Literature on Social Stratification," *AJS*, 58:392, 1953; and Walter Goldschmidt, "Social Class in America—A Critical Review," *American Anthropologist*, 52:483–98, 1950.

all Negroes and no whites are service workers. Similarly, all Negroes may have lower prestige in a community than any white. If this situation truly exists, then these two groups are social classes. Another consideration is that of caste, which means the same as social class except that caste is fixed at birth and cannot be changed.

It is obvious from the above that a pure social class will almost never be found in American society. In other words, in the example used, some Negroes will almost always make more money than some whites and will have reached a higher occupational status. The problem then becomes at what point in the overlap between distinguishable classes can one no longer identify classes. A correlate of this problem is whether the total community is stratified in terms of classes or whether most of the community is characterized by continuous status differences with a few classes distinguishable.

How much overlap is needed to destroy the identity of a social class? This problem has not been solved in research and can only be considered in terms of common observation. Most American communities are not characterized by a class structure. The differences in income, prestige, and so on, are continuous, rather than observable with natural breaks occurring in the distribution. There is a correlation between various status characteristics, that is, those who have high income are generally those who are high in the occupational structure, have high prestige, have more power, and so on. But the correlation is not high enough to prevent a considerable number of cases being found where positions on one status variable are high and positions on another are low. Thus, the prestige of the school teacher is relatively high, but the income is relatively low. The teacher's place in the occupational structure is high, but in the power structure is relatively low. Skilled workers in present-day American communities have high income, rank as medium in the occupational structure, and are low, as individuals, in the power structure. It may therefore be tentatively concluded that the total community population cannot be stratified in terms of disjunct, distinguishable classes. Stated in another way, there would be too many people who would have to be arbitrarily classified for the social scheme accurately to describe the status structure. This means that status differences are present, but the distribution is continuous.

The second problem, namely, whether there are any social classes in the community, may be answered pretty much in the affirmative. For example, in many Southern communities the Negroes represent a social class. In large urban centers, the managers of large businesses represent a social class. In a college community, college professors and students probably represent social classes. The difficulty here is that, since the total community cannot be described in terms of social classes, the attention given to any one class represents an incomplete picture of the community structure.

From what has been said it follows that "upper middle class," "upper class," and the like are merely crude summary terms for a number of people who generally fall in a particular hierarchical position with respect to most of the status variables. But the foregoing discussion also suggests that in some areas of the country, such as the South, there may be some communities where social class situations exist.[9]

Prestige

Prestige includes social honor and respect and is expressed through deference and title. The experienced community development worker will know the importance of associating the names of prestige persons with the community development program to foster an air of respectability.[10] In this sense, prestige may also be viewed as one type of power.

Prestige in large communities is primarily based on position in some formal structure. For example, within an industry the person with the highest authority usually has the highest prestige. Further, some types of formal positions carry a halo effect beyond the areas of activities in which the positions are directly involved. The medical doctor, as a case in point, has high prestige within the health organization, but his prestige also carries over into all other realms of human activity. One interesting consequence of this principle is that a specialist is often called upon to give "expert" advice in areas where he is really a layman.

In smaller communities where more intimate acquaintance with everyone is possible, the factor of personality enters into the determination of prestige. Thus, a physician may still have high prestige, but it will decrease if he does not conform, say, to moral codes of conduct. This would also be true of the large community if the undesirable personal trait became public knowledge.

Prestige is positively correlated with all other status variables, such as authority, income, occupational status, and style of life, but the correlation

[9] For further consideration of the problem see Otis D. Duncan and Jay W. Artis, "Some Problems of Stratification Research," RS, 16:17–29, 1951.

[10] For an excellent summary of several studies concerned with the stratification dimension in middle-sized and urban communities, see John F. Cuber and William F. Kenkel, Social Stratification in the United States, Appleton-Century-Crofts, Inc., New York, 1954.

is not perfect. Therefore, one may find a person with high prestige who is not a power in the community and who does not have many of the resources needed for deliberate action programs. On the other hand, one is likely to find someone who has a great deal of power in the community but who has low prestige. Usually this latter group of persons will have, in addition to power, many of the resources needed for community development programs. It is obvious from this that wherever names are associated with a program to give an atmosphere of respectability and honest intention, prestige is the more important of the status variables. Likewise, a person who has prestige is ordinarily a person who exhibits all the value orientations of the community.

The importance of external conformity in determining prestige is indicated in a study of a small rural community in Pennsylvania. The study was designed to show the relationship between status variables and social participation. In the process of obtaining data on the prestige of persons in the sample, an effort was made to determine the value criteria for high and for low prestige. The study indicated that value conformity was a criterion. The particular criteria used (in words of the respondents or close paraphrase) were as follows: *

Criteria of Higher Standing

(a) *Money, wealth, high material level of living.* This category was the most easily recognized and unambiguous. The answers tended to run to the stereotyped form, more money, but a number of alternative phrasings and nuances appeared:

Better fixed
Better place to live in
Don't have to work or do anything
Wealthy
Financially higher standing

Well-to-do
Own their own homes
Inherited a lot
Have things up to date

(b) *Activity and leadership.* The central emphasis here was on civic interest and activity, with a subemphasis in a small minority of the responses on power and influence:

Takes part in more things

Civic activity, such as leaders
Civic interest
Very active in community affairs

Has more to do and say about the clubs and organizations
Social activities
Runs the community
Seems to be into everything

* Otis D. Duncan and Jay W. Artis, "Social Stratification in a Pennsylvania Rural Community," *Pennsylvania AES Bulletin 543*, State College, Pa., 1951, pp. 16–19.

(c) *Religious worthiness.* These responses stressed participation in church activities and living a Christian way of life:

Good church worker

A good Christian life

Good religious life

Does a lot of church work

(d) *Positive moral characteristics.* The leading ideas here were friendliness and neighborliness, sobriety and industriousness, and general high moral character:

Always helping others

Good neighborliness

Tries to get along—honest

Honesty and loyalty

Have amounted to more and help others

A better life so that you are an example to others

Friendly with everyone

Industrious, sober, neighborly

High morals, good lives

(e) *Education.* The attainment of a high educational level and the exercise of training in one's occupation:

A good education and can hold a good position

Better education—kids all graduated from high school

More highly educated

(f) *Old families.* Belonging to a family of good name and resident in the community for a long time:

Older residents

Family name

Longer time in community

(g) *Usurpation.* The explicitly expressed notion that higher standing is partially or largely a matter of pretensions to such a position:

They think they are better

A lot is just thinking you are

Because they think so

Some put on a front

(h) *Occupation.* Mention of occupational status as a condition of higher standing, primarily in reference to doctor, minister, teacher, and business man:

Is a doctor

Higher because of profession

Better job

Business man has higher standing

Professional—preacher

In business

Minister and school teacher have high standing

(i) *Personability.* Desirable personality traits, of the pleasant, likeable sort:

Pleasant disposition

Talks better than I can—lots of friends

Personality

Sociable, agreeable, not snooty

(j) *Miscellaneous.* The following is a virtually complete listing of the responses coded as miscellaneous; many of these responses, if more fully qualified, doubtless could have been coded in the preceding categories. The ideas of social prominence and standing of associates could well have been made the basis of another category, except for the small number of responses involved.

Not handicapped—smaller families

Better prepared for the work they're doing

If you have good health you're pretty well off

Better view of life

Higher socially

Up-to-date farmers who are younger

People they associate with

Social standing in community

Way people look up to them

Environment . . . experience

More talent

More prominence

Great sportsman

Way of living

Better position socially

High social standing

Criteria of Lower Standing

(a) *Poverty, poor material level of living.*

Poor people

Don't have enough to eat, poor housing

Have a hard time to get along

Not well off

Isn't doing very well

On relief

No money

(b) *Immorality.* The principal traits mentioned referred to drinking, criminality, illicit sexual relations, and general immorality:

Unmarried mothers

Disreputable character

Steal, not trustworthy

Run around with other men

Drink and gamble

Drunkard

Husband in prison

Liars and trouble-makers

(c) *Irresponsibility.* The main items concerned family neglect, lack of ambition and effort, and carelessness with money:

Don't provide for their families

No attempt to get ahead—just exist

Sponging on government

Wasteful, shiftless

Choose to be lower—spend money foolishly

Don't feed kids; out till morning; don't pay bills

They just won't work

Too damn lazy to do anything

Lack of self-respect

(d) *Not active in community life.*

No civic interest

Poor attitude toward community betterment

Don't take active part in welfare organization

Doesn't associate with other people

(e) *Irreligious.*

Never go to church

Won't even let their children go to Sunday School

People with no religion at all

Unchristian

(f) *Lack of education.*

No education

Never see them in a school

Can't read or write

Aren't as well educated

(g) *Dirty.*

Filthy, dirty   Just plain sloppy
Live like hogs   Not neat and clean

(h) *Dull mentality.*

Mentally deficient with many chil-   Lacking in ability
   dren in same shape   Feeble-minded
Aren't very intelligent

(i) *Misfortune, lack of opportunity.*

Bad luck   Lot of sickness
Never got a good start in life   Didn't get the breaks

The prestige structure will follow occupation to a great extent in any community, although in a smaller community an intervening variable will be personality. Since prestige and occupation are closely associated, the findings from a study by Mapheus Smith are presented here. Numerous replications of his work not only lend support to the notion of prestige accompanying occupation, but show a surprising correspondence in the ranking of occupations themselves. This is particularly true of the very high and the very low status occupations. This is not quite so noticeable in occupations in the intermediate range of status, although the differences among studies and among sample members are usually not great. The findings from the Smith study are presented because they not only give occupations of considerable relevance to community work, but place these occupations in a frame of reference within the total society. Of course only a few of the approximately 35,000 occupations in American society are listed, but many of the most frequently found occupations are in the list of 100.

TABLE II

Mean Prestige Status Ratings of
100 Representative American Occupations *

Rank Order	Description	Mean
1.	U.S. Supreme Court Justice	99.02
2.	U.S. ambassador to foreign country	97.56
3.	U.S. cabinet secretary	97.08
4.	U.S. senator	96.21
5.	Governor of state	95.25
6.	College president or chancellor, 3,000+ students	92.30
7.	Banker, large city	89.41

Rank Order	Description	Mean
8.	Mayor of city of over 500,000 population	88.76
9.	Medical doctor, city of over 500,000 population	88.19
10.	State prosecuting attorney	85.36
11.	Captain ocean-going merchant vessel	82.17
12.	Criminal lawyer	81.32
13.	Architect	79.40
14.	Author, poet; has published poems	78.12
15.	Actor, motion pictures, above rank of extra	77.91
16.	Aviator, transcontinental airline	77.52
17.	Clergyman	75.88
18.	Certified public accountant	73.78
19.	Postmaster, city	73.35
20.	Radio entertainer, any except announcer	72.94
21.	Inventor, working alone on patentable devices	72.13
22.	Cashier of bank	70.47
23.	Building contractor	70.46
24.	Editor-owner, small town newspaper	69.56
25.	High school administrator, 1,000+ pupils	68.43
26.	Trained nurse	67.59
27.	Justice of peace	66.92
28.	Professional baseball player, major league	66.46
29.	Interior decorator	65.89
30.	Owner and operator, department store	65.79
31.	Radio operator	65.59
32.	Owner and operator, any type mine	65.04
33.	Retail jewelry dealer	63.90
34.	Undertaker	63.28
35.5	Owner of log or timber camp	63.01
35.5	County sheriff	63.01
37.	Social or welfare worker	61.81
38.	Supervisory position, railroad	60.98
39.	Real estate agent	60.93
40.	Retail dealer, five and ten, variety store	59.73
41.	Mate, ocean-going vessel	59.72

DIMENSIONS OF THE COMMUNITY

TABLE II

Mean Prestige Status Ratings of
100 Representative American Occupations ° (*continued*)

Rank Order	Description	Mean
42.	Manager or other official, log or timber camp	59.66
43.	Private secretary to executive	59.50
44.	Manager or official, any type of mine	59.04
45.	Foreman, supervisor, factory	57.75
46.	Electrician, own business	57.42
47.	Hotel keeper or manager, city under 25,000	56.89
48.	Policeman, city of over 15,000	54.91
49.	Watchmaker, factory	53.96
50.	Owner-operator general farm	53.64
51.	Owner-operator dry-cleaning establishment	52.86
52.	Linotyper	52.06
53.	Locomotive engineer	51.45
54.	Oil well driller	51.32
55.5	Conductor, steam railroad	49.90
55.5	Railway mail clerk	49.90
57.	Bookkeeper	47.48
58.	Typist	45.60
59.	Ticket agent, railroad	44.81
60.	Rural mail carrier	44.69
61.	Practical nurse	43.78
62.	Carpenter, general business for himself	41.93
63.	Structural iron worker	41.77
64.	Pawnbroker	39.43
65.	Salesman in store	39.41
66.	Dressmaker, own business conducted at home	38.45
67.	Telephone operator	37.61
68.	Telegraph or telephone lineman	37.17
69.	Painter, house and other non-factory	34.47
70.	Barber	33.95
71.	Cook, hotel or metropolitan restaurant	31.70
72.	Farm tenant, operates for share of profits	30.51

Rank Order	Description	Mean
73.	Baggageman, railroad	30.04
74.	Semiskilled worker, automobile factory	28.15
75.	Chauffeur, private family	27.36
76.	Semiskilled worker, building trades	27.21
77.	Semiskilled worker, clay, glass, pottery	27.11
78.	Semiskilled worker, cotton mill	26.19
79.	Auto filling station attendant	25.24
80.	Waiter, hotel or metropolitan restaurant	24.03
81.	Taxicab driver	23.70
82.	Manual worker, stone quarry	20.81
83.	Miner, coal mine	20.75
84.	Porter on pullman or dining car	20.57
85.	Woodchopper or sawyer at lumber camp	18.89
86.	Farm laborer	18.44
87.	Unskilled laborer, railroad	17.59
88.	Janitor, public building	17.07
89.	Longshoreman, unskilled heavy work	15.71
90.	Unskilled worker, automobile factory	15.58
91.	Unskilled worker, construction	15.24
92.	Unskilled worker, woolen mill	14.66
93.	Newsboy	13.59
94.	Huckster or peddler	9.30
95.	Scissors or other tool grinder, house to house	9.26
96.	Unskilled worker, odd jobs	7.70
97.	Scrub-woman	7.27
98.	Garbage collector	6.80
99.	Unskilled migratory worker	3.76
100.	Professional prostitute	1.62

* Mapheus Smith, "An Empirical Scale of Prestige Status of Occupations," *ASR*, 8:185–92, April, 1943. Used by permission.

The ranking itself represents a deference gesture toward the word or symbol standing for the occupation. It would be interesting to note the differences in prestige conferred if the word "janitor" instead of "custodian" were used. It should be pointed out that the qualification as to size of city in

Smith's findings on certain occupations such as "medical doctor" (number nine) should not be taken too seriously. In studies where only community occupations are listed, the doctor nearly always ranks first in the prestige listing, although he is sometimes equaled or surpassed by the judge.

Occupations which are consistently found to have high prestige in communities are those of the doctor, banker, lawyer, judge, editor, and school administrators. As mentioned previously, the cooperation or merely the names of these persons, in association with a community program, brings an atmosphere of respectability as well as special talents and knowledge to the work of the community organizer. The consistency of the findings with respect to subsequent studies of the sort done by Smith indicate the reliability of the generalizations for theoretical work.

It appears also that the prestige dimension of the occupational structure does not change much over a period of time. A study done by Deeg and Patterson in 1946 indicated that during a twenty-one-year period the ranking of occupations had shown almost no change with a correlation of .97 (almost perfect) between the rankings in 1925 and 1946.[11] Of the few changes which did occur, the farmer dropped three ranks, the traveling salesman dropped five ranks, and the insurance salesman gained four ranks. All other occupations in a list of twenty-five changed no more than two ranks, and many of them experienced no change. The remarkable similarity between the rankings of the two periods, with a depression and major war occurring in between, indicates that the prestige system has changed very little over the period of time covered. In both periods, of course, the findings were very similar to those presented previously from the study by Mapheus Smith.

Economic Position

Many social thinkers have distinguished "class" as having an economic basis while other types of stratification are based on social honor, position, and other social characteristics.[12] That the economic basis of stratification is important cannot be denied. It is particularly important where the history of the community is dominated by one type of economy. This is the case in the South and the Southwest. This fosters the type of status structure referred to as social class. As mentioned previously, the outstanding features of a class structure are twofold: (1) There is a high correlation between any

[11] Maethel E. Deeg and Donald G. Paterson, "Changes in Social Status of Occupations," Occupations, The Vocational Guidance Magazine, 25:205–9, 1947.
[12] Gerth and Mills, op. cit., p. 181, and Oliver C. Cox, "Max Weber on Social Stratification: A Critique," ASR, 15:223–27, 1950.

two variables in stratification, that is, high economic position, high prestige, much power and authority are associated. Similarly, a low position on any of these variables usually means a low position on any of the others. (2) The other feature is the disjunct nature of the distribution of status variables.

In the United States the most clear-cut case of class difference is the Negro as mentioned previously. While the difference between Negro and white on the defining criterion is actually race, or the social definition placed on this, much of the difference between Negroes and whites in their ability to realize their life chances is based on difference in economic power. In a study by Beers and Heflin in Kentucky in 1946, some of the differences readily known by most people between Negroes and whites were shown with more precision.[13] They found that nearly three-fourths of the Negro males were employed in only four occupational categories: operatives, farm laborers, other laborers, and service workers. It was further found, as has been found in many studies of urban communities of the North and South, that Negroes were employed in these four occupational classes proportionately far in excess of whites. As indicated by the Census, generally the situation in Kentucky found the educational status lower by approximately one and a half to two grades as compared to whites, whether it was in the total population, urban, rural non-farm, or rural farm. Negro housing was more often tenant-occupied than among the whites in owner-occupied dwellings in the rural non-farm areas. The need for repair of houses was considerably higher among Negro families than among the white families. While no data were available on informal interaction, as well as institutional interaction, the general picture in nearly all Southern communities and many Northern ones finds Negroes in different churches and different schools. Often voting is difficult, although Negroes legally have the franchise, and intermarriage is found almost nowhere in the United States. This, of course, perpetuates the class system, since the status of the children is largely determined by the status of the parents.

The explanation of the differences in these two classes is largely, but not entirely, a matter of the economic history of the South. A one-crop economy, with slaves introduced as almost necessary to profitable enterprise in cotton-growing, fostered perpetuation of class distinction long after the economic basis for it had disappeared. That the economic basis is an important one is indicated by the fact that a similar class structure existed between the dons and peons in the Southwest, with large ranches and many landless employees being characteristic of cattle-ranching. Leonard and Loomis de-

[13] Howard W. Beers and Catherine P. Heflin, "The Negro Population of Kentucky," *Kentucky AES Bulletin 481*, Lexington, Kentucky, 1946.

scribed the situation in the Southwest, although the class situation had largely disappeared by the time they did their study. The dons in the local villages, who owned all the cattle, controlled the surrounding land, and employed the other residents, had disappeared along with their holdings. The holdings were very large and the gap that separated the dons and peons was also very large. It is a general characteristic, as it was in the case Leonard and Loomis were describing, that when a class situation exists, intermarriage occurs within the class rather than between the classes. This perpetuates the class system. While much is made of the intermarriage of the "poor little girl" to the wealthy man in American society, it is probably true that even in the majority of American communities where the status structure is continuous, intermarriage is relatively homogeneous with respect to status.[14]

A still further test of the economic basis of the class situation is indicated by the study by Holt of rural neighborhoods and communities in Alabama.[15] He found that "social difference between owners and tenants as a rule is definitely greater than anywhere in the United States." He was talking here only about white owners and tenants. It is common knowledge now that the "poor whites" have little more in the way of respect and other life chances than do Negro tenants.[16] A more detailed analysis of the class structure among the whites is given below from a study done in Harmony, Georgia, in a series of bulletins called the "Culture of a Contemporary Community." Several studies of this kind were done throughout the country.

Class Structure [*]

Class structure in the Harmony Community, as in other farm communities of the county and of the South generally, has two bases: the one is radical, the other is farm ownership. The pattern of class structure based on race as a determinant is too well known to warrant more than the statement that racial lines in the community are strictly drawn, and strictly adhered to, as they are in other communities of the cotton South.

The Harmony Community with respect to farm ownership among white farmers

[14] Olen Leonard and C.P. Loomis, *Culture of a Contemporary Rural Community: El Cerrito, New Mexico*, United States Department of Agriculture, Bureau of Agricultural Economics, Washington, D.C., 1941.

[15] John B. Holt, *Rural Neighborhoods and Communities of Lee County, Alabama*, Bureau of Agricultural Economics, United States Department of Agriculture, Washington, D.C., 1941.

[16] E.A. Schuler, "Social Status and Farm Tenure—Attitudes and Social Conditions of Corn Belt and Cotton Belt Farmers," *United States Department of Agriculture Social Research Report IV*, Washington, D.C., 1938.

[*] Waller Wynne, *Culture of a Contemporary Rural Community: Harmony, Georgia*, Bureau of Agricultural Economics, Washington, D.C., 1943.

is not typical of southern farming communities generally in that nearly all its white farmers are owners. The community does not have a white tenant class. In fact, among the approximately twenty white families actively engaged in farming, only four do not own all or part of the land they operate.

Among white farmers, owners have a higher social status than do tenants. Furthermore, some owners have a higher social status than other owners—those who are descended from families that have been in the community for generations set themselves apart from owners who are relatively new in ownership. The existence of social lines between owners and non-owners and between owners themselves is obvious in the pattern of personal association within the community. Old families among the owners do not usually "accept" the new owners who have climbed the agricultural ladder, and if the culture of the new owner is markedly different from that of the old families he is never accepted. Even a second-generation owner is not accepted by the inner circle if he retains the same culture as his parents. In contrast, descendants of old families do not find their social position imperiled when they yield, through necessity or choice, their ownership of land. New owners, and tenants as well, are aware that their social standing in the community is not so high as that of their neighbors who have a long family history, closely connected with, if not a part of, the planting tradition.

But the old families do not have the characteristic of snobbishness. They give to the new owners, and to tenants, the same friendly and neighborly treatment they give to each other. Furthermore, the sympathies of the old families are wide, and in time of adversity they are always ready to help.

Owners who have climbed the agricultural ladder identify themselves as members of the owning class but they generally associate with members of their own group, that is, with those who have risen to ownership in the same way. To a very limited degree they associate with members of the tenant class.

The extent of farm ownership among Negro farmers stands in sharp contrast with that prevailing among white farmers. Of the approximately fifty Negro families engaged in farming, only one owns the land it operates. The others are rather evenly divided into renters, sharecroppers, and wage hands.

This colored family that owns its farm has a higher status than other Negro families have, and this fact is recognized by the white families. This family does not associate with the tenants except as to the institutional life of the community. There are no apparent social differences among Negro tenants, renters, croppers, and wage hands.

Among the older white residents of the community, and of the county as well, there is the growing complaint that the high social character of the county is rapidly declining owing to the "low" character of recent comers to the county and to the influence of the governmental work programs which they believe have encouraged among certain persons an increased sense of dependency upon others and a decreased sense of dependency upon themselves.

Commenting on the type of person who has but recently come into the county, one white owner, whose family has lived in the county for generations, said: "I'm not bragging but we used to have good people around here. There was no scum of the earth in this community. They were just large farmers and their helpers. The community didn't know the one-horse farm we have today. You don't care to have as neighbors people with whom you don't want to associate." This owner had particular reference to clients of the Farm Security Administration, but he also had reference to other families that have moved into the county. This man's attitude is typical of the community as a whole.

Citizens who have always somehow managed to get through trying economic times and have never sought relief under any of the governmental relief programs are practically unanimous in their opinion that such programs have a deleterious effect upon the individual who participates in them and upon the communities of the county. Governmental relief programs, these citizens declare, encourage the participating individual to become forever dependent upon governmental work, which is, they hold, less demanding upon the individual than farm work. Furthermore, they think that government work too often encourages farm owners to shift to the government the responsibility for the solution of problems that farmers, individually and collectively, should solve for themselves.

In the Harmony Community some elderly persons receive old-age assistance and public relief from the county, but apparently not one of its residents was employed on WPA projects at any time during the course of the study. Apparently farmers, with possibly one or two exceptions, will not rent a tenant house to a family of which any member is employed by the WPA.

The attitude of farm owners toward newcomers to the county derives not only from a sense of social difference between themselves and the recent arrivals but also from an awareness that the dominant position the older residents held unchallenged in the past is now seriously threatened. Probably not all would agree that the older families are now at the bottom of the heap and that the newcomers are on top, as one resident said in effect, but they would agree that the present trend of things is rapidly in that direction.

While historically the explanation of the class situation is usually an economic one, its perpetuation occurs in other institutions. For one thing, the lack of intermarriage prevents the type of social mobility dependent upon marrying above one's status. This of course depends upon the institution of the family, where in most class situations intermarriage between classes is strongly interdicted. Second, political power is lacking in groups who have low class standing and their legal protection in other types of activities which would enhance their status must await action on the part of the dominant group. Votes, of course, represent strong encouragement to politicians to pass measures for the legal protection for the lower classes.

Status and Participation

In two ways, participation is a status variable: (1) the leadership relation is a power relation, to be discussed in the next chapter, and (2) membership and attendance allow a person's views to be recognized by those in power.

In another sense, participation is a human relationship affected by other dimensions and elements of the social structure, including status. There is no factor of the social structure more important than status in determining participation in formal organizations. In a study in one small urban community in 1941, Mather found adults in families earning less than $100 per month participating in all types of organizations to a lesser extent than higher income families. The findings were true of religious, fraternal, recreational, patriotic, political, and "cultural" organizations as well as service clubs. As compared to the men earning $100 per month or more, the men in the lower income grouping were ten times as likely to belong to no formal organization. The relationship between income and participation was somewhat lower among women than men, but still quite high.[17]

Using a combined classification of occupational status and income, Komarovsky arrived at essentially the same conclusions as did Mather. Generally, higher occupation-income status was associated with (1) a high proportion of persons who belonged to at least one organization, (2) a higher proportion of persons who belonged to many as opposed to few organizations, and (3) a higher proportion of persons who belonged to particular types of organizations, such as economic, political, civic, and so on.[18]

There are other studies verifying these research results. It appears that regardless of which status variable is used for measurement, regardless of what measure of participation is employed, regardless of the type of participation, and regardless of the type of community studied, the higher the status the more the participation in the formal organizations of the community. This means that the course of events in the community is determined by and in conformity with the values of the upper status groupings.

PRINCIPLES

The foregoing description of social stratification assumes three basic principles upon which the study of the phenomenon is based:

1. *Persons, groups, organizations, races, and nations, as well as any other social unit of analysis, are ranked as higher or lower on some characteristics.*

2. *This ranking is important in and of itself—it is pleasant to have our fellow men think well of us and unpleasant to have them look down upon us.*

3. *The ranking is important in achieving other goals which we may have.*

---

[17] William G. Mather, "Income and Social Participation," *ASR*, 6:38–81, 1941.
[18] Mirra Komarovsky, "The Voluntary Associations of Urban Dwellers," *ASR*, 11:686–98, 1946.

SELECTED REFERENCES

Bendix, Reinhard, and Seymour Martin Lipset, *Class, Status and Power*, the Free Press, Glencoe, Illinois, 1953.

Cuber, John F., and William F. Kenkel, *Social Stratification in the United States*, Appleton-Century-Crofts, Inc, New York, 1954.

Davie, Maurice R., *Negroes in American Society*, McGraw-Hill Book Company, Inc., New York, 1949.

Davis, Kingsley, *Human Society*, The Macmillan Company, New York, 1949, Chapter 14.

Gerth, H.H., and C. Wright Mills, *From Max Weber: Essays in Sociology*, Oxford University Press, New York, 1946, Part II.

Kaufman, Harold F., "Prestige Classes in a New York Rural Community," *Cornell University AES Memoir 260*, 1944.

Kaufman, Harold F., Otis Dudley Duncan, Neal Gross, and William H. Sewell, "Problems of Theory and Method in the Study of Social Stratification in Rural Society," *RS*, 18: No. 1, 1953.

Merton, Robert K., Ailsa P. Gray, Barbara Hockey, and Hanan C. Selvin, *Reader in Bureaucracy*, the Free Press, Glencoe, Illinois, 1952.

Miller, Herman P., *Income of the American People*, John Wiley and Sons, New York, 1955.

Mills, C. Wright, *White Collar: The American Middle Classes*, Oxford University Press, New York, 1951.

Pfautz, Harold W., "The Current Literature on Social Stratification: Critique and Bibliography," *AJS*, LVIII: 391–418, 1953.

Veblen, Thorstein, *The Theory of the Leisure Class*, the New American Library of World Literature, Inc., New York, 1953.

Vidich, Arthur J., and Joseph Bensman, *Small Town in Mass Society*, Princeton University Press, Princeton, New Jersey, 1958.

Warner, W. Lloyd, and Paul S. Lunt, *The Social Life of a Modern Community*, Yale University Press, New Haven, 1941, Chapter 6.

Various articles in "Civil Rights in America," *The Annals of the American Academy of Political and Social Science*, Vol. 275, May, 1951.

CHAPTER 9

Power and Leadership

Both power and leadership reflect the ability to influence the action of others; however, there is a distinction to be made between them in terms of the ways in which that influence is exercised. Power implies the ability to compel others to behave in the desired manner. Leadership, on the other hand, implies the ability to help a group determine the desirable response which they then follow voluntarily. It is by definition, then, that those who hold power in a community will generally determine its course of action. In the present chapter we shall continue the study of inequalities by considering power, its function in general, and its influence in the community structure. This is most noticeable in considering political control since it may not involve the same area and people as the community structure itself, particularly in the small community.

THE FUNCTIONS OF POWER

Factions

Conflicting interests frequently develop in the relations between men and between groups and institutions. This was recognized long before the scientific study of human relations was deemed possible or appropriate. One of the clearest presentations of the importance of conflict of interest in human society was presented in *The Federalist*.[1] The point of view was taken that as long as men were not of the same mind and as long as liberty to disagree was accepted, men who were united by some common interest would strive for what they believed right, or to further their own interests. According to *The Federalist* this was inevitable, and since the causes of "faction" could not be removed without losing liberty, the only alternative was to be sought in the control of the effects of factionalism. This control was posited as necessitating a larger and ultimate power to control strong

[1] *The Federalist*, Modern Library, New York, pp. 53–62.

factions in their oppression of weaker ones. Further, it was thought that this stronger power, the political institution, was necessarily a republican or representative form of government; otherwise the stronger faction could merely legalize its control and oppression of the weaker opponent.

This control has worked especially at the federal and state levels. The operation at the community level will be discussed in the chapter on the political institution. At this point it is necessary only to point out that in an earlier chapter it was seen that community boundaries are irregular and fluctuate from time to time. This is intolerable for the political unit, since jurisdiction of legal agencies must be relatively constant and well known by the public. Community areas usually do not in fact correspond to political areas.[2]

In the problem of factionalism it is thought necessary to have an established authority. In the previous chapter, power was defined as the ability to bring about behavior in others even against their own wishes. When this ability is made legitimate, either through legislation or through common acceptance that such a relationship is morally right, this power becomes authority. Since legal legitimation depends upon some well-defined and predictable political unit, it is obvious that authority on this basis must necessarily be lacking for the community structure as a whole. How, then, is difference in interest settled among factions in the community structure? Is there a complete lack of authority? How are decisions made and who makes them at the community level? If this is power without legitimation, is it rampant?

The Bases of Authority

Before moving to an attempt to answer these questions it is helpful to look at the bases upon which power may be exercised and made legitimate. Weber furnished much insight into power relations when he formulated a theory that there are three ways in which power may become authority.[3] The first of these he called charismatic leadership. In this kind of power the basis of authority rests upon attributing extrahuman characteristics to the leader as a person. While a charisma seldom occurs in its pure form, it can be seen in some degree at many levels of human relations. Farsightedness,

[2] See C.R. Wasson and Dwight Sanderson, "Relation of Community Areas to Town Government in the State of New York," Cornell University Agricultural Experiment Station Bulletin 555, Ithaca, New York, 1933; and Dwight Sanderson, "The Community as an Administrative Unit," Rural America, March, 1930.

[3] Hans H. Gerth and C. Wright Mills, editors, From Max Weber: Essays in Sociology, Oxford University Press, New York, 1946, Part II.

qualitatively superior intelligence, experience, and the like are often attributed to a leader as if he were somehow beyond the range of the average human and possessed of a qualitative superiority. A very important aspect of charismatic leadership in the community structure is that ability is generalized beyond the particular situation in which the leader has special talents.

The second basis upon which power is legitimized is that of tradition. In many societies, and in many communities of American society, the superior position in a power relationship is assigned on the basis of tradition. This would be the case particularly of sacred-type communities as described in the chapters on social change and the value system. Traditional power may be assigned to a family whose successive generations assume the role or it may be assigned to a position, such as that of the minister, the editor, or the banker. Again, pure cases of traditional power are seldom seen in American society, but a person who assumes a role with power deemed morally right may often get that power because it has always been assigned to his position.

The third basis is that of legal enactment or prescription of power. The government and bureaucracy are the best examples of this basis of authority. As previously mentioned, this type does not usually exist for the American community, but its existence within an element of the community may often be generalized to the remainder of the community structure. Efficiency, the act of deliberating and then rationally implementing policy, and the division of labor are concepts of "proper" power relations in the legalized or bureaucratic base. That these criteria are transferred to the community situation in many cases cannot be denied.

In a study of the questions listed above, Floyd Hunter described some of the ways in which the operation of power relations among groupings in a very large community operate. The following review of the book answers some of the questions raised above.*

Decision-Makers of an American Community

Viewing the community as a number of face-to-face groups made up of interacting individuals, it is not difficult to be hopeful about the fascinating and almost infinite possibilities of educating for intelligent and democratic decision-making; such groups have relatively little structure and their emotional energies can, with skill, be channeled into breaking down ineffective structure and creating a more fluid and democratic one. The structure of power relationships in such informal

* Harry L. Miller's review of Floyd Hunter, *Community Power Structure*, University of North Carolina Press, Chapel Hill, North Carolina, 1953. The review appeared in *Adult Education*, 4:167–75, 1954.

groups has been very little studied, for the possibly good reason that it does not seem to matter much.

If one switches spectacles, however, and views the community not as a series of groups but as a socially patterned whole, the problems of what decisions are important, how they get made, and how the process of getting them made can be influenced by wider segments of the community, become very different ones. Most of the data available on the process has until now been impressionistic or based on informed hunch. Floyd Hunter's study is important because it takes a scientifically methodical look at the power structure of an American city, at the forces and people which converge at the central point of decision-making, and provides us with precisely the data needed to plan intelligent action if adult education is to be successful in doing what it so often talks about—helping the community solve its own problems.

The account of Hunter's finding which follows is highly selective; what seemed important was to pass along the data most relevant to adult education for those who must read on the run, and bring the study to the attention of others who might find it significant enough to go to the original study for the full account.

The Decision-Makers of Regional City

Regional City is the name Hunter has given to a large city in the eastern United States, in the South but not deep South. It is a focal point in its region for transportation and finance, a center devoted "to finance, commerce and industry in about that order of importance." The enormously complex activity of such a city would be impossible without system, without a network of relationships which can be abstracted as a structure. Hunter has analyzed those relationships to determine in whose hands power lies, using the following definition: "Power is a word that will be used to describe the acts of men going about the business of moving other men to act in relation to themselves or in relation to organic or inorganic things."

Using what has become relatively standard sociological procedure (asking a large number of knowledgeable people in the community to name power figures and selecting those which occur above a certain order of frequency), the writer arrived at a group of forty persons who might justifiably be assigned to the top level of power in the community. Here are the kinds of people they are:

Eleven direct large commercial enterprises.
Seven direct banking and investment enterprises.
Six are professionals (five lawyers, one dentist).
Five have major industrial responsibility.
Four are government personnel.
Two are labor leaders.
Five are leisure personnel, i.e., they do not have offices or conduct businesses.

Clearly, the major economic interests of the community are overwhelmingly represented in this group, and Hunter concludes, after some discussion, that "the pattern of business dominance of civic affairs in Regional City is a fact." Not only are the social roles restricted to a rather narrow band of the spectrum of community roles, but if the community is zoned in terms of highly desirable, desirable, and undesirable residential sections, all but two of these top-flight leaders live in the first zone. This tends further to isolate the group from the mass of citizens not only because the most desirable section is somewhat removed, but because the routes taken to and from work condition people's images of their community.

In general, Hunter finds that the top leaders interact with one another on community projects, and select one another as leaders of them, with an important structural exception. The leadership group itself is divided into cliques which Regional City calls "crowds." Asked to explain the meaning of the term, one of the respondents said, "I simply mean that there are 'crowds' in Regional City—several of them—that pretty well make the big decisions. There is the crowd I belong to (the Homer Chemical crowd); then there is the First State Bank crowd—the Regional Gas Heat crowd—the Mercantile crowd—the Growers Bank crowd—and the like."

How Decisions Get Made

Representatives of each of these crowds are drawn into any discussion of a major community decision, so the division within the top slice of the power pyramid appears to reflect no basic conflicts in important community matters.

It is important here to draw a careful distinction between policy-making and the carrying out of policy after it has been set. One gets the picture from Hunter's data of a small group of policy-makers who devote considerable amounts of time to interaction among themselves as a group, but who carefully maintain their exclusive status in a number of ways. Endless luncheons make for solidarity as a group, but they are held in places never entered by what Hunter calls "understructure personnel." Meetings of top-flight leaders to discuss policy decisions are held in private clubs or homes; for example, one group known as the "Grandview Club crowd" gets together in the most exclusive athletic club in the city, a place where many important decisions are made.

Understructure personnel attend to the carrying out of policy, this group consisting of the kinds of people listed in the last three categories of the following structural layers:

1st rate: Industrial, commercial, financial owners and top executives
2nd rate: Operations officials, bank vice-presidents, public relations men, small business owners, top-ranking public officials, corporation attorneys
3rd rate: Civic organization personnel and board members, newspaper and radio commentators, petty public officials
4th rate: Professionals, personnel directors, small business managers, etc.

Policies, once made, are transmitted through two institutions, the committee and the luncheon club. The importance of the committee for power relations, Hunter believes, cannot be overstressed. There appears to be a stable base of understructure personnel who devote large proportions of their days [to] meetings. While most top personnel are rarely seen at meetings attended by understructure personnel, these meetings carry a large share of the work of carrying out major policy decisions. The luncheon clubs, on the other hand, operate as a unifying force, as a creator of morale through a mixture of "ham, hocum, and horseplay." They are important as a meeting place for selected members of the understructure and some of the upper structure, and, though big policy is not decided in this framework, the clubs are a part of the chain of command by which things get done in Regional City.

Let's look at the process of decision-making as it goes on against this background. Generally, the process includes the following steps:

1. A series of informal meetings, within the "crowd" or inter-"crowd."

2. A policy committee is formed when it appears that the time for action has arrived, for example, when money must be raised.

3. The policy committee is composed of selected top men, chosen by a system of mutual choices, and in the early stages of policy formation a few of these men will make the basic decisions.

4. As the project is made manageable, some top-ranking organizational and institutional personnel will then be selected by the original members to augment their group.

5. The civic associations and formalized institutions (churches, government, etc.) will next be drawn into some phases of planning.

6. The newspapers will finally carry stories of the proposal, the ministers will preach sermons, the association members will hear speeches regarding the plan.

There are some variations of this basic theme. In some cases the men who set policy may wish to remain anonymous in relation to the action phases of a particular program, in which case the policy group remains informally intact and second-rate or third-rate men are advertised as the sponsors. At other times projects that do not originate in the policy-determining group are allowed to proceed with the tentative blessings of a few of the top decision-makers "if their interests and dominant values are not threatened by the proposed activity."

A specific example of this process can be seen in the decision to make Regional City the headquarters for the International Trade Council. The idea occurred to "Homer," one of the top men, who called in his own "crowd" for discussion of the project. Tasks were assigned various members of this inner group; for instance, specific persons agreed to involve in the project groups of other "crowds" to raise money for the project; into this meeting the initiators of the plan went with a Board of Directors already selected, a constitution written, and an executive picked, "a third-string man, a fellow who will take advice." The public was then informed of the project through a number of publicity channels, as though it were a proposal up for consideration. Civic organizations were brought in on the idea at this stage to help get the Council established.

"Don't Rock the Boat"

Clearly, such power to control the decision-making processes as revealed in the patterns just described must be socially sanctioned in a systematic way, and must be maintained against attack. The policy-making group holds the structure intact by the use of three devices: control of state and local politics, coercion, and propaganda.

The control of political power permits the only available use of "legitimate force" and it is difficult to overstress the importance, therefore, of maintaining such control. In Regional City the top group holds key posts in one or another faction of the major political party, and is therefore in a position to influence the naming of gubernatorial candidates. According to Hunter: "All candidates are financed largely by the big business interests who control the elected governors. These facts of political life in the state are carefully kept from the rural electorate—as carefully kept as possible. The rural people are under the impression that they control state politics and in some measure they still do. At least an appeal must be made periodically to the rural electorate for their support of chosen candidates. The tried and true formula for a successful campaign that appeals to the rural voters has been to raise the 'race issue.' "

The study uncovers some evidence of a struggle between "crowds" for control of the political machinery, but although there may be heated rivalry, the accession to office of the candidate of a rival "crowd" produces no basic change in governmental policy. The awarding of lucrative contracts to one "crowd" or another seems to be the extent of the change.

Rivalry is forgotten in the face of a commonly perceived threat. For example, the attempt of the Progressive Party to get on the ballot in 1948 brought action by at least six of the top leaders for a special session of the state legislature, the only purpose of which was to make it impossible for the party to get on local ballots. The constitutionality of the law passed by the special session was questionable, but as one of the respondents put it, "By the time the courts get around to passing on the question of constitutionality the election will be a thing of the past and who will then care what the courts say? If they say the wrong thing we can always pass another law!"

The aggregate influence of these men on the political institutions of the state does not mean, as Hunter points out, that any one individual has authority over them. Only one of the group, as a matter of fact, "James Treat," seemed to be in a position to manipulate the Governor, the only one of whom people would say, "The Governor would come to Treat" if commanded. The others could exert influence, but would ordinarily go to see the Governor to do so, or use more indirect methods.

Nor can one make a simple interpretation of the fact of this influence. Says Hunter: "The men who hold the power structure intact through policy decision are firmly convinced that their decisions are correct more times than incorrect, and that their decisions are made with the whole community and nation, for that matter, in mind. That the system holds together and that the interests continue to dominate the political situation is the pragmatic test of the success of the policy-making group's ability to meet the minimum requirement for satisfying all interests in the community. The men who have been described have met such crucial 'political' tests for many years."

Informal methods of maintaining power involve a range of coercive or threatening pressures. Many of them operate as the control of expenditures by contributors; more subtly, the actions of top men attending meetings of lower echelons are watched acutely. Even grunts of disapproval are carefully recorded. Professionals are kept in line by the coercive threat of dismissal; for those in the understructure who are not insulated from violence, force may be used.

One interesting case of the use of coercion is given in detail, that of "Brown," a writer for a local trade journal, who wrote an editorial piece mildly opposing the lifting of price controls. "Cruther," one of the top forty, called and poured considerable abuse and threats on him. "Brown" had a talk with his employer, who urged caution, and the next issue carried a "toned-down" article on the same subject, though "Brown" refused to retreat to the extent of writing a retraction. From then on "Brown" was a "controversial figure," a dangerous thing to be in Regional City. He heard that "Cruthers is out to get you," and somehow his relations with his employer deteriorated steadily. "Brown" finally found another job.

The use of propaganda appears to be only a milder form of coercion. Once a decision is made with the pattern described, a 'principle of unanimity" swings into action, and pressures toward conformity are initiated in the press and radio. Sometimes, on decisions which are set only tentatively, discussion is permitted down to the association level; but on large issues which affect land policy, private enterprise, and other established interests, the general theme is "don't rock the boat." Boat rocking of this kind is generally avoided by choosing carefully the committee chairmen for "hot" subjects, e.g., housing, men who "have their feet on the ground," and who can skillfully maneuver a committee into paralysis. When issues are considered to be "dynamite," an aggressive committee can usually be handled by a labeling device, getting the word around that it is controversial, or worse, subversive.

Big and Little Policy

Do American communities really look like this? Is the decision-making structure as tight as it seems in this picture? As a matter of day-to-day living, of course, it is not. Hunter's evidence indicates that a policy decision does not fall within the structural grid we have been discussing unless the matter is important in itself, or unless it challenges some tenet of the established order. New policy must be consistent with the general scheme of the old.

In matters of big policy this established order involves the following assumptions: taxation favorable to corporations, anti-labor policy, restraint in the expansion of services such as education, public health, and welfare, and segregation of the Negro. All other matters are lesser policy. Big policy on national or international issues is set by a public pronouncement of one of the top men; if a lower echelon person speaks out of line, sanctions are applied. Once the line is set he may speak in favor of it, but he must be cautious with any hints of dissatisfaction. Should he have a serious objection, he may voice his opinion to someone near and above him in the informal hierarchy. An exception to this generalization was a court fight instituted by Negroes for equal school facilities. Hunter points out that here settled policy is being challenged by a group organized to the point where it must be heard because the older methods of intimidation no longer work.

Lesser policy involves specific programs devoted to community welfare, for example, funds for scholarships, medical supplies for clinics, etc. The value of many projects of this kind is clear enough, but Hunter introduces the concept of "diversionary activity" to describe many others, such as Patriot's Day: "It is not suggested that there is a conscious design on the part of the leaders to get men involved in 'popgun' activities when more potent approaches to community problems are indicated, but it remains that much activity in civic affairs in the community is devoted to relatively useless projects, and such undertakings are encouraged by the power leaders.

"When many of the associational leaders became interested in slum clearance a few years ago, there was a slight division between the top leaders as to the worth-whileness of an aggressive program of housing reform. The compromise arrived at by the leaders finally revolved around aiding a woman's group which had as its platform, 'paint-up and clean-up the undesirable neighborhoods.' This program had all the support of the press, and a great deal of organizing activity went into the explanation and promotion of the program. Paint and brooms were not the answer to Regional City's housing problems. Bulldozers were indicated . . . The ladies who were strong for the cleaning methods finally became discouraged. The slum dwellers showed little interest in cooperating, and the owners of the properties, when they could be located, showed the same lethargy. The publicity died out, and the ladies were off on another project which had to do with helping girls who got into the city stockade on moral charges."

Fear, Pessimism, and Silence

The top leaders, according to Hunter, are riddled with fear, fear of danger to the American way of life, fear that the power structure may become known, fear of reform, not unmixed with some guilt at holding the power they wield. The professionals are almost uniformly pessimistic. They are isolated from the effective power source, and also from the average citizen, yet most are dedicated to the social improvement of the underprivileged. Their professional principles often conflict with power group decisions, and must consequently be set aside in a drearily continuous frustration. Their files are crammed with studies and reports of experts about what could be done to relieve some of the tensions in the city, which never reach an action point.

From the top leaders, fear; from the professionals, pessimism; and from the citizens, silence. If these could be dispelled, Hunter believes, the organized structure of the community could operate more effectively. His thesis generally holds that power is necessary in modern community life and relations; the crucial question is, "How can policy be determined so that it takes into account the interests of the largest number of people?" While it is difficult to summarize his views in brief, and yet do them justice, what seemed to me to be the main line of argument is given below. Readers who are interested in the problem of community strategies are strongly urged to read in full Chapter 9, "The Organized Community and the Individual."

Associational groupings in the community appear to be the logical place to center hopes for increasing the power participation base. "It is here that all economic and political structures cross, and it is here that the policy-making machinery might be strengthened effectively to channel an individual's activities to aid in meeting the problems of community life that are involved in modern urban society." Unfortunately, the associations of the community, luncheon clubs, councils, fraternal organizations, generally have boards which are controlled by men who use influence to keep down public discussion, in the name of being practical, on all issues except those which have the stamp of approval of the top power structure. The professional staffs, as we have seen, are subject to coercion.

From the review by Miller of Hunter's book it is apparent that the formal leader is not entirely free to make decisions; but likewise, he is not entirely powerless either. The power discussed here is in part institutionalized or legitimized, not through legal authority but through the mores. It is true that some of the self-interests of the decision-makers are evident, and at this point the power relation is not authority. Conformity is produced by fear on the part of the secondary leaders of personal loss. However, when issues arise which threaten the basic mores, the actions of the decision-makers are perfectly consistent with those mores and would be deemed morally right by the populace if the nature of the power relation were recognized and understood by them.

It is perhaps important also to see that the same positions (or at a given time the same persons) make decisions for the community which are sometimes authority or institutionalized power, and at other times represent "naked power" or self-interest. This is an example of the generalization of power given to persons or positions in excess of the situations in which their talents and the value system define power for them as appropriate.

The situation of power and authority is not as simple as it often appears. Authority is limited by the informal power structure as in the case of a leader in a formal organization who may be effective or ineffective due to his ability or inability to elicit active cooperation from members and from other organizations interested in the same problem. It is much more severely limited by the subtle nature of the power structure itself.

Perhaps the most important consideration in the discussion of power and authority in the present context is the use which may be made of persons in important positions in community organization work. One approach to the organization of community resources around a problem is through the leaders of the community. This is most easily accomplished by the use of the more obvious formal leaders.[4] But the foregoing treatment, while pointing out the importance of such leaders, implies that the community organizer should be aware of possible patterns of more subtle power. Those patterns, if present and ignored by the organizer, may well defeat community development programs.

[4] Bryce Ryan, "Social and Ecological Patterns in the Farm Leadership of Four Iowa Townships," *Iowa AES Research Bulletin 306*, Ames, Iowa, 1942.

Another approach in gaining support for community action is through power as exhibited through the occupational structure. Such procedures are widely used already. Not only power but special talents and skills accompany special occupations. Thus, a banker may bring with him knowledge and skills relevant to the financial aspect of a community development program as well as his general influence in the community. Likewise, a lawyer may bring his informal power and his needed legal knowledge. While prestige is conceptually different from power, the two are correlated. The discussion on prestige presented in Chapter 9 may be used in drawing inferences about the power structure of communities as well as the principles of prestige as such.

LEADERSHIP

Most power relations do not involve basic mores and do not involve the kind of conflict of interest that must be resolved by some higher and more ultimate authority. Rather, relationships are more often found as problematic where a person or persons need, within the structure of a single organization in the community, to accept responsibility for seeing that a job is done. This is, as it actually operates, a type of power. Not coercion, but persuasion, is used. Sometimes this involves merely the distribution of duties to members, sometimes it involves mere concern for the forms rather than the content of organizational action, as in a discussion, and sometimes it involves a dictatorial role played by a person. There is perhaps more discussion of leadership in the literature about the community than about any other social unit.

Weber's bases of institutionalization of power referred to previously in the chapter are not adequate to explain the variation in types of leadership at this level of the power relation.[5] The problem is to have more concrete illustrations with regard to the difference such variations make in community work.

Within American communities there are essentially four types of leadership: [6]

[5] For theories of this order see Dwight Sanderson and Robert A. Polson, *Rural Community Organization*, John Wiley and Sons, New York, 1939, Chapter XII; Dwight Sanderson, *Leadership for Rural Life*, Association Press, New York, 1940; Alvin W. Gouldner, editor, *Studies in Leadership*, Harper and Brothers, New York, 1950; and Paul Pigors, *Leadership or Domination*, Houghton-Mifflin Company, Boston, 1935.
[6] These leadership types were identified by Wayland S. Hayes, *The Small Community Looks Ahead*, Harcourt, Brace, and Company, New York, 1947, pp. 74 *ff*. See also Coolie Verner, "Leaders and Leadership," *Extension Service Review*, 28:81–82, 1957.

(a) *Institutional leadership.* Persons holding office in a community, whether elected, appointed, or otherwise designated to carry out routine functions, are institutional leaders. It is the position that carries the leadership responsibility rather than the individual person who occupies the position. Thus, teachers, ministers, agricultural and home agents, or political officeholders are assumed to be leaders because of the position they occupy. The leadership function associated with the position will continue, even though the persons occupying the position may change. Such leadership is rarely progressive or democratic. The prime function of such leaders is to assist the group maintain its customs, purposes, and attitudes.

(b) *Situational leadership.* When the existing social structure becomes inadequate for one reason or another, drastic changes in the structure may be required. Because the institutional leaders are themselves a part of the inadequate social structure, they are incapable of providing the constructive guidance necessary to achieve changes in the structure. In such instances, leadership may arise from the community without reference to the existing leadership pattern. Such leaders become a product of the situation that requires leadership.

(c) *Dictatorial leadership.* Both institutional and situational leaders may develop into dictatorial leaders. This is the type of leadership which Pigors has identified as domination.[7] Dictatorial leadership is often found in those communities that are burdened by the paternalism of an old family, or by a political boss, a perpetual officeholder, or the manager of a dominant business. Dictatorial leaders exercise power as discussed earlier and may have virtually complete and paralyzing control over the life of the community, as has been pointed out in the review of Hunter's study presented above.

(d) *Creative leadership.* This is the ideal of democratic leadership. The essential ingredients are a genuine vision of the potentialities of human society and a desire to encourage and help others to develop their own abilities. A creative leader derives his greatest satisfaction from releasing power in others rather than in exercising power for his own personal aggrandizement. When the creative leader has helped his group achieve its goals they are unaware of the role of his leadership in their success and they do indeed say, "We have done it ourselves."

A community's acceptance or tolerance of one or another of these types of leadership depends upon the degree of maturity in the processes of democracy which that community represents. An immature community is

---

[7] Pigors, *op. cit.*

one which rejects the responsibility of self-determination and allows its leadership to make all decisions and dictate its behavior. A mature community is one which accepts the responsibilities of democracy and makes its decisions for itself. In such a community dictatorial leadership is not tolerated. American communities fall somewhere between these two extremes along a continuum of maturity.

The designation of a leader is accomplished in a number of different ways:

(a) *Appointive leader.* He may be appointed from above. The principal, the preacher, and the home agent are appointed leaders. In general, appointed leaders occupy institutional leadership positions and the individual person can be appointed or removed without seriously influencing the continuity of leadership. Such leaders have a difficult task of making followers out of the group they are working with. They must build an esprit de corps so the group will give willing service in a common cause that is not usually selected by it.

Appointive leaders are quite common in American society, but not easily recognized. When the home agent selects a woman for leadership she makes an appointed leader whose success is dependent upon the ability to create a cooperative group. This is the middle ground of leadership and, while it is not representative of the best democratic leadership, an appointed leader can operate by the principles of the democratic process. The range and latitude within which such a leader may operate is controlled by the higher authority that appointed him; however, he can develop real democracy within those limits.

(b) *Self-constituted leader.* Any individual with an intense will to be a leader, with some skill, and fortunate enough to be in the right place at the right time can make himself a leader. This is the type that is usually (and incorrectly) called a born leader. Such a person has an assertive ego and a strong, domineering personality.

Self-constituted leaders are primarily interested in their own development. They have a strong determination to achieve their personal goals regardless of the cost to the group, the organization, or the community. They operate in such a way that they make people subservient to them. This kind of leader is found in every form of activity—business, politics, local affairs, and clubs and organizations. Leaders of this type are successful for a time because people are misled by them; however, in our democracy they are eventually disowned.

(c) *Group-selected leader.* The third type is that leader which the group selects for itself. This is, of course, the most democratic means of achieving leadership. It has an advantage over all other forms in that the group is predisposed to follow a leader they have chosen for themselves.

Such a leader starts with reasonable agreement among those he is leading, but he must sustain and deepen the support and cooperative intent of his group. He will be most successful when he can help the group get what it wants with the least dissension and the greatest sense of unity and self-realization.

There is a precaution which must be observed, however, in the process of group selection. Too often, the choice of a leader becomes too mechanical. Roberts' Rules of Order and the majority rule can be misused by too rigid adherence to the majority concept. Many organizations split or fail because a large minority may break away when an unacceptable leader is chosen in this way. It is much wiser—particularly in smaller organizations —to select leaders on the basis of agreement rather than by vote, through what the Quakers call "the sense of the meeting."

Regardless of the types of leadership or the ways in which people become leaders, the actual nature of leadership is not clearly defined. In general there are three basic theories explaining the nature of leadership. In one instance, leadership is considered to be an accumulation of traits that an individual is born with; however, there is insufficient evidence to support this theory completely. Another theory insists that leadership is a function of the group, and a third theory states that it is a function of the situation in which leadership is required. Hendry and Ross in their synthesis of research on leadership conclude that "any truly adequate conception of leadership involves elements from all three conceptions." [8]

Leadership is in some ways only a shorthand expression for the leadership-membership relation. In this sense it is important to consider not only leadership but the nature of membership as well. Further, the relations between leader and member vary from situation to situation, and this means that the values, the existing structures, and the interests of the entire group come into play.

Formal Leadership

The type of leadership most like the authority relations previously described is referred to as formal leadership. In this situation the patterned relations among members of a group become so well recognized that mem-

---

[8] Murray G. Ross and Charles E. Hendry, *New Understandings of Leadership*, Association Press, New York, 1957, pp. 17 *ff*.

bership qualifications are defined, specific names given to various positions, and written codes of conduct for the group as a whole and for members within the group are prescribed.

Generally, research has shown formal leaders to come from higher status in the income, prestige, and occupational worlds.[9] By the very nature of the definition of the role, leadership is general rather than specific to a given situation. A leader with certain special talents and lacking in others can effectively lead the group in the areas of his or her weakness only through calling upon those who do have the necessary talents, that is, the delegation of authority and responsibility. This process allows temporary leadership to rest with a person who has the required abilities, but it is limited in time and also to the specific problem at hand.

It would appear, then, that in the case of formal leadership the leader is not a person who is selected to fit the particular situation because of his special talent, but rather someone who has generally high status. It would be difficult for a large formal organization to change leadership to fit each situation except through the process of committee work, that is, delegation of responsibility.

Therefore, in large formal organizations the leadership relation can be characterized as the placement of ultimate responsibility for the success of the organization upon the person or persons in the leadership positions. But this is done through allowing the leader to select persons to act as leaders for specific problems.

Informal Leaders

People cluster in terms of friendship and interest, and as a result of frequent and intimate contact learn from one another many attitudes, skills, and items of information. Since these informal groups persist over a period of time, the influence of one member on another becomes progressively greater. Often this influence is felt at times when the group is not present, a concept known as the reference group.[10] This means that the values of

[9] Harold Kaufman, "Participation in Organized Activities in Selected Kentucky Localities," *Kentucky AES Bulletin 528*, Lexington, Kentucky, 1949; Joseph A. Kahl, *The American Class Structure*, Rinehart, New York, 1957, p. 147; Donald G. Hay and Douglas Ensminger, "Leader-Follower Patterns in Selected Maine Towns," *RS*, 14:2:160–63, 1949; Bernard Barber, *Social Stratification*, Harcourt, Brace and Company, New York, 1957, pp. 183–85; Emory J. Brown, "Elements Associated with Activity and Inactivity in Rural Organizations," *Pennsylvania AES Bulletin 574*, 1954; and W.A. Anderson and Hans Plambeck, "The Social Participation of Farm Families," *Cornell University AES*, Department of Rural Sociology Mimeo., *Bulletin 8*, March, 1943.

[10] For consideration of this theory see Robert K. Merton and Alice S. Kitt, "Contributions to the Theory of Reference Group Behavior," in Robert K. Merton and Paul F.

the group are internalized by the individual and are used as criteria in making decisions even when other members of the group are not present.

Some members have more influence of this sort than do others. These are referred to as leaders, although they differ from other types in many ways. These leaders are more likely to be specific to the situation than are formal leaders. This results from the fact that talents are more easily observed in a group situation when group members' knowledge of one another is not limited to the "public personality." Since talents are better known, the particular talents the individual possesses are likely to be called upon for a particular situation, with the result that he is given a leadership role which is limited to some particular task.

There is evidence, however, that certain persons may be given a kind of general status which might be called leadership. A person of higher respect in the group may be called upon to lead more often, and he may be called upon in situations where the correspondence between problem and talent has not been established. Research has shown that members of a group are willing to select one of their number as a leader, and that in any given group, there is a large measure of agreement as to which member is the leader.

The characteristic required to be a general leader in a small informal group is the possession of those values which are similar to those of the group. Unlike the formal leader, who may take his position because of "outstanding" characteristics, the informal leader must be truly a group spokesman. He expresses the values and attitudes of the group members, and exerts his leadership not through changing the group but through defining the situation for it so members will know which of their values to draw upon. An example of this is the definition of a particular course of action as "socialism" rather than "progress" or vice versa. Thus, a course of action would be defined in negative rather than positive terms. While this example is obvious, the definition of the situation operates universally and in very subtle ways.

If the leader is at the core of existing group values, what about change? Behind nearly every informal leader is the farsighted person who may actually be liked only by the leader himself.[11] This person may see far ahead, and therefore not be like the rest of the group. It follows that his ideas may be put into operation only through leadership relations of which he himself is incapable. His imagination and critical aptitude is then im-

Lazarsfeld, *Continuities in Social Research, Studies in the Scope and Method of "The American Soldier,"* the Free Press, Glencoe, Illinois, 1950, pp. 40–106.

[11] Helen H. Jennings, *Leadership and Isolation: A Study of Personality in Interpersonal Relations,* Longmans, Green and Company, New York, 1950.

plemented by the leader through the slow process of changing group values and attitudes by means of persuasion. If the leader himself goes too far ahead of the group he no longer meets the criteria of group leadership.

The leader is not an "idea man." In a study of diffusion research, it was found that the first to adopt recommended farm practices were the innovators; the next, the early adopters; and the third, leaders, followed by the masses.[12] This distinction between innovators and leaders is an important one. In a discussion with professional experts working in various counties, one of the authors asked, "How can you identify leaders when you cannot know the groups in the counties very well?" An answer was that "at a county picnic, the leaders would congregate at the same table." This is an example of the confusion between innovators and leaders. The concept of the leader given here is quite the contrary—that is, the leaders will be found with their respective groups. Indeed, an innovator will not be followed by others because he is an innovator. The leader will be considered to be conservative by his group, the members of which believe that anything which will work for him will work for them.

Classification of leadership relations given in the earlier discussion describes the types with implications as to group success and group values.

Characteristics of Leaders

Two misconceptions exist in the common-sense theory of leadership which have a great effect upon the ability of organizations to elicit leadership in the community. One is that leadership ability is inborn, whereas there is much evidence to show that the characteristics for a leadership position are learned. In fact, leaders can be deliberately trained. Also, there is a common fallacy that a certain type of personality makes for good leadership. No such general list has been successfully derived from evidence, and probably will not be. The reason is that different characteristics are needed for different groups and for different situations.

It follows from the discussion immediately above and from the concept of leadership discussed in previous sections that a leader in one group may or may not be a successful leader in another. This is less correct of leaders in formal organization than of leaders in informal groups, where the transfer is almost impossible.

There are various roles in any group, formal or informal, which take on leadership characteristics. Sanderson lists five such roles:

[12] North Central Rural Sociology Committee, Subcommittee for the Study of the Diffusion of Farm Practices, "How Farm People Accept New Ideas," *Special Report 15*, Agricultural Extension Service, Iowa State College, Ames, Iowa, November, 1955.

The planner—the person who can look ahead and see the long-range effects of group action and who can point out immediate problems.

The executive—one who carries out the group policies.

The educator—one who can help the group see alternative solutions to its problem and helps in arriving at a concensus.

The spokesman—the role of representing the group in its relations with other groups.

The harmonizer—the role of identifying the areas of agreement in the group and bringing cohesion through this agreement.[13]

All these roles may be played either by individuals or groups of individuals, and the same individual may play several roles. It would be expected that the division of labor in these five roles would be greater in the large formal organization than in the small informal group.

Leader-Member Relations

There are several ways of classifying leader-member relations and a number of these have been implicit in the discussion so far. For example, one of the more frequent classifications bears upon democratic, authoritarian, and *laissez faire* leadership, and these are implicit in the discussion of types of leaders earlier in the chapter. Another method of classification is the formal and informal, as suggested in the discussion of types of groupings in which leadership is problematic. It is important in understanding these various relations, however, to note that there are formal aspects to an informal leadership relation—certain things, for instance, are prescribed and rigid—and there are informal aspects to formal leadership relations. Friendship, informal clique groupings within the organization, and recreation-type activities affect the nature and effectiveness of the formal leadership a great deal.

Similarly, no leadership is entirely authoritarian or democratic. There are limits beyond which the authoritarian leader cannot go, and these are set by the willingness of the membership to avoid the threat implicit in authoritarian leadership. On the other hand, there are times when the democratic process is too slow and an immediate decision must be made. In this case the democratic leader may act for the group without a group decision.

While none of the aspects of leadership are found in their pure form, it is of great help to consider the predominance of one over the other in a given situation. The reason is that, first, the type of leadership makes a great difference in the ability of the group to achieve its goals. The democratic

[13] Dwight Sanderson, *Leadership for Rural Life,* Association Press, New York, 1940.

process results in a slower take-off but continued progress toward its goal, while the authoritarian leadership makes a more dramatic beginning but soon levels off, falling behind the democratic group in achievement.[14] Secondly, the type of leadership is important because of the value placed on certain means themselves. For example, democratic leadership is valued in American society, not for its effectiveness, but for itself.

PRINCIPLES

1. *Conflicting interests result in a relationship among units of a community structure in which one person, group, institution, or the like is able to bring about behavior in another even against the wishes of other units.*

This relationship is referred to as power and it exists throughout the structure of the community as a dimension.

2. *Power relations become legitimate (deemed morally right) on the basis of superhuman characteristics attributed to the leader through tradition or through legality. Legitimate power is called authority.*

3. *Since the community does not correspond to any political unit, the legal basis of authority is not generally characteristic of community structure.*

This means that various combinations of the other two bases of authority as well as unlegitimized power characterize community structure.

4. *Leadership is a combination of factors of the person, the group, and the situation.*

No one of these alone is an adequate explanation of the phenomenon of leadership.

5. *The character of leadership in a community reflects the degree of cohesion of the community itself.*

Communities will vary from irresponsible to responsible and their leadership will vary accordingly from authoritarian to democratic.

SELECTED REFERENCES

Bendix, Reinhard, and Seymour Martin Lipset, *Class, Status, and Power,* the Free Press, Glencoe, Illinois, 1953.

[14] Kurt Lewin and Ronald Lippitt, "An Experimental Approach to the Study of Autocracy and Democarcy: A Preliminary Note," *Sociometry*, I:292–300, 1938.

Gerth, H.H., and C. Wright Mills, *From Max Weber: Essays in Sociology*, Oxford University Press, New York, 1946, Part II.

Gouldner, Alvin, *Studies in Leadership*, Harper and Brothers, New York, 1950.

Hunter, Floyd, *Community Power Structure*, University of North Carolina Press, Chapel Hill, 1953.

Hunter, Floyd, Ruth Connor Schaffer, and Cecil G. Sheps, *Community Organization: Action and Inaction*, University of North Carolina Press, Chapel Hill, 1956, Chapters 3 and 4.

Millis, Walter, *Individual Freedom and the Common Defense*, the Fund for The Republic, New York, 1957.

Nelson, Lowry, *Rural Sociology*, American Book Company, New York, 1955, Chapter 11.

Pigors, Paul, *Leadership or Domination*, the Riverside Press, Cambridge, 1935.

Sanders, Irwin T., *The Community*, The Ronald Press Company, New York, 1958, Chapters 6, 9, 12, and 20.

Sanderson, Dwight, *Leadership for Rural Life*, Association Press, New York, 1940.

Sanderson, Dwight, and Robert A. Polson, *Rural Community Organization*, John Wiley and Sons, New York, 1939, Chapter 12.

Whyte, William H., *The Organization Man*, Doubleday and Company, Inc., 1957.

CHAPTER 10

Age and Community Structure

There is perhaps no single factor more important than age in explaining why people act the way they do. While studies often do not show age differences, this may be explained by the fact that the age of respondents is usually limited in such studies. Children do not take the important role in the community's affairs which adults do, a point which is not so obvious when consideration is given to statements concerning age as a mere "background factor" or as merely "census-type" data. That broad age differences are crucial in understanding the social structure cannot be denied.[1]

AGE-RELATED PROBLEMS OF THE COMMUNITY

Most of the problems concerning the relationship between the community and its individual members may be classified according to an age base. In the family one of the important problems is the socialization of the child, by which is meant the assurance that as the child grows up, he will accept the predominant values and codes of conduct deemed right in the community. As the child matures, the problem of his relationship to the educational institution becomes important, both as to the quality of his response to learning knowledge and skills and as to his continuation in school after the legal age of compulsory attendance. The matter of continuation is intricately bound up with the way he relates himself to the occupational structure of the community.

As an individual enters the labor force, the quality of his work, his satisfaction with his work, and his social mobility up and down the occupational ladder become important to the community. His relationships to community institutions and services undergo changes as age changes. At different times in life individuals stand in differing relationships with the school, church, government, and so on, and have need for differing kinds of services. This

[1] Ralph Linton, *The Cultural Background of Personality*, D. Appleton-Century Company, New York, 1945.

193

gives rise to problems associated with designing institutional programs and services to meet the needs of broader age ranges in the population. Thus, the addition of evening adult programs to the public school or a children's section to public libraries is indicated, although such expansion is by no means accepted by all institutions or their leadership.

The increasing numbers of older retired people in the population brings additional problems to the community, particularly the need to provide non-work related activities of interest to those relieved of the necessity of work; supplemental work for those with insufficient retirement income; and the continued use of the talents, skills, and experiences of old people for the general welfare of the community. It is apparent, then, that the relationship of the individual to his community changes drastically with age.[2] In the present chapter, some of these problems are discussed within the context of societal change.

Interpretations of Age

Age is usually measured precisely in terms of the number of years a person has lived. Measured this way, it relates empirically to many of the variables in human behavior and values. The ways in which age may be interpreted as affecting human behavior differs from various problems encountered and the approaches taken to solve them.

Age may be interpreted as an index of *maturation*, particularly when applied to youth. Maturation is the physiological development of an individual which is a necessary prerequisite to certain types of behavior. Athletic prowess or sexual competence, for example, cannot be expected until an individual achieves a certain stage of physical maturity. Likewise, intelligent conversation or ambition for cultural goals are dependent upon reaching a point of intellectual maturity. The exact chronological age at which maturity is reached will vary, of course, from individual to individual. Interpreted this way, age is a necessary condition to certain types of relationship between the individual and the community, and is most important during the first two decades of life.

A second interpretation that is placed upon age in many studies is that of social experience. The longer a person has lived, the greater his experience with the goals and the means to achieve those goals that are acceptable to the community. Looked at in this way, the amount of social experience

[2] See, for example, Talcott Parsons, "Age and Sex in the Social Structure of the United States," *ASR*, 7:604–16, 1942.

a person has had is related to human behavior from early youth throughout life. One example of this type of relationship is the increased conservatism in people as they proceed from adolescence to an older age.

A third way in which age is interpreted in many studies is in role definition. This is particularly important in societies where certain well-defined roles are assigned on the basis of age, such as the delegation of authority to the elders. The absence of precise role definition on an age basis is found in the ambiguity of the adolescent role in the American community. The adolescent is too young to be given the responsibilities of an adult, yet too old to be treated as a child. Many problems of adolescent adjustment are attributed to this fact.

A fourth interpretation of age that relates to the individual's integration into the community is in the concept of senility. This refers to the decreasing mental alertness on the part of the very old, and is assumed to have a physiological basis.

An age group also may be interpreted as a predictive factor over a period of time, that is, today's youth are tomorrow's adult citizens. The loyalties and ambitions of youth, therefore, are important not only as today's problems, but also as a groundwork for predicting the future ability of communities to solve their problems.

Age also reflects the past. One example of this is the negative relationship between age and educational attainment. Older age groups have consistently lower levels of educational attainment than younger age groups, and this is entirely a function of the gradual increase in school attendance historically. A less quantitative example, but no less important, is found in the values and behavior patterns which have resulted in part from the fact that a person was reared during a depression or a war.

SOCIALIZATION OF THE CHILD

The factors which influence the internalization of community values and traditions are discussed in the chapter on the family.[3] It is important here,

[3] On the process of socialization with special reference to primitive societies, see Margaret Mead, "Research on Primitive Children," in Leonard Carmichael, editor, *Manual of Child Psychology*, John Wiley and Sons, New York, 1946, pp. 667–706; also her *Growing Up in New Guinea*, William Morrow and Company, New York, 1930, and *Coming of Age in Samoa*, William Morrow and Company, New York, 1928. On socialization in American society, see Allison Davis, "American Status Systems and the Socialization of the Child," Chapter 33 in Clyde Kluckhohn and Henry A. Murray, editors, *Personality in Nature, Society, and Culture*, Alfred A. Knopf, New York, 1950.

however, to point out that in the relationship between the child and the community there is some reason to believe that the amount of adjustment in children is decreasing, which would indicate that the family is failing to develop members of the community who will conform to its codes of conduct. Over the long range, this creates an extremely important problem in community development, since many of the problems with which communities are concerned center around childhood and adolescence. Moreover, since the children of today are the adults of tomorrow, a community's future ability to solve problems will depend upon the values and loyalties developed by the families of today.

Empirical evidence on adjustment is contradictory and imprecise. Most authorities on the family believe that it has lost all its functions except that of affection, but on the other hand, they also claim that certain adjustments of the child to the family have decreased, particularly those relating to the primary group aspect of the family. If this is so, it would be expected that the later adjustment of the child to the community would likewise be seriously affected. In a study in a rural community in Minnesota, the attitudes of children in the same community were compared in 1939 and 1952 to see if any changes had occurred. These attitudes were measured and classified according to total adjustment to the family and to six different types of adjustment within the family, including agreement between parents and children on ideals, a sense of obligation to the family, and the expectations that parents have from their children. The results indicated no significant change in adjustment in that community over the thirteen-year period. Of course, this study alone cannot be assumed to prove that the contention of poorer adjustment is false. However, the authors discussed the findings in the light of other evidence available and found that there is no evidence in this study to support the hypothesis that there were changes in family adjustment or in their values and attitudes toward specific family relations, except that the girls in the 1952 sample had less of a sense of obligation to the family than those in the 1939 sample:

Without presuming to generalize beyond the universe of the study, the authors are led to speculate briefly on the possible explanation of the results. Among other factors of importance previously mentioned, the high rates of divorce and separation during this period led many observers to regard the American family as notably unstable, especially in an urban environment. The first suggestion is that the family is achieving a successful adaptation to what are often called urban influences; that is, whatever changes may take place in other family functions, the basic confidence and loyalties of members to each other are not measurably affected. The second suggested explanation is that the age group included in this sample is not influenced in attitudes by changes in the social "climate"; their lives are sheltered from the changes in the economic and social order—changes which may be more immediately reflected in modified attitudes of adults.

Whether or not the findings of this study are established in subsequent research, it is apparent that the alarms sounded from press, lecture and pulpit about the problems of the family have little or no effect in discouraging youth from entering matrimony. More of them are marrying than ever before and doing so at younger ages, apparently undeterred by much discussed "uncertainties" of family life.[4]

While the data of the study itself as well as the other evidence cited by the authors are observed during late adolescence, the point of interest is in the early years of socialization. It is during these years that the groundwork is laid for later adjustment. If the researchers are correct, this problem is not a serious one.

PROBLEMS OF LATE ADOLESCENCE

The problem most important during the period of late adolescence is the way in which a person relates himself to the three institutions of the family, the school, and the economic structure. These come as problems of family adjustment, school drop-out, and occupational choice. The problem of school drop-out is considered in the chapter on the educational institution, and the problem of family adjustment may be seen in the previous section and in the chapter on the family as a consequence of earlier socialization.

The literature abounds in studies of occupational choice.[5] From the point of view of the community, the reason for all this attention is that many persons irrevocably commit themselves to careers which mean loss of special talent to the community, either through school drop-out or through the individual's investment of time in school and college courses which lead him away from more appropriate occupations. By appropriate occupations are meant here (1) a matching of the occupational role with personal ability so that quality work results, (2) a matching of the occupational role with personal interest so that job satisfaction results, and, given the first two conditions, (3) a sufficient number of applicants in occupations which are functionally necessary in the community and for which there is a need for a greater number of workers, such as in medicine, nursing, teaching,

---

[4] C.E. Ramsey and Lowry Nelson, "Change in Values and Attitudes Toward the Family," ASR, 21:605–9, 1956.

[5] See, for example, Eli Ginzberg et al., Occupational Choice: An Approach to a General Theory, Columbia University Press, 1951, for excellent review of the literature; and H.M. Bell, Youth Tell Their Story, American Youth Commission, Washington, D.C., 1938.

social work, and, on a societal rather than community basis, scientists and engineers.

A higher proportion of persons in American society are white collar workers, professional and clerical, than ever before, which has brought additional importance to this problem. In spite of this, the increased demand for workers has exceeded the increase in the number of persons entering these fields. Earlier research on the problem of occupational choice found that a higher proportion of youth preferred white collar jobs than were available. This was sometimes referred to as the "hitch your wagon to a star" philosophy. The criterion of available jobs was the proportion of the labor force in these occupations. The fallacy in this criterion was that using the proportion of persons so employed to measure availability of jobs did not allow for societal change such as the tremendously increased demand for personnel to fill such occupations.

The complicated problem of increased demand for health personnel is discussed in another chapter. The demand for school teachers and similar community professional personnel is comparable. The rural community suffers a shortage in these occupations more than do urban communities.

A study conducted at Washington State College, where much of the work on occupational choice has been done, demonstrates many of the factors which influence the decisions made by youths concerning their occupational choices. This study was based on a random sample of 35 of Washington's 265 high schools, where questionnaires were completed by nearly 2,000 high school seniors. The material follows.*

The senior year in high school marks an important transition for most teenagers, farm and non-farm alike. Decisions made then to enter the labor force immediately after graduation or to obtain further education may have far-reaching consequences for the entire work life of the individual. It is not easy for a young man or woman to make a rational occupational choice. As this study demonstrates, many high school seniors are somewhat confused with respect to their future plans.

Family Background

Because much of the early social training of children is received in their homes, the nature of relationships within the family should have considerable influence on the occupational decision-making of individuals. Family relationships are materially influenced by family values and standards. These, in turn, may be indicated or reflected to some extent by such factors as education of parents, income level, occupational status of the male parent, rural versus urban residence, and the pattern of family management used by the parents.

* W.L. Slocum, "Occupational and Educational Plans of High School Seniors from Farm and Non-farm Homes," *Washington AES Bulletin 564*, 1956.

Education of Parents

One indication of the importance of family values as an influential factor in the plans of teenagers is found in the striking relationship between the educational level of the parents and plans for further education. Nearly seven out of ten of those whose fathers were college graduates were planning to attend college the following fall, compared with less than three out of ten of those whose parents had only an eighth grade education or less. At the other end of the scale, it seems the lower the educational level of the father, the more likely it was that the individual would be planning to enter the labor force immediately or to be uncertain about plans for next year. The same relationship held true for educational level of mothers.

Income

Seniors were asked to report the 1954 income of their parental families. Seventy-nine per cent of the boys and 59 per cent of the girls did so. In an effort to check the reliability of the data, these boys and girls were requested to indicate how certain they were of the information provided. Considering only those who said that they were positive or reasonably sure that they had provided reliable information, it appears that those who made rather definite plans for enrollment in college immediately after high school tend to come from families having somewhat higher incomes than do others. It was somewhat surprising to find that girls who planned immediate marriage and who provided information about income tended to come from higher income families than did others. However, this may have been due to the low rate of response in this category.

Occupational Level of Father

When the occupations of the fathers of the seniors are classified into white collar, agricultural, and blue collar categories, the differences in plans for the year following graduation are very striking. Those whose fathers were employed in white collar occupations were much more likely to be planning to enter college. Those from blue collar families were more likely to be planning on immediate entrance into the labor force or to be uncertain about their plans for next year. Those whose fathers were employed in agriculture occupied an intermediate position but were somewhat closer to the blue collar than to the white collar category.

Pattern of Family Authority

The pattern of family management utilized by parents indicates the pattern of intra-family relationships generally. A family utilizing what might be termed a democratic plan of management would emphasize permissive relationships rather than the "ordering and forbidding" technique. It might be expected that such families would stress the initiative of the child in solving problems involved in his occupational and educational planning.

Classification of seniors according to their plans for 1954–55 and their own perceptions of family authority types indicates: (a) that most students considered their families to be democratic and (b) that a considerably higher percentage of those from homes classified as democratic were planning on college attendance the following year than was the case among those from homes classified as intermediate. Also, the difference between democratic and undemocratic was very pronounced. Conversely, a higher percentage of those from undemocratic and intermediate homes were planning on working or were uncertain about their plans.

Family Composition

It has been assumed by many that an individual reared in a normal home encounters fewer complications in personal and social adjustment than one reared in a broken home, particularly a home separated by divorce or desertion. A recent study by Landis indicates, however, that in many respects children from broken homes are likely to be just as well adjusted as those from normal homes.

The importance of studying the impact of broken homes is emphasized by the fact that 25 per cent of the seniors were not living in normal homes with both biological parents. Farm homes (82 per cent) were more likely to be normal than non-farm homes (73 per cent).

When the classification is made according to post-high school plans, those who lived in a normal home with both father and mother were most likely to be planning to go to college immediately. They were followed by those who lived with one of their biological parents. Those who lived with neither parent were least likely to be planning to go to college immediately. Seniors in the latter category were also somewhat more likely to be uncertain of their plans.

School Factors

Next to the family, the school probably has the greatest influence on the development of education and occupational attitudes and values by adolescents. Hence, it may be expected that various aspects of individuals' school experiences would have a considerable bearing on plans for the future. Those who considered that they had done well scholastically were more likely than others to be planning to attend college.

Size of School

Size of school, as reflected in the number of seniors in the class of 1954, apparently was an important influence on plans for next year. Although there were exceptions in particular schools, there was a definite tendency for those in the larger schools to be more likely to plan on immediate college attendance. Conversely, those from the smaller schools were more likely to plan on immediate entry into the labor force. Since the larger schools are found in metropolitan centers, this may be a reflection of urban attitudes concerning the value of higher education.

Satisfaction with School

Satisfaction with school also had some influence on plans of seniors for the immediate future. Satisfaction with school is closely related to scholastic achievement in many cases. Students who liked school were more likely to be planning to go to school the following year. Those disliking school were much more likely to be planning to seek immediate employment, to enter the armed forces, or to be uncertain about their plans for the following year.

Participation in Extracurricular Activities

Almost all students had participated in one or more extracurricular activity. The more active the individual, the higher the probability that immediate college entry was contemplated. The less active the individual, the higher the probability that immediate entry into the labor force was contemplated. This was especially pronounced among farm youth.

The type of activity did not seem to have had very much influence on plans for the following year, except that seniors from farms who had participated in 4-H and/or FFA were less likely than other farm seniors to be planning on immediate college attendance.

Attitudes Toward Work

The responses of the high school seniors to a series of questions indicate that most of them had wholesome attitudes toward work. In response to the question, "Do you think of work as a pleasant activity?" 71 per cent responded in the affirmative. In answer to a further question, perhaps even more penetrating with respect to basic attitudes toward work, "If you were independently wealthy and didn't have to work, would you work anyway?" 57 per cent answered "yes," 10 per cent answered "no," and 33 per cent answered that they were undecided.

The distribution of answers to "What do you want most from your life work?" shows that 28 per cent indicated that the most important goal desired from a job was security. A somewhat larger number (31 per cent) indicated that they wanted work that continues to be interesting. Fourteen per cent indicated that they would like to have a chance to be of service to humanity. Only 10 per cent indicated that they were motivated principally by the money that might be obtained through work. The latter porportion may surprise those who think of American society as being one in which the primary motivation of most individuals is the accumulation of wealth.

Occupational advancement is of considerable importance in contemporary America. In fact, even the very young are aware of the desirability of "getting ahead." The traditional view is that promotion on the job is gained by hard work. In order to ascertain the views of young people on this important issue they were asked, "What is the best way to get ahead on the job?" The responses show a generally high degree of conformity with the traditional definition of the situation: slightly more than half indicated that the best way to get ahead was by working hard, 27 per cent indicated "by learning many jobs of the business so that you become more valuable to it," and 18 per cent checked additional training.

YOUNG ADULTHOOD AND MIDDLE AGE

The young adult is primarily concerned with his vocational and family objectives and his involvement in community affairs is generally limited to activities in these areas. His participation increases, however, during his thirties when his relationship to the community becomes more extensive. His relationship to the labor force and voluntary organizations in the community is treated intensively in the chapters on social stratification and communications and the various discussions on leadership, participation, and change.

In the middle years of life an adult's motivation changes from the concentration on vocational and family objectives that characterized the earlier years to an intensified concern for community welfare and his own personal development. As a result, his interest in community activities and participation in local organizations increases. By middle age an adult generally accepts his achievement occupationally as final and his family has usually left the home. In this period his interest in status and position decreases. As a result of this, not only does this participation increase but the nature and range of his interests are modified so that his organizational affiliations are different from those that characterized his earlier years.

THE AGED

The way in which the aged relate themselves to the community is of crucial importance, since they have more experience, knowledge, and skills than younger persons. Nevertheless, the loss of this talent may be increasing as retirement increases. This problem is described in the following excerpt * from the point of view of societal change, in a foreword written by N.L.

---

* N.L. Whetten in a foreword to "Old Age and Retirement in Rural Connecticut" by Walter C. McKain, Jr., and Elmer D. Baldwin, Storrs AES Bulletin 278, 1951.

Whetten of Connecticut, where much of the research on the aged has been conducted by Whetten, Walter C. McKain, and others.

Among the many important changes taking place in the United States in recent years, perhaps none has more far-reaching implications than the gradual aging of our population. There is now a much greater proportion of old people than formerly; and demographers tell us that we can expect the proportion in the older age groups to increase in the future.

This aging of the population is due to a number of factors, including a reduction in infant mortality, better control of communicable diseases, generally improved medical care, and higher standards and levels of living. All of these circumstances have enabled a greater proportion of children to reach adulthood and even to attain a ripe old age. This is especially emphasized by data regarding changes in life expectancy. In 1900, for example, the average person at birth in the United States could expect to live only forty-nine years. The person born in 1950 has a life expectancy of approximately sixty-eight years.

The growing proportion of elderly people in our society is accompanied by a number of developments which require increasing attention. The problem of retirement becomes more important especially in view of our shift from a predominantly agricultural to a highly industrialized civilization. The family has gradually cast off much of the responsibility of caring for dependent relatives and has tended to shift this burden to public and private agencies. Industry frequently discards the older worker; and the problem of financial independence during the declining years looms large. Diseases of older people become more conspicuous and cry for greater attention. The problems of recreation, of leisure-time activities, and of avocations that will absorb the energies of both body and mind during the later years are considerations that need to be planned long before the individual expects to retire.

Problems of Retirement

The two-way problem of the person's adjustment to the community, and the community's need for his experience and knowledge is one of the more crucial problems both in participation and in leadership for community development. This problem results from an increased value placed on rewarding the older persons by giving them less responsibility and more leisure during a long retirement.[6] At the same time, the community suffers

[6] A voluminous literature on aging and its social, economic, and medical problems has appeared in recent years and much research is being sponsored which it is hoped will lead to some solutions. Examples of many excellent studies are Robert J. Havighurst and Ruth Albrecht, *Older People*, Longmans, Green and Company, New York, 1953, and John J. Corson and John W. McConnell, *Economic Needs of Older People*, the Twentieth Century Fund, New York, 1956. For a general survey of aging problems with an excellent bibliography, see Bernard Kutner, David Fanshel, Alice M. Togo, and Thomas S. Langner, *Five Hundred Over Sixty*, Russell Sage Foundation, New York, 1956.

the loss of talent and leadership when the older person retires. In the community, power is held mainly by older persons, and this has two implications for the point being made here. First, even though a person retires, he may well retain part of the power that he held, although this will not be as closely associated with the occupational structure of the community. Second, insofar as the power structure needs to be retained to be consistent with values, the loss of power which results from retirement is a loss that must be filled by some deliberate action on the part of the community. The problem then becomes that of determining how the older person adjusts to the community in retirement and possibly after he moves from the community of his work to one for retirement.

This relationship between the older person and the community was intensively studied in New York by Philip Taietz, Gordon F. Streib, and Milton L. Barron. They give some detail as to the way in which this integration occurs.*

Background and Significance of Rural Retirement

Studies of the economic, psychological, and social problems of aging in the United States have been concerned largely with the urban industrial population. There have been relatively few studies of the aged in rural areas.

The research emphasis on the urban segment of the aging stems from two causes. First, an explanation is to be found in population trends. Since 1930, persons over sixty-five years of age who live in urban communities have exceeded numerically those in rural areas. By 1950, approximately two-thirds of all persons sixty-five years of age and over in the entire country were living in urban communities.

A second reason for the greater attention given to urban than to rural aged is to be found in the assumption that problems of aging are an urban phenomenon and that the social and economic conditions of rural life are favorable to the status of the aged.

A closer examination of these reasons raises some doubt as to their validity. Despite the shift from rural to urban communities in the distribution of the total population and of the population sixty-five years of age and over during the first half of this century, it is nevertheless true that the absolute numbers of the rural aged have approximately doubled in the past fifty years. In 1900 there were about two million persons over sixty-five years of age. By 1950, this figure had increased to almost four and one-half million.

It is also true that in the past self-sufficient agriculture and the large family with its deeply ingrained tradition of familial responsibility guaranteed the basic

* Philip Taietz, Gordon F. Streib, and Milton L. Barron, "Adjustment to Retirement in Rural New York State," *Cornell AES Bulletin 319, 1956.*

necessities of life and emotional security for the aging farmer and his wife. But social and economic changes have brought about emotional and economic insecurity. Family ties have weakened. Agriculture has become commercialized and mechanized. Studies have shown that farmers themselves feel that farming is no more secure than other occupations in terms of preparing for retirement.

There are many strong hints that aging in rural areas is not as idyllic as we have been led to believe. For example, Warren's survey in Almond, a rural township in upstate New York, indicates that the rural aged in that community may have greater "primary group" resources than the aged in urban communities, but they have fewer organized recreational facilities, fewer commercial facilities, fewer public and private agencies, less transportation, and less opportunity to participate in retirement plans.

Meaning of Retirement

To most people in this country, retirement means "administrative" retirement, a form that developed during the era of rapid industrialization early in this century and received an added impetus in 1935 with the passage of the Social Security Act. When an employed individual reaches a given age or has worked a specified number of years, or both, he is required to terminate his employed status. Retirement in this sense is an aspect of the personnel policy of an organization and usually includes the provision of reduced payments to the retirant in the form of a pension. Without this financial provision, retirement would hardly differ from being discharged or "laid off." Although retirement in the United States is not completely institutionalized from a normative standpoint, it can safely be postulated that the status of the retired person is higher than that of the unemployed person of the same age who still considers himself to be part of the "labor force."

The form of retirement experienced by those who are self-employed is quite different from administrative retirement, which is compulsory and applies largely to employees. When the self-employed retire, it is usually a voluntary decision, for by definition, the self-employed determine their own work status. The decision to retire is usually personal, although often it is conditioned by such factors as health, sufficiency of financial resources, family attitudes, and the feasibility of disposing of the business or farm.

Not all the respondents in this study of the rural aged were retirants. Therefore, the term "active" is used to designate those who, at the time of the survey, continued to play occupational roles in their work, either as employees or as self-employed persons. The term "retired," on the other hand, refers to those persons whose connections with their occupational roles have been severed as a result of the company's personnel policy; or, if respondents were previously self-employed, they have drastically reduced participation in their occupations or have withdrawn from them, so that by self-definition, as well as by the definition of others, they are retired.

It must be emphasized that as the terms "active" and "retired" are used in the subsequent analysis, they refer primarily to gainful occupational employment, not to functions such as formal organizational participation, informal friendship, clique participation, and hobbies. It should not be assumed that respondents referred to as retired are completely inactive, or that those in the active category are necessarily active in either formal or informal associations, or in hobbies and avocations.

One of the primary purposes of the rural study was to compare the farmers' problems of adjustment in retirement with those of the rural aged in other occupations. But the widely divergent economic statuses and social positions of farmers call for considerations of a more precise subgroup in the farm population. In this report attention is focused upon owner-operators, since all but a few of the farmers in the study group were in that category. Elsewhere the point has been made that the farm owner-operator is financially in a more favorable position to retire than is the farm tenant or laborer, but because of the owner-operator's emotional tie to the land, he is psychologically less prepared to do so. In many respects the situations of the farm laborer and tenant are similar to those of industrial workers.

Adequacy of Income

One method of assessing the adequacy of an individual's or family's income is to measure it in terms of some criterion established by the Bureau of Labor Statistics or by some other professional agency. Another method, and no less useful because it is subjective, is to question the individual himself. Indeed, a useful measure of the adequacy of income is the individual's own satisfaction with it.

The respondents were asked: "Is your present income enough to meet your living expenses?" A higher proportion of those active than of those retired replied in the affirmative. This is to be expected, for a decline in income usually accompanies retirement. In this survey, 84 per cent of the respondents stated that their current income was less than it was when they were gainfully employed. Similarly, more of both the active and the retired farmers than of the active and retired non-farmers considered their present incomes adequate. Almost nine out of ten active farm owner-operators considered their incomes adequate, whereas active non-farmers and retired farm owner-operators were virtually tied for second place in self-evaluation of income adequacy. Lowest of all in evaluating their incomes were retired non-farmers, for little more than half of them thought their present incomes were enough to meet their living expenses.

It is clear that one of the blunt realities of life confronting many retired persons —whether rural or urban—is the necessity of adjusting to a reduced income. An important question which follows logically is, "What are the specific ways in which people reduce their living expenses in order to live on their limited income?" Although 41 per cent reported no change, 54 per cent claimed they were compelled to curtail expenses. Almost 11 per cent were doing part-time work and 3 per cent were living with relatives as a means of adjusting to a reduced income. It is significant that reductions are made in the three basic necessities: food, clothing, and shelter. Clothing economies were made by 28 per cent, food and recreation cutbacks were undertaken by 26 per cent, and 18 per cent turned to more modest housing.

Work Span of the Rural Aged

Farmers continue to be occupationally active long after rural non-farmers. In fact, almost twice as many farm owner-operators as non-farmers among the respondents waited beyond the middle of their seventh decade of life to retire. This is a reflection of the significant difference between farming and non-agricultural occupations discussed in the introductory section. Theoretically, farm owner-operators can persist in their work almost as long as they wish, subject only to self-defined restrictions and those that may be imposed upon them by their families. Many of the other aged, on the other hand, are subject to administrative retirement.

Sixty-two per cent of the non-farmer respondents no longer working retired voluntarily, 21 per cent of them were compelled to retire because of employers' policies, and 17 per cent were "laid off" or stopped work for unknown reasons. On the other hand, all the farm owner-operators who were no longer working had retired voluntarily, not being subject to administrative retirement. The proportions of those who had retired because of poor health and difficulty in doing their work were quite similar in both occupational groups.

Another characteristic in the pattern of occupational withdrawal of farmers is that they can reduce their work load gradually. More than twice as great a proportion of the retired farmers as of non-farmers experienced gradual retirement. Almost twice the proportion of the former as of the latter worked as long as they could. Furthermore, non-farmers are much more likely to mention the need for money as a reason for continuing to work. Other motives for continuing to work are the desire to keep busy and the intrinsic enjoyment of work. In this study no differences were found between the retired farm operators and the retired non-farmers in this respect.

If it is true that a higher proportion of retired farm operators than retired non-farmers worked to an advanced age and as long as they could, one would anticipate that the work expectations of active farm operators and non-farmers would conform to the same pattern. The active respondents were asked: "We would like to know what your prospects are for the next five years regarding your work. Do you expect to continue in your present work, stop work, or do something else?" Almost nine out of every ten active farm operators expected to continue work, in contrast to slightly more than six out of ten active non-farmers. More than three times the proportion of non-farmers as of farm operators expected to retire (33 per cent, as compared with 10 per cent).

Significant differences appear in the reasons given by active farm operators and active non-farmers for their work prospects. The reason most often given by the former for expecting to continue working is enjoyment of work; the need for money is the most frequently named reason for the latter.

The outstanding reason given by farm operators for not expecting to continue working is the difficulty of their work. Non-farmers, on the other hand, refer to "wanting more leisure time" more than any other reason. Although the number of cases is limited in the analysis, it is interesting to find that a larger proportion of non-farmers than of farmers reported that the desire for more leisure time was a reason for stopping work. This points out again that farming is more of a total way of life than is true of non-farmers.

Social Participation in Leisure-time Activities

One of the problems of readjustment that many older people are said to face is the increasing availability of unscheduled time. This can be of crucial importance to those individuals whose lives heretofore revolved mostly about their work and for whom inactivity may have a serious disintegrating impact on personality.

What are the noneconomic activities of older people in rural areas, and which of these are most significant and satisfactory to them? Has there been any change in activities and their meaning for the individual in the course of time?

Each respondent was asked to state whether he engaged in any of the twelve leisure-time activities. The activities were classified as solitary (i.e., typically engaged in by a person alone); spectator (i.e., involving merely passive attendance); interpersonal (i.e., involving interaction with another person or persons); hobbies; and other activities.

Of the 248 respondents who indicated what their activities were, 206 reported that they talked with friends more frequently than anything else. Listening to the radio ranked second, followed in order by working in the garden, reading, going to town to shop, taking rides in the country, watching television, playing cards, hunting and fishing, taking walks alone, talking with friends on the telephone, and lastly, attendance at movies. The older persons in this study, like those reported in other investigations, differ widely in their activity patterns. The range of activities reported by individual respondents was from none to all twelve activities.

Another area for analysis is whether participation in activities is associated with background characteristics such as the amount of education, place of residence, and occupational status, and also social-psychological factors such as whether one plans or does not plan for retirement. The first step in testing hypotheses in this area is to differentiate those who participate in few or many activities. Respondents were classified into three categories: low if they reported none to three kinds of activities (65 persons); medium for four to six activities (128 persons); high for seven or more activities (55 persons). The following correlations were thereby uncovered:

(1) There is a significant relationship between extensiveness of activity and amount of formal education. One of the consequences of education is the broadening of the individual's horizon and a stimulating of his interests and participation in a variety of activities. Not only are educated people more aware of the opportunities about them, but they are more frequently in a position to take advantage of those opportunities. Thus, it is expected that they will engage in a greater diversity of leisure-time and recreational activities than those with less education. Some of the activities in the list, such as reading, assume a certain

educational level and it is obvious that people with little education do not read as much nor as widely as do those with more education. The relationship between education and diversity of activities is operative throughout the life span so that, whether the person is old or young, it would be expected that with more education he would engage in a greater diversity of interests and activities. Consequently, the significant relationship, between activities and education is not surprising. The proportion of those respondents in the low activity category declined steadily from those with grammar school education to those in the high school and college groups. Conversely, the proportion of those in the high activity group increased steadily from the low to the highly educated groups.

(2) There is a significant relationship between extensiveness of activity and place of residence. A much smaller proportion of village residents than of open country residents were in the low activity category, and conversely, a greater proportion of village than of open country residents were in the high activity category.

(3) There is a significant relationship between extensiveness of activity and type of occupation. A much greater proportion of non-farmers than of farm operators were in the high activity category, whereas a significantly greater proportion of farm operators than of non-farmers were in the low activity category. Perhaps this can best be explained by the fact that more rural non-farmers than farm operators live in villages. Inasmuch as extensiveness of activity and place of residence are directly correlated, it stands to reason that there would also be more extensive activity by the preponderantly village-dwelling non-farmers than by the preponderantly open-country-dwelling farmers.

(4) There is no significant difference in the amount of activity between those rural aged who are retired and those who still are occupationally active. This tends to substantiate the point made earlier that the terms "active" and "retired" refer primarily to gainful employment, not to participation in activities such as informal friendship groups, leisure-time activities, and hobbies. Respondents classified as retired are not always completely inactive, nor do those in the active category necessarily participate either in formal or informal associations, or in hobbies and avocations.

(5) There is a significant relationship between extensiveness of activity and socioeconomic status. Why do people of high socioeconomic status tend so much more often to take part in a variety of activities than those of lower socioeconomic status? The answer may lie in the fact that socioeconomic status implies more education, a wider range of interests, and possibly greater opportunities and resources. It is in effect a difference between a style of life which is more likely to be characterized by psychological and social isolation.

Leisure-time Activities and Satisfaction

In addition to their range of activities, the respondents were also asked to indicate what activities gave them the most satisfaction in life. The satisfaction items and the number of persons who named them are listed in declining order as follows:

TABLE III

Optimum Satisfaction Items

Satisfaction Items	Number of Respondents
Just being with your family at home	121
Keeping house (working around the house and yard)	90
Doing things you like to do yourself at home	77
Having relatives visit you	68
Your work outside the home	67
Spending time with close friends	49
Your religion or church work	49
Visiting with your neighbors	43
Just sitting and thinking about things	31
Your reaction outside the home	26
Getting out to visit relatives	25
None of the above	4
No answer	4

Respondents gained the most satisfaction from activities centered in the home, for the four leading satisfaction items were clearly domestic in nature.

Change in Leisure-time Activities with Age

To determine the effects, if any, of the aging process on participation in leisure-time activities, the respondents were asked whether they had done certain things more often when they were fifty years of age or more often now.

In general, the findings indicate a trend toward the curtailment of activities among the respondents after the age of fifty. Activities involving family associations (seeing children and relatives) were especially affected over the years, closely followed by such activities as club and organizational affiliation and hunting and fishing. It is interesting to note that passive activities, such as reading and listening to the radio, tend to increase with age.

Formal Participation

Formal participation is herein defined as taking part in one or more of the following phases of an organized group: being a member, attending meetings, paying dues, serving as a member or officer. Formal participation has a function similar to that of the leisure-time activities discussed previously, in that both are ways in which older persons can fill their unscheduled free time. Both types of activities provide opportunities for sociability, creativity, and diversion. It is evident that the person who participates in formal organizations is also more likely to be active in other types of leisure-time activities. This finding has significance for the sociopsychological theory of the interrelationship between a person's self-image and his attitudes toward others and his social behavior. The person who conceives of himself as a sociable, creative person who seeks to avoid boredom participates in a variety of activities, both formal and informal. Participation in these activities in turn reinforces the person's image of himself.

In another respect, however, formal participation is a type of activity that differs from the above-mentioned cluster of leisure-time activities. This difference is a consequence of the function of formal organizations in American society. The manifest function of formal organizations is to serve as sociability centers and to provide a channel for community service in the broadest sense. But formal organizations also have the functions of social mobility and economic and political control. Formal participation affects the participant's behavior and attitudes, and is related to his position in the social structure. Furthermore, many studies have shown that the participation pattern in formal organizations reflects the social stratification system of a community. In every instance, the higher status group tends to dominate the organizational activity in the community. The data in this study corroborate these findings.

A significant relationship between socioeconomic status and formal participation is shown. Almost twice as many of the high status, as compared with the low status, older rural men participate in formal organizations.

Formal Participation and Education

As already noted, there is a significant relationship between participation in formal organizations and taking part in a diverse number of activities. It has been shown also that the older rural men in this study who had high school education and above were more often active in a broad range of activities than those with less than high school education. Older rural men with higher education participate more often in formal organizations than do those with less education.

Occupation Status and Participation in Formal Organizations

As pointed out earlier, in addition to the function of sociability and service, formal organizations also serve as vehicles for social mobility and power. Some formal organizations emphasize occupational improvement, while others emphasize sociability and interpersonal satisfactions. If this analysis is accepted, it follows that retirement will bring about a reduction in formal participation. The retired will tend to drop out of occupationally oriented organizations and to retain their membership in those organizations that provide face-to-face group satisfactions. The data in this study indicate that 51 per cent of the active older men belong to formal organizations, as compared with 40 per cent of the retired men. The relationship is not statistically significant, but is in the expected direction.

PRINCIPLES

1. *Nearly all the relationships between the individual and the community are strongly affected by age.*

As the individual goes through the process of maturation and social conditioning from infancy to old age, his position in the community passes through many changes.

2. *Age is an important criterion for assigning role and status within any society, and to a large extent sets the limitations on the relationships between the individual and the community.*

3. *It is the contention of some observers that the adjustment of youth to the institutions of the community is becoming less favorable, an observation that foreshadows trouble for the community if age can be regarded as a factor predictive of the behavior of the future adults.*

Insofar as this applies to the family there is some evidence against the hypothesis.

4. *Appropriate occupational choice influences an individual's relationships to the community, but this may be influenced by many nonrational factors.*

The proper matching of ability and interest to job role is directly associated with the relationship between an individual and the economic institution and indirectly with his adjustment to other institutions.

5. *The increasing proportion of the aged in the population is a significant social change that is influencing American communities.*

6. *Care of the aged has been assumed by the economic and governmental institutions and the family no longer performs this function.*

7. *Size of community influences the participation of older people in the formal and informal life of the community.*

In very large urban communities the older retired person tends to be isolated from the stream of community activity; however, smaller communities tend to encourage his continued participation. This may or may not result in the loss of community leadership and experience through the retirement of the older person.

SELECTED REFERENCES

Carmichael, Leonard, editor, *Manual of Child Psychology,* John Wiley and Sons, New York, 1946.

Committee on Aging and Geriatrics, *Fact Book on Aging,* Federal Security Agency, Washington, D.C., 1955.

Davis, Kingsley, "The Sociology of Parent-Youth Conflict," *ASR*, 5:523–34, 1941.

Davis, W. Allison, and Robert J. Havighurst, *Father of the Man*, Houghton-Mifflin Company, Boston, 1947.

Gesell, Arnold, Henry M. Halverson, Helen Thompson, Frances L. Ilg, Burton M. Castner, Louise Bates Ames, and Catherine S. Amatruda, *The First Five Years of Life*, Harper and Brothers, New York, 1940.

Havighurst, Robert J., and Ruth Albrecht, *Older People*, Longmans, Green and Company, New York, 1953.

Linton, Ralph, "Age and Sex Categories," *ASR*, 7:589–603, 1943.

McKain, Walter C., Jr., and Elmer Baldwin, "Old Age and Retirement in Rural Connecticut," *Storrs AES Bulletin 278*, Storrs, Connecticut, 1951.

Parsons, Talcott, "Age and Sex in the Social Structure of the United States," *ASR*, 7:604–16, 1942.

Piaget, Jean, *The Language and Thought of the Child*, Routledge and Kegan Paul, Ltd., London, 1952.

Piaget, Jean, *The Moral Judgment of the Child*, the Free Press, Glencoe, Illinois, 1948.

Tappan, Paul W., *Juvenile Delinquency*, McGraw-Hill Book Company, Inc., New York, 1949.

PART THREE

Elements of the Community

In Part I the nature of community structure was
described along with some of the concepts necessary
to the understanding of this structure. In addition,
certain conditions were described which exist outside the structure itself, but are extremely important in understanding community structure and
change. In Part II the discussion of community structure, as such, was introduced. Several all-pervasive
dimensions of community structure were described.
In the succeeding chapters, less pervasive, although
not less important, elements of community structure
will be analyzed. Elements are those aspects of the
community which may be viewed more in isolation
from the remainder of the structure than may values,
communication, and the like. An example of an element is the relationship between the educational and
economic institution, let us say, in the sense of the
educational function of personnel selectivity through
grading students. All the dimensions of community,
values, communication, stratification, age, and so
on are intimately bound up with the grading function. However, most other elements will not be related. An example of an element which is not closely

related to grading would be the recreational function of some formal organizations in the community. The distinction between dimensions and elements, then, rests on the general importance of the dimension and the specific importance of the element.

While elements are not manifested throughout the community structure, they are related. In the example given, a change in the grading system will not only influence the personnel selection process, but it will also influence the family institution. Parents also wish to know the relative standing of their children in school. Or conversely, they may wish grades to be substituted by a measure of achievement in terms of potential. This would not serve the purpose of the economic institution in personnel selection. In this way, many elements are intimately bound together.

There is an old adage in the social sciences to the effect that a change in one feature of the social structure will produce changes throughout. In the change of a dimension, this principle holds. In the change of an element, it must be qualified. In either case, the change of an element or dimension brings more changes in other elements or dimensions than are usually anticipated.

In Chapter 11, the elements involving the relationships among small, intimate, and informal groups and the community are discussed. Groups of this sort are found throughout the community structure, but no one group is so pervasive. (Power "groups" are best understood in terms of the power dimension rather than in terms of groups.) Any one group can be identified and located at a specific place in the community structure.

As these groups increase in size, they tend to become formalized. Further, many formal organizations had their origin as an effort to meet a particular need not satisfied by the institutional structure. These organizations are numerous, but each one functions in only specific ways, therefore qualifying as an element. These are discussed in Chapter 12.

The remaining chapters of Part III deal with institutions. The functions of each institution are elements of community structure in the sense that they are the specific relations between and among other substructures in the community, that is, among institutions, or between institutions, groups, and formal organizations. Because institutions function in ways considered fundamental to the value system, their functions resemble dimensions in times of crisis. For example, a serious economic depression is likely to influence the entire community. However, except in times of extreme crisis, institutional functions are more specific than dimensions.

CHAPTER 11

Informal Groups and the Community

Small informal groups are found throughout the community structure, but no one group is pervasive in the entire structure. In addition, any one group can be identified and located at a given point in the community structure. However, aside from any one group, informal cliques, friendship groups, and other intimate face-to-face relationships may be seen to influence all other aspects of the social structure.[1] The influence or functions of groups may be more fully understood in terms of types of group relations, if the internal structure and the range of variation are first described.

THE NATURE OF GROUPS

A group is the set of relationships resulting from the active or suspended interaction of two or more persons. The generalizations found in research on group relations do not apply to other social relations and therefore it is important to distinguish the group from other social phenomena.[2]

There are three distinguishing characteristics of the group: the size, the psychological nature of interaction, and informality. The mere size of a group, as measured by the number of persons interacting, is important in and of itself. For example, intimacy, so important to the shaping of ideals and attitudes of members, is much less likely in a large than in a small group. Again, in group participation the smaller group may be more satisfactory. This is the reason a large college class may be divided into small

[1] A. Paul Hare, Edgar F. Borgatta, and Robert F. Bales, editors, *Small Groups*, Alfred A. Knopf, New York, 1955; Maria Rogers, "Autonomous Groups," *Handbook of Adult Education in the United States*, Bureau of Publications, Teachers College, Columbia University, New York, 1949, pp. 143–52; Hurley H. Doddy, *Informal Groups and the Community*, Bureau of Publications, Teachers College, Columbia University, New York, 1952; and various issues of *Autonomous Groups Bulletin*.

[2] For different definitions see the readings in Hare *et al., op. cit.*

219

discussion sections. Still another example is that a group of two persons (called a dyad) is different from a group of three persons (called a triad) in the full participation of members. A triad usually takes the form of a dyad with an onlooker.

A second distinguishing feature of the group is the psychological nature of the interaction. This means that each person modifies his own behavior on the basis of his anticipation of how the other person will react. This anticipation of the other person's behavior involves the covert or psychic action. Mentally, we base our prediction of the other person's reaction on our knowledge of his peculiarities, on the situation, and on the mores and folkways guiding the interaction at this point in time. This anticipation of the other's behavior usually happens in much less time than it takes to describe the mental process. However, sometimes one may deliberate or plan—as in the case of a trial attorney preparing his questions for the next day or the instructor preparing his lecture. While the basic question is, how will he (or they) react to what I say, the form the question takes in the process being described is, how would I react if I were he? This process we call role-taking.[3] This means we put ourselves in the place of the other and predict how we will react—modifying our own actions to get the reaction we wish. In other social entities, the social relationship between two persons may occur through representatives. For example, the relationship between the people of one country and another may occur through ambassadors, that between a plaintiff in a law suit and the defendant is through their lawyers, and that between two formal organizations through their leaders or representatives.

The third distinctive feature of the group relation is its informality. This distinction is more difficult to make clear, for although the word is frequently used, the difference between formality and informality has not been adequately conceptualized and studied. The dictionary definition includes the main sociological aspects, namely, that an informal relation is one which is not done in accordance with established and prescribed rules. These relations are referred to as informal or autonomous groups.

These are the essential elements of groups. It is obvious that the Negro race, the United States, the middle class, the Farm Bureau, the Grange, and the Methodist Church are not groups, for the members are not in psychological interaction. The importance of this point is that the generalizations described below are applicable to groups and only to groups. In addition,

---

[3] This concept is different from role-playing, by which is meant conforming to the expected behavior patterns associated with a given status. See Walter Coutu, "Role Playing vs Role-Taking: An Appeal for Clarification," *ASR*, 16:180–87, 1951. For the theory of interaction described here see George H. Mead, *Mind, Self, and Society*, University of Chicago Press, Chicago, Illinois, 1934.

a transitory interaction may occur in which all the criteria of the group are met. In terms of interest, however, the more permanent arrangements described below are of greatest importance.

Group Description

Because of their basic importance, groups have received much attention from sociologists. They are amenable to use in deliberate social change in the community. Likewise, the course of action in larger social units is often predetermined by the power group within the organization. Groups are not, however, as simple to understand as they first appear. The following outline * proves this point and also serves as a frame of reference for the study of groups. The real importance of these structural features is that a difference in structure makes a difference in function.

The objective of any science is a description of its phenomena.

Until we take the trouble to describe different kinds of groups with the same care that a biologist describes a species, genus, or family of plant or animal life, we shall fail to have any adequate understanding of the nature of the group. How far would zoology advance if its students merely talked about sparrows, bugs, or squirrels, with no exact descriptions?

An adequate description of a group seems to involve five major sets of characters: (1) identity—what limits it or sets it apart from other groups; (2) composition—the individuals composing the group; (3) intergroup relations— whether the group is independent or is controlled from without; (4) intragroup relations—forms of interaction between members; and (5) structure and mechanism—the established procedures and division of labor for performing specific functions.

Identity

What is it that delimits a group, that gives it a sort of boundary, or sets it off from those who do not belong?

Groups may or may not have prescribed limitations to membership. Thus, some are (a) exclusive, such as fraternities, social clubs, organizations of stockholders; others are (b) restricted, that is, open to all who will conform to certain conditions, as subscribing to a creed to enter a church, or being a college alumna to join the Association of University Women; while some are (c) inclusive, or open to all, as a political party, parent-teacher associations, most civic organizations.

Entrance and exit. One enters a club voluntarily, but he is a member of a family or of a community involuntarily. To some groups he must be elected, while others may be joined without the knowledge of the members.

Identification of members. A member of a family is recognized by his name;

* Dwight Sanderson, "Group Description," *Social Forces,* 16:309–19, 1938. Used by permission.

a member of a religious order, the army, or a police department, by his garb; and members of many fraternal orders and fraternities are known by their insignia, pins, keys, or fobs.

Composition

Size and elements; the number of persons in a group. Some are limited, such as families, fraternities, and card clubs, while others desire as large a membership as possible. Some groups are composed of individual persons, while others are composed of individuals who are representatives of their groups.

Homogeneity. Some groups are confined to one sex, age, or nationality, while others include all types of people. A social club will probably have little social distance between its members, but social distance between the membership may be a limiting factor of a parent-teacher association.

Stratification. Certain groups very definitely recognize differences of social strata, as in the army between privates and officers, or between freshmen and seniors in a college. Others seek to make stratification impossible, as in a veterans' organization, or a political club.

Permanency. Some groups, such as the church, have a relatively stable membership; some groups are specially for a certain age or period, as Boy Scouts and the college class; while in some loosely organized groups the membership is short-lived.

Intergroup Relationships

A social club is an entirely independent autonomous group. Groups which become federated with others lose some of their independence through the effect of the opinion of the larger group, even though they profess their autonomy. Groups which receive their charters from a higher authority, such as fraternities and fraternal orders, certain churches, and trade unions, thereby limit the form and behavior of the local group to certain prescribed standards.

Intragroup Relationships

These involve the forms of interaction between members.

The nature of the relationship may be personal as in a family or social club, or impersonal as in a business corporation; it may be representative, as in a legislative body or in many councils or federations; or it may be fiduciary, as in the board of directors of a building and loan association or the trustees of a church.

Contacts of members of a group range from the hourly association of members of the family to weekly or monthly meetings of many groups and annual sessions of national organizations. The nature of these contacts ranges from those which involve all members of the group, as in the family, to those which include only a limited portion of the membership.

Participation in the group varies from that which is universal and intimate, as in a family, fraternity, religious order, or military company in war, to the type of passive participation involved in paying annual dues and having practically no active part in the work of the group, as is common in so-called welfare organizations.

The quality of participation is equally varied, from the domestic attitudes of the family to the competitive attitudes of a bridge club. The neighborhood is characterized by neighborliness, the fraternity by brotherhood, the cooperative association by cooperation, and so on.

The solidarity of groups, or the degree of awareness which each member has of the group and his loyalty to it, may be almost nil, as in a national learned society, or at a maximum, as in a gang or a family feud.

Some groups have almost absolute control of the behavior of their members, as in a religious order or in the army; some control their behavior only on matters affecting the special interests of the group, as in a cooperative marketing association; while some have practically no control over behavior outside of the meetings of the group, as would be the case with many special interest groups, such as a philatelic club, or a social club.

Many groups have folkways or mores peculiar to them. Members of the Grange and some fraternal orders call each other "brother" or "sister"; some churches seat women on one side and the men on the other; every family has its own folkways and mores; freshmen in colleges must wear caps; games of chance are prohibited in some churches and exploited by others.

Certain groups have language peculiarities, most obvious in groups of foreign nationality, but also in evidence in the "thee" and "thou" of the Quakers.

The roles of individuals characterize or are peculiar to certain groups, notably in the formation of a football team, in an orchestra, a band or a quartette, and in the husband and wife relation in the family.

Most groups have definite spatial relationships. The area covered by the group may be as small as a neighborhood, or as large as a state or nation. Density and dispersity will vary according to the area covered. Many groups own buildings which are the homes of such groups as churches, lodges, fraternities, and the like.

Temporal Relationships. Some groups are but temporary and plan to dissolve upon the accomplishment of certain purposes, such as a campaign committee. Others are of relatively short duration, as the college class. Some groups are seasonal, like baseball, football, and skiing clubs. Most groups are presumably continuous, although the mortality is high and many become quiescent and then revive. Whether the group has a long and well-preserved history and established traditions is a considerable factor in determining the behavior of the present group.

Structure and Mechanism

Every group has certain established means of carrying on its life by the assignment of a division of labor to its members and by certain accepted means of procedure, which form its structure and involve definite mechanisms. One of the most common of these group mechanisms is the leader.

Does a group have a recognized leader, is he employed or voluntary, is he elected or does he obtain his position by his own efforts?—these are the questions which reveal the leadership characteristics of different sorts of groups.

Some groups have recognized subgroups. Thus a Scout troop is composed of patrols, and a Sunday school of classes; churches have various auxiliary groups; and the work of many organizations is largely handled by committees.

Some groups have stated aims or purposes which dominate their existence, such as a reform group or political party. Other groups entirely lack any avowed aim. Parent-teacher associations have rather definite aims, but largely confined to matters of education, whereas the aims of the Grange are very broad and diverse.

If a group has a definite code of behavior for its members, it is a mechanism for group control. The discipline of the Methodist Episcopal church is such a code, as is that of a religious order, or the regulations of the army.

Groups which do not have frequent contacts must have means of arriving at a consensus of opinion so that they may be able to act collectively. For this purpose meetings are held, at which discussions take place; a record is kept of the procedure so that the actions may be consistent and cumulative; parliamentary procedure is used to ensure fairness in discussion and voting. These are but mechanisms of group procedure.

Means of developing and maintaining morale. These may be journals or group publications; letters to members; persons in charge of newspaper publicity; banquets; reunions; special events.

Old groups which have become highly institutionalized often develop a very elaborate system of ritual and ceremonial, with the use of insignia and symbols, as in certain churches, in Masonic orders, in European universities. The degree to which a group is dominated by such usages or by custom or tradition, as over against an entire informality of procedure, is a difference in group structure.

Certain mechanisms of groups are chiefly for the maintenance or preservation of the life of the group, and are sufficiently indicated under the subheads in the outline above. Certain of these mechanisms are characteristic of some groups and are entirely lacking in others.

Physical bases or essential physical equipment. In the case of certain groups the physical conditions associated with them are essential for understanding them. Thus the farm family cannot be adequately described except as associated with its work on the farm, and a factory group of employees has its existence because of its relation in and to the factory. Likewise the physical equipment of certain groups is essential for their existence and they cannot be conceived without it, as yachts for a yacht club or a golf course for a golf club. Such essential physical equipment would seem to be a part of the group structure.

TYPES OF GROUPS AND THEIR FUNCTIONS

The outline above presents a comprehensive way of looking at groups in terms of structure. When several of the characteristics in the outline are found to be highly correlated, types of groups are constructed. For example, it may be found that restricted membership, small size, personal interaction, and frequent contacts more often go together. The type of group described in the example has been developed into a typology based on C.H. Cooley's work on the *primary group*.[4] Later, sociologists found this so useful that they added the concept of the secondary group whose characteristics are opposite to those described.

The functions of the primary group are many. First, it fulfills the affectional need of people, which is met by no other social unit. This is assuming that the family may be looked upon as a primary group as well as an institution. Second, the primary group furnishes an outlet for frustration on the part of the individual through exchanging confidences. Third, and very important for the community, is the fact that the primary group produces common ideals and values on the part of the individual members. Fourth, the primary group serves as a communication device for those items of information, skill, and attitude which are not communicated at the mass level. Thus, rumors, gossip, and so on are transmitted through the primary group.

The functions of the secondary group are highly specialized and are more properly considered under the chapter on large formal organization. The relationship between the primary group and the secondary group is also important, since the community-wide organization designed for a program of deliberate change of the community is likely to fit many of the generalizations of the secondary group. The primary group clique may hold the power to control the actions taken by a secondary group. This point, also, is of great relevance to community structure and change.

The family, neighborhood, and play group more often than not represent primary groups. Generally, research has been done without determining whether any given neighborhood or family actually involves primary group interaction. Nevertheless, the generalizations which apply are quite often the functions of the primary nature of the neighborhood, family, and play group.

Another classification of groups was constructed by Sumner very early in the history of social science. This typology consists of the in-group and the out-group.[5] The in-group is exclusive and restricted with involuntary entrance. It resembles the primary group in many of the other characteristics.

[4] Charles H. Cooley, *Social Organization*, Charles Scribner's Sons, 1909.
[5] William G. Sumner, *Folkways*, Ginn and Company, Boston, 1906, especially Chapter 1.

It is usually homogeneous and relatively small, although this latter point may not hold during certain times. In fact, in a traditional society, a community may exhibit the characteristics of an in-group. The in-group almost always has permanency, has a high degree of solidarity and of awareness and loyalty. Perhaps the major characteristic of the in-group is ethnocentrism, described in the previous chapter on value systems. This type of intergroup relation is extremely important to community development where the professional worker may come from another culture and might be considered a member of the out-group.

Still another type of group relevant to the field of community behavior is that of the reference group. The reference group is applicable to situations where only one member of the group is physically present. For example, if a situation arises in which the person must make a decision which might affect his relations with an important group, he may make that decision on the basis of anticipation as to how the group would react. A person "refers" to the group values in making a decision even though the group may not be physically present.[6] For example, a person may be in a committee which is attempting to consider the problem of developing a sewage disposal unit. His discussion in this group, the committee, is not only influenced by the problems and values facing the committee but by problems and values from other groups of which he is a member. Around the conference table there will be many interfering variables resulting from the group membership and loyalties of each member. In a parent-teachers association meeting discussing the problem of building a school, a person may be influenced by the fact that he is a member of both "parents" and "taxpayers." Therefore, the reference group notion is applicable not only to groups, but to formal organizations as well. The concept of the reference group has been rediscovered in recent years, but it is a very old one. Indeed, the concept of the representative in the governmental institution is identical in nature. A member of the House of Representatives "represents" a district (his reference group) that may influence him to vote a certain way, even though from the federal point of view a different decision is clearly more desirable. The reference group influence is stronger when the conditions under which it is operating are similar to those of committee work. The committee, as opposed to the group from which the reference values are taken, is relatively impermanent, has little intimacy, and is specialized in purpose.

The function of small groups generally in the social structure of the com-

---

[6] Robert K. Merton and Alice S. Kitt, "Contributions to the Theory of Reference Group Behavior," in Robert K. Merton and Paul F. Lazarsfeld, *Continuities in Social Research,* the Free Press, Glencoe, Illinois, 1950, pp. 16–40.

munity, and in the change of that structure, is varied and subtle. A summary discussion of this relationship was made by Wayland.*

Relationship of Small Groups To Larger Social Systems

In this area two different types of problems have been studied: (1) the function of small groups as a basic unit in larger generalized social systems, such as communities or societies; (2) small groups or units within formally organized social systems, such as an industry, the army, or a school system.

The Small Group in Generalized Social Systems

As a basic unit in a larger generalized social system, the small group has been studied from four essentially different approaches: its role as a basic unit in the status system of a larger social system; its role as a basic mediating unit within which the societal forces and influences are interpreted and reacted to in terms of the values of the group members; patterns of responses (structural and operational) of different kinds of small groups to social change in the larger social system; impact of small groups of various kinds on the structure and dynamics of a larger social system.

Role of the Small Group as a Basic Unit in a Social Status System

In the numerous studies of social statuses, the members of a particular family are commonly identified as having the same social position. Although the place of other small groups has not always been recognized, there seems to be increasing awareness of the importance of such groups in defining the status system and understanding the operation of the system. Warner says in the Yankee City study: "We eventually became convinced that the clique was next in importance to the family in placing people socially." [7]

Hollingshead also found the clique to be a subunit of his class formulation, within which "commonly shared sets of likes and dislikes . . . tie the members together, within which persons worked out most of their intimate, personal relationships during periods of leisure and recreation." [8]

In Miller's study of the process of decision-making experienced by communities in connection with the Hill-Burton Hospital Construction program the pattern of action of small groups with high prestige was analyzed.[9] It was found, for example, that the energetic backing of a small friendship group, composed of

* Sloan Wayland, "Functional Roles of Small Groups in Large Social Systems," *Teachers College Record*, 55:359–68, 1954. Used by permission.
  [7] W.L. Warner and P.S. Lunt, *The Social Life of a Modern Community*, Vol. ı, Yale University Press, New Haven, 1941, p. 110.
  [8] August B. Hollingshead, *Elmtown's Youth*, John Wiley and Sons, New York, 1940, p. 80.
  [9] Paul A. Miller, "The Process of Decision-Making Within the Context of Community Organization," *RS*, 17:153–61, 1952.

high prestige persons who had established themselves through previous action as a unit with community welfare interests, was the decisive factor in the reaching of a positive decision.

In addition to the identification of small groups as units within class structures, the function of different kinds of small groups has been identified in numerous studies in rural communities. In one such study the differentiation is made between the coterie and the casual congeniality group, in terms of both status composition and function in the community.[10]

Role of the Small Group as a Basic Mediating Unit

In exploration of the problem which was originally formulated as the individual versus society, sociologists have recognized that the individual usually interprets and reacts to experiences as a member of a group rather than as an isolated individual, and that not all members of a society interpret and react in the same manner. The function of the small group is that of a mediating mechanism through which the individual selects from his total experiences those he deems significant, and works out patterns of response which are acceptable among persons who are socially significant to him, while developing his own self-concept which will be at the same time functional in his society. This is obviously an extremely complicated problem and many aspects have not been explored. Selected examples of the level of current development are given below.

In a number of community studies the mediating role of small groups has been indicated. Hollingshead, in the study referred to above, described this role for adolescent peer age groups. In another study the function of the informal small group is defined as a "basic social mechanism for moulding public opinion, steering local gossip, generating social pressure, transmitting news and developing leadership." [11]

Studies of the pattern of social interaction and participation in urban settings have indicated the insignificance of the small group for working class families who have a low rate of participation in formal associations. This has been pointed out in Hurley Doddy's study [12] of informal groupings in a low income area in New York and in a study by Floyd Dotson [13] in New Haven. Recognition of the importance of such groups for urban residents of low economic status has brought into question the assumption of some urban scholars that all of urban life is characterized by impersonality, contractuality of relationships, and lack of (or very limited) continuing association.[14] Doddy found about two hundred small groups with varying degrees of formality of organization in a multiethnic group

[10] P.J. Jehlik and R.E. Wakeley, "Rural Organization in Process," *Iowa State College AES Research Bulletin 365*, Ames, Iowa, 1949, pp. 179–81.

[11] P.J. Jehlik, and J.E. Losey, "Rural Social Organization in Henry County, Indiana," *Purdue AES Bulletin 568*, Lafayette, Indiana, 1951, p. 37.

[12] Hurley H. Doddy, *Informal Groups and the Community*, Bureau of Publication, Teachers College, Columbia University, New York, 1952. See also *Autonomous Groups Bulletin*, Vol. vi, No. 4, Summer, 1951.

[13] Floyd Dotson, "Patterns of Voluntary Association Among Urban Working Class Families," *ASR*, 16:687–93, 1951.

[14] Wilbur Hallenbeck, *American Urban Communities*, Harper and Brothers, New York, 1951, and Saul Alinsky, *Reveille for Radicals*, University of Chicago Press, Chicago, 1946.

area of New York which has poor housing and a rapidly changing population. In rural areas, action programs are being developed by such agencies as the Agricultural Extension Service in which friendship groups, identified through sociometric studies, serve as basic operating groups.[15]

The mediating role of the small group in handling events arising in the larger society has been explored in several other behavioral areas. In their study of political behavior, Lazarsfeld and his colleagues discovered the importance of the small group as the unit within which decisions are made.[16] This function of the small group is of particular significance in the determination of political behavior when individuals are subjected to cross-pressures growing out of their identification with segments of the society, such as ethnic or economic groups, which have conflicting positions regarding appropriate political behavior. This pattern has been extended by Merton and others to political opinions and to general consumption attitudes and standards.[17]

Patterns of Response of Different Kinds of Small Groups to Social Change

The statement of the problem implies that the characteristics of small groups are related to the characteristics of the society of which they are a part. As Shils has pointed out in his excellent review of the study of primary groups, many sociologists assumed that small groups were meaningful in a preindustrial society, but would pass from the scene as industrial society reached its mature form.[18] With the discovery that small groups still play a major role in societies which have highly developed industrial characteristics, small groups have been examined anew in terms of their response to the changing forms of that society. The best documented studies of this kind have used the family as the focus of study. Specific attention has been given to such factors as the changing patterns of reproduction, disorganizing forces having a cultural origin, and the comparison between families in subcultures which have incorporated urban industrial values.[19]

A number of studies have been made by rural sociologists of the changes in the composition of small groups as a result of improved communication facilities, enlarged farms, and development of more specialized interests among rural residents.[20] In the area of urban sociology, similar problems have been con-

[15] Edmund deS. Brunner and E. Hsin Pao Yang, *Rural America and the Extension Service*, Bureau of Publications, Teachers College, Columbia University, New York, 1949.

[16] Paul Lazarsfeld and Associates, *The People's Choice*, Columbia University Press, New York, 1948.

[17] Robert Merton, "Patterns of Interpersonal Influence and of Communicative Behavior in a Local Community," in Lazarsfeld and Stanton, editors, *Communication Research 1948–49*, Harper and Brothers, New York, 1949, pp. 180–219.

[18] Edward A. Shils, "The Study of Primary Groups," in Lerner and Lasswell, *The Policy Sciences*, Stanford University Press, Stanford, California, 1951.

[19] James H. Bossard, *The Sociology of Child Development*, Harper and Brothers, New York, 1950, and E.W. Burgess and Harvey J. Locke, *The Family—From Institution to Companionship*, American Book Company, New York, 1945.

[20] Noel P. Gist, "Decentralization and Rural-Urban Relationships," *RS*, 17:328–35, 1952; J.H. Kolb and Edmund deS. Brunner, *A Study of Rural Society*, Houghton-Mifflin Company, Boston, 1952, Chapters 12, 13; Selz Mayo, "Testing Criteria of Rural Locality Groups," *RS*, 14:317–25, 1949; and Frank D. Alexander, "The Problem of Locality-Group Classification," *RS*, 17:236–45, 1952.

sidered. For example, Merton and his associates have examined the pattern of development of small groups in public housing projects. In describing the life patterns of adolescents in Elmtown, Hollingshead identified cliques with somewhat different membership bases: school cliques, recreational cliques, and institutional cliques based on affiliation with such institutions as churches. Problems of role conflict become increasingly important as the society develops more specialized bases for association.

The development of small groups with very little overlapping in membership has produced problems of appropriate and consistent behavior for individuals who are members of several such groups whose values are in conflict. The concepts of role conflict and reference groups have been developed to study the means by which the difficulties growing out of this situation are resolved. One study of this problem was made in the area of political behavior, in which cross-pressures were felt by individuals because of identification with different reference groups, that is, social units whose values are accepted as guides, which were in conflict regarding the candidate deserving support.

The current interest in group development may be viewed as associated with the increased frequency of formal meetings in which the individuals involved are not personally acquainted. One of the basic themes of research and action in this area is the development of means by which small *ad hoc* groups may move rapidly to acquire some of the qualities of the autonomous group. The intent is to develop a high degree of intimate relationships in a short time, while anticipating that the group will not continue to function after the occasion for its formation has passed. In such situations, the problem of role conflicts may be intensified, as loyalty to the *ad hoc* group is not usually high enough to supersede the individual's commitments to his other, more permanent social roles. It is in such situations that the development of role-playing has peculiar relevance, because role behavior developed in other social relationships and not understood in the new setting may be clarified for both the actor and others. The degree to which, and the conditions under which, these *ad hoc* groups manifest characteristics of small groups have not been fully established, although the assumption is frequently made that small *ad hoc* groups have or may quickly develop the characteristics of small groups.

The nature of the relationships between the characteristics of small groups and the social context in which they operate has been by-passed by many of the contemporary investigations of small groups. Homans' *The Human Group* represents one notable exception to this.[21] In addition to the identifying three elements of group life—activity, interaction, and sentiment—he emphasizes the significance of the social environment, the external system, the "given" factors. As Shils points out in his study, "The primary group will be adequately understood scientifically only when its interconnections with the ecological and corporate context have been perceived and given proper emphasis alongside the variables which the new analysis has rendered visible to our eyes."[22]

[21] George Homans, *The Human Group,* Harcourt, Brace and Company, New York, 1950.
[22] Shils, *op. cit.,* p. 69.

The Impact of Small Groups of Various Kinds on the Structure and Dynamics of a Larger Social System

The problem here is the converse of the issue discussed earlier and is alluded to in the above question from Shils when he refers to the *interconnection* of small groups and the society. Because of the magnitude of the problem, analyses of the functional role of the family and other small groups in a cultural system have been largely speculative to date. An exception to this is a recent study of the role of small groups as mechanisms for integrating new immigrants into the Israeli society, which has indicated the significance of such groups in meeting a problem faced by the whole society.[23]

The general assumption on which much work has been based is that the maintenance of a democratic society requires the development of meaningful small-group relationships of a democratic character. But the differences in the relationship of small groups to the larger society in democratic and nondemocratic cultures have not been explored. For example, what is the role of the small group within a totalitarian state? Shils advances the hypothesis, based on his study of the German Army and Leighton's investigation of the War Relocation Center for Japanese in Arizona, that "authoritarian leadership can indeed be a crucial component in primary groups composed of persons with personality needs which can best be satisfied by authoritative protection or in primary groups operating in situations which bring these needs for paternal protection to the fore. . . . With certain types of personalities in certain types of situations (tasks and threats) primary-group solidarity might well be disintegrated by democratic leadership.[24] Extension of analyses on a cross-cultural basis is urgently needed at this stage. Leadership in this direction is being furnished by rural sociologists such as Charles Loomis, T. Lynn Smith, Bryce Ryan, Olen Leonard, and Irwin Sanders, who are studying rural social organizations outside of the United States.

In considering the functional role of small groups in society, Homans advances the thesis that small groups "tend to produce a positive surplus, a margin of safety in the qualities the group needs for survival (morale, leadership, control, extensions of the range of social contacts) and that this surplus may be used, not simply to maintain the existing adaptation of the group to its environment but to achieve a new and better adaptation."[25]

Small Groups as Units in Formal Social Systems

Although much of the study of small groups in formal organizations has been focused on the analysis of such groups in industry, other areas, such as military organizations, religious education, and medical institutions have also been explored.

---

[23] S.N. Eisenstadt, "The Place of Elites and Primary Groups in the Absorption of New Immigration in Israel," *AJS*, 56:222–32, 1951.

[24] Shils, *op. cit.*, p. 65.

[25] Homans, *op. cit.*, pp. 271–72.

In industrial settings, the study of small groups and other sociological aspects has developed very rapidly since World War II. Until recently, industrial leaders gave little recognition to the social variable associated with work performances. The failure of workers to respond to incentives which management assumed were important led to the discovery of how small groups form patterns of behavior with values which are meaningful to workers but different from the values management expects them to hold. Research has been focused on the factors that make for such differences and on means for adjusting them. The concept of the alienated small group has been introduced to refer to those groups which resist incorporation into the formally organized social system. For example, Warner explained the long strike in Yankee City in terms of the development of a bureaucratic system which threatened the small-group pattern and impersonalized the relationships of members of such groups.[26]

Literally dozens of studies emphasizing small-group operations in industry are being conducted annually. An illustration of recent work of this kind is the analysis by Donald Roy of a machine shop, in which the author describes the behavior of his colleagues in a workshop, including the restriction of output, in accordance with goals set up by the group and the development of a pattern of goldbricking —loitering or engaging in unproductive activities—as a socially sanctioned means for quota restriction.[27] In this framework, the "rate buster" may be defined as an individual who rejects membership in the small group and is willing to flout group-established goals in full knowledge of the pressures which will be brought to bear on him.

In the studies of small groups in military organizations[28] many of the same problems are raised and many of the same concepts used as in the study of small groups in industry. As in industry, communication and execution of commands were most successful when the leadership patterns were the same for both informal and formal organization. Further, the abstract goals of the military had as little effect in determining the behavior of its personnel as the goals of management had in industry. As Shils points out in his summary of this research, ". . . the soldier's motivation to fight is not derived from his perceiving and striving toward any strategic or political goals; it is a function of his need to protect his primary group and to conform with its expectation."[29] In an interesting study of the German Army, Shils and Dicks reached essentially the same conclusions, although they found that the small groups in the German Army were much more leader-oriented than similar groups in the American Army.

Investigation of small groups in other kinds of formal organizations has been rather limited. In educational systems, considerable attention has been given to the sociometric patterns among classroom members. In an unpublished study of moral values among elementary school children in a midwestern urban school,

[26] W.L. Warner and J.O. Low, *The Social System of the Modern Factory*, Vol. IV, Yankee City Series, Yale University Press, New Haven, 1947.
[27] Donald Roy, "Quota Restriction and Gold Bricking in a Machine Shop," *AJS*, 57:427–42, 1952.
[28] S.A. Stouffer *et al.*, *The American Soldier; Adjustment During Army Life*, Vol. I.; see also Shils, "Primary Groups in the American Army," in Merton and Lazarsfeld, editors, *Continuities in Social Research*, the Free Press, Glencoe, Illinois, 1950, pp. 16–39.
[29] Shils, *op. cit.*, p. 64.

A.W. Foshay has found that children tend to exhibit such traits as helpfulness, considerateness, and responsibility toward members of their own friendship group, but do not show the same traits when dealing with persons who are not in these groups. Hollingshead, in his study of adolescents in Elmtown, recognized the importance of the peer age groups in the schools. In his concern with class position, however, he did not follow through on the ramification of clique membership for differential behavior in the school.

PRINCIPLES

1. *Groups represent the most frequent type of social behavior experienced by man. Thus the shaping of values and behavior occurs in groups in an important way.*

2. *Groups vary in structure in many different ways, and differences in function and group behavior may be expected from each of these variables.*

The exact difference in function resulting from the variation in structure has not been established for most of the twenty-nine variables listed by Sanderson.

3. *The small, intimate face-to-face groups, called primary groups, function to teach the value system to individual members of the community.*

Insofar as alternatives are allowed within the value system, the particular alternative value internalized by the individual will be largely due to the particular groups of which the person is a member.

4. *In-group, out-group relations are characterized by ethnocentrism.*

Accompanying difficulties are involved for the man of action in community development. Communities which fit the criteria of the in-group not only resist the "outsider" but resist change generally.

5. *The references to one's group values in making judgments occur even when the person is not actually in the group at the time.*

This concept of the reference group is of utmost importance in explaining "peculiar" behavior and attitudes of individual members of a committee or other situation in which there is little intimacy, lack of permanence, and little pressure to conform to the same ideals.

6. *The small group may function to place individual members in the social system, as a unit in which the individual interprets codes of conduct and behavior accordingly, as an influence in the individual's response to social change, and as one mechanism of problem solution in the community.*

SELECTED REFERENCES

Bales, R.F., and P. Slater, "Role Differentiation," in T. Parsons, R.F. Bales, et al., Family, Socialization, and Interaction Process, the Free Press, Glencoe, Illinois, 1955.

Blumer, H., "Psychological Import of the Human Group," in M. Sherif and M.O. Wilson, editors, Group Relations at the Crossroads, Harper and Brothers, New York, 1953, pp. 185–202.

Cartwright, D., and A.F. Zander, editors, Group Dynamics: Research and Theory, Row, Peterson and Company, Evanston, Illinois, 1953.

Cooley, C.H., Social Organization, Charles Scribner's Sons, New York, 1909.

Festinger, L., and J. Thibaut, "Interpersonal Communication in Small Groups," J. Abnorm. Soc. Psychol., 46:92–99, 1951.

Homans, G.C., The Human Group, Harcourt, Brace and Company, New York, 1950.

Lippitt, R., Training in Community Relations: A Research Exploration Toward New Group Skills, Harper and Brothers, New York, 1949.

Loomis, C.P., W.B. Baker, and C. Proctor, "The Size of the Family as Related to Social Success of Children," Sociometry, 12:313–20, 1949.

Moreno, J.L., Who Shall Survive? rev. ed., Beacon House, Beacon, New York, 1953.

Sherif, M., The Psychology of Social Norms, Harper and Brothers, New York, 1936.

Sherif, M., and H. Cantril, The Psychology of Ego-Involvements, John Wiley and Sons, New York, 1947.

Simmel, G., "The Number of Members as Determining the Sociological Form of the Group," AJS, 8:1–46, 158–96, 1902–03.

Whyte, W.F., Street Corner Society: The Social Structure of an Italian Slum, University of Chicago Press, Chicago, 1943.

Wolff, Kurt H., The Sociology of Georg Simmel, the Free Press, Glencoe, Illinois, 1950.

CHAPTER 12

Formal Organizations

As autonomous groups become larger they tend to introduce formal structure, with roles defined, written constitutions, membership lists, and often a formal alliance with some state or federal organization with similar interests. These groups are often referred to as special interest groups, voluntary associations, or formal organizations.[1] They operate in the community structure to supplement the functions of institutions and to meet needs created by change to which institutions may not adjust. They become one of the channels through which action may be taken most frequently by the community as a whole, splintered as it is by jurisdictions and legal districts which are not coterminous.

The forming of associations has always attracted attention from the writers interested in describing American society, either contemporary or historical.[2] From house-raisings, husking bees, the vigilantes, and hobby groups to citizens' associations and parent-teachers associations, Americans solve their problems mainly through organizing themselves.[3] These types of organizations are often referred to as special interest groups, since such activities are usually specialized as to the problems they try to solve and often even as to the means they use to solve them.

THE ORIGIN OF THE LARGE FORMAL ORGANIZATIONS

Formal Organizations and Institutions

Institutions are structures of human relationships which have relatively specialized functions in the total community. These functions cluster around

[1] For a discussion of the theoretical aspects of formal organization see Robin Williams, *American Society*, Alfred A. Knopf, 1952, especially Chapter 12.

[2] Alexis de Tocqueville, *Democracy in America*, J. and H.G. Langley, New York, 1843–45.

[3] Warner and Lunt report 900 formal organizations in a city of 17,000. See W. Lloyd Warner and Paul S. Lunt, *The Social Life of a Modern Community*, Yale University Press, New Haven, 1941, Chapter 16.

problems.[4] For example, the economic institution is a structuring of human behavior around problems related to the production and distribution of goods and some services. The political institution is concerned with problems in the area of social control. An institution has a heavily codified set of rules, where means are often raised to the level of ends. Thus, the institution cannot change rapidly; it is, on the one hand, a creator of stability and dependability in the community, and on the other hand, it may itself create problems because of its inability to change rapidly when adjustments are needed as a result of changes in some feature of the environment.

Certain aspects of institutions account for the need to create large formal organizations. The first is that only the more basic functions needed for human goal-seeking are performed by the institutions. The governmental and the economic functions were used as examples above. The family perpetuates the community through teaching children the value system of the community. This latter process is called socialization. The family also is one of the predominant consumer units in the community, thus supplementing the economic institution. The religious institution has the function of worship and also supplements the government in social control.

Adjustment to Change

In addition to these basic functions there are many others that are important to individuals and groups in the community not usually considered basic to all. Institutions sometimes are broadened to cover these kinds of problems, but usually they are not flexible enough to do so. This gives rise to the need for another type of activity organized around the particular function or problem left untouched by the institutional framework of the community. When values are being violated through lack of means for achieving the goals, membership interest and leadership activities are mobilized, and a new formal organization comes about.

Institutional Effectiveness

The second aspect of the institutional structure which gives rise to large formal organization is that the institution may be ineffective in the fulfillment of its function, either as a whole or in one particular aspect of it. This may result from the inability to meet changing demands placed upon it by the community or it may come from a breakdown in the institution itself. The Parent-Teachers Association is an example of the first type, where the

[4] Hans H. Gerth and C. Wright Mills, *Character and Social Structure*, Harcourt, Brace and Company, New York, 1953.

"total" approach to the child's further socialization called for the family and the school to cooperate in the problems of learning. Obviously, the school could not take care of total socialization, if for no other reason than the fact that the child was in school only a short time during the day.

A breakdown in institutional performance may be defined as failure on the part of only one subculture within the community. For example, lobbyists and pressure groups or tax associations may define the governmental institution as having failed, and may bring pressure to bear for an adjustment, or work toward a new definition of functions within the governmental structure.

The Community-wide Organization

One of the best examples of the large formal organization which supplements the institutional framework of the community is the community-wide organization directed toward the solution of an unspecified set of community problems.[5] These go under various names, such as the Planning Committee, the Citizens' Council, or the Advisory Board. They perform many of the functions in particular situations which are assigned to institutions, thus supplementing them. They may work on educational, governmental, economic, or family problems. They may service institutions through identifying and defining new problems, offering alternatives, pressuring the institution to take a course of action, and implementing institutional policy. They are less powerful than the institutions, but they are not without power. Their support is often necessary for those in control of institutional relations to maintain their control. Thus, a political party may lose control unless it brings political institutional resources to bear upon a problem defined by the community, although this change in parties does not mean a change in the institution itself. Rather, the political institution is structured to encourage this kind of activity.

Institutional Traditionalism

Moreover, the need for the supplementary formal organization sometimes arises from the fact that means are raised to the level of ends within the institution. For example, the political institution is limited in the solution

[5] Floyd Hunter, Ruth C. Schaffer, and Cecil G. Sheps, *Community Organization: Action and Inaction,* University of North Carolina Press, Chapel Hill, 1956; Dwight Sanderson and Robert A. Polson, *Rural Community Organization,* John Wiley and Sons, New York, 1939; Dwight Sanderson, *Rural Sociology* and *Rural Social Organization,* John Wiley and Sons, New York, 1942, Part III, Section D; and Irwin T. Sanders, *The Community,* The Ronald Press Company, New York, 1958, Part III.

of problems of social control and service by the jurisdictional boundaries. Since problems often extend beyond these lines in the local area, the political unit may find itself unable to ameliorate the problems. An interesting example of this happened in the Northeastern part of the country, where a county passed a sales tax. One village center, however, was half in that county and half in another. The county line ran through the middle of the business district. Since there was a sales tax for half of the businesses and not for the other half, the families in the community area traded with the businesses which were located in the county without the sales tax. A local community organization was set up to bring some adjustment in the situation. This presented an extremely difficult problem, since the community structure extended its influence into both counties, crossing the county line as if it did not exist.

Hobby Groups

Another source of origin of the special interest group is the hobby interest. While this interest is not particularly relevant to community structure in all cases, there are two relationships which do exist and may be found to be important. On the one hand, the hobby interest group furnishes the unique type of community resources which allows for more kinds of specialization in modern-day American communities. These organizations have the recreational function which is largely left out of other institutions.

Another characteristic of the hobby group is the tendency for formal organizations, once organized, to broaden their activities. Thus an organization originally directed at recreational interest may decide through discussion by its members of problems of common concern to operate for a very serious purpose, not directly related to the hobby interests that brought it into being.

THE CYCLE OF ORGANIZATIONS

Kolb and Wileden describe the stages through which organizations move, the human relations involved at each stage, and some of the generalizations which can be made at each stage.[*]

[*] J.H. Kolb and A.F. Wileden, "Special Interest Groups in Rural Society," *Wisconsin AES Bulletin 84*, Madison, Wisconsin, December, 1927, Section v, Natural History of Interest Groups, pp. 74–79.

Interest groups have much in common. They all depend upon leadership and some form of membership. Thus all groups, regardless of their professional names or functions, their geographical location or size, follow certain general principles and tendencies. Certain variances in these principles and tendencies, however, are sure to be found in the different classes of groups. Furthermore, no two groups even of the same general class and form are identical. The more general principles and tendencies are here presented in terms of life-cycle characteristics, and illustrated by case histories of selected groups.

Like other living things, groups follow cycles. These cycles consist of rather definite stages through which the group passes, the periods being of longer or shorter duration, depending upon the nature of the group and its surrounding conditions. In this section is presented a sort of composite narrative of what happens in the various periods of the life cycle. There are four of these periods: stimulation, rise, carrying-on, and decline.

Stimulation

All groups depend upon people and their ability to act together. Proximity or the ability to overcome topographic barriers is essential. Likewise, various similarities such as religion, nationality, previous place of residence, and education are helpful. These are pregroup requirements which must be considered.

Certain prerequisites must be fulfilled. The one prerequisite which was found least frequently fulfilled is that a sufficient number of people are essential for the existence of an organized group. Thus in the northern county, where the soil was poor and the means of subsistence hard to obtain, the characteristic response, "People moved away," told the story. There was no longer a sufficient number of people to maintain the group of the type and structure set up, so the organization died. This was not an unusual condition. When the group was started it was believed in all confidence that there would be more people rather than fewer as time went on. The pregroup conditions changed and the prerequisites were no longer present. In a similar way but to a much lesser degree, trouble was encountered when nationality and religion were not sufficiently taken into account. A group must ever be watchful of the past as well as of the future.

Purpose Comes First

The excuse for the existence of a group is its avowed purpose which, according to the way of organized groups, comes first. This purpose is usually stated in the form of a thing or things to do. This is the rational procedure. When sufficient interest and sentiment have been aroused around the expressed purpose (the real purpose may remain unexpressed, or even unknown for the time being) crystallization will begin to take place. Just like the chemical reaction, this often becomes quickly noticeable at the basket social at the school, or at some promoted meeting where definite organization was entirely unexpected by most of the people present. This entire process usually takes place very quickly, except in those groups where a certain amount of stock or a certain number of memberships must first be sold. Even there it is usually put on as a drive and gotten over in a hurry and with a considerable emotional excitement.

Promoters Are Evident and Active

There is much of promotion (usually on the part of a few people), and a great deal of talking. Someone from outside of the local group has practically always supplied the idea. Very frequently an outsider is one of the most active promoters, either as representative of some professional group or because he likes to promote things and "seems to have a genius" for it. In the minds of the people, the organization becomes a reality. It becomes a shibboleth whereby pressing the magic button "presto" what they think they most want is accomplished.

Rise

People who never thought of another organization in that community now approve it. Frequently they do even more—they request it. They ask for help in getting it started and an organization is started.

There Are Frequent Meetings and Large Crowds

Small wonder it is, then, that the early meetings are well attended. These meetings are held more frequently than they will be later, and special meetings are called to decide upon such important matters as a constitution and election of officers. Enthusiasm runs high. Everything is new and there are plenty of ideas, although the people are probably reticent in expressing them. So, of course, the promoters have their way at the start. "Everybody" joins—ninety-two of them— everybody at that first meeting who is eligible. Twelve more join at the next meeting, and seven at the next. Jim Brown said he "wouldn't join no county agents' organization," but he is called "peculiar."

The Organization Takes on a Form

Meanwhile, the structure of the organization is becoming "set." A constitution (probably a printed form received from the promoter) has been accepted. This specifies that this organization shall meet once a month during the school year. It shall meet at the school house. It shall have four officers: a president, vice-president, secretary, and treasurer, to be elected annually at the first meeting in January. Anyone who is interested may become a member on payment of a fee of 50 cents a year to the treasurer. To change this constitution in any way, it is specified that the approval of two-thirds of the total membership shall be necessary. The constitution thus becomes the almost unchangeable code or method of procedure for the organization from that time on.

A Pace Is Set for the Future

Likewise the first programs set the pace for programs that are to follow. They start with a business session of at least a half hour duration, because there are numerous items of business to be discussed. There is also some group singing, a couple of good musical numbers, and a reading or recitation. These may very probably be presented by someone "from town." There is then, of course, a talk by a Mr. Brown from a neighboring organization, the county seat, or the state headquarters. Following this, coffee and doughnuts are served by "the committee" while the adults visit and the young people start a few games. These first meetings have been set up by the promoters or suggested to the first officers by the promoters. After the first two or three meetings, however, the officers must "go it" alone in planning meetings. Occasionally, the officers assume this responsibility regularly, but most frequently they cast around for a method of assistance, and decide upon the plan of appointing a committee at one meeting to plan the program for the next. This method, of course, immediately discourages debates and plays which require longer time for preparation. Also, since these types of programs involve more people and necessitate more teamwork, they are found less frequently. . . .

The Inner Circle Begins to Function

It is noticeable from the very start that practically every organization has its select group (officers, committee chairmen, and volunteer speakers from the floor) which virtually runs the organization. The officers may change about, and new committees may be added, but this inner circle remains about the same. Radical changes in this inner circle usually mean equally radical changes in the nature of the organization, and vice versa. The problem from the beginning, then, becomes one of creating loyalty to the leaders and through them to the organization. This process is well under way by the time the organization reaches its peak when the structure is well "set," the ideals and purposes codified, and custom has begun to play its part. The unquestioned reason for not doing different things or for not doing the same things differently is "because we have always done them this way."

Carrying-on

The testing time for every organization comes after the promotion period is over and the newness has worn off. It is then that the group must "carry on."

A Shift in Leadership Responsibility Takes Place

In most types of organizations by this time the early outside promoters disappear almost entirely from the scenes, the burden from then on being shouldered by local people, usually the officers. It is then that leadership inadequacies and leadership jealousies arise. New leadership loyalties and new group loyalties must be created if the group is to carry on. Any time from now on, disillusionments begin to take place, for frequently certain promises have been made and objectives held forth by the promoters that apparently are not (and frequently cannot be) fulfilled. Factions develop within the group, and conflicts between these factions occur over numerous things. Some of these conflicts become very serious and often threaten the very life of the group itself. Frequently friction over excessive social activities, particularly dancing or card playing at the meetings, is most critical.

Discovery of Conflicts with Other Groups

It is discovered at this time, too, that the group is possibly conflicting with the standards or ideals of other groups, such as the school or church. Consequently, members of the group may be denied the use of the school building, or the clergy may forbid their young people to take part in the group. Or, the new group may discover a head-on collision, that is, may find that it is trying to do about the same things as an already existing group in the same area, and is using about the same group of people to do it. These conflicts being discovered, certain adjustments are necessary and methods of establishing working relations with these other groups must be devised. If these needs are ignored, results are often fatal.

Attempt to Help and Reform the Community

Meanwhile the group, under its leadership, must carry on its program of help and reform for the community of which it has become an integral part. The leaders must keep on the aggressive, planning new things, and finding new and ingenious ways of presenting old ideas and plans. If they do not, the membership will drop out, as they frequently do, because "there is nothing to interest them any more." Rather dramatic things must sometimes be undertaken, campaigns and drives put on, and special events arranged. The constituency must know that this group is "doing things" and feel proud that they are a part of it. Besides, the general public must be favorably impressed by it. Some of these "outsiders" must be continually seeking to join in membership to replace those who are always dropping out, if decline is not to set in.

Difficulties Arise within the Group

From the time it starts, but particularly during this carrying-on period, the changing demands of the people concerned must be carefully noted. There are seasonal fluctuations in the nature of the programs and activities to be watched. But what is more often overlooked are the larger cyclical fluctuations. People tire even of pie after a while, although it may be the much coveted pumpkin pie. Likewise, even debates or plays run their course and something else must be supplied. This constantly brings before the organization and its leaders the suggestion of a change. But about half of the time the constitutionalists or the fundamentalists win and the proposed change is not made. However, those organizations that do change secure thereby a new lease on life. They are able to move on toward other goals.

Organization Tends to Grow Up with People

Added to the difficulties of this period is the tendency for organizations to grow up with people. As a new organization it starts with people unfamiliar with the organization. They gradually mould the organization to conform to their way of doing things. The embryonic leaders gain confidence gradually and their efforts become more perfect. Newer people coming in later cannot experience this same give-and-take process. They must more largely take things as they find them. This they occasionally refuse to do, particularly a younger generation. Thus, it is not at all unusual to find separate organizations for the various age groups, or to see a new organization cycle start with each succeeding generation.

Adaptations Are Attempted

When decline once sets in, there are about two avenues of adaptation for organizations other than demise. One of these is specialization. Thus the old general club may become the strictly social club, or it may become the women's welfare organization, the cemetery association, or the farmers' lecture club. The present tendency is toward these specialized groups. The other avenue of adaptation is in the form of a complete reorganization when the group is "on its last legs," into the form of a newer movement just coming in. Thus, the women's clubs which were practically inactive have reorganized and become active homemakers' clubs; community clubs have become parent-teacher associations, and equity societies have become shipping associations.

Decline

When the period of disintegration once sets in in earnest, it is difficult to head off without some rather drastic measures. There are certain characteristics of this period which are inescapable.

It Becomes Difficult to Keep the Membership in Line

Members lose interest in the organization and are no longer willing to attend its meetings or participate in its activities. Things are done halfheartedly. Special events, if any such are planned, "fall flat." There is much complaining both on the part of the officers and members, and criticism of each other. They find fault with their organization, and with other organizations which they believe are competing with it.

The Leadership Seems Inadequate for the Situation

It is generally agreed that if it could get some "strong" leaders, the organization would come back on its feet all right. But such leaders are not available, or if they can be found, they will have nothing to do with the organization.

It Becomes Difficult to Meet or to Transact Business

Gradually, special events and projects are omitted from the calendar. Meetings become less frequent and may not be held regularly. Finally, for a long period, no meetings are planned or called. An attempt may be made to revive the organization, but revivals are seldom seen during this period. The organization just ceases to meet and carry on its regular activities. In the minds of many of the people it will not be dead for a long time, because they still have their constitution and records, and some money in the treasury. Frequently the building is still there, unused for other purposes, and there is frequently other property. The organization simply is "inactive."

THE STRUCTURE OF LARGE FORMAL ORGANIZATIONS

Since the social entities dealt with here have generally more members than the groups considered in the last chapter, the effects of size are evident. Indeed, the formal nature of the relationships itself is in part a consequence of size. Within the large formal structure, however, there exist many small groups, or informal patterns of relationship, which affect the behavior of the organization itself. Sometimes this informal patterning of human relationships may even bring about organizational behavior much different from that which could be expected from limiting the analysis to the formal structure alone. Nevertheless, the formal structure is important in understanding the relationship between the organization and other elements of the community.

The first aspect of the structure of large formal organizations is the recruitment of membership. Unlike most institutions, the formal organization depends upon voluntary participation. There is no moral indignation associated with failure to belong nor with withdrawal after membership is established in a formal organization. This means that the relations within the formal organization must be satisfying to the individual or family. Furthermore, this satisfaction must come from the way an individual or family defines the rewards expected from the organization. This keeps the formal organization in line with member interests, and since the interests are diverse, the formal organization must remain flexible and sometimes compartmentalize to meet varying interests of the membership. The internal structure of the organization must integrate the purposes of the organization and the diverse member interests, since interests set the requirements of the organizational structure. In fact there are probably few large formal organizations, whatever their purpose, which do not include, either as an integral part of their activities or as extraneous to those activities, some recreational functions.

A second aspect of the structure of large formal organizations is the division of labor. This is made possible by the larger membership and is demanded by the requirements of achievement set by the nature of voluntary participation. At the highest level, some members are leaders and some are followers. In the chapter on power and leadership it was seen that leadership roles themselves are specialized, with some roles being those of executive, planner, harmonizer, and so on. Membership roles are likewise divided as to special talents and characteristics. The artist in the membership list, the hard workers, the expert on some narrow subject all are used at some time to achieve organizational objectives.

Another variable on which large formal organizations are structured is the relationship among members. This permeates all other relations. In one organization, leader-member relations will be rigidly patterned, while in another they may be casual and informal. Members themselves may have to follow certain patterns of relationships, quite formalized, within the organization meeting. They may, in addition, be obligated to help each other more than they would help non-members outside of organization meetings. Certain ritualistic means of identification, such as a secret handshake, may be used to foster this mutual aid. Formalization of member-organizational relationships is a product of the age and size of the organization, by and large. Generally, when formal organizations reach this point they are approaching institutionalization.

The structuring of the formal organization may vary as to its temporary or relatively permanent character. Institutions almost never die, but formal organizations often do. In times of drastic change, institutions remain, but change, if slowly, with the times. On the other hand, particular formal organizations may almost completely disappear within a few years under conditions of rapid change in the environment. It is unlikely, however, that formal organization as such will ever disappear as an important element of community structure.

The relationship of the formal organizational structure to pan-community forces is also an important aspect of the community structure. The federation of clubs within a county or even on a national scope brings change to the community that perhaps would not occur if the rules and behavior patterns were determined entirely within the community.

The membership of the large formal organization is likely to be more heterogeneous than is true of informal groups, but the formal structuring of relationships itself depends upon some outstanding homegeneity, either in interest or in the definition of problems.

Large formal organization may have a subculture of its own value system which may at times vary from the total value system of the community. This is of little consequence, as these codes and objectives refer to relations within the organization. However, when they concern change in the community as, for example, in a community-wide citizens' council, the values may differ from those of the community itself and bring about problems of relationship between the organization and its community.

FUNCTIONS OF LARGE FORMAL ORGANIZATIONS

The concept of the community employed in this book involves the relationships among institutions, large formal organizations, small informal groups, and other subunits as elements of the community structure. Thus, part of community structure is the patterning of relationships between, say, the school and the family, or the school and the parent-teachers association, or the political institution and a clique group of power figures. If these relationships prohibit the changing, say, of the school by the PTA, or involve the control of the political institution in meeting problems by certain groups who desire to keep the status quo, the community structure may be characterized as sacred. In other communities, where change of one institution by another or by a group is encouraged, that is, where the value system calls for change, the community structure may be characterized as secular. What role does the large formal organization play in this total structure? What functions are assigned to it? The mechanisms through which these functions can be fulfilled were described in the section on structure. It remains to see the relationship between large formal organizations and the rest of the community structure. This relationship can be described by listing the functions as relationships between organizations and groups, institutions and the like.

Supplementing the Institutional Framework

The first function of large formal organizations follows from its source of origin. The value system defined the problems or goals in human activity and these are sought by means also prescribed in the value system, which then become patterns of human activity and are given a high value in the system. These activities on areas of problems are assigned to the institutions. But institutions, because they are so heavily endowed with prescribed goals and means, may not be flexible enough to change with the changing nature of the problems. Thus the first function of the large formal organization is to supplement and assist the institution in solving the problems assigned to it. The educational institution, as it operates in classrooms certain hours of the day, cannot solve the problem of the need for continual education which grows out of the rapidly changing times. As a result, organizations come into being to supplement the work of the school in this respect. If this organization works well as defined by the value system, and if the problem persists, then it is either integrated into the educational institution, as happens in the case of the night class, or it becomes institutionalized as a separate but closely related institution, as occurs in the case of the agricultural extension service, the evening college, and similar institutions.

Meeting New Problems

A second function of the large formal organization also follows from the relationship between the value system and the institutional framework of the community. Not only is the institution tied down by prescribed means in solving its assigned problems in changing times, but qualitatively new problems arise. For example, the development of better means of transportation has allowed youth to escape from its home community and the resultant social control of gossip, so that youth is required to behave only within the limits of the formal social control imposed by the legal structure of the community. This places a heavier burden upon the socialization agencies, since the need for internalization of the value system is greater. Thus, delinquency is increasing and neither the family, the government, nor the school alone is capable of coping with the problem. Relations among these three institutions have not been so defined as to allow unified action. As a result a new formal patterning of relations occurred through such organizations as youth commissions (legal-family relations). As time passes, these organizations in between two or three institutions may be integrated into one of the institutions or become separate institutions. We can generalize these two functions in that they make the institutions more responsive to the needs defined in the total community. Organizations achieve this through assistance, supplementary work, and pressure.[6]

Recreational Function

A third function of the large formal organization is recreational. In this relationship to institutions, the large formal organization may exist within the institution, as a bowling league in a business, or this function may be achieved as a part of the activities of an organization that is entirely separate from institutions, such as the recreation hour in a sewing club. Then, too, it may be a recreation-oriented organization entirely outside the framework of an institution, such as a hobby club. In any event, this recreational function of organizations competes with the economic institution and commercialized entertainment.

If we assume interests to cause rather than be elicited by formal organizations, institutions would have great difficulty trying to satisfy all the diverse interests represented by formal organizations. For example, Kolb and Brunner list the number of organizations by type for the rural farm population. Parent-teachers associations, farmers' clubs, community clubs, 4-H clubs, homemakers' clubs, cooperative associations, spray rings, breeders' associations, horticultural societies, and shipping and producers' associations are listed. These certainly do not exhaust the list even in a rural farm society, and are greatly added to when other occupational strata are included in the population. By type of interest, Kolb and Brunner list social enjoyment, better farming, helping school and teacher, better business, youth interests, health and social welfare, home improvement, public and

---

[6] Buckman identified thirteen techniques used by clubs to influence institutions (and vise versa):
(1) Let them alone.
(2) Cooperate with them.
(3) Ask for what we want.
(4) Bring pressure through friends and superiors.
(5) Impress and thereby influence them.
(6) Give them a job to do and recognition for it.
(7) Tie them to regulations and "channels."
(8) Bring out the voters on our side.
(9) Absorb some of the leaders in the group.
(10) Remove their leaders.
(11) Stage a slow-down strike.
(12) Dictate to them—lay down the law.
(13) Employ sanctions—make life uncomfortable for them.
Rilma O. Buckman, *Interaction Between Women's Clubs and Institutions in Greater Lafayette, Indiana,* Unpublished Doctoral Dissertation, University of Chicago, 1952 (microfilm), p. 162.

civic affairs, community betterment, helping church, and so on. This indicates the diversity of interests served by formal organizations. It should be noted that the classification scheme is heuristic, but that in the real world the diversity is much greater than indicated by it. For example, youth interests alone could be subdivided into many types.[7]

Insofar as the large formal organization results from value conflicts within the community, it gives, on the one hand, concrete expression to these conflicts, and on the other, serves to integrate conflict through promoting compromise with other elements in the community. A taxpayers' association and a parents' group may have conflicting interests on the issue of increased public support of education, and through the organized effort of both groups it may be possible to reach a compromise fairly satisfactory to both sides.

Another function of the large formal organization results from the fact that political and educational institutions are limited by relatively arbitrary boundaries. Problems associated with these institutions that cross the lines of legal jurisdiction of the institution can be and are attacked by the large formal organization. While these organizations are usually locality-bound, they are also capable of adjusting to the fluctuating community boundaries and of crossing over the limiting and arbitrary legal boundary.

Large formal organizations also serve as channels to communicate individual opinions and needs to the controlling forces in the community structure. This is achieved in two ways: In the first place, the isolated individual cannot influence the power structure of the political, educational, and economic institutions because there is no channel through which he may contact persons in these structures. He exercises only a vague influence through his vote in the case of political institutions, and through his purchases in the case of the economic institution. These are generalized reactions, however, and are not expressions of reaction to a given aspect of the governmental policy or the product. However, through the formal organization he may present his argument, elicit support, and receive attention from the power structure.

In some cases, he may find that there are already many people of like mind. This is the second way in which the large formal organization serves as a communication channel. It tells others to some extent the number of individuals concerned with a given problem. Of course this also may be misleading, since the power group of a given organization may report its own opinions as representing organizational opinions.

In either communication or pressure, the large formal organization provides protection for freedom of expression through the operation of the old

---

[7] John H. Kolb and Edmund deS. Brunner, *A Study of Rural Society*, Houghton-Mifflin Company, Boston, 1952, Chapter 15.

axiom that there is safety in numbers. Not only is there safety but strength in numbers, and 100 persons individually expressing complaints not only run more risk of retaliatory action, but are less effective as individuals in gaining response to their complaints than through organized communication and pressure.

Another function of large organizations involves adult education. In this respect, organizations operate on three levels: the education of the membership about the organization; the education of members about the community and its problems; and the education of the community about the organization and its role in the life of the community. Few, if any, organizations recognize adult education *per se* as one of their functions. The degree to which an organization recognizes adult education as a function depends upon the realization that it is necessary to implement organizational objectives. Thus, adult education becomes a means rather than an end in itself. Organizations will utilize adult education when it becomes necessary to educate the membership or the community about organizational objectives, but very few organizations actually conduct educational activities for the sake of education.

Organizations vary considerably as to whether their educational activities are directed toward their membership primarily or toward the community at large. Some organizations conduct various kinds of cultural events and programs for the community. Other organizations, particularly business and professional associations, carry on educational programs to familiarize the public with the services provided by their members. Every organization conducts educational activities of some kind designed to improve the internal processes of the organization through membership education. Such educational activities are rarely as extensive or valuable as many organizations insist.

The scope and objectives of adult education activities of organizations reflect the dominant value systems of both their leadership and membership. The methods, content, and procedures followed by organizations in developing educational activities is determined by the patterns of organization within the association. Any educational activities developed within associations must be directly related to the perception of the mission of the local association that is held by its leadership.

SOCIAL PARTICIPATION

Since membership in large formal organizations is more voluntary in nature than is participation in most of the substructures of the community, it is important to see whose interests and problems are likely to be taken up by such organizations. This is especially important in predicting the elements of community structure from the nature of large formal organizations and for seeing the dimensions of the community as they operate in these organizations.

Most authors agree that the concept of community development implies a broad participation by members of the community.[8] In fact, the concept of community development may be identified with or measured by the participation base. Similarly, the concept of democracy is more directly measured by social participation than by any other single variable, provided a wider view of participation is taken than mere attendance at meetings of formal organizations.

Social participation includes many aspects, each of which is important to community structure and change. Chapin [9] pointed out five of these in constructing a scale for the measurement of participation. From low to high they are: membership, attendance at meetings, financial contributions, membership on committees, and leadership positions. To these may be added several other important dimensions, such as the contribution in time and effort to the work of the organization. This, of course, is measured in part by the upper three levels of the Chapin Scale, but there is considerable variation at any given level of the scale. Much of the work of organizations is done outside of committees and, further, a leader or committee worker may take his job quite seriously or do only the minimum amount of work.

Another dimension of social participation not measured by the Chapin Scale is that of the participation of individuals in the affairs at a meeting. It is one thing to have regular attendance at meetings and quite another to have true group participation in decision-making. Group decisions require discussion involving most of the members of any organization with particular attention paid to the expression of minority opinions. Quite often this process is confused with voting. Voting itself may be the result of group discussion and group decision, but not a replacement for it. A leader may be effective although quite authoritarian and persuade his followers to vote favorably for his own decision. Thus, it may be that every decision by the group results from voting, which is not necessarily a decision reached democratically.

[8] For example, see Benne, Brownell, and Hallenbeck, "Participation for Democracy," in *Planning Better Programs*, Adult Education Association of the United States, Chicago, 1955, pp. 41–47; Hurley H. Doddy, *Informal Groups and the Community*, Bureau of Publications, Columbia University, New York, 1952; Wilbur C. Hallenbeck, "The Problem of Participation," *Teachers College Record*, 52:232–38, 1951.

[9] F. Stuart Chapin, *The Social Participation Scale*, University of Minnesota Press, Minneapolis, 1937, and "Social Participation and Social Intelligence," *ASR*, 4:157–66, 1939.

Still another important dimension of participation is that of overlapping membership. If there is a heavy overlap in membership so that there are several people in attendance at one organization who also will attend meetings of other organizations, it is more likely that decisions will be reached which are in substantial agreement with those of other organizations. This overlap in membership has not been studied sufficiently, but it can be quite important in community development programs using a community-wide council that must fit into the existing organizational structure of the community.

One of the most important consequences of a broad participation base is the wise representation of opinion that is available in such a situation. This is particularly important when one considers minority opinion. If minority opinion is expressed and considered before a decision is reached, then the decision is more apt to be a compromise without which the decision might otherwise meet strong resistance from minority groups in the community. Of course, the other facet of this point is that minorities will be protected against programs which might work a hardship on their ambitions and goals.

Research has shown also that conformity to a decision is greater when the decision is made by the group, rather than imposed on it. Interest increases as each person feels his own involvement in the decision, and similarly, his agreement with the conclusion is more likely. A broader participation base, furthermore, will bring to any given organization, such as a community council, a greater number of human resources to use in achieving the goal. It is obvious, of course, that leaders are not necessarily competent in all areas, and specialized talents can be drawn from a broad sampling of community members as they are needed.

A tremendous amount of evidence has been compiled showing that participants in large formal organizations come mainly from middle and higher status groupings. Compared to nonparticipants, the members and those who attend meetings in large formal organizations have a higher educational attainment, have higher incomes, come from white collar rather than blue collar jobs, and have a higher level of living. Since the value orientations of individuals vary according to this status, the greater participation found among higher status groups means that the kinds of problems defined in higher status subcultures will be those most likely to receive attention from large formal organizations.

Organizations are for solving problems, and as such one of their most important functions is social change. However, the kinds of changes produced by the solution to the particular kinds of problems defined in these organizations is likely merely to adjust the status quo rather than bring drastic changes in community structure. Higher status people are not likely to approach problems nor find solutions which would upset a structure in which their success and achievement are relatively secured. The risk of losing status in a new order will prevent the higher status members of the large formal organization from promoting drastic changes in community structure. This is reinforced by the fact that the positions of leadership in large formal organizations are filled generally by persons of even higher status in the community than are the members. Thus it may be seen that conservatism is likely, since members come more often from middle and higher status positions, and leaders from still higher positions. Large formal organizations, then, produce more stability than disruption as a result of the relationship between participation and status.

Factors Associated with Participation

In the many studies of social participation one consistent finding has been the positive association of formal participation rates with certain variables that are measures of socioeconomic status. The relationship between these variables and participation rates will differ from one community to another, so that status variables that appear to be most significant in one community may be least significant in another.

In urban communities occupation is a major determinant of both rates and types of formal participation. This is less applicable to rural areas where there is less differentiation by occupation; therefore, the rates of participation are less uniform among occupation types, but the type of association is uniform. Thus we find that business, professional, and civic organizations involve those from professional and managerial occupations chiefly; labor unions draw from skilled and semiskilled; and farm organizations involve farmers and businessmen in market towns. Some organizations such as fraternal, veteran, or church-related draw their membership from all occupation types.

Income is related to participation, but this probably results from the increased status that income brings and the fact that low income would probably indicate longer working hours and therefore less time to participate. Certainly income cannot be taken alone to indicate participation rates.

Educational levels are highly significant in the extent, intensity, and pattern of participation. Participation increases with education, but beyond the high school level the increase is greatest in nonchurch-related organizations. Organizational leadership tends to be heavily concentrated among the better educated in the community. Effective participation obviously requires communicative and human relational skills which must be learned; hence those who are better educated would be better equipped for participation.

Place of residence in the community influences participation to some extent. People who live in neighborhoods with high participation will be more active in organizations. The importance of neighborhoods tends to increase with residential segregation, but with increased urbanization the neighborhood grows less important and consequently tends to counteract this influence.

Participation in formal associations is generally low for young adults, increasing sharply in the late twenties and early thirties, remaining fairly constant to about age fifty, and then declining slowly until age sixty, when the rate of decrease accelerates rapidly.

Differences in participation between the sexes are related to other variables. Socioeconomic status seems to affect the participation of women more than men. Women tend to be more active in church-related associations than men and less active in nonchurch-related organizations. Women will go to more meetings but men will be members of more organizations.

Married persons are generally more active participants than single people. Parents of school age children are generally more active than any other group. Family patterns of participation tend to be repetitive in that children whose parents are active participants tend to be more active.

Length of residence in a community influences participation but, of course, there will be wide variations among communities as to the length of time required before new residents are accepted in the community. This time element is a reliable index of the adjustment of migrants to the new community environment.

The Nonparticipant

The number of nonparticipants in any given community varies from study to study, from ½ to about 5 per cent. Probably this variation is due in part to the number of organizations studied, but much of it may be due to differences in the loyalty and involvement found in the community itself. There are some consequences of nonparticipation which are important for community structure and change as well as community development. For one thing, it is believed that nonparticipation not only results from but brings about greater apathy and indifference.[10] Some authors also feel that not only does apathy arise in many cases, but frustration and the inability to overcome difficulties through organized activities bring about

[10] Benne *et al., op. cit.*

more critical or negative opinions toward programs designed to solve the problems of the community. It is true, of course, that no one program can completely solve a problem, and negative opinions toward such programs probably result from an overemphasis on the deficiencies of the program. It is also sometimes suggested that nonparticipation can encourage dependency, so that when decisions are habitually left to others, this forms the habit or inability to make any decision involving the community. This likewise is associated with a mass escape into commercialized entertainment where emotional satisfactions are obtained from recreational rather than community-oriented activity.

Trends in Participation

It is extremely difficult to assess the trends in participation in American society. On the one hand, it is well known that there are many more specialized organizations available now than formerly. It is not known whether there are more nonparticipants among the citizenry than was formerly the case. There are, however, certain indications that there are factors operating in American communities which may work to decrease the amount of democratic decision in community problems.

One of the most important general trends which may be diminishing the amount of general participation, particularly as it applies to group decision, is that of specialization, or the value of relying on the expert. This is particularly so in certain areas of life such as areas of health, education, and personal conflict, where reliance is placed upon physicians, teachers, and attorneys, respectively. Part of this, of course, is due to the complexity of American society, where a greater amount of specialized knowledge is needed to solve the problems facing communities. Insofar as the expert is allowed to make the decision, rather than being used as a resource person helping a group make the decision, this of course represents a weakening of the democratic position. An interesting result of this specialization in the affairs of the community is the movement from a direct to a republican form of democratic decision-making. This, of course, has always been true on the national scene, but it is expanding to include the operation of many institutions such as the school and the church. In this way decisions are not made on a broad membership basis, for the authority to make a decision is delegated to someone who is considered to represent the values of the membership. While this is not assessed here as good or bad, it does represent a trend away from democratic action. To some extent this is the result of the increasing size and complexity of American communities. There is an undetermined optimum size beyond which it is difficult—if not impossible—for the membership of the community to meet together to make decisions on matters of common interest.

Another trend in American society is that crucial problems are no longer purely local in nature and origin, so that many of them are solved at a higher level than before. Formerly, problems relating to local schools, road building, public health, and so forth were solved almost entirely by local units; today, with federal aid to welfare services, Supreme Court decisions on segregation, and federal aid on road building, as well as the new types of roads being built, these decisions are being made more and more at levels higher than the local community. Again, without attempting to assess this trend as good or bad, it may be pointed out that it represents a less democratic basis for decisions. It also represents consideration of other groups in other communities with a broader area of problems involved in a solution of any one problem.

Commercial entertainment is another factor that influences participation rates. While participation may be influenced primarily by an intrinsic interest in community welfare, it is encouraged also by the sociability occurring at meetings. With the increased use of television, radio, and cinema, however, the entertainment aspects of participation are less influential, with the result that individuals may choose recreation in preference to duty as citizens. This decline in the sociability function performed by community meetings has contributed to the declining interest in participation. To counteract this trend, most organizations now depend upon interesting and entertaining programs to attract the membership to the meeting because the pull of duty and citizen responsibility are not alone sufficient to insure participation.

On the other hand, such broad mass media as television and movies are increasing the awareness of what is being done in other communities and are probably having a leveling affect on American culture and values. Thus, not only are the goals and the means of other communities influencing those who are the audience or viewers of the mass media, but precedence or experience is exchanged much more broadly than before in solving community problems.

The authors do not mean to imply from the above that the trend is definitely downward in terms of participation, but they do suggest that these factors probably operate to decrease participation, and if there are any canceling factors which may keep broad participation in community activities, they are very subtle factors which have not been studied to any great extent. This holds true despite the increase in special interest groupings.

While the number of organizations is increasing, these are highly specialized and often have little to do with community action.

PRINCIPLES

1. *The large formal organization arises in response to needs which are not satisfied through the institutional framework of the community.*

2. *One type of need results from the relationship between institutions and social change.*

The advent of new associations from time to time indicates that as new social problems are recognized, associations come into being to resolve them. Thus, formal organizations help reduce the lag between the needs of society that are undergoing rapid change and the adaptability of institutions to meet those changing needs. There are many illustrations of ways in which organizations mobilize community resources to meet emergency situations to which the institutional structure is unable to respond quickly.

3. *In another way, organizations perform an "adhesive function" in that they serve to harmonize and adjust the relationships between the institutions and the community at large.*

Through institutionally related associations, the institution is personalized and "humanized," although such associations play a very subordinate role in the parent institution.

4. *Organizations have recreation as either a manifest or a latent function.*

5. *Organizations pass through a life cycle, including stimulation, purpose, form, and shifts in form due to the necessity of adapting, and then either decline or become institutionalized.*

6. *Organizations often express the interests of middle and higher status groupings because of selective participation.*

SELECTED REFERENCES

Baxter, Bernice, and Rosalind Cassidy, *Group Experience—The Democratic Way*, Harper and Brothers, New York, 1943.

Brunner, Edmund deS., David S. Wilder, Corinne Kirchner, and John S. Newberry, Jr., *An Overview of Adult Education Research*, Adult Education Assoc. Chicago, 1959, Chapters 6 and 13.

Chapin, F.S., *Contemporary American Institutions*, Harper and Brothers, New York, 1933.

Gerth, H.H., and C. Wright Mills, *From Max Weber: Essays in Sociology*, Oxford University Press, New York, 1946, Chapters 4, 8–10.

Kolb, John H., and LeRoy J. Day, "Interdependence in Town and Country Relations in Rural Society," *University of Wisconsin AES Research Bulletin 172*, 1950.

Kolb, J.H., and A.F. Wileden, "Special Interest Groups in Rural Society," *University of Wisconsin AES Research Bulletin 84*, 1927.

MacIver, R.M., "The Multi-Group Society," in *The Web of Government*, The Macmillan Company, New York, 1947.

Merton, Robert K., Ailsa P. Gray, Barbara Hockey, and Hanan C. Selvin, *Reader in Bureaucracy*, the Free Press, Glencoe, Illinois, 1952.

Payne, Raymond, "Organizational Activities of Rural Negroes in Mississippi," *Mississippi State College AES Circular 192*, 1953.

Sanders, Irwin T., *The Community*, The Ronald Press Company, New York, 1958, Chapter 7.

Sanderson, Dwight, "Group Description," *Social Forces*, 16:309–19, 1938.

Sanderson, Dwight, and Robert A. Polson, *Rural Community Organization*, John Wiley and Sons, New York, 1939, Chapter 11.

Vidich, Arthur J., and Joseph Bensman, *Small Town in Mass Society*, Princeton University Press, Princeton, New Jersey, 1958, Chapter 10.

CHAPTER 13

Family-Community Relations

The relationship of the family and the community may be described in five general ways: first, the structure of the family influences the way in which the community behaves and limits the ways the community can change. Second, the family as an institution has the task of fulfilling certain social needs. When the family fails to fulfill these needs, community action may be necessary to do so. Third, the family is an institution and the community is not; therefore, the potential competition between family and community may always be expected to involve less change in the family than in the community. Fourth, the family may be an important influence for deliberate community change, provided family structure and function are fully understood by community leaders. Finally, community structure limits and serves as a resource in family functions.

FAMILY STRUCTURE

The Nucleated Family

One of the most obvious features of family structure in the United States today is that aunts, uncles, and in recent years, grandparents no longer live in the home. This is referred to as the *nucleated family,* as opposed to the extended family, which includes most of the relatives from either the female or male line of the family through several generations. The relationship of this aspect of the family to community structure and change has not been studied to any great extent. Perhaps the most important influence of this aspect of family structure on the community is that a closely knit extended family is a strong deterrent to the development of the community. Indeed, the extended family may perform the same functions that the community does in a society where the family is nucleated. This may also extend to the point where the extended family appropriates the identification and loyalty which are so important to community development.

One manner in which the extended family may interfere with community

259

development is illustrated by George E. Spencer from an experience in the Near East.°

In the Near East a community development project had been selected on the basis of a survey of rural schools. Over a period of twenty-five years, these schools had institutionalized the idea of school gardens as a means to implement functional education. Representatives of the ministry of education, and the local school teachers, in discussions with the village had decided to establish a poultry unit as a project in which the villagers too would participate. The unit was to be built on the local school grounds where it could supplement the school garden in teaching agriculture and at the same time supply at cost improved poultry stock for the students' home projects. A detailed estimate of the total cost and budget were prepared. These costs were prorated among the agencies involved, including the community.

When the project was less than half finished, it was found that labor costs were exceeding the original estimates by nearly 100 per cent. This particular item in the total budget was assumed by an agency outside the village in order to stimulate the local economy. Representatives of the agency were concerned about the high cost of labor since this project was an experiment with implications for future community development projects.

Upon investigation, one of the village intelligentsia found that competition between families for the "ready cash" provided by the project had created a practice of "slow down," and this was the cause of the increased labor costs. In seeking a solution to the problem this native suggested: "Get a head master of the school to hold a conference which includes the elder member of each of the four families which comprise this village. Have him remind them of the moral obligation they have assumed in accepting the responsibility for the project. Tell them that this authority was delegated to them by governmental officials who could have given it by contract to outside interests. Assure them that the success of their project will be pointed to by other villages as an example of what can be accomplished without intervention by outside supervisors."

The fact that subsequent work was completed within the estimated budget substantiated the hypotheses implicit in the advice on this particular occasion. The principles were also verified in subsequent community development projects.

Not only is the principle of family-community conflict found in this story, but always the importance of a full understanding of the role of family organization in community development is indicated. That the situation is not hopeless, when at first the interests of community development and those of the family seem to contradict one another, is apparent from the sequence of events related by Spencer.

Authority

The seat of authority within the family is another feature of family structure which is of considerable importance to community organization and

° Written especially for this book.

development. In some societies, and in the United States until recent years, the male head of the family holds or held almost complete authority over actions of every other member of the family as well as over the family as a unit. Historically, societies have existed where the family members were explicitly recognized as the property of the male head. In other societies, fewer in number, the oldest female exercises similar authority. In the United States the democratic family, in which all adult members of the family have equal influence in family decisions, is generally considered to be ideal, but this is probably far from realization in actual fact and may not even be acceptable to most of the population. It is only in recent years that the vows for the female marriage partner have omitted the expression, "love, cherish, and obey."

The empirical situation may be understood as it varies from or approaches extreme and logical types. In a study in rural New York, Sanderson and Foster [1] were able to isolate two distinct types of family structure which illustrate how various characteristics seem to go together by type. In the first type, referred to here as the "authoritarian," decisions are made by the male head; child-parent affection is divided between the parents as individuals; family labor is assigned with particular tasks for particular people (division of labor); few activities are conducted within the home; and there is infrequent individual or family unit participation outside the home. This latter point is of particular importance in those instances where community development programs involve the authoritarian family, since participation of women is low in such situations.

The second type of family described by Sanderson and Foster may be described as the democratic family. This type is characterized by the participation of all family members in the making of decisions; the affection of children is given to parents undivided as individuals; a division of labor is accepted but not assigned; there are many activities within the home, and there is active participation in community organizations.

Family Participation

The problem of increasing participation is directly related to the authority structure of the family. Knowing the explicit authority structure is not always sufficient information to diagnose the situation with respect to participation. A study made by Anderson in New York illustrates this point, and brings out an important principle of both theoretical and practical importance. Using rather complicated and rigorous statistical techniques, Ander-

---

[1] Dwight Sanderson and Robert G. Foster, "A Sociological Case Study of Farm Families," *The Family*, 11:107–14, 1930.

son found that of all individual members of the family, the mother's participation in formal organizations is most highly correlated with the participation of the other members of the family. Unfortunately, this important study has not been replicated in other areas to verify this fact sufficiently to permit generalization.*

The First Approach to Obtain Family Participation Can Best Be Made Through Wives and Mothers

The suggestion that the social participation of the individual is largely the result of family participation practices and that there is stimulation to individual participation from the family pattern, leads to the question, "Do some family members exhibit this participation trait to a greater degree than others?" Organization workers who know which family members are the best participators can approach the problem of influencing the nonparticipating or partially participating family through this person.

Studies at Cornell show that the wife and mother is the most active organization participator of the family members, that daughters are next, sons next, and husbands and fathers last. This statistical conclusion that women, especially wives and mothers, show most interest in organizations and take the most responsibility for promoting them with other family members is in accord with practical experience.

If, then, it is desired to obtain more participation in community activities, the initial approach can best be made through wives and mothers. The promotion of local community activities which call for family action, such as participation in cooperatives, working in the Grange, the development of special interest programs for individual family members, such as 4-H Clubs, rural scouts, young adult activities, can obtain encouragement and promotion from these mothers. Their support and enthusiasm can be used to spread interest to all the family members.

Here a caution must be given. Because of the folkways in some regions, it is not possible to approach the wife in the family directly. Program promoters may find it necessary to make initial approaches to the husband. But they should develop the situation so the wife and mother will exert her influence in support of the program.

The findings of this study indicate not only that the woman's participation is crucial in the American family, but also that family member participation is a function of the family rather than the individual.[2] The importance of the woman's role in family participation may be due to a subtle influence exerted by women even in a male-dominated family. While the woman's

---

* W.A. Anderson, "Some Participation Principles; Their Relations to the Programs of Rural Agencies," *Cornell Extension Bulletin 731*, 1947.

[2] W.A. Anderson, "The Family and Individual Social Participation," *ASR*, 8:420–24, 1943.

subtle "manipulations" are often joked about by men in American society, the hypothesis of this type of influence by the subordinate marriage partner has not been tested sufficiently to draw a conclusion one way or the other. Whether this principle holds true in other than American communities is not known.

In a study conducted at Washington State University, the relationship between parental authority patterns and teenage adjustments was studied.[3] It was found that children from democratically controlled families were less anxious to migrate from the home community than those from non-democratic families; however, this was characteristic of children from urban rather than from rural areas. A high proportion of both boys and girls who had been reared in authoritarian families expressed an actual dislike of their home community. The investigations concluded that this was due, perhaps, primarily to the association of their family with the home community. Associating a lack of freedom with the community environment was probably influenced by the adolescent's attitude toward his community. It may be that in a culture where the authoritarian family is almost universal, this same influence is not felt.

One of the most striking findings of this research was that among farm girls from democratic families, approximately two-thirds expressed a feeling of loyalty to their community, while only half this proportion did so among those who had been reared in authoritarian families.

Another aspect of this family authority structure is that of willingness to accept change. This study found that a teenage youth's admiration for his parents was related to his family's authority structure, and indicated, in common with other studies of family roles, that the authoritarian family fosters a rebellious attitude in children. This indicated that, generally, children reared in democratic homes would "like to be like their parents," while this is less apt to be found true of children reared in authoritarian homes. It is believed that the child reared in a democratic home is usually better prepared to make decisions for himself, and this study indicates that these decisions will result from the values learned in the family.

It is a plausible inference, therefore, that change is more easily accepted by those individuals whose negative attitudes toward their families are generalized to negative attitudes toward all existing traditions. Furthermore, when the desire for change comes from those with rebellious attitudes, they are more apt to lean toward radical changes involving most of the elements in the structure.

[3] Paul H. Landis and Carol L. Stone, "The Relationship of Parental Authority Patterns to Teenage Adjustment," *Washington State AES Bulletin* 538, 1952.

The Broken Home

The broken home is a third aspect of family structure important to community development in industrial societies. The broken home is an important factor in determining the ability of the family to perform the functions of socializing the child. This is so whether the broken home results from divorce, desertion, or the death of one of the marriage partners. In recent years in the United States, it may be noted that approximately one in every five marriages ended in divorce.

The normal child in American society is one whose personality, attitudes, ideals, and adjustment patterns are influenced by the presence of both parents, with the father usually working and the mother at home all day. Thus, if one assumes the influence of both parents on the development of the child, the absence of one would produce different results. Both the assumption and the conclusion have been demonstrated adequately through research on child development.

A relatively clear-cut illustration of this principle is the problem of delinquency. This is of particular importance here because delinquency is a community problem. The child or adolescent who commits a delinquent act usually does so within his own community area, which has assumed some responsibility both for prevention, through recreational and other programs, and punishment, through its legal organization. Divorce or death of a parent seems to produce delinquent behavior more often than the complete family.[4]

PRINCIPLES OF FAMILY STRUCTURE AND COMMUNITY

1. *Family structure refers to relations among persons, positions, and sub-groups within the family.*

2. *The extended family is that type of family structure where aunts, uncles, cousins, and grandparents interact with the immediate family with a greater frequency and intimacy than is the case of the nucleated family, with all of them sometimes sharing the same domicile.*

3. *The extended family in some societies often performs the functions assumed by community organizations in other societies.*

[4] Paul W. Tappan, *Juvenile Delinquency*, McGraw-Hill Book Company, New York, 1949, Chapter 7. It has also been found that poor discipline in the home generally produces more delinquency. *Ibid.*, p. 137.

The basic institutions of economic production, education, worship, and social control may all be organized within the extended family, and the needs defined in such cultures may therefore be supplied largely by it.

4. *The extended family may often have the loyalty which otherwise might be shared by the community.*

As in the case related by Spencer, this loyalty to the extended family sometimes results in competition among families. This in turn inhibits the development of the cooperation so necessary to successful community development. Supra-family loyalties must be established so that each family will see that its individual welfare prospers as a result of cooperation among the families.

5. *In situations where the authority for family actions rests with a male (or female) head, cooperation with and participation in community development programs must be established in a different manner than where family decisions are made democratically.*

As Anderson indicates, participation is a family function even in a democratic society; therefore, the approach to the family for purposes of community development must be adapted to the authority pattern of the families involved.

6. *Broken homes, which produce abnormal children, may create problems for the community.*

The exact course of the abnormality taken may or may not be defined as "bad" by all cultures, but some of the behavior patterns of children from broken homes are undesirable from the point of view of American communities. Many community development activities in the area of social work have been directed at just such problem behavior.

FUNCTIONS OF THE FAMILY

The institution of the family performs two manifest functions. First, the society is perpetuated through the control of sexual relations so that children will be born into a setting where they will be cared for during the long period of dependence. During this time the children will be trained in and indoctrinated with the mores and folkways to which the parents subscribe. Thus, a society may be assured not only of a continuing membership in time but also of the preservation of its approved ways of doing things.

In addition to these two manifest functions, the family is the principal consuming unit in American society. It is the family which uses most of the material goods and nonmaterial services produced by the economic and political institutional organizations.

Another latent function of the family is that it relates its members to the larger society, giving the members status and fostering or discouraging social participation.

The change and development of community organization is dependent upon the process by which the family performs these functions perhaps even more, or at least in more ways, than it is upon family structure. The general relationship between community and family functions may be described in the following propositions:

(*a*) *Community development programs often are or could be in support of family functions.* When the family fails to develop conformity to the basic mores or fails to develop leadership ability in children, the community may substitute for the family through programs of delinquency prevention and leadership training. An example of this was the recent attempt by some schools in the United States to prevent mischief by delegating to the "bad boys" the responsibility for traffic control at busy school intersections. The Parent-Teachers Association, now widespread in the United States, is an example of a community organization that strengthens and supports the work of the school in substituting for certain functions of the family.

(*b*) *Community development programs must always supplement rather than contradict the process through which the family performs its functions.* The method of operations used by individual families must be fully understood by persons interested in community development lest the activities that tend to support the family functions actually conceal the success the family is already having.

(*c*) *The need for support should not be mistaken for the need to substitute the community for the family in performing a given function.* There are several reasons why this principle is more than simply a value judgment. First, it is assumed that the aim of community development is really to develop communities that can better serve the needs of people. This is usually achieved through the deliberate organization of the elements into a smoothly operating social system. Since much of this organization is already in existence in some form any change in existing patterns of organization must be examined carefully lest it foster changes in other aspects of the social system not intended originally. The family is a basic institution and most of the social structure has evolved in organization with already existing family functions. Any rapid change in the relationship between the family and existing community structure is therefore likely to create more problems of social disorganization than it solves.

Second, most of the functions remaining in the province of the family can be accomplished better by the family than by other structures. For example, the socialization of the child is more effective when it is done by those who have intimate acquaintance, love, and continuing contact with him which is most likely to be found within his family group. Efforts on the part of other elements of the social system to perform this function meet with difficulties resulting from the impersonality of the relationship established with the child.

Third, while the institution of the family is not "organized" in the formal sense as is a labor union or an association of business men, it does have those aspects that provide stability and continuity. This results from two factors: first, the institutional nature of the family gives it stability in the culture, and second, as most individuals are members of a family unit, they protect it against other interests. When community development programs appear as an attempt to usurp the functions reserved to the family, the program will likely meet with very strong opposition.

Perpetuation of the Group

The replacement of members of the society is dependent upon a family type of unit because of the prolongation of human helplessness after birth. If promiscuity were allowed, the care of children through the helpless stage would not be assured. Likewise, any behavior which weakens the family is disapproved.

More attention has been given to the closely related topic of the birth rate itself. Three general problems have been associated with this topic: overpopulation in countries such as those in Southeast Asia, underpopulation in countries such as Ireland and France, and the quality of the population.

The problem of overpopulation immediately attracts the attention of persons interested in community change. Most foreign community development programs are located in countries where overpopulation accompanied by a low level of living is considered to be the main problem. While much of the work to raise the level of living and decrease population density is not truly community development, it is closely related. Certainly from the point of view of the influence of mass society on the community, overpopulation and low level of living are factors influencing community change and development.

The low level of living characteristic of many countries is attributed directly to population density. It is possible that there is an optimum population per unit of resources, although this has not been computed with any degree of accuracy.[5] From the standpoint of the community, the most important aspect of this problem is the effects one may expect to result from a program of action to reduce the population density.

Industrialization is often considered to be a causal factor in the decrease of population, but there is no evidence to indicate that this is necessarily true. In the first place, the level of living tends to increase as industrialization brings higher wages. Mortality rates decline as a result of better health care and a greater number of physicians, so that fewer babies die either at birth or during the first years. Second, people live longer as a result of the better health and nutritional care associated with industry, and as a result over-population will continue. Third, longevity of life has increased among the older age groups owing to the same factors. Thus, as the level of living and industrialization increases, the overpopulation or the population density is also likely to increase, especially in the short run. Over a period of time, industrialization in the past has had a deterrent effect on population growth.

While this problem has not been studied sufficiently to draw any ironclad conclusions, it appears that the factor which is most important in decreasing the birth rate sufficiently to decrease the population pressure is that of education. Birth control, while it is against the mores in some countries, tends to follow education and therefore is considerably longer in coming to a society than is industrialization and level of living. The sequence appears to run something like this: First the level of living is increased and there is increased desire for items pertaining to a higher level of living. This makes possible programs of industrialization which in turn bring more money, more leisure time, and still higher aspirations. The last three variables in turn seem to bring about a greater desire for formal education and for recreational life. These two in turn change the value toward having children and encourage birth control methods and therefore reduce the population density.[6]

Another process that follows the sequence from increase of level of living to decrease in population pressure is that of the system of organization for population replacement within urban communities. In American society, as urban communities have increased in number and size, the personnel to fill the necessary jobs came from the rural communities. Rural communities usually produce a greater population than is needed to maintain stability and this results in a tremendous rural-to-urban migration. Such population movement has solved the problems of labor supply for urban communities to a

[5] For example, Ogburn found no relationship between level of living and density; see William F. Ogburn, "Population, Private Ownership, Technology, and the Standard of Living," *AJS*, 56:314–19, 1951.

[6] Joseph J. Spengler and Otis D. Duncan, editors, *Population Theory and Policy*, the Free Press, Glencoe, Illinois, 1956, Parts 5–8.

great extent and urban families tend to a lower birth rate. The crowded, compact conditions of family living in an urban center are less suited to large families than are conditions in rural areas, so that urban families tend to limit family size to that which can be accommodated and sustained conveniently in the urban home.

Migration has also brought problems of heterogeneity to the urban community and of adjustment to a different environment for the migrant. Although this rural-to-urban migration is still occurring in the United States, a countertrend is found in the increased movement of city workers to the suburbs—usually a forty mile radius from the urban center.

Another factor of considerable importance to community change and development results from the differential birth rate with respect to social status. Traditionally, in American society the upper status groupings have not replaced themselves while those groups on a lower status level have had birth rates far in excess of replacement needs. Thus, the upper status groupings have had to depend upon selectivity in upward social mobility from the lower status groupings for replacement. While this in itself is an important area of study, its main implication for community change and development is the effect that it has upon the course community action will take. This relationship has two features: the first is the conformity to traditional norms of the socially mobile person, and the second is the problem of the quality of the population. From the standpoint of community development, this matter of quality is of importance because of the need for leadership.

The differential birth rate with respect to status groupings leads to the conclusion that the community average in respect to the talent and ability of the population will decline if one assumes that those of lower status have less talent and ability than those of upper status. This assumes further that the family transmits, either through genetics or training, the talents and ability necessary for leadership in the community.

American social scientists have never determined whether or not the quality of the American population is decreasing. Duncan considers the various techniques social scientists have used in attempting to determine if there is a trend in any direction concerning the quality of the population, but he concludes that it is still a moot point as to whether the quality of the population is declining. He arrives at his conclusion because of the fact that the generalizations made in the original research studies are based on, as he calls it, a "hypothetical construct twice removed from direct observation." [7]

In any event, the short-range view of the declining talents and ability of

[7] Otis D. Duncan, "Is the Intelligence of the General Population Declining?" *ASR*, 17:401–7, 1952.

the population due to a differential birth rate need not cause alarm. Leadership talents as well as specialized talents and abilities in community development appear to be more or less random with respect to cultures. What is probably more important is that leadership ability, while it is not fully understood, is probably much more extensive than that actually used in community development programs today.

The Function of Perpetuating the Culture

A second major problem of a society is the perpetuation through oncoming generations of beliefs, values, mores, folkways, and customs that are treasured by the culture. To a large extent, this function traditionally has been left to the family. While in American society other institutions perform part of this function, the family is still the primary institution influencing a person's ideals, religion, politics, and allegiances as well as his personal adjustment to the community. The school provides him with much of the knowledge of the world that is necessary to solve the problems he will meet throughout his life; nevertheless, the family still is the institution in which he learns the language, is disciplined to obedience, and is encouraged or discouraged in his levels of aspirations. It is in the family that the child receives his first orientation to the value system of his society.

Orientation to the value system by the family includes not only the transfer of ideals and folkways, but also the conditions under which the child is most likely to begin his adjustment to the many limitations imposed upon him by society. In this way the child begins to acquire the elements that determine his social adjustment in the formative years and throughout life.

Perhaps as much effort in the last century has gone into understanding the socialization of the child as into any other aspect of sociology. One theory which has gained wide acceptance among scholars is that of the influence of infant training practices.[8] This theory holds that the way in which the family influences the adjustment of the child is through bowel training, weaning, and similar kinds of infant training. Of course, such training represents the first important adjustments the child must make to his culture, but the theory insists that since such adjustments are made in the most formative period of life, the way in which this training is accomplished becomes a major influence in the adjustment of the individual to problems and situations which he encounters in later life.

This, the neo-Freudian theory, has been severely attacked on scientific

[8] For a summary of literature see Harold Orlansky, "Infant Care and Personality," *Psychological Bulletin*, 46:1–48, 1949.

grounds. First, Harold Orlansky summarized the scientific evidence and con- cluded that there was nothing to support it; [9] then William H. Sewell de- signed a study to test the theory.[10] The theory maintains that differences in adjustment result from these weaning practices regardless of any sociocul- tural differences. Sewell kept these sociocultural differences constant by studying only children of white, old American families in a rural area of Wisconsin, which added validity to his test of the theory. He found no re- lationship between the adjustment of individuals and their early weaning and bowel training. Scientific caution would lead most sociologists to with- hold judgment, yet the theory has been discarded by most as inadequate and of little use.

A second theory of socialization is that of "symbolic interaction," which stems from the work of George Herbert Mead [11] and Charles Horten Cooley.[12] This theory maintains that personal adjustment, including the internalization of folkways and mores, is influenced by the face-to-face inter- action that occurs between members of small groups. Furthermore, the most important such group is the family, although at particular periods in the development of the individual the playgroup (treated here as the in- formal group) and the neighborhood are also of primary importance.

This theory too, has been subjected to much testing and the results of such studies generally tend to support it. One study by Leland H. Stott il- lustrates this theory of how the family solves the problem of socializing the child. It was done in Nebraska in the late 1930's and was one of the earlier rigorous tests of the symbolic interaction theory. In his conclusion Stott wrote:

1. When all the correlations were taken into consideration, the homelife factors, grouped roughly according to their importance, were:
    a. Those which involved to the greatest extent the activities, participation, and person-to-person interaction of the youngsters themselves. Some of the items of this group were: an attitude of welcome on the part of parents toward the child's friends in the home, having enjoyable times together in the home as a family group (playing games, music, stories, etc.), frequency of punishment, and affec- tionate and confidential relationships with parents.
    b. Those items concerned with the activities and the health, physical and emo- tional, of the parents, such as the extent to which the mother participated in the work outside the home, the amount of nervousness, as judged by the youngster, in mother and father, and illness of parents.

[9] *Ibid.*
[10] William H. Sewell, "Infant Training and Personality of the Child," *AJS*, 58:150–59, 1952.
[11] George H. Mead, *Mind, Self and Society*, University of Chicago Press, Chicago, 1950.
[12] Charles H. Cooley, *Human Nature and the Social Order*, Charles Scribner's Sons, New York, 1902.

c. The physical aspects of the home environment, i.e, the economic level of the family.[13]

In addition, he listed the factors influencing the adjustment of boys and girls:

. . . some of the more important characteristics of the successful farm family from the standpoint of the personal development of the boy and of the girl, according to the results of this study, are roughly in the order of their importance as follows:

Boy	*Girl*
1. An attitude of welcome on the part of parents toward the child's friend in the home.	1. An attitude of welcome on the part of parents toward the child's friends in the home.
2. Frequently to have enjoyable times together in the home as a family group.	2. Infrequent punishment.
3. Infrequent punishment.	3. Nothing in the behavior of the mother which she particularly dislikes.
4. An affectionate relationship between the boy and his mother (expressed by frequently kissing the mother).	4. A minimum of participation of the mother in the work outside the home.
5. A minimum of nervousness manifested in the mother.	5. A confidential relationship between the girl and her father.
6. A minimum of nervousness in father.	6. An affectionate relationship between the girl and her mother (frequently kisses mother).
7. Nothing in the behavior of the mother which he particularly dislikes.	7. A confidential relationship between the girl and her mother.
8. Nothing in the behavior of the father which he particularly dislikes.	8. Frequent family excursions (picnics, visits, church, etc.) in which she participates.

In general, our results from the farm group are in agreement with the findings of previous investigations. We may conclude, therefore, in much the same words as the White House Conference report, that "the subtler and more intangible aspects of family life," including the intimate person-to-person relationships and the various forms of social interaction and participation, are most important in relation to the personality development of the children, and hence to the "success" of the farm family.[14]

It is apparent from Stott's findings that the adjustment of youth, or the internalization of the value system, is a function of the family. It is further

---

[13] Leland H. Stott, "The Relation of Certain Factors in Farm Family Life to Personality Development in Adolescents," *Nebraska AES Bulletin 106*, 1938, p. 3.

[14] *Ibid.*, pp. 45–46.

indicated that such socialization results from frequent and intimate interaction which can occur only in the family or a group similarly structured, and therefore that the training of individuals in what "ought" to be done and the internalization of attitudes which bring guilt feelings on the part of the deviant are primarily a family function.

Where the family cannot handle the problem of socialization adequately as a unit, other components of the community may supplement or reinforce the effort. It is difficult to compare the relative influence of the community and the family in the process. It may be that community influence is minor, yet just enough to insure success to the family which otherwise might fail. In any event, community action must build on, and thus depends upon, the personality previously created through family interaction. If the problem is delinquency, reformation of character begins with values learned in the family. In some instances where family values fall short of community expectations, it may be necessary to alter those values through community action before individual rehabilitation can succeed.

It is a perennial problem in community development to find those persons who deviate from the normal pattern of values so as to furnish insights that can lead to social progress. An action program designed to accomplish social change in a community requires persons with an acute perception of their own values. These persons may be scientists and statesmen at the societal level, but often are viewed as merely nonconformists at the community level. Such persons are not necessarily leaders, for leaders are more often conformists who for various reasons exert an influence over others. A study by Helen Jennings offers some insight into this phenomenon.[15] She found that the leaders of youth groups in a girls' school were not often perceptive individuals. Behind each leader, however, there was another girl who, while not well liked by the rest, exerted influence on the leader. This phenomenon of the power behind the throne is seen in many types of situations, as in the power structure of a modern city, influence upon adoption of newer agricultural practices, and in many instances at the nation-state level throughout history.

The necessity of obtaining conformity through the socializing process inhibits the development of the nonconformist. With acute perception of this problem Thomas Gray in his Elegy wrote: "Full many a flower is born to blush unseen and waste its sweetness on the desert air." Such unseen and wasted personalities should be brought into community development programs, yet how is talent recognized and developed when it may differ from

[15] Helen Jennings, *Leadership and Isolation,* Longmans, Green and Company, New York, 1950.

the value system of the community? How can such creative individuality be nurtured in a setting where conformity is a necessity?

Community development itself may be a way to recognize and develop creative leadership. Since community development is democratic action by definition, it develops leadership and uses special talents. Nevertheless, this involves adults, and the nurture of talent and leadership in childhood is wanting.

The Consumer Function

The distribution of goods and services is important to an industrial society. From the point of view of production, this distribution is the main function of the economic institutions, and from the point of view of consumption, the family is the major institution performing this function.

Research on this subject, under the concepts of level of living and socioeconomic status, shows generally that the quantity of material goods held by families is so important in the social structure that it correlates with practically every other social and economic characteristic of families. Furthermore, these correlations are higher than with most other variables, and no others are more important. This reflects the materialistic value system of the American people.[16]

The consumption of material goods is related to other family functions. As we have mentioned earlier, a high birth rate is associated with low income and lower levels of living. Since values differ among various status groups, the particular sets of values internalized by children of low status families will differ from those of children from middle or high status families. Then, too, social participation occurs at a much higher rate among the higher status families than among those of low status.

This emphasis on material welfare in the American value system shows up in the community development program itself. Material comfort, like health and long life, is not an inherent good but it is held as a value-goal by some families and not by others. The fact that more people value material comfort than, say, progress or security, makes it no less a value learned through being a member of a particular social system. Therefore, levels of living must always be considered in the light of values as follows:

[16] See Lowry Nelson, *Rural Sociology,* American Book Company, New York, 1955, Chapter 16, and Bibliography contained therein for a summary of literature on rural levels of living. For urban communities see Elizabeth E. Hoyt, *American Income and Its Use,* Harper and Brothers, New York, 1954; and Hazel Kyrk, *The Family in the American Economy,* University of Chicago Press, Chicago, 1953.

(*a*) *The level of living of a family must be compared to the level of aspiration for material comfort before the level of living can be defined as a problem.* The level of aspiration, from the community point of view is the *standard of living.* The difference between the level of aspiration of individuals and the standard of living in a community may create problem situations.[17]

(*b*) *The goals probably move upward, staying beyond the level attained.*

(*c*) *When a discrepancy exists between the level and the standard of living, the relationship between the family and the economic institution must be changed to allow avenues to increasing the level of living if the gap is to be narrowed.* This may involve a change in the economic institution alone, as, for example, bringing an industry into the community. It may also involve a change in the process through which the family performs the consumer function. In a money economy such as ours, the male head of the family usually works for money which is exchanged for consumer items that the family desires. Where the standard of living and the family goals outstrip the earnings of the family head, the addition of the wife to the money-earning position may be required, or the male head may accept two jobs, as is found in some large Latin-American cities and to a growing extent among certain white collar groups in America.

(*d*) *A change in the family structure that is sometimes necessary to increase family income must be weighed against the cost to other family functions if social organization is to be maintained.* In those instances where both parents are employed or the male parent holds two jobs, the effects may be costly in terms of the value placed on socialization of the child. Such costs are rarely anticipated or considered when the family plans a program to increase its level of living.

In community development programs this conflict of values presents a perplexing problem. This is illustrated in the case of a Peruvian village where a community development project to provide a new well conflicted with other values. In this case (1) the village had insufficient water—at least by our standards; (2) the people opposed the digging of the well; and (3) they would not use the well when it was completed. The community development specialist must be careful to avoid imposing his own value system on the community. It is necessary to bring into harmonious relationships the conflicting values of the community before self-help programs are inaugurated. Thus, the people themselves must desire change and improvement in order to avoid the imposition of such changes by external force.

[17] Carl C. Taylor, "Social Theory and Social Action," *RS,* 5:17–32, 1940.

When the desire for change is created within the group by specialists, the conflicting values are reconciled and the change is accepted.[18]

The Participation Function

A fourth function of the family is the relationship between individual members and their social world. This is of primary importance in community study and development. The nature of this function and how it is performed is indicated in the following study by W.A. Anderson: *

The hypothesis presented in this paper is that the social participation of an individual is to a considerable degree a function of the social participation of the family. It says that if husbands participate, wives usually do, and if husbands and wives participate, children usually do, so that participation is chiefly a family trait.

In order to discover the association between individual and family participation, one of the methods used has been to compute Chapin Participation Scores for 1,176 farm families and the 2,014 individuals ten years of age and over of which they were composed, living in Cortland and Otsego Counties, New York.[19] This scoring technique uses measures of five aspects of participation. It allows one point for each organizational membership held by each family member; two points for each organization attended at least once during the year by each member; three points for each organization to which a contribution is made for support; four for each committee membership held; and five for each office held. The total number of points thus given to each person for these activities in the different organizations is that person's score, while the total family score is obtained by adding all the scores of the family members. In Chapin's score sheet, the average family score is computed by totaling the points made by the husband and wife and dividing by two. In our study the average family score is computed by averaging the points made by all family members ten years of age or over. This score is a measure of both the extensity of participation and of its intensity, since it includes memberships, which indicate extent; and attendance, officerships, committee activities, and contributions, which indicate intensity. The reliability of the Chapin score as a measure of participation has been pointed out in other papers; [20] it is necessary for us to deal with this problem here.

Is it factually true, then, that extensity and intensity of the participation of the individual family members are closely related to the extensity and intensity of

* W.A. Anderson, "The Family and Individual Social Participation," ASR, 8:420–24, 1943. Used by permission.

[18] Allan R. Holmberg, "The Wells that Failed," in Edward H. Spicer, editor, Human Problems in Technological Change, Russell Sage Foundation, New York, 1952, Case 7.

[19] W.A. Anderson and Hans Plambeck, The Social Participation of Farm Families, Cornell AES Rural Sociology Mimeo. Bulletin No. 8, Ithaca, New York. Children less than ten years old were omitted, since most formal organizations do not include them.

[20] F. Stuart Chapin, The Social Participation Scale, University of Minnesota Press, 1937; F. Stuart Chapin, "Social Participation and Social Intelligence," ASR, 4:157–66, 1939; H.R. Cottam, "Methods of Measuring Level of Living, Social Participation, and Adjustment of Ohio Farm People," Ohio AES, Dept. of Rur. Soc. Mimeo. Bulletin 139, pp. 18 ff., July, 1941.

the participation of the rest of his family? If so, we may expect that these would show high correlation. That the relationship between participation of the individual family members and the other family members is fairly close is shown by the size of these coefficients, which are uniformly high.[21] Likewise, the relationships between the participation scores of the individual family members are consistently high, especially those between the husband and wife, the wife and the daughters, and the brothers and the sisters. The relationship of the participation of the husbands and the wives seems to be the strongest, while that of the husbands and the daughters seems to be the weakest. But the relationship between the participation of the other family members and of any given family member is consistently strong and supports the original hypothesis.

Further indication of this influence of family participation on the individual's activities may be given by showing to what extent all the family members participated in the five ways that are included in the participation scale. There are two ways in which the family may behave as a unit in this participation. If none of the family members participate in any way, non-family participation is illustrated. If all of the family members participate in all five ways, then positive participation of the family as a unit is illustrated. Families in which some members participate in some ways while others do not, show only partial participation and if this were the general situation, then one could not infer influence between family members in these activities.

Another condition has bearing on the relationships. All persons ten years of age or over in the area studied had opportunity to become members, to attend meetings, and to make contributions to a number of different organizations. But organizations have only a few officers and usually only a few committees, and these are usually limited to active members. . . . Only three out of every ten families had one or more members who held some organization office. Committee memberships were even fewer. Opportunities to participate in these two ways are thus limited, so that participation in these activities is not directly comparable to participation through attendance, membership, or contributions.

If it can be shown, in large proportions of the families studied, that either all family members do not participate through membership, attendance, and contributions, or that all members participate in these three ways, there would be strong evidence, in addition to the correlations between the participation scores, that unit family participation is characteristic. . . . In the families including two persons, in 13 per cent neither member participated in any of these three ways, so there is uniform family participation in the 13 per cent. In 47 per cent both members participated in all three ways, so there was unit positive participation in the 47 per cent. In four out of ten families there was participation in some of the three ways when the other member did not participate, so that 40 per cent are partially participating families. In each of the other sizes of family, in one-half or more of them all family members either did not participate in any of the three ways or all participated in all three ways when the unit negative and the unit positive participation is combined. When all of the families are added into one grouping, the negatively participating and the positively participating families

---

[21] In each case, in order to avoid spurious relationships, the average family score was computed after excluding the score of the particular family member under consideration.

totaled 57 per cent, while the partially participating families were 43 per cent. In these generally available participation opportunities, therefore, the majority of the families behaved as a unit, either not participating at all or participating in all three ways.

If the base of these comparisons is broadened and the families are compared as to the participation of members in organizations in one or more of the five possible ways, another aspect of family influence is emphasized.

In the families composed of only two persons, in 13 per cent neither person participated in organizations in any way. In 22 per cent only one of the two persons participated in some of the five ways, while the other members did not participate at all; but in 65 per cent both persons participated in one or more of the five possible ways. In each different size of family up to and including those composed of six persons ten years of age or more, in over one-half of them, all family members participated in one or more of the five possible ways. When the percentage of the families in which none of the members participated in any way is added to the percentage in which all of them participated in some ways, the percentage of positively participating families and negatively participating families ranges from 59 per cent of the six-person families to 78 per cent of the two-person families. In only 22 to 41 per cent of the families was there participation by some members of the family, while others did not participate at all or partial family participation. In the majority of instances, therefore, either the families did not participate at all or all the family members participated in some ways.

Membership, attendance at meetings, and contributions toward support, it has been indicated, are the three most common ways in which individuals participate. Since comparison shows each of these to give the same general results, attendance at meetings will be used to illustrate family influence in a specific type of activity. In 48 to 54 per cent of the families of specific sizes, all of the members attended one or more meetings of organizations during the year. In 8 to 25 per cent of the families of specific sizes none of the family members attended, so that in this particular there was non-family participation. When complete lack of attendance is added to attendance by all family members or complete positive participation in this regard, the range in the percentage of families in which all members attend plus those in which none attend is from 60 per cent in the families composed of five members to 79 per cent in the families including two persons. In other words, only 21 to 40 per cent of the families are partially participating families as far as attendance is concerned. In the great majority of the cases either all attend or all do not.

Family members hold offices or serve on committees of organizations in not more than three out of each ten families. As stated, offices and committees are not numerous and are not, therefore, available to many individuals. In spite of this fact, it appears that even with respect to participating in this way the influence of the family is present. If office-holding is used as our illustration, it is observed that in those families where at least one member holds an office, as the size of the family increases, the proportion in which only one of the family members holds an office decreases and the proportions in which two or more members hold offices increase. It is, of course, true that as the number of persons in the family increases, the statistical chances of more than one member holding an office would be increased. In 49 per cent of the families of three persons, only one member holds an office, while in 51 per cent either two or all three members hold office. In the four-person families where at least one person holds office, 46 per cent number one member as an office-holder, while in 54 per cent two or more hold offices. There are only a few families of six members, and so the percentages may be chance percentages. But in 35 per cent of them where at least one member is an officer, one member only holds an office, while in 43 per cent three or more hold office. In one of the fourteen families five members, and in one all six of the members, hold office. Now the chance possibilities of as many as five out of six or of all six members in such a family being organization officers in a given year are very slight, yet in two out of the fourteen families such is the case.

Since offices are available to only a small proportion of the individuals, they act as a selective factor. Those individuals with the highest social status in the group probably get the offices. Social status, as far as the younger family members are concerned, is to a considerable degree a matter of the family social status and leadership position, so that, in the larger families where the family heads have achieved officerships, the younger members may get them through the reflective process and as a result of the leadership qualities they absorb in their family environments.

All of these statistics appear to confirm the hypothesis suggested, that the social participation of individuals is closely associated with the participation of other members of the family and that participation is to a considerable degree a family characteristic.

PRINCIPLES OF FAMILY FUNCTIONS

The relationship between family functions and community development may be described in the following propositions.

1. *The family itself may change in its relationship to other sociocultural elements, thus ultimately changing the social system of the community.*

During the past two centuries, the functions of the family in American society have changed tremendously. The family surrendered almost completely the function of economic production, and has given a large share of its responsibility for the socialization of the child to the educational institution. The function of meeting the need for affection, not discussed in this chapter, is still with the family, but it has narrowed to the nucleated family.

2. *The specialized sociocultural elements arising to meet the needs no longer met by the family change the community, making the social system more elaborate.*

This occurs in two ways. First, the relationship between two institutions is more elaborate than relations within an institution. Thus, as a function such as socialization is shared with the educational institutions, new relationships are introduced in the social system. Second, codes of conduct arise through generations of experience in solving problems, so that new sets of relationships between institutions create new problems; not only, therefore, do the original institutions or organizations themselves change, but still other organizations may come into existence merely to solve the problems created by the new relationships that are established. For example, the presence of the school is a change, as is its socializing function. But neither the school board nor the Parent-Teachers Association is directly involved in performing this function. Rather, these two organizations serve to smooth out the relationships between the family and the community on the one hand and the family and the school on the other. In many instances the creation of such new institutions or organizations may lag behind the need for them even to the extent of not developing at all. This will accentuate the maladjustment between the older institutions which may resist the acceptance of the changes in their relationships. Community development is an important procedure for reconciling such differences or for facilitating the establishment of conciliatory instruments.

SELECTED REFERENCES

Brown, James S., "The Farm Family in a Kentucky Mountain Neighborhood," *Kentucky AES Bulletin 587*, 1952.

Burgess, Ernest W., and Harvey J. Locke, *The Family*, Second Edition, American Book Company, New York, 1953.

Frazier, E. Franklin, *The Negro Family in the United States*, University of Chicago Press, Chicago, 1951.

Kirkpatrick, Clifford, *The Family: As Process and Institution*, The Ronald Press Company, New York, 1955.

Loomis, Charles P., and J. Allan Beegle, *Rural Social Systems*, Prentice-Hall, Inc., New York, 1950, Chapters 2-4.

Mercer, Blaine E., *The American Community*, Random House, New York, 1956, Chapter 9.

Ogburn, W. F., and M. F. Nimkoff, *Technology and the Changing Family*, Houghton-Mifflin Company, Boston, 1955.

Sanders, Irwin T., *The Community*, The Ronald Press Company, New York, 1958, Chapter 14.

Sirjamaki, John, *The American Family in the Twentieth Century*, Harvard University Press, Cambridge, 1953.

Smith, T. Lynn, *The Sociology of Rural Life*, Harper and Brothers, New York, 1947, Chapter 16.

Wilkening, Eugene A., "Adoption of Improved Farm Practices as Related to Family Factors," *Wisconsin AES Research Bulletin 183*, 1953.

CHAPTER 14

The Religious Institution

THE NATURE OF THE RELIGIOUS INSTITUTION

In no other area in sociology is it more important to point out the difference between science and other thoughtways than in the sociology of religion. An illustration will make this distinction clear. Sociologists find that many rural churches have too small a membership to support a full-time minister. This proposition is susceptible to scientific testing with resultant proof or disproof. A recommendation following from this testing that individual churches in the rural areas should close their membership and be combined in a community church is not scientific. Such a decision would involve beliefs and doctrines, and therefore is a matter of whether the theological doctrines of different denominations are mutually compatible, which is not subject to scientific test. Perhaps the words "unscientific" and "nonscientific" would better indicate these kinds of statements. If the first statement were incorrect (that is, if there were not many churches which did have too small a membership base), the statement would be unscientific. Since the second statement is not subject to scientific test, it is nonscientific. Other examples of nonscientific statements are those referring to whether there is or is not a God; or that Jesus was or was not divine. In this chapter, of course, we are interested only in those statements which are scientific and therefore part of the substance of the sociology of religion. The criterion, then, is whether or not a statement is subject to scientific test.

The religious institution is composed of four parts and is an institution in the sense that these parts are systematized into a single acting unit. First, there is an exclusive organizational structure in which active members are identifiable and distinguishable from non-members. Second, there is an edifice with various types of symbolisms, such as statues, crosses, and so on, which represent the beliefs of, and furnish a place of worship and other activity for, the membership. Third, there is a system of codes of conduct with positive and negative sanctions for insuring conformity to them. Most of these codes govern the relationship between man and some Supreme

Being, but some govern the interactions among men. Fourth, there are theories which furnish explanations for the otherwise unexplained, such as the origin and purpose of life, and continued existence after death.

It is important to view religion as a part of the community, influenced by other elements of the community, and in turn influencing them. Many social theorists in the past have considered the importance of such influences. One of the more popular theorists, Karl Marx, believed that all social structure and culture are a function of the economic institution, with religion serving only to pacify the underprivileged elements of society and characterized by the famous phrase he applied to religion as being the "opiate of the masses." Another social theorist, Max Weber, showed that since a cause must precede an effect, Marx's position could not be correct, because in many instances the code of conduct of a particular religion changed before the economic system changed. In particular, the Protestant ethic preceded in most places the rise of capitalism. The position taken was that certain codes of conduct in the Protestant religion were necessary before capitalism could develop.[1]

In the present chapter consideration will be given first to the necessary conditions of religious behavior, namely, the membership components of the institution; second, to studies showing the influence of religion on other aspects of the community; and third, to some changes which have occurred in religious organization over several decades.

Church Membership and Centralization

The religious institution, like the educational, economic, and governmental institutions discussed elsewhere, is becoming centralized. This is illustrated by the decline in the number of rural churches which results from the closing of churches in the rural areas surrounding community centers. In a study of sixty-two closed Protestant churches in Pennsylvania, Scheifele and Mather report: "Major factors responsible for the closing of rural churches were: (1) population decline; (2) changes in type of population or to another religious faith; (3) too many churches; (4) congregational disputes; and (5) unsatisfactory professional leadership."[2]

At the same time that rural churches are closing there is a relative decline in membership and attendance in the remaining rural churches with an accompanying increase in urban churches. This is so in spite of an increase

[1] Max Weber, *The Protestant Ethic and the Spirit of Capitalism*, George T.F. Unwin, London, 1930, and R.H. Tawney, *Religion and the Rise of Capitalism*, the New American Library, New York, 1947.
[2] Theodore C. Scheifele and William G. Mather, "Closed Rural Pennsylvania Churches," *Pennsylvania AES Bulletin 512*, 1949.

in rural church membership which lagged behind rural population gains. Those churches which extended their functions to include social and educational activities showed the most gain in membership.[3]

THE INFLUENCE OF RELIGION ON OTHER ASPECTS OF THE CULTURE

As was mentioned earlier, religion has proved to be a prior condition to changes in the economic organization of societies. The following study, "Religion in a Rural Community of the South" by Frank D. Alexander,[*] shows the influence of the church on the family and many of its practices. While such practices are declining, they are still carried on in many of the rural areas in the United States, and perhaps much more so in other countries which are predominantly rural and sacred.

The analysis of religion presented here is only one aspect of a broad cultural study of Ruralville,[4] an open-country community in southwestern Tennessee. A modified anthropological approach was followed in securing and analyzing the data. There were approximately 252 families in the community area. Cotton farming is the dominant type of agriculture. Small farms predominate. Though not excessive, tenants are more numerous than owners. With the exception of one Negro family, the population is entirely white. Throughout the study, emphasis was placed on comparison of owners and tenants to present the tenancy problem in its cultural setting.

Religion in the Family: Religious Ritual in the Home

The rural family has often been considered a stronghold of religion. The facts of this study do not always support this conclusion. Investigation was made of several simple religious practices which appeared to be within the sphere of family religion. Table [IV] summarizes the results of this investigation.

While local ministers might be discouraged if they knew the extent of their ineffectiveness in maintaining the virtues of religious observance in the family, they could find compensation in the fact that for some there is the chastening voice of conscience for neglecting family religious rites. One tenant farmer remarked in answering the question whether or not he said grace at the table: "No, used to do that. Feel bad and cramped for not doing it." The wife of an owner commented: "We ought to be ashamed not to, but I can't get my husband to." A wife of a

---

[*] Frank D. Alexander, "Religion in a Rural Community of the South," *ASR*, 6:241–51, 1941. Used by permission.

[3] Lauris B. Whiteman and William G. Mather, "The Rural Church of Four Pennsylvania Counties," *Pennsylvania AES Bulletin*, 1952.

[4] A fictitious name, Ruralville, is used throughout this article.

tenant commenting on the same question said: "I'll bet you don't find many that does. I think everybody ought to be ashamed that he don't."

TABLE IV

Percentage Distribution for Tenant, Owner, and All Families on
Observance of Certain Religious Rituals

	Tenant Families			Owner Families			All Families		
		Per cent			Per cent			Per cent	
Ritual	Number	Yes	No	Number	Yes	No	Number	Yes	No
Say grace at table	103	20	80	53	28	72	156	23	77
Recite verse from Bible at table	91	1	99	49	2	98	140	4	96
Have family prayers	97	8	92	42	5	95	139	7	93
Read Bible as group	95	28	72	50	34	66	145	30	70

The Religious Sect

The power and pervasiveness of religion in influencing and determining the behavior of the family is also present in the behavior of the community as such. In many instances, the community lends support and provides cohesiveness to the perpetuation of subcultural behavior patterns far beyond anything which could survive the pressures of the surrounding culture in individuals or families. This is clearly illustrated in the following study by Eaton, where a religious sect perpetuates its own subcultural patterns quite different from the majority culture surrounding it.*

What are some of the factors related to the survival of ethnic minorities in America? The question is usually posed indirectly because it is studied in cultures in the process of disorganization. The Hutterites offer an opportunity for a somewhat more direct study of this problem. In-group cohesion and cultural autonomy are preserved in this American minority to a high degree.

Overt family conflicts are rare. We know of only one divorce and two separations. The aged, the ill, and the infirm are generally well protected and cared for. We did not find any case of major crime, psychopathy, severe physical assault, or other forms of severely antisocial behavior, but the group is not free from neurosis and psychosis. The picture of the Hutterite community as an unspoiled rural Utopia, which led us to study them, is impaired. Our study shows them to be unusual at least with respect to their effectiveness in maintaining a social system relatively free of individuals who are neglected or who engage in severely

* Joseph W. Eaton, "Controlled Acculturation: A Survival Technique of the Hutterites," ASR, 17:331–40, 1952. Used by permission.

antisocial acts, against their own group or the larger American society. The question arises: How is it done?

Religion is a major cohesive force in this folk culture. The Hutterites consider themselves to be a people chosen by God to live the only true form of Christianity. Like the Mennonites and other Anabaptist sects which have similarities with the Hutterites, they believe in adult baptism. They are vigilant pacifists and emphasize simplicity in every aspect of living. Had Thorstein Veblen studied them, he would not have found, then or now, much evidence of conspicuous consumption.

The homogeneity is further enhanced by the high rate of in-group marriage which has been practiced by these people for over a century. Their voluntary isolation from outside social influences has been all the more effective because their way of life is well integrated around a strong value system. Hutterites indoctrinate their children in a generally well-planned educational process. We do not wish to run the risk of overstating the degree of homogeneity. Hutterites are not made out of one mold—the degree of variation is currently increasing. But by comparison with American or western European cultures, they can be characterized as relatively uniform.

The Hutterites have unusual features, some of which are of considerable current scientific and political interest:

1. A family with little more than procreative and affectional functions. Economic support, preparation of food, and much of the education after the age of about three are community responsibilities.

2. A communal system of sharing property and products of labor.

3. A high degree of security, both economic and spiritual.

4. A predominance of the primary-group type of social relationships. Colonies generally stay about 100 in size.

5. Fertility is high. It comes closer to the theoretical level of fecundity than in any other observed society. The median completed family in 1951 had ten children.

6. There is a narrow range of prestige variations, leaving virtually a "classless society."

7. Integration around an absolute value system. The culture is "totalitarian," if this term is used without its contemporary political and antihumanistic connotations. Hutterites abhor all use of physical force and are fanatically devoted to the humanistic principles of an Anabaptist type of Christianity. They are totalitarian only in these respects: no major deviations from central beliefs and socially approved practices are tolerated; each generation is indoctrinated systematically to grow up to believe and act close to what their traditions believe; considerable subordination of the individual to the needs of the group is expected.

Processes of Change

What is somewhat distinctive about social change in this culture is its gradual nature and the institutionalized techniques that have been developed to deal with pressure for change in an organized fashion. Hutterites tend to accept cultural innovations before the pressure for them becomes so great as to threaten the basic cohesiveness of the social system. We shall illustrate this process of change (which will be defined later as "controlled acculturation") primarily by references to the written rules of the Schmiedenleut Hutterites, one of three cliques of colonies which constitute administrative and social subunits of the larger ethnic group.

These written rules constitute no systematic guide to living, as does the Shulhan Aruk of Orthodox Jews. Most problems of behavior among the Hutterites are dealt with on the basis of ancient traditions, which are transmitted to succeeding generations through example and oral communications. When people are sure of one another, no written laws are needed. Families, friendships, cliques, and other primary groups order their affairs on the basis of mores, supported by common consensus. Rules tend to be written down only when this common consensus starts to break down.

New rules, among the Schmiedenleut Hutterites, are usually proposed at an intercolony meeting of elected lay preachers, and are intended to combat a specific innovation in personal behavior of some members which some of the preachers regard as a violation of the unwritten mores. The new practice must be more than an isolated deviation of the sort which is controlled effectively through the normal processes of community discipline—punishment of the offender by admonition, standing up in church, and temporary ritual excommunication. Only when a deviation becomes widespread in one or more colonies are the leaders likely to appeal for a formal statement of the unwritten community code.

If such a formal rule is adopted by the preachers, it is read to the governing assembly of male members in every colony. Adoption or rejection is by majority vote of all baptized males. Hutterite leaders have their ears to the ground. Their grass-root consciousness is indicated by the fact that in the entire history of the Schmiedenleut colonies, no formal ruling of the preacher-assembly has ever been voted down.

The Schmiedenleut do not usually repeal a rule. When the pressure for change becomes strong enough among the members to threaten harmony and unity, the rule ceases to be enforced. In time a new rule will be passed to give formal recognition that a new practice is now authorized. What started as a violation becomes a law. The Hutterites are not fanatic. In this they differ from most groups which have established colonies involving communal ownership of property or unusual religious principles. They do not expel a member for deviating a little from the narrow path of custom. Disagreements, new ideas, and personal idiosyncrasies are not completely repressed, although they are not encouraged. Taking their cue from the dogma that man is born to sin, they do not expect perfection from anyone.

The Principle of Austere Simplicity

It appears that the Hutterites are careful not to be excessively severe in restraining strong drives. They reduce the temptation to violate rules by not forbidding all enjoyment of food, drink, sex, and adornment. Hutterites enjoy eating. They are encouraged to get married. "Simple" decorations and colors in clothing are authorized. Wine, beer, and occasional hard liquor are distributed in moderate quantities. The rules are only directed at what the culture considers excesses.

This principle of moderation is well illustrated by a 1925 rule to put an end to what are considered excesses at weddings, when the community provides quantities of alcoholic beverages for the celebration of festivities:

"When there is a wedding, nobody shall take the liberty of carrying home drinks or taking away from the wedding that which he could not drink. This because human natures are different. And everyone shall drink only so much that his conscience remains clear, because all excess and misuse are sinful. Only if somebody, because of his need to work, cannot be present when drinks are poured, can he come later to the person charged with pouring and ask for his share. But he must not take it home. If somebody is sick, however, and cannot attend the wedding, the manager shall give him his share in all fairness."

The largest number of austerity rules are concerned with clothing. Hutterite clothing is the visible symbol of their autonomy. The forces of assimilation are most easily brought to bear against this form of symbolic segregation. It is external to the person, and its change seems to be just a trivial matter. Changes in dress often symbolize the beginning of a major break with the past.

One Hutterite regulation exhorts members that they should ". . . start no new styles . . ." But the style urge is strong and one can expect many rules on this subject to be issued to keep up with the genius of younger Hutterites for expressing themselves. Hutterites needed to be reminded in 1909 that they must not make "rolled caps" for children, nor add colored strings or bands. Black hats were the only kind permitted by a 1936 rule which added that "recently purchased white or grey hats should be worn out this year," indicating that they were contrary to the unwritten tradition. Two years later, another regulation was necessary to include pith helmets in this prohibition, since some Hutterite children had begun to purchase them because "there is nothing in the regulations against them."

Schmiedenleut tradition required the use of hooks and eyes to fasten clothes until 1926, when it was decide that buttons on winter clothes "could be retained." The ex post facto regulation acknowledging this change in fashion also sets clear limits: "Only black buttons could be used, except on white garments, where there should be white buttons." But the tendency to use buttons in colors contrasting with the cloth persisted, and twelve years later the 1926 regulation had to be virtually repeated. Emphasizing that buttons should be of the same color as the garment, the preachers added: "Let everyone be warned of the dangers of misfortune and eternal damnation."

Concessions are being made. When the pressure for change becomes too great we find here as previously a willingness to change a little. In the long view of history, these changes may accumulate into a lot.

Principles of Self-Sufficiency

For Hutterites, the preference for self-sufficiency has always had more than an economic motivation. It functions to keep down the frequency of business contacts between members of the colony and outsiders. It also reflects the religious emphasis on austere simplicity.

The effective system of communication throughout America, with its modern roads, its radio, and its press, as well as the economic pressure for the use of technological improvements, made it impossible for the Hutterites to maintain the degree of isolation that had been possible when they lived among Russian peasants. The group is now adjusting itself to these technological and social forces. Very much unlike the anti-machine-age Amish people, Hutterites have no religious taboos against new inventions as such. Their basic attitude is to be tolerant of the use of technology in production, but to be more insistent upon home-made products in consumer goods.

Controlled Acculturation and Personal Adjustment

The strong communal organization which enables the Hutterites to make a planned retreat in the direction of assimilation in the form of controlled acculturation, probably contributes to the good adjustment of individuals. Unlike the natives in the Pacific Islands or the Poles of America's ghettos, Hutterite individuals are not being forced, almost overnight, to make a transition from the security support of their "Gemeinschaft," with primitive peasant values, to an unfamiliar "Gesellschaft" society with twentieth-century American values. They make the change slowly enough to enjoy community support in the process.

Many members of American minority groups have become marginal and disorganized when caught in a culture conflict. Immigrants lose confidence in their ancestral culture. Their children tend to reject the old-fashioned practices in which their parents no longer believe, but to which they adhere for lack of alternative. They become what Stonequist calls "marginal men"—people without secure roots or values. The high rates of crime, delinquency, prostitution, venereal disease, and other indices of social disorganization commonly found in this marginal second generation of immigrant groups can be viewed as a social price of their rapid assimilation, without much in-group support.

No such pronounced tendency of individual demoralization was observed among the Hutterites. Hutterites are generally self-confident about their group membership. There are few signs of self-hatred and the sense of deep personal inferiority commonly found among assimilationist Jews, who feel ambivalent about their relationship to the Jewish group.

The factors responsible for this phenomenon are no doubt numerous and are beyond the scope of this paper, but controlled acculturation is one of them. This controlled process of adjustment to social change gives group support to the Hutterite individual who must adjust his way of life within the conflict of his own sixteenth-century Anabaptist peasant traditions and the twentieth-century American values of his environment. Hutterites are making the adjustment, both as a total culture and as individuals while maintaining a considerable measure of functional adequacy and self-respect.

While the research by Eaton was done on an atypical religion, the advantage is that the relationships between the religious institution and other elements of the community are more distinctly drawn. Other research studies have shown various features such as stratification, to be related to religious affiliation. It is probably safe to say that in a rural community of more traditional bent, religion permeates the codes of conduct and the actions of the person in all the elements of the community and in community activity itself. It is probably also safe to say that in larger communities and more industrial societies, religion has much less influence, although this certainly would not be true of all large industrialized communities.

Trends and Change

While religion may exercise influence upon various aspects of community life either to induce or retard change, the religious institution, in keeping with all other social institutions, is itself subject to change. In his study of religion in South Dakota, Kumlien illustrates many of the changes in religious organization over several decades.*

Purpose

The purpose of this study is to portray as simply and clearly as possible the basic trends in the religious organizations of South Dakota.

Scope and Method

This study attempts to cover the main phases of religious organization emphasizing particularly changes in the number of churches, of church members, and also changes in the services of the church to the community. Data have been secured from the Federal Census of Religious Bodies for the years 1890, 1906, 1916, 1926, and 1936, from Denominational Year Books where available, and in a few instances from the federal and state census of population.

Participation in Church Affairs

The number and kinds of people who take part in church activities greatly influence the number and kinds of churches in the state and also their organization. In this section we will attempt to show what changes have taken place in church participation.

(1) Both church and Sunday school members have declined in numbers and in proportion to the total population. The number of church and Sunday school members increased from 1890 to 1926 but declined between 1926 and 1936.

Church and Sunday school membership increased much more rapidly than did the population or the number of churches throughout the period from 1890

* W.F. Kumlien, "Basic Trends of Social Change in South Dakota: Religious Organization," *South Dakota AES Bulletin 348,* 1941.

to 1926. Between 1926 and 1936, the number of church members declined less than did the churches themselves, but the number of Sunday school members decreased more rapidly than the number of churches. All showed a greater decline than did the total population.

Before 1926 the population of South Dakota grew rapidly. It was one of the most prosperous periods in the history of the state, and property value, income, and standards of living were all rising. At the same time relatively large amounts of Home Mission money were sent into South Dakota from various denominations to bolster up weak churches.[5] As a result, there was a tendency for the churches to overexpand.

The greater decline in church members than in population is reflected in the decreasing ratio of members to population.

There are several reasons for this decline. A smaller number of children has probably caused a decrease in Sunday school membership.

The depression and drouth, with the consequent lack of money, have also cut church and Sunday school membership. Farm tenancy, which is generally not conducive to church attendance, has increased. As farm tenants frequently move from one community to another every few years, there is a tendency for them to lose interest in the church.

Paralleling this has been the gradual breakdown of the neighborhood which has long served as a strong influence for building up church membership and attendance. This breakdown is especially evident in the open-country churches, where the neighborhood consciousness has been strong until recent years.

In addition, the widespread use of the radio and the competition of commercial amusements on Sunday have reduced church attendance.

Although there were churches of forty-five different denominations in South Dakota in 1936, 84.5 per cent of the total membership was found in the five largest churches and 94.1 per cent of the membership was found in the ten largest churches. Similarly, the five leading denominations had 74.1 per cent of all church units under their jurisdiction and the first ten denominations had 85.4 per cent of all church units in the state.

A few denominations merged between 1926 and 1936. Some denominations which had church organizations in 1926 no longer listed them in 1936, and certain other denominations not represented in 1926 had established churches by 1936.

(2) A distinct relationship between denominational preference and nationality background has developed. Immigrants into South Dakota, whether from foreign countries or other states, brought with them their customs including religious affiliations.

Very soon after coming here these people established churches of their preference. The settlers who came from south Germany, south Ireland, France, or Poland established Catholic churches. The settlers from north Germany and the Scandinavian countries soon formed flourishing Lutheran churches. The Hollanders founded congregations of the Christian Reformed Church or of the Reformed Church

[5] W.F. Kumlien, "The Social Problem of the Church in South Dakota," *South Dakota AES Bulletin 294,* May, 1935, p. 24.

of America. The British people and many of the migrants from other states established churches of British origin such as Methodist, Baptist, Presbyterian, Protestant Episcopal, and Congregational.

The Russians who settled in South Dakota were originally of German stock. Their ancestors left Germany in the eighteenth century and settled in Russia to obtain religious freedom. This group founded mainly Roman Catholic, Lutheran, and Mennonite churches.

In recent years certain denominations of United States origin have established churches in South Dakota. These churches are largely evangelistic. The only one to have more than 1,000 members in South Dakota by 1936 was the Assemblies of God, General Council. This particular group had no churches in the state in 1926.

A comparison between the denominations and nationality groups as related to the total church membership shows a close relationship. For instance, the people of Scandinavian and German backgrounds make up a large proportion of the population; the proportion of the total church members who belong to the Lutheran churches is correspondingly high.

(3) The number of church units in the state has decreased since 1926; the average number of members per church has increased. During the early years of settlement the number of churches increased quite rapidly, although never as rapidly as did the population. Since 1906 the increase in the number of churches has been even less rapid, and between 1926 and 1936 they declined more rapidly than the population did.

There was a total loss of 294 churches during these ten years, but this loss was apparently entirely in towns of less than 2,500 population and in the open country. The urban places of the state gained 24 churches, while the rural areas lost 318. The decline in the rural areas no doubt occurred in both the towns and open country.

A decreasing number of churches was an expected development of the last ten years. The drouth and depression of the early 1930's greatly reduced the income of families in South Dakota, and it became more difficult to secure sufficient money with which to support as large a number of churches as were present in South Dakota in 1926. In addition roads and automobiles have been so greatly improved that it is possible for people to travel much farther in order to go to church. At the same time that the income of farm families declined there were fewer farm families. This further reduced the amount of money available to support the churches.

However, there is some indication that the number of churches may have increased slightly since 1936, or at least that there has been no noticeable decline. This may be true even of open-country churches, but their services probably have been decidedly curtailed because of their limited financial resources. The leading denominations in the state indicate little or no abandonment of churches, either open-country or town.[6]

Despite the fact that both the number of churches and the number of members decreased between 1926 and 1936, the average number of members per church in-

[6] Returns from a questionnaire sent to leading denominations in the state.

creased. This indicates that even though a number of churches were forced to disband, many of their members joined churches of other denominations or else went greater distances to reach a church of their preference. Many members from the open country are attending church in the villages and towns.

Nearly all ten leading denominations in South Dakota show an increase in the average number of members per church between 1926 and 1936. The only exception was the Protestant Episcopal Church.

The greater average membership per church should somewhat lessen the financial burden upon individual church members and should also help to develop a better church program and more cooperation between churches. With fewer churches there is less competition between churches for members. Consequently each church can serve a wider area.

(4) Church comity [7] has slowly decreased denominational overlapping and overchurching at certain crucial points in the state. There has been considerable denominational overlapping in the state, especially where there have been one or more distinct nationality groups in the same community. However, the number of different denominations has been decreasing since 1906. There were fifty-seven different denominations in the state in 1906 as compared to forty-five in 1936. This represents considerable change in the particular denominations in the state, since some denominations die out and new ones appear.

The various denominations are beginning to recognize that the very small towns cannot support a large number of churches. Approximately 60 per cent of the towns with less than 250 population had only one church, and only eight towns had as many as four. However, some of the larger towns had a large number of churches in relation to their population. Half of the towns of 2,500 population and over had more than ten churches. Only two had as few as seven churches. Some of the smaller towns between 250 and 2,500 population also had an excess number of churches for the number of people served.

The Role of the Clergy

Much of the relationship, although not all, between the church and the community occurs through the medium of activities of the clergy. This occurs not only through the orientation of sermons toward social versus strictly religious affairs, but also through the clergy's relations with the membership and their leadership activities in nonreligious problems. The expectations of the clergy with regard to these relationships often differ as between the membership, the clergyman himself, and his superiors in the church hierarchy. Samuel W. Blizzard [*] analyzed these differing role expectations to determine their nature and effect.

[7] Church comity in this connection refers to the process of centralizing or combining churches of one or more denominations so that a church of adequate size is maintained in the community.

[*] Samuel W. Blizzard, The Christian Century, April 25, 1956. Copyright 1956 by The Christian Century Foundation and reprinted by permission.

The Minister's Dilemma

The new American culture has resulted in a change in what people expect of the minister. In the past the parish clergyman has performed his functions as a general practitioner. Now, increasingly, he is expected to be a specialist. Parishioners who are confronted by a complex and chaotic world want to be counseled rather than to receive a social call from the minister. They look for a perceptive prophet who is able to make sense out of the crisis of the current week rather than for a preacher who merely assures them that all is well with the world. They seek the help of a priest who uses liturgy, rites and sacraments in a way that is meaningfully related to the issues of life rather than letter-perfect administration of the church ordinances. They want a professional organizer rather than an amateur promoter. They expect the minister to be an efficient manager of the business affairs of the parish rather than a laissez faire administrator.

But what parishioners and community residents expect from the minister is only one side of the picture. The other side is the minister's picture of himself. He too defines the roles he is expected to play. Research now under way among 690 clergymen representative of the theologically trained American Protestant parish ministry suggests that Protestant parish clergymen in the United States face a basic dilemma. The theology they hold and the seminary instruction they received place the roles they perform in the parish in one priority order. But they actually spend most of their time doing those things they feel are least important. Denominational goals and programs and local parish needs determine the use of their time. But these activities bring the least satisfaction. Hence the various offices of the ministry are normatively in one order of priority, and functionally in another order of priority. Therefore there is much ambivalence about those offices.

The Practitioner Roles

For purposes of analysis, six practitioner roles have been distinguished within the work of the parish minister: administrator, organizer, pastor, preacher, priest, teacher. In the *administrator* role the minister is the manager of the parish. At the local church level this involves official board and staff meetings, publicity, clerical and stenographic work, financial administration and promotion, physical plant supervision and general church planning. Related denominational and interdenominational assignments enter here, too. The *organizer* role involves leadership, participation and planning in local church associations and community organizations. The *pastor* role involves interpersonal relations. This is distinguished from the intra- and inter-group relations in the organizer role. The pastor does the visiting among the parishioners and prospective members, ministers to the sick and distressed, and counsels all who seek his guidance.

The *preacher* role involves the preparation and delivery of sermons. The *priest* is a liturgist. He leads people in worship and officiates in the rites of the church. The *teaching* office involves church school instruction, confirmation classes, study group leadership and preparation for teaching. Throughout this article the six roles are used in these specific meanings.

Some of the practitioner roles of the parish ministry may be classified as traditional, others are neo-traditional, still others may be called contemporary. The roles of preacher, priest and teacher are those which the Protestant clergyman *traditionally* performs. There is a biblical definition of these roles. Furthermore, there is a theology (or religious ideology) associated with the traditional offices. Church tradition also supplies patterns for these roles. Role definitions, expectations and ideology are all present. Hence the parish minister knows how to legitimate the way he fulfills the roles of preacher, priest and teacher.

The pastor role is *neo-traditional.* It has a biblical tradition and an ideological definition. However, new developments in clinical psychology and counseling procedures are giving a new outline and new direction to this role.

The *contemporary* roles are those of administrator and organizer. These roles are newer to church practice and tradition. The ideology of these offices is not as clearly defined in scriptural tradition. There is little agreement on the legitimate behavior in these roles. Men who are recruited for the ministry usually have an image of the preacher, priest, teacher and pastor as a servant of God. They lack a religiously oriented image of the minister as organizer or administrator.

Norms and Motives

Each of the 690 clergymen participating in our current study of the Protestant ministry was asked to evaluate these six roles from three perspectives: importance, effectiveness and enjoyment. It was assumed that when the ministerial informant rated the tasks in order of importance, he would reveal his concept of an ideal ministry and the goals he has as he functions in the parish. By rating the importance of each job he was stating the norms for the minister's professional behavior held by the church as an institution.

This normative view of the six roles, as seen by the parish minister informants, goes from most important to least important as follows: preacher, pastor, priest, teacher, organizer, administrator. Rural ministers rate the roles normatively in the same order as do those serving urban churches. This is the status hierarchy for a normative view of the roles of the parish minister.

In the next stage of the self-analysis procedure, the clergymen were asked about their sense of effectiveness in performing the various tasks of the ministry. The intention was to ascertain the ministers' level of personal involvement in relation to each professional role. Each man's sense of effectiveness in performing the various roles was used as one clue to his ministerial motivation—what was pushing him and what he was driving at as a minister.

Generally the ministers felt most effective as preachers, but their sense of effectiveness in this role was not as strong as the importance they attached to it. They felt next most effective in the pastor role, and their sense of effectiveness as pastor was stronger than the importance they attached to the role. From most effective to least effective they mentioned the roles as follows: preacher, pastor, teacher, priest, administrator, organizer. Urban parish ministers felt much more effective in the administrative role than did rural clergymen.

Informants were also asked to assess their feelings of enjoyment in performing their professional roles. Their sense of enjoyment was viewed as another index of motivation in the various roles of the ministry. The pastor role was most enjoyed, but the preacher role was enjoyed almost as much. Medium enjoyment feeling was associated with the teacher and priest roles. The organizer and administrator roles were least enjoyed. The enjoyment pattern of urban and rural ministries differed very little. Urban men got greater satisfaction in the liturgical office than did rural clergy. The organizer role was more enjoyable for rural men than for their city colleagues.

The Minister's Work Day

The normative indoctrination may furnish the minister with an ideal goal, and personal involvement may motivate him as he seeks to perform the role in a normative manner. The choice a minister makes regarding the use of his time, however, gives some evidence of how the normative and the motivational are expressed at the operational level in the parish.

To check this, the daily activities carefully reported by 480 rural and urban ministers have been classified as professional or nonprofessional (personal and family). All professional activities were classified according to the role being performed. To avoid arbitrary decisions, the preaching and priestly activities were considered as a unit.

The professional work day of the cooperating ministers averaged a few minutes less than ten hours. Rural men reported a work day of nine hours and 17 minutes. That of the urban minister was ten hours and 32 minutes. Considering all ministerial informants, almost two-fifths of their total work day was spent as administrator. Slightly more than one-fourth was devoted to the pastor role. Preaching and priestly activities took up almost one-fifth of the work day. Organizing consumed more than one-tenth of the work day. The residual time (about one-twentieth) was devoted to teaching. This order of priority from most time to least time (administrator, pastor, preacher and priest, organizer, teacher) was the same for both urban and rural parish ministers.

An incidental but revealing item of intelligence is the time parish ministers devote to sermon preparation and to stenographic work each day. The average time devoted to sermon preparation is 34 minutes for rural men, 38 minutes for urban clergymen. The time taken up by stenographic tasks is one hour and four minutes for both country and city men.

When the functional demands of the parish are considered, it is apparent that the six practitioner roles are in one order of priority. The normative and the motivational orientations place these roles in a quite different order of priority. With the exception of the pastor, those roles rated high normatively and motivationally tend to be rated somewhat lower functionally. Roles that are rated low by norms and motives tend to be rated higher on a functional basis in the parish.

The educational implications of the conflict between the normative-motivational and the functional orientation is seen when a fourth orientation is added—adequacy of seminary preparation. Clergymen were asked to evaluate their seminary preparation in the light of their experience in the parish ministry. An analysis of their comments was made using the six practitioner roles. The order of priority for additional knowledge and further training, from most mentioned to least mentioned, is as follows: pastor, administrator and/or organizer, preacher, teacher, priest. The requests from the rural and urban men are closely alike with one exception. Rural men expressed a greater need for more training as teacher than did urban ministers. Over-all, the training needs support the functional rather than the normative and motivational orientations to the practitioner's roles.

The traditional roles (preacher, teacher, priest) are those in which the minister feels most adequate. The roles that he finds most troublesome are those that are neo-traditional (pastor) or contemporary (organizer and administrator). In the traditional roles he functions in the world of ideas. However, the neo-traditional and contemporary roles are those in which the minister is most involved in relations with people. These latter roles do not have the sanction of universal understanding in religious ideology that the more traditional roles share. Nor are there generally accepted behavioral ways of performing the neo-traditional and contemporary roles.

The Required Motivation

The problem of the parish clergyman who holds a normative view of the ministry is to secure motivation and training that will aid him in becoming the minister his parishioners will count on his being. The roles a minister performs in present-day American society are basically equivocal. On the one hand, the church has a traditional set of norms by which he is expected to be guided. On the other hand, the parishioner has a set of functional expectations by which the minister's professional service is judged. This is the minister's dilemma. He faces basic ambiguities in performing the practitioner roles.

For the Protestant parish minister practitioner, these data about normative, motivational and functional orientations reflect the various influences and pressures created by those who guide and those who seek his professional services. The normative orientation apparently reflects his religious ideology and the way in which he is theologically indoctrinated. The motivational orientation reflects his personal commitment and involvement in the profession. The functional orientation (with the support of expressed educational needs) reflects the extent to which the minister tends to perform the practitioner roles within the parishioner's expectations and the community's definition. It also reflects the extent to which the local parish minister follows programs promoted by the national denominational headquarters.

No matter how different ministers' ideas of what is important in the ministry, all wind up doing substantially the same thing. It is perfectly apparent how largely the social roles of Protestant parish ministers are conditioned and defined by the requests of parishioners, the denominational program and the culture of the community. It is not nearly so clear at the parish level, however, how much a minister's religious ideology or normative orientation has to do with what he actually does as a minister. Furthermore, there appear to be basic ambiguities in the church structure itself. The minister is urged to spend much time organizing and administering programs. The national church body is at the same time failing to give him an adequate theological understanding of these offices. That is the minister's dilemma.

PRINCIPLES

1. *The importance of the sociology of religion as it bears upon community structure and change is in the interrelationship of religion and other components of the community.*
This has several aspects: Religion as a nucleated institution is an organization of people recognized by themselves and by others as different from non-members. In this sense, the structuring of the religious institution in America into many denominations has brought problems of potential conflict in the community and of difficulty of support of several independent churches in smaller communities.

2. *Religion as an institution not only includes codes of conduct for relations between man and Deity but also between man and man, man and other elements of the community. Thus, religious codes of conduct limit and foster certain types of activity in the economic and family structure.*

3. *In this sense the religious system limits and promotes certain types of change in these other elements of the community and in the community itself. (See chapters on values.)*

4. *The influence of the religious institution on community structure and change is decreasing.*
This involves a smaller church membership, less attendance, less dogmatic conviction on theological issues, and less competition among churches.

SELECTED REFERENCES

Abell, Aaron I., *The Urban Impact on American Protestantism, 1865–1900,* Harvard University Press, Cambridge, 1943.

Bower, William Clayton, *Church and State in Education,* University of Chicago Press, Chicago, 1944.

Gerth, H.H., and C. Wright Mills, *From Max Weber: Essays in Sociology,* Oxford University Press, New York, 1946, Part III.

Goldschmidt, Walter R., *As You Sow,* Harcourt, Brace and Company, New York, 1947, Chapter 5.

Goldschmidt, Walter R., "Class Denominationalism in Rural California Churches," *AJS,* 49:348–60, 1944.

Landis, Judson T., "Social Action in American Protestant Churches," *AJS,* 52:517–22, 1947.

Mercer, Blaine E., *The American Community,* Random House, New York, 1956, Chapter 11.

Nelson, Lowry, *American Farm Life in the Twentieth Century,* Harvard University Press, Cambridge, 1954, Chapter 8.

Nuesse, C.J., and Thomas J. Harte, *The Sociology of the Parish: An Introductory Symposium,* The Bruce Publishing Company, Milwaukee, 1951.

Sanders, Irwin T., *The Community,* The Ronald Press Company, New York, 1958, Chapter 14.

Smith, T. Lynn, *The Sociology of Rural Life,* Harper and Brothers, New York, 1947, Chapter 18.

Vidich, Arthur J., and Joseph Bensman, *Small Town in Mass Society,* Princeton University Press, Princeton, New Jersey, 1958, Chapters 9 and 10.

Yinger, J. Milton, *Religion in the Struggle for Power,* Duke University Press, Durham, North Carolina, 1946.

The Catholic Digest, St. Paul, Minnesota. Various issues commencing in November, 1952.

"Organized Religion in the United States," *Annals of the American Academy of Political and Social Science,* No. 256, March, 1948.

CHAPTER 15

Political Organization

Political institutions provide social control and certain necessary common services. These two functions are essential elements in any well-ordered community. Both of these functions are performed on several levels by differing levels of governmental organization. Our concern here is primarily with the political institutions in the local community. The performance of these functions by the political institutions of the community is generally accepted at the present time, although the degree and intensity of the performance have evolved slowly through the centuries. In some instances the performance by government in some areas of community life is still questioned by large segments of the population. The general trend, however, is consistently toward the increased involvement of government in a growing number of community activities. Such growth and expansion of the functions of government is inevitable in a rapidly expanding and changing community.

All social organizations exercise some types of social control in the community. The family exercises discipline over children, the church enforces conformity to moral standards, and managerial bureaucracy controls economic institutions. In modern societies the ultimate control is exercised by the political institutions, and the need for such ultimate authority results from conditions that have developed out of the nature of modern society.

In the first place, every society has codes of conduct that are considered by the members of that society to be morally right. Particular individuals or groups, including large organizations such as corporations, may violate these mores. As a result, government, through the use of violence or the threat to use violence, punishes and prevents such violations of the rules of the society. In industrialized societies such as ours, many of these mores and folkways are codified and preserved as laws, which the government enforces through the use of a specialized enforcement machinery such as police, courts, or administrative and executive orders. These laws generally represent the basic values of the society in such a way as both to enforce conformity and to insure the exercise of individual liberty. Thus, we find that the law will punish crime, yet not compel an individual to participate in any

300

organized form of worship, even though our society generally holds that the worship of God is morally right. In the one case we have the enforcement of a law and in the other the protection of individual rights by law. In the second place, large and powerful groups or corporations may have conflicting interests. Only through the intervention of an organization which has some ultimate control over both parties could these interests be arbitrated. In fact, this ultimate authority of the governmental organization may prevent the outburst of violence or civil war among competing groups. In the third place, subsidiary groups or corporations within a federal state may not be able to safeguard their members against threats from external sources, so that protection must come from the government which is the most powerful organization in the social structure.

Many services that are essential to the well-being of the community or the society cannot be provided adequately by subsidiary organizations, so that it becomes necessary for government to provide these services. Some services have always been considered to be a legitimate function of the government, such as the postal service, schools, and public roads. There has been an increasing tendency, however, for functions previously carried out by subsidiary organizations to become governmental functions, as, for example, care of the aged, which was previously a family function but is now more and more a governmental function through social security legislation and state institutions for the aged.

The use of governmental machinery as a means to attain certain goals collectively has been increasing rapidly in recent decades, so that many services which were at one time performed by private enterprise have become public responsibilities. This has resulted in those instances in which the particular service becomes so essential to the well-being of the society that government must assume responsibility for that service to preserve the common welfare and protect the public against unscrupulous private groups or corporations.

As a result of the convergence of a number of factors both historic and environmental, the people of the United States have a rather complex governmental structure. The devotion of people to the idea of local autonomy, which dates from the very beginning of the nation, is manifest in the variety of types of governmental organizations in the various states. It is true that there are universal elements that appear in all these forms, but it is clear that local people have exercised wide discretion as to the form which their local governments ultimately attain.

The increased demand for services from governments, whether local, state, or national, has had two consequences: first is the growth in size of state and national units, because of the inability of the local unit to meet the needs, and second is centralization of government because of the demand for services by the people which can only be met by the national or state governments.

ESSENTIAL CHARACTERISTICS OF A GOVERNMENTAL UNIT

While governmental units on the local level may assume a variety of different forms, there are certain essential elements that characterize a unit. These are discussed in the following selection from the Bureau of the Census.*

A government is an organized entity having governmental attributes and sufficient discretion in the management of its own affairs to distinguish it as separate from the administrative structure of any other governmental unit.

To be regarded as a government, any entity must possess all three of the attributes reflected in this definition: Existence as an organized entity; governmental character; and substantial autonomy. Following are some of the characteristics which are taken as evidence of these attributes.

Existence as an Organized Entity

Evidence on this score is provided by the presence of some form of organization and the possession of some corporate powers, such as perpetual succession, the right to sue and be sued, have a name, make contracts, acquire and dispose of property, and the like.

Designation of a class of units in law as "municipal corporations," "public corporations," "bodies corporate and politic," and the like indicates that such units are organized entities. On the other hand, some entities not so specifically stated by law to be corporations have sufficient powers to be recognized as governmental units.

Obviously, the mere right to exist is not sufficient. Where a former governmental unit has ceased to operate—e.g., receives no revenue, conducts no activities, and has no officers currently—it is not counted as an existing government.

Governmental Character

This characteristic is indicated where officers of the entity are popularly elected or are appointed by public officials. A high degree of responsibility to the public, demonstrated by requirements for public reporting or for accessibility of

* "Local Government Structure in the United States," *Bureau of the Census,* Washington, D.C., 1954.

records to public inspection, is also taken as critical evidence of governmental character.

Governmental character is attributed to any entities having power to levy property taxes, power to issue debt paying interest exempt from federal taxation, or responsibility for performing a function commonly regarded as governmental in nature. However, a lack of these attributes or of evidence concerning them does not preclude a class of units being recognized as governmental in character, if it meets the indicated requirements as to officers or public accountability. Thus, some "special districts" exist which have no taxing powers and are empowered only to provide electric power or other public utility services also widely rendered privately, but are counted as local governments because of provisions as to their administration and public accountability.

Substantial Autonomy

This requirement is met where, subject to statutory limitations and any supervision of local governments by the State, an entity has considerable fiscal and administrative independence. Fiscal independence generally derives from power of the entity to determine its budget without review and detailed modification by other local officials or governments, to determine taxes to be levied for its support, to fix and collect charges for its services, or to issue debt without review by another local government. Administrative independence is closely related to the basis for selection of the entity's governing body.

Accordingly, an agency is classified as an independent unit of government if it has independent fiscal powers and in addition:

(1) Has a popularly elected governing body;

(2) Has a governing body representing two or more State or local governments; or

(3) If its governing body is appointed, it performs functions that are essentially different from those of, and are not subject to specification by, its creating government.

Conversely, separate existence is not attributed to entities which lack either fiscal or administrative independence. Some local government agencies having considerable fiscal autonomy are therefore classified as being parts of other "parent" governmental units where integration is evidenced by characteristics (usually more than one) such as the following:

(1) Appointment of agency officers by the chief executive of the parent government, or control of the agency by a board composed wholly or mainly of parent government officials;

(2) Control by the agency over facilities that supplement, serve, or take the place of facilities ordinarily provided by the creating government;

(3) Provision for reversion of agency properties and responsibilities to the creating government after agency debt has been repaid;

(4) Requirements for approval of agency plans by the creating government; or

(5) Legislative or executive specification by the parent government as to the location and type of facilities the agency is to construct and maintain.

Other Factors

Although application of the foregoing criteria involves little difficulty in many instances, the infinite variety of provisions regarding local government entities and particularly the shadings of autonomy which they exhibit leave the classification of some types of entities subject to considerable judgment. In such cases, the Census Bureau has taken account of (1) local attitudes as to whether the type of unit involved is independent or not and (2) the effect of the decision upon collection and presentation of statistics of governmental finances and employment.

Such considerations apply, however, only where other criteria leave room for alternative decisions. As indicated below under "Relation to Other Classifications and Listings," regard for local terminology or traditions as to the nature of particular types of governmental entities has been subordinated, wherever necessary, to the need for uniform classification of entities of similar nature as among various States and areas.

Other Common Characteristics of Governmental Units

The foregoing description of essential characteristics makes no reference to certain other attributes which are possessed by many governments but which are not essential criteria for the identification of governmental units.

Area and Population

Most but not all governments exist to serve, and operate primarily within, an explicit geographic area for which a population can be determined. However, some entities having all essential characteristics of local governments do not possess this attribute but at best can be associated only with an undefined general location or area, rather than an explicitly defined territory. Examples of this are districts providing toll road and bridge facilities.

Even those governmental units which can be directly associated with a defined territory for certain purposes, such as property taxation, often own and operate facilities outside or provide services on one basis or another to residents of adjoining territory.

It should be noted also that, in connection with governmental operations, various types of geographic areas are established or recognized which lack characteristics of independent governments. These constitute in most instances devices for the conduct of elections, administration of justice, or performance of particular public services by governments serving the total area of all the particular types of districts concerned. Although these are useful for administration and are significant for the analysis of particular services and operations of government, such minor geographic areas and "districts" have no place in a count of governmental units.

Taxing Power

Most units of government are vested with authority to impose taxes. Again, however, this is not an essential or critical attribute, since some types of local entities which in every other respect can properly be viewed as independent units of government lack such authority, but derive a considerable degree of fiscal independence through powers to impose assessments for improvements, to charge for services, or to incur indebtedness. Some of the very largest special districts, such as the Port of New York Authority and the Chicago Transit Authority, are of this nature, as well as numerous other special district governments.

Uniformity of Taxation and Services

Even for those units of government which have property taxing powers and serve a precisely determined area, it cannot always be said that a single level of taxation and standard of services applies throughout the area concerned. Differential taxation often occurs legally where annexation or other boundary changes place a burden of debt service on some but not all of the territory; and subordinate "districts" which lack independence from the parent government are sometimes provided for with regard to particular types of improvements or governmental services, with resulting differences of tax level within the total area served by the government.

Relation to Other Classifications and Listings

A similarity of terminology appears as between some major types of local governments and certain local areas for which population data (and certain other statistics) are reported. This is particularly true as to entities here termed "counties," "municipalities," and "townships and New England towns."

This report is concerned with the governmental units so designated, however, rather than with the geographic areas to which similar terminology applies. Here, reference is to operating governments; areas similarly designated in other statistical reports include some areas without an organized local government of the type concerned. The difference between county areas and county governments reflects the fact that in fifty-four county "areas" no distinct county government exists.

THE NUMBER OF GOVERNMENTAL UNITS

The multiplicity of governmental units is a distinctive characteristic of American society. These units vary widely both in form and in function, with many special districts that are very narrow in purpose. Few people realize the extent to which this breaking up of the governmental structure has resulted in isolated units. The following research study reports the extent to which this isolation of elements of the local community is accomplished by the governmental organizations.*

Governmental units in the United States numbered 116,743 in 1952—fewer by 38,000 than in 1942. Local school districts, numbering 67,346, made up three-fifths of the 1952 total. In addition to the Federal Government and the forty-eight State governments, there were 49,348 local governments other than school districts. These consisted of 17,202 townships, 16,778 municipalities, 12,319 special districts, and 3,049 counties. The average number of governmental units per State was 2,432, but Rhode Island had only 89 while Minnesota had 9,026.

Figures in this report for nonschool governments are as of June 30, 1952; school district figures are for the 1951–52 school year.

Each of the following ten States had over 5,000 governmental units in 1952:

Minnesota	9,026	Kansas	6,933
Nebraska	7,981	Michigan	6,766
Illinois	7,723	Iowa	5,857
Wisconsin	7,258	New York	5,483
Missouri	7,002	Pennsylvania	5,156

Together, these ten States account for more than one-half of the total number of governmental units in the Nation. Nine of the ten have numerous town or township governments and all have large numbers of local school districts.

In the ten years since the enumeration of governmental units for the 1942 Census of Governments, the total number of governments has declined 25 per cent. Changes since 1942 in numbers of each of the various types of governmental units are summarized below:

TABLE V

Changes in Number of Government Units, by Type: 1942–52

Type of Government	Number of units 1952	1942	Per cent Change
Total	116,743	155,116	−24.7
U.S. Government	1	1	0.0
States	48	48	0.0
Counties	3,049	3,050	(†)
Municipalities	16,778	16,220	3.4
Townships	17,202	18,919	−9.1
School districts	67,346	108,579	−38.0
Special districts	12,319	8,299	48.4

* "Number of Local Government Units in the United States," *Bureau of the Census,* Washington, D.C., 1954.
† Less than .05 per cent.

The most striking change from 1942 to 1952 was the elimination of 41,233 school districts. Extensive school reorganization produced most of this 38 per cent reduction in the number of local school units. Special districts, on the other hand, increased 48 per cent in number during the ten-year period. There were 4,020 more special districts in 1952 than in 1942.

TABLE VI

Number of Governmental Units by State: 1952

State	All Government Units
UNITED STATES TOTAL	116,743
Alabama	548
Arizona	367
Arkansas	1,089
California	3,764
Colorado	1,953
Connecticut	363
Delaware	108
District of Columbia	2
Florida	617
Georgia	976
Idaho	938
Illinois	7,723
Indiana	3,050
Iowa	5,857
Kansas	6,933
Kentucky	796
Louisiana	489
Maine	664
Maryland	328
Massachusetts	584
Michigan	6,766
Minnesota	9,026
Mississippi	693
Missouri	7,002
Montana	1,598
Nebraska	7,981
Nevada	243
New Hampshire	551
New Jersey	1,151
New Mexico	289
New York	5,483
North Carolina	608
North Dakota	3,968
Ohio	3,936

TABLE VI

Number of Governmental Units by State: 1952 (*cont.*)

State	All Government Units
Oklahoma	2,771
Oregon	1,723
Pennsylvania	5,196
Rhode Island	89
South Carolina	413
South Dakota	4,917
Tennessee	435
Texas	3,963
Utah	385
Vermont	414
Virginia	366
Washington	1,539
West Virginia	350
Wisconsin	7,258
Wyoming	519

COUNTY DISTRIBUTION

One-third of all county areas have fewer than ten units of government. On the other hand, each of 274 county areas, or about one in every eleven, contains at least 100 local governments. These facts are evident from the following distribution of county areas by number of governments they include:

TABLE VII

Variation in Government Units by County

Number of Units	Number of County Areas	Per cent of Total
U.S. total	3,103	100.0
200 or more	16	.5
150–200	46	1.5
100–150	212	6.8
75–100	250	8.1
50–75	345	11.1
25–50	602	19.4
10–25	596	19.2
5–10	618	19.9
Less than 5	418	13.5

TABLE VIII

The 16 Counties Having 200 or More Governmental Units Each

County	State	Number of Local Governments
Cook	Illinois	422
Otter Tail	Minnesota	334
Dane	Wisconsin	292
Custer	Nebraska	276
Stearns	Minnesota	271
Grant	Wisconsin	255
Allegheny	Pennsylvania	247
Polk	Minnesota	237
Suffolk	New York	233
Holt	Nebraska	226
Marathon	Wisconsin	218
Fillmore	Minnesota	214
Kent	Michigan	214
Dodge	Wisconsin	205
Fond du Lac	Wisconsin	204
Knox	Nebraska	201

In the ten-year period 1942 to 1952 the number of county areas containing more than 200 local governments declined from 54 to the present figure of 16, largely because of reorganizations of local school districts. In Illinois alone, there were 25 counties containing 200 or more local governments in 1942 as compared with only one—Cook County—in 1952.

The average number of local governments per county area for the Nation as a whole decreased from 50 in 1942 to 38 in 1952.

CHANGES IN GOVERNMENT

The preceding section provides a general view of the complexity of the governmental structures in the United States. Each unit of government represents a measure of control over the citizens within its jurisdiction, whether a school district, road or bridge district, a township, village, city, county, state, or nation. The individual citizen thus is subject to many governmental jurisdictions. While our interest is the local community, as the following selection by Kumlien * points out, the local unit is affected greatly by the action of the units above it. In addition, problems and trends in local government are well described, including the expansion of governmental services, the multiplicity of units, overlapping jurisdictions, and the inefficiency of old forms of local government which the new technology of communication and transportation makes obsolete.

Some of the more marked trends in government are the changes in participation of individuals, increasing costs, and changing relationships between units of government.

More active participation in government during periods of economic stress and social crisis. Between 1890 and 1918 the percentage of potential voters who actually voted decreased almost 60 per cent. Beginning with the presidential election of 1920, however, this trend has been reversed. In the general election of 1940, 81 per cent of the potential voters in the state voted. This was a higher percentage than at any time except in 1900, and was a 25 per cent increase over 1920 and a 27 per cent increase over 1930. More interest is displayed in the presidential elections than in purely state elections, as evidenced by the fluctuations in the proportion voting each year.

Increasing centralization of government. Government is becoming increasingly centralized, and local government units are losing more and more of their responsibilities and functions. Numerous instances of this trend can be found in South Dakota.

Reasons for the decline of township functions. (1) The number of incorporated towns has increased rapidly in the last fifty years. When a town incorporates it ceases to be a part of the township for governmental purposes. The number of towns with more than 1,000 population is increasing and they are becoming the important community centers. These towns offer more services to people in and outside of the town than do the smaller towns and thereby diminish the functions of the township.

(2) Most of the townships were originally laid out in arbitrary six-mile squares without regard for physical barriers or community or neighborhood groupings. It frequently happens that personal contacts with the majority of the people of a township are largely for voting purposes, and little for educational, religious, or social purposes. In no case do the community boundaries coincide with the township or county lines. Not only do community boundaries disregard township lines, but also county and state lines, especially where towns are located near the border of the county. However, people still maintain considerable contact with the county seat, because of the business which must be transacted there.

Much attention is now being paid to the organization of services upon a community basis. In some places the working units of institutions are organized somewhat on a community basis, even though the main administrative unit may be

* W.F. Kumlien, "Basic Trends of Social Change in South Dakota," *South Dakota AES Bulletin 347*, Brookings, 1941, pp. 6–25.

the county. Libraries and health units, for example, are sometimes organized this way.

The suggestion has been made that the whole local governmental unit might be based advantageously upon the community. The town would be the community center and most of the social institutions would be located in this town, but the rural area around the town would help support and would use the services offered. The set-up would be flexible enough to suit different situations.

(3) Improved roads and means of communication have made many of the counties smaller than necessary, since they were laid out with the idea that all persons residing in the county should be able to drive a team of horses to and from the county seat in one day. It now has become possible for more and more business to be transacted in the county seat, thus decreasing further the importance of many of the township officers, such as justices of the peace.

(4) The multiplicity of functions recently assumed by governmental agencies makes it imperative that the unit of government be larger. Even the county, in many cases, has far too limited resources for the maintenance of many of the desired services. As a result, many more state grants-in-aid are being made to the counties, but not to the townships.

(5) There is a growing belief that the great number of local governmental units, including school districts, incorporated villages, towns and cities, and counties and townships, are a strong factor in the mounting tax burden.

The people in the incorporated towns find themselves in three taxing units, as do those who live in the open country. The tax burden of the incorporated towns is especially heavy, however, since many of them have a very small population and the tax base is so limited that a very high levy must be made in order to secure enough money to carry on the functions of the town. This is especially true where small towns have bonded themselves for the purpose of making improvements.

(6) The development in recent years of many types of federal grants-in-aid has helped further to weaken the townships and even the counties. Previous to the depression one of the largest items for which these grants were made was the road item. Since this was formerly the main expenditure of the township governments, and since now the township is limited to the building of side roads leading to highways, there seems to be less and less reason for their existence. These federal grants to the state have increased the authority of the state over the counties and townships, just as they have increased the authority of the federal government over the state. This has been one of the major factors in the centralization of government during the past decade.

Changes in population are gradually modifying government services. More stable population conditions which followed the period of settlement probably have influenced the functions of government.

There is a much larger proportion of older persons in the population now than there was in 1890. This tends to make government more conservative except in matters pertaining directly to legislation benefiting the aged. As an example, a large-scale program of old age assistance has been developed in the last five years and no doubt will continue to be a permanent part of the services of the government.

In the same period the sex ratio has become much more nearly equal. In 1890 there were 119 men for every 100 women in South Dakota, but by 1940 this ratio had declined to 107 men for every 100 women. More of the social services of government, such as public health, education, and social welfare, have been established as the number of women became larger. A predominantly male population does not feel the need of these services as keenly as does a more stable population with a larger proportion of women.

Not only has the age and sex composition of the population changed, but also the occupational composition. The proportion of agricultural workers in the population has declined, although they still outnumber all other workers.

Paralleling this change is the decline in the population living on farms. As towns have grown, a much greater variety of occupations has come into the state and many more people have left the farms.

The amount of money expended for education has increased rapidly, and taxes for public school purposes now make up a large proportion of the taxes paid by each property owner. More education, together with faster means of communication, has made the people more conscious of what is happening in the world, and consequently they demand from their government more services than they have had in the past.

As the population becomes more stable, and its rate of growth declines, the number of government units is not likely to increase even though certain functions do expand.

Transfer of functions of other social institutions to the government. Some governmental services have been greatly expanded. This is especially true of general welfare, which includes expenditures for the various institutions for the care and education of special groups, as well as for the Child Welfare Commission, Social Security Commission, State Health Laboratory, the State Chemical Laboratory, the penitentiary, and the state training school. Although many of these services, the Child Welfare Commission and the Social Security Commission excepted, have been in existence practically since the state was established, they have been greatly expanded in recent years and many more now are being cared for in institutions.

Education has also been greatly expanded. No doubt, the expansion of education has been greater than that of almost any other function of government. Although common schools had been made available for most people by the time South Dakota was established as a state, there has been an increasing demand for more education, especially in the secondary education field. Between 1890 and 1938 the proportion of South Dakota high school students among all students of the state increased from 1.3 per cent to 24.4 per cent. At the same time college enrollments rose from 1.0 per cent to 5.3 per cent of the total.

In several other fields there has been a gradual expansion of appropriations. Certain fields such as agriculture and transportation have been receiving increasing aid from the government. A State Department of Agriculture was established in 1921 and various boards were maintained to assist the agricultural industry of the state and to regulate the products sold. The increased appropriations for transportation are due largely to increased state aid to the counties for highway construction. These functions formerly were left almost entirely to the individual or to local governmental units, but increasing demands and more centralization of government made it more expedient for the state government to perform them.

It would seem that most of the functions which were transferred to government from other social institutions were originally transferred because of a lack of facilities and money to meet the increasing demands for certain services.

Government, being the only institution which could easily raise the necessary money and have the authority required to enforce regulations, was naturally the one to which people turned. Gradually there has developed a feeling that many functions which were originally considered the legitimate functions of other institutions really should be a responsibility of government. This accounts for a more rapid transfer of functions in recent years.

Shift of functions from one unit of government to another. There has been a decided trend in South Dakota toward the shifting of various functions from one unit of government to another. Most of the functions of the township have been taken over by the county; certain functions exclusively the duty of the county have been turned over to the state; and to some extent the federal government is helping out with some of the functions of the state.

The operation of democracy has become more complex. As our civilization has become more complicated the smooth operation of democracy has become more difficult.

The many changes which have taken place in ideas, both political and social, and the great increase in inventions and industrialization have created many problems for our democratic form of government. With much faster means of transportation and good roads the problems of maintaining law and order are greatly increased. This is true to some extent even in the most rural areas where previously little more than the force of neighborhood opinion was necessary to keep law-breaking at a minimum. The problem is more intensified in the large towns of the state.

With the development of labor-saving machinery there is less chance for the surplus youth of the state to secure employment, which not only increases the problem of government aid to the needy, but also tends to form a discontented group within the population.

Even our local government is showing the effect of certain urbanizing influences. This is especially noticeable in the increasing complexity of political party organization. The major political parties have greatly expanded their organization, so that political patronage, vote gathering, and selection of candidates for office are largely under the control of a local county chairman. This organization has become very effective and, if not working for the best interests of the people, can be very disastrous.

Public office does not always attract the best-qualified officials. The qualifications for either state, county, or township officials as set by law are general, requiring little more than that the person has resided in the state for a short time and is a qualified voter. The governor and lieutenant-governor must be at least thirty years of age. The attorney general of the state, all judges, state, circuit, and county, and the state attorney of the county are required to be learned in the law.

These very general qualifications for office allow some poor officials to be elected. Other reasons are probably equally important as causes of such incompetence.

Salaries are not high and the tenure of office is limited (in most cases they serve not more than two terms of two years), so that often the more successful people are not attracted by public office.

Another reason for inefficiency and waste in county government is the lack of a centralized authority to which the county officials are responsible. At present they are responsible only to the electorate, although the county commissioners do exercise some control over the other officials.

Improvement in the qualifications of public officials. Although it is hard to say definitely that public officials today are any better than they were in the early days of statehood, there are some reasons to believe that persons holding public office as well as electors are becoming better qualified than previously.

First, illiteracy has now almost disappeared, illiterate persons being only 1.2 per cent of the population in 1930. The proportion of illiteracy in the state has never been high, however.

Second, the extent of education has increased considerably.

Third, a system of merit examination has been established for employees of two divisions of the state government, the Unemployment Compensation Commission and the Social Security Commission. These two commissions employ only a small proportion of the public employees in South Dakota, but it is an encouraging trend toward securing better qualified personnel.

GOVERNMENT-COMMUNITY RELATIONS

As we pointed out in the selection by Kumlien, the township is losing many of its functions, some of which are being taken over by the county and the state. Furthermore, the federal government is becoming integrated with local units through grants-in-aid and the creation of central services which have to be administered locally. In some ways this increases the importance of the local unit since the federal grants-in-aid give considerably more service than could be offered on the basis of local taxes alone. However, it also decreases local autonomy because the locality must conform to the codes and criteria determined on the federal level.

The relationship between the governmental organization and other types of service organizations is complicated and there have not been many research studies on this relationship except for those showing that the jurisdiction of governmental units does not necessarily correspond to the community area served by other organizations and elements. This factor complicates the operation of the political process and accentuates differences among component groups.

To resolve the conflicting interests of the variety of groups that compose the community requires the operation of a community decision-making process that we generally refer to as the political process. Problems and issues are analyzed and discussed by the community, and the major decisions are settled by ballot in accordance with the wishes of the majority. The political process, however, frequently breaks down because of the inability of citizens to understand adequately the problems, issues, and alternate courses of action that are involved. As a result, decisions tend to be the product of group interests that may not be always the best for the community as a whole. Political decisions in a democracy depend upon enlightened citizenship competent to evaluate problems and reach decisions on the basis of intelligent concern for the common welfare rather than group interests. The breakdown of this political process provides one of the major areas of concern for community development where the emphasis is on the study and understanding that should precede decision-making. The difficulties existent in communities on this matter of the political process are illustrated in the following study by Hoffer which describes the various interest groups and the conflicts and tensions in a somewhat heterogeneous community.

The Community Situation and Political Action *

If "the situation" means the configuration of factors conditioning the behavior reaction,[1] it is a convenient concept for considering political activity within a community, for political action is peculiarly responsive to the multiplicity of forces in community life. This is the case to such an extent that it reflects the degree of integration as well as the quality of the various social processes occurring within a community. It is idle to condemn the nature of political processes without attempting to analyze their origin in community situations. This paper, therefore, examines the circumstances in modern community life which affect political action and the significant political results that emerge because these circumstances prevail.

The term "community" will be used to indicate a group of people living in a contiguous area having common interests and activities which result from such habitation. Although the word has been used for a long time, this connotation of the term has received increasing emphasis since C.J. Galpin demonstrated the physical reality of the rural communities in Walworth County, Wisconsin, and numerous social surveys were made in different parts of the United States.

Due partly to this new connotation of the term and its application to social organization, many adults have only a vague understanding of the nature of

* C.R. Hoffer, "The Community Situation and Political Action," ASR, 4:663–69, 1939. Used by permission.
[1] W.I. Thomas, "The Behavior Pattern and the Situation," Publications of American Sociological Society, Vol. 22, 1927, p. 1.

community life and have even less definite ideas about the social processes occurring within it. They do not think of the community situation as being the foundation for the political processes that occur, nor do they see the relationship between the two. This unfamiliarity with community life is one characteristic of the community situation which affects political action. People understand neither the cause nor the methods used in carrying on their political affairs and hence are unable to control them.

Another circumstance which has confused the relationship between the community situation and political action is the ecological nature of the community. Its physical boundary varies, depending upon the interests that are being considered and the circumstances affecting the length and shape of the borderline at any particular time. The community is in part a product of natural forces, whereas political areas are socially determined and relatively fixed. When governmental or political units were being formed in this country, there was a tolerable degree of correspondence between the so-called natural community and the political area. This natural unit, commonly called the neighborhood, corresponded closely with the one-room school district. Township government fitted this type of social organization well, but modern communication and transportation have changed these relationships. The community area has enlarged while the legal units have remained static. A recent study of high school communities in Michigan showed that there were 6,671 school districts in the state but only 533 high school communities. In Lower Michigan, high school districts had an average of thirteen square miles but served an area of eighty-eight square miles.[2] It is estimated that if these districts were enlarged on an average of seven times they would approximate the areas actually being served by them.

A detailed listing of the governmental units in a single rural-urban type of community (Howell, Michigan) shows that the center was an incorporated city of 3,615 and that the trade area covered parts of four townships. The city was provided with various services, like fire protection, police protection, public health, etc., and personnel to perform the necessary duties. However, these did not extend beyond the territorial limits of the town corporation. In addition to the town, there were townships and school districts and these were all overlaid with a system of county government. This situation is not exceptional, but occurs repeatedly in various parts of the United States wherever town and township governmental units exist.[3]

Since the geographical units for political action have not expanded with the territorial increase of the community, proposals are made frequently that they be enlarged to correspond more closely with community boundaries, but several circumstances prevent or greatly retard this adjustment. Changes in the size of the community area and diversity of interests within it complicate the situation. Usually, people are inclined to be loyal to existing forms of government and are suspicious of plans which would change them. Proponents of a change are necessarily put in a defensive position. They must demonstrate the superiority of the

[2] J.F. Thaden and Eben Mumford, "High School Communities in Michigan," *Michigan AES Special Bulletin 289*, 1938.
[3] C.R. Hoffer, "Cooperation as a Culture Pattern," *RS*, 3:153–58, 1938.

new in comparison with the old. Moreover, the politicians intrenched in the existing patterns of government urge their continuance for selfish reasons.

The inhabitants of modern communities have a variety of interests affecting political activity. These divide along occupational and cultural lines. To a laborer confronted with uncertain employment and low wages, it may seem as though a community in the sense of common interest scarcely exists, unless he is obliged to call upon its charitable agencies for assistance. Only within recent years has the labor group become a factor of importance in the local political affairs of a great many communities, but it is doubtful if systematic community development is definitely a goal in the political ideology of this group. Likewise, the business group becomes aware of community relationships largely as they relate to business success. Thus, it is difficult also for business men to appreciate the value of a well-balanced program of community development and the political action necessary to attain it.

The heterogeneity of cultural patterns in many communities also tends to prevent a clear understanding of political processes. Even though the arrival of new immigrants in most communities has ceased, many cultural traits of foreign groups persist. The continuation of these traits of foreign cultures, though they may be laudable in many respects, tends to set foreigners and their immediate descendants apart from the remainder of the community. This segregation retards their participation in political affairs unless, perchance, such groups become assertive politically and wrest political control from the others, as some urban groups of foreign descent have done. Ordinarily, however, foreigners have regarded themselves as only a small part of the community and have not been active politically except when the realization of an immediate need concerned them.

Even in communities where the identity of foreign groups has disappeared and the cultural characteristics are predominantly American, the diversity of interests still persists and impedes political action. The differences between the labor group and the business group in community situations have been alluded to already and have received elaborate treatment in such studies as *Middletown*. Diverse interest groups also appear in the field of religion, recreation, and morals. Those who have read *The American Community in Action* will be impressed by the fact that a majority of the cases cited there deal with conflicts and tensions which have come to be dominant in the life of the community. There is, for example, the community of Ferrum where the management of civic affairs was left to the merchants, professional groups, and the industrial population, but even with this diversity of participation, the leaders were unable to control factional interests. So powerful had these become that a Republican school superintendent was kept in office for three years by four Democratic members of the school board while the three Republicans voted against him on every occasion.[4] In this book we find that neighborhood rivalry prevented school consolidation in Long Creek; in the Daytona community, religious conflict prevailed; Big Lick was divided against itself; Roxbury had passed through the cycle from village

[4] J.F. Steiner, *The American Community in Action*, Henry Holt and Company, New York, 1928, p. 138.

homogeneity to urban heterogeneity. Yet in spite of all these differences, the political interest which was concerned, at least theoretically, with the common good had to be expressed in some manner or other.

In addition to such differences in community life, there is still the dominating influence of the *laissez faire* theory and its corollary, individualism, which make any kind of community organization and concerted action difficult. Adherents of the doctrine of individualism do not carry their theory far enough to see that it would be advantageous to participate in political affairs, at least to the extent of voting, even though the connection between the act of voting and the benefits to be derived from it are not direct nor definite. Many of the values associated with voting are abstract in nature, and in addition to questions of finance, involve education, health, recreation, or general community services which still will be provided even though a considerable number of individuals do not vote at all. Certainly, there are other and often more definite interests than the political competing for the time and attention of the voters. In fact, a study of the interests of people in local community affairs as reflected in the newspapers in thirty-five Michigan communities showed that the political interest was eighth in a list of twelve topics.[5] It was preceded by neighborhood news, personal items, agricultural topics, school news, church news, civic and patriotic affairs, and announcements of various kinds.

In view of the foregoing situation, one may ask, What are the patterns of political action which exist in our communities? F.S. Chapin has recently called attention to the fact that there are three patterns of government in the local community: "the legalistic pattern of government exemplified in the county, the village, the town or city; the quasilegal pattern of the party system, whose activities are partly regulated in the law, and partly a matter of private and even secret understanding; and third, the extra-legal pattern of the unseen government which consists of alliances that range from predatory business to the criminal underworld." [6]

Generally speaking, the so-called average citizen is aware of the legal pattern but is only vaguely familiar with the quasilegal pattern and knows little or nothing about the extralegal pattern. As Chapin points out, for a long time it was considered not nice to recognize or even admit that the extralegal pattern existed. It somehow cast a shadow upon the theory of democracy so dear to the heart of every American. However, a realistic attitude toward community life plus abundant evidence from racketeering and the occasional prosecution of it in courts make it clear that this is a significant pattern. The form of government, the legalistic pattern, is one thing; the actual process of government is another. It is entirely possible that the same form may provide the framework for a number of very different processes. Certainly, a study of government emphasizing form only will not adequately nor realistically acquaint the student with the way political action occurs in his community. It is not only a question of what the duties of

[5] C.R. Hoffer, "The Interests of Rural People as Portrayed in Weekly Newspapers," *Michigan AES Special Bulletin 298,* 1939, p. 12.

[6] F.S. Chapin, *Contemporary American Institutions,* Harper and Brothers, New York, 1935, p. 27.

the various officers are but how they are elected and how they discharge their official duties.

The existence of the quasilegal and extralegal patterns has given rise to what is generally known as the politician and the political gang. As popularly understood, politicians are individuals who become interested in political affairs and manage them in such a way that they themselves are benefited. Benefit to the community, while desired and welcome, is secondary to the interest of the selfish political group. In other words, the politician, unlike the statesman or civic-minded citizen, makes a business of politics and, given a particular set of circumstances, he behaves in a particular way. Under other circumstances, that is, in another community situation, he may behave differently, possibly quite contradictorily to his previous course of action. Generally speaking, it is safe to assume that the politician would prefer to do the right thing for his community rather than to follow some other course, but he must have a good "political" reason for doing so. This circumstance makes the participation of citizens in political affairs indispensable if good government is maintained.

A study of the politician and the political group as social units in a way similar perhaps to the study of the gang by Thrasher is greatly needed. Certainly, the political group manifests the characteristics of a social group from the standpoint of formation, personnel, leadership, control, morals, and group loyalties. The assumption, for instance, that the morals and loyalties of individuals belonging to the political group are always similar to those of individuals belonging to other groups is not a safe one. The evidence points in a different direction, as the occasional reports of business patronage, political scandals, and questionable acts of public officials indicate.[7]

The circumstances creating the political group favor its frequent alliance with the criminal group. Community sentiment severely condemns this relationship, but its repeated existence suggests that there are certain underlying factors in the present community situation which favor its development. Both are social groups within a community which strive to achieve benefits for themselves, frequently at the expense of the community. The political group needs votes and the "vice-criminal" group needs protection. What could be simpler than a clandestine alliance between them? Tannenbaum puts considerable emphasis on this relationship and points out that it matters little whether or not the politician desires this relationship.[8] He probably does not, because the politician is not a criminal. He is, however, realistic about political processes in community life and uses the instruments at hand to gain his ends.

The public has the impression that the alliance between politicians and criminals occurs in the realm of state affairs such as, for example, the granting of parole, but this is a fallacy, as recent treatises on criminology point out. The major control of political affairs by the criminal element occurs in local community situations through appointment of police officials, election of mayors, the behavior

[7] See for example, "Teapot Dome Scandal," *The Outlook*, January 30, 1924, pp. 136–66.
[8] Frank Tannenbaum, *Crime and the Community*, Boston, Ginn and Company, 1938, Chapter 5.

of court attendants, and the failure to enforce laws or ordinances controlling vice.[9]

It follows from these statements that the alliance between these two groups occurs most easily in an urban community where relationships between officers and citizens tend to become impersonal and secondary. As the density of population in the community decreases, such alliances become more difficult. In a rural environment, the relationships of citizen and officer tend to be personal and their activities are more easily observed by the public.

In contrast to the influence of the criminal element on the political group, the dependent or relief population in a community may be cited. The latter group, if it can be considered as such, consists of individuals who through some turn of circumstances must seek assistance from the public relief agencies. They are practically unorganized and helpless, and have a questionable status in the estimation of other groups in the community. Hence they are at the mercy of the politicians who seek to maintain control of relief for whatever political advantages it may have. The rise of social case work techniques and efficient administration now being adopted is not favored by many politicians because these improvements do not permit the use of tactics to which the politician is accustomed. This opposition was so strong in one state (Michigan) that the State Association of Township Supervisors forced a statewide referendum on a law designed to provide a modern centralized system of public welfare. Politicians do not distinguish clearly between social work and social workers and interpet the social workers' insistence on modern standards as a means of securing tenure of office for the social worker rather than as a desire to help clients in the most effective way.[10]

As the political group has endeavored with a considerable degree of success to control the political affairs of the community, individuals not belonging to this group have become skeptical of politics and political activity. This attitude is widely prevalent and makes improvement difficult, even when sponsored by the political group itself. Some people argue that control by the political group is inevitable and consequently they favor decentralized control and administration of community service rather than a more efficient centralized one because the latter, they believe, gives more opportunity for graft. Graft is inevitable anyway, they say, so let it be distributed widely and locally. Such a procedure might be designated as a democratic process working in reverse. The public is suspicious of any change in governmental organization lest it may further intrench the politicians. A corollary attitude, therefore, is avoidance. This attitude explains in a large measure the apathy of many citizens to the political affairs of their community.

Changes come slowly and not without opposition, as already pointed out, because the distinction between administrative responsibility and the policy determining function of government is not always clear. People fear that if they relinquish control over administration they will lose also the power to determine policies, but this result is not necessary nor inevitable. People lose control over

---

[9] See E.H. Sutherland, *Principles of Criminology*, Philadelphia, J.B. Lippincott Company, 1934, pp. 213–14.

[10] For a detailed statement of this controversy, see William Haber, "Social Work and Politics," *Survey Midmonthly*, 74:138–42, 1938.

the policy-making function when they cease to think and vote on issues presented to them. Civil service aids citizens in distinguishing between the administrative functions of government and its policy-determining functions. Its development will help to make clearer the nature of political action. All of these changes portend a new pattern of political action in the United States in which the possibility of control will be made available to the people in a simpler form, but so long as democracy endures, the community situation will determines the nature of political action.

The Relation Between Government and Community Development

The resemblance between goals and means of the political organization of the community on the one hand and community development on the other requires noting a careful distinction between the two. This distinction must be made in terms of the relative facility with which the two types of organization can be expected to solve certain types of community problems.

Of particular importance in discussing the nature and trends of governmental organizations is the similarity and character of many of the local governmental units with community-wide organizations designed for community development programs. It is usually thought that in order to accomplish their purpose, the governmental organizations must have ultimate power, particularly a monopoly on the threat of violence. They also must have written compulsory codes for citizens. Third, the governmental organizations, which reinforce norms of a broader nature, are in turn reinforced by them. In other words, legislation must correspond to mores, and often is a direct result of the feeling that this is the only means of achieving conformity to those mores. A fourth characteristic of governmental organizations is a requirement that a specific population or jurisdiction be made explicit. This characteristic is relatively unchanged over a course of time, so that growth or decline in population or in size is not met by changing the definition of legal units. The annexation of suburban areas to cities is a sample of such adjustment, but it is obvious that this adjustment does not follow lines of change as quickly as voluntary membership in organizations.

The community development organization has only one of these requirements, namely, that it reinforce norms of a broader nature and in turn be reinforced by them. This means that in any type of program where ultimate power, written codes, or a specific population are required, the governmental organization may be of more service in intelligent social change than community organization. However, in problems of immediate adjustment to change, where the desire to change is found among the people so that no power is needed, and where the exact boundaries of the area affected are not to be determined or do not correspond to an area of interest, the community organization may well solve a problem which has traditionally been left to the government.

Whether a given problem confronting a community is to be met by government or by voluntarily organized citizens depends on the nature of the problem and the adequacy of the government unit or of the voluntary organization to accomplish the purpose. Generally, government units change very slowly and are often found to be inadequate to meet a particular situation. This may mean appeal to a higher level of government. The gradual transfer of functions from the local township to the county or state, discussed by Kumlien, indicates that changes do come about, even if they result from indirect forces. The form of the township remains, but its functions change, or even disappear. Community development often cannot wait for the slow adaptation of government units to the needs of the times. Under such conditions voluntary community action is called for.

PRINCIPLES

1. *The primary functions of political institutions are social control and social service.*

2. *The general need for social control rests on the specific needs arising out of violations of the codes of conduct, the conflicting interests of powerful organizations within the society, and extra-community relationships.*

3. *The general need for social service rests on specific needs arising from the failure of other institutions to perform their functions for the general welfare and the discovery of new social needs not met by any existing institutional program.*

4. *A major feature of the structure of government in America is the multiplicity of governmental units, with specific needs being served and well-defined populations included.*

As a result of this the community structure is broken down into independent particles which are not well integrated. Thus a solution to a problem in one aspect of the community is not always accomplished with due regard for consequences which may accrue to some other aspects of the community.

5. *A major trend in political organization is the centralization of governmental function, thus taking from local government much of the control and service previously assigned to it.*

6. *The administration of federal programs at the community level cancels some of the loss of functions in the local governmental unit, but also decreases the autonomy of the local unit through the necessity to conform to federal codes in the administration of these programs.*

7. *The relationship between the legal pattern and other patterns of social control and social service in the community is subtle and it is difficult to consider in nongovernmental action programs in the community.*

This is particularly so of quasilegal patterns, as pointed out by Hoffer, and the extralegal patterns, as pointed out in the chapter on power and leadership. Yet this relationship is important in social change and in the success of deliberate action programs.

8. *There are often elements within the community which are government-like in character, particularly in the service function, but have to operate without some of the institutional sanctions of government.*

Of particular importance is the example of a voluntary organization for community development. The voluntary nature of support for such organizations makes their job more difficult than that of the government. However, because the government is an institution, it is less responsive to newly defined needs and to newly discovered means of achieving its aims than is the community-wide organization.

9. *Inherent in the nature of government is an inflexibility and institutionalization that often retards the provision of adequate control and services.*

10. *Community development is an extragovernmental pattern of organization through which citizens can initiate programs of both control and service.*

It supplements and strengthens government through its emphasis on the spread of knowledge about problems and issues as a basis for decision-making in the political process.

SELECTED REFERENCES

Anderson, William, and Edward W. Weidner, *State and Local Government in the United States,* Henry Holt and Company, New York, 1951.

Baltzell, E. Digby, "Urbanization and Governmental Administration in Lower Bucks County," *Social Problems,* 2:38–46, 1954.

Chase, Stuart, *Democracy Under Pressure: Special Interests Versus the Public Welfare*, Twentieth Century Fund, New York, 1945.

Lancaster, Lane W., *Government in Rural America*, Second Edition, D. Van Nostrand Company, New York, 1952.

Mercer, Blaine E., *The American Community*, Random House, New York, 1956, Chapter 12.

Merriam, Charles E., *Public and Private Government*, Yale University Press, New Haven, 1944.

Merton, Robert K., Ailsa P. Gray, Barbara Hockey, and Hanan C. Selvin, *Reader in Bureaucracy*, the Free Press, Glencoe, Illinois, 1952.

Sanders, Irwin T., *The Community*, The Ronald Press Company, New York, 1958, Chapter 12.

Smith, T. Lynn, *The Sociology of Rural Life*, Harper and Brothers, New York, 1947, Chapter 19.

Snider, Clyde F., "American County Government: A Mid-Century Review," *American Political Science Review*, 46:66–80, 1952.

Vidich, Arthur J., and Joseph Bensman, *Small Town in Mass Society*, Princeton University Press, Princeton, New Jersey, 1958, Chapters 6 and 8.

Wager, Paul W., editor, *County Government Across the Nation*, University of North Carolina Press, Chapel Hill, 1950.

Weidner, Edward W., and Jack Preiss, "Rural Local Governments and Politics and Adult Education," in *Rural Social Systems and Adult Education*, Michigan State College Press, East Lansing, 1953.

CHAPTER 16

School–Community Relations

It is the general frame of reference of this book that the relationships between an institution and the remainder of the community constitute elements of community structure and that these relationships may be examined in terms of functions performed by the institution. Thus, the relationship between the educational institution and the community will be looked at from the viewpoint of the functions of education. In addition, there are several problems created by the structure of the educational institution which also relate to community activity. Both the functions of education and these problems will be discussed in this chapter.

The major function of the educational institution is the training of the younger, and to a growing extent, the older members of the community in the knowledge, skills, and values necessary and desirable to life in that community. It is a major means of transmitting the culture to the new generation. Knowledge includes information necessary to occupational contribution to the community, leisure time, and health. The skills include proper speech, writing, numbers, and some types of occupational skills. The values include the codes of conduct and the goals, or the mores and the folkways. Examples of these are patriotism, intellectual curiosity, and ambition.

The educational institution as now constituted in the United States is, perhaps, the youngest of all the basic institutions. Formal education as an institution by itself, differentiated, say, from the family, is younger than written history, while the institution of the family, some form of political authority, and economic as well as the institutional organization around religious worship are doubtless older than written history. However, the function of teaching and training the young in the culture of the group is also very ancient. What is perhaps more important is that mass education of all the people in a community regardless of their position in the stratification system is very recent. One implication of this is that many of the means used in the educational institution have not yet become ritualized and desirable for their own sake, but are still judged in terms of their relative effectiveness in achieving the ends or functions for which the educational institution exists. This

325

does not mean that effectiveness in achieving objectives is always or even often the criterion used in making changes in the educational process. Rather, it means that the structure of the school is an issue, and the relationship between structure and effective function serves as a major criterion in decision-making.

STRUCTURE

Church-School Relations

Certain influences in American society operate to modify or condition the structure of the educational institution. In the first place, private and public schools operate side by side. This is the result of two major factors. Private schools, for one thing, antedate the development of public free education. Thus, in the early period of American history, practically the only schools available were those operated under private auspices. These "private auspices" were usually churches. Most of these early church-supported schools at the elemntary level disappeared with the development of the public schools. However, since the constitutional separation of church and state forbids religious instruction in the schools, some denominations maintain parochial schools in which not only the religious values but the entire formal school curriculum can be taught.[1]

Age Specialization

In the second place, the school's structure is characterized by the organization and specialization based upon age of the learner. Education during the first five or six years, during which many of the most basic values and skills and some knowledge are learned, is a function of the family. The school then takes over the teaching process and continues this function until the person is somewhere between sixteen and twenty-five. Up to this point formal sanctions force the person to learn in the family and the school. After he leaves school, less formal sanctions are employed but the institutional function is still operating.

However, adult education is not itself a recognized responsibility of any single institution or organization within the community. Organized educa-

---

[1] Robert J. Havighurst and Bernice L. Neugarten, *Society and Education*, Allyn and Bacon, Inc., Boston, 1957, Chapter 6, and Robert M. Bear, *The Social Functions of Education*, The Macmillan Company, New York, 1937, Chapter 8.

tional opportunities for adults are provided by many community institutions either as an extension of their normal function to include the adult population or because they need to educate adults in order to fulfill their manifest function.[2] For example, the public schools offer evening classes for adults in such areas as vocational training, general education, or literacy as an extension to the adult population of their normal responsibility for formal education. Health and welfare agencies, on the other hand, provide organized educational opportunities for adults in order to improve the health or welfare of the community. The Extension Service engages in adult education in order to interpret agricultural and homemaking research and thus improve farm and home life. Such programs of adult education are generally isolated both from each other and from the major operation of the institution itself.

School Administration and Control

In most small communities in the United States, there is no single enterprise either in the world of business, government, or elsewhere which has so large a budget or involves so large a number of people as does the school. Particularly in those very small communities where there exists a centralized school or a consolidated school, as it is sometimes called, the school superintendent or principal in charge handles a budget far in excess of any other enterprise in the community. This means that the people in charge of the school must center most of their activities and have most of their training in budgetary and personnel matters, and are deprived of the opportunity of giving full attention to the educational functions of the school. While the school's functions are performed at the classroom level for the most part, there are many decisions which may have to be made in connection with the teaching process which are made in terms of the budget rather than the educational function. It is not a function of the school to keep expenses low, of course, but budgetary concern does indicate that the relationship between the school and the community may be seen in large part in terms of the budget. The school tax is one of the largest of the local taxes, and therefore this sponsorship of the school at the community level is again a very important aspect of school-community relations.

A third factor is that local autonomy in educational control gives the community more power and authority over the educational institution than

[2] Howard Y. McClusky, "Adult Education and Community Relations," in J.E. Grinnell and Raymond J. Young, editors, *The School and the Community*, The Ronald Press Company, New York, 1955, Chapter 19, and Bibliography contained therein; and Edmund deS. Brunner, *Community Organization and Adult Education*, University of North Carolina Press, Chapel Hill, 1942.

over most of the other institutions. The township trustees, the school board, and other similar types of local groups make decisions regarding their own school, and thus the correlation between school and community is very high.[3] By correlation between school and community is meant that the curriculum, teaching methods, and aims of the particular school meet the expectations of the community. This makes another function extremely difficult, namely, the leadership of the school in social change. But it does foster the satisfaction of community needs as defined by the community in furnishing either liberal arts or vocational courses, counseling or strict attention to subject matter, heavy emphasis or de-emphasis on sports events, and so on.

Teacher Specialization

Still another aspect of the structure of the educational institution in American society is that teachers are specialized and trained personnel. This factor is different from the family, the government, and in some cases the economic institution. This means that many of the decisions which are made about teaching and other educational problems have been studied much more intensively by the agents of the community than by the other members of the community.

Teachers play a double role in that they are members of the community at the same time that they are its agents in matters of education.[4] In moments of conflict between school and community, the better trained teachers are more apt to identify themselves with the school.

Conflicts between school and community often arise over matters of function and method. Community members are apt to consider themselves as qualified to make decisions in these matters as their professionally trained agents, with the result that changes in the institution will be slow and the adaptation of the institution to the changing needs of society will be retarded. Many educators encourage the use of groups made up of professional educators and lay citizens to study school problems and make decisions for changes.[5] This tends to reduce conflict and maintains a balance between educationally desirable and locally acceptable modifications to the function and method of the institutions.

The Parent-Teachers Association illustrates one such cooperative decision-making group, although it does not always operate effectively. In communi-

[3] Havighurst and Neugarten, *op. cit.*, Chapter 8.
[4] *Ibid.*, Chapter 17.
[5] G.D. McGrath, "Citizen Interest and Participation," and Raymond J. Young, "The Parent-Teachers Association and Other Parent Groups," both in Grinnell and Young, *op. cit.*, Chapters 7 and 8.

ties where the PTA is active, many difficult decisions can be made with a minimum of conflict and confusion. In other instances, the PTA may become so involved with petty issues that it will not consider basic problems, with the result that this process of decision-making breaks down.

The Community School

In American society the concept is changing as to the role of the school as an educational institution, with increasing emphasis upon its responsibility for the lifelong education of community members.[6] This newer concept is popularly referred to as the "community school," although as we have used "community" here any school is a community school.

Under this new concept there are several different or additional activities included in the function of the school. First, learning is organized more around problems and situations in the community itself than knowledge in isolation. As a result, resources within the community are utilized to a greater extent to enhance the learning process and add first-hand experiences. Second, groups and individuals from the community become more deeply involved in the learning process as educational resources and as advisory planning groups. Third, closer communication between school and community is effected, with the result that the community participates more actively in making decisions respecting the function of the school. Fourth, educational opportunities for adults are made a normal part of the schools' function so that adults can continue learning. Fifth, school facilities become generally available to the community at large, becoming the center for the active social life of the community. This last point was traditional in the neighborhood schools in the past, but through consolidation it was almost eliminated, so that the new concept of the community school is a revival of a long tradition in American society.

SCHOOL FUNCTIONS

There are many lists of functions of the educational institution which range from a carefully worked out summary, such as the two presented below, to a

---

[6] For a description of community schools and their programs, see Edward G. Olsen, et al., The Modern Community School, Appleton-Century-Crofts, New York, 1953, and Elsie R. Clapp, Community Schools in Action, the Viking Press, New York, 1939. Also see Maurice Seay and others, The Community School, the Fifty-second Yearbook of the National Society for the Study of Education, Part II, University of Chicago Press, Chicago, 1953.

detailed list of several hundred specific aims of education. Early in the twentieth century, the National Education Association appointed a committee to prepare a list of principles to "guide the reorganization and development of secondary education in the United States." [7] These are referred to as the seven cardinal principles. This list, which has received much popular acceptance, at least at the verbal level, is as follows: Health, command of fundamental processes, worthy home membership, vocation, civic education, worthy use of leisure, and ethical character. As may be seen from this list, the traditional concept of the school as imparting knowledge and the later concept of the school as teaching skills is superseded, and the ideas of civic education and ethical character imply all that was suggested in the first part of this chapter in the reinforcement of mores and folkways.

The function of command of fundamental processes is the traditional and perhaps the major function of the formal educational institution. It is major because the school is the only institution whose function it is to teach these basic skills. Primarily, these skills are represented by the three R's, but they also extend in present-day schools to include skills in artistic fields, athletics, handling vocational problems, and refinements on the three R's, including expression as well as writing and higher mathematics as well as arithmetic.

It is the aim of democracy that these skills should be possessed by all of the population, for it is inconceivable that a democracy can exist without an informed public competent to make decisions on matters of common concern. An informed public must be literate, but literacy alone is not enough, and hence the schools must teach more than the basic skills.

Not only does the political institution demand the teaching of basic skills, but all other institutions except the family demand them also. Even the family requires the teaching of the fundamental processes indirectly. The religious institution requires these skills through its sanctions on reading the Bible; the economic institution requires those in the labor force to be trained for their vocations; and the family requires training, since the division of labor in the American family precludes the time necessary to teach the essential skills.

Institutional Relationships

The other items listed in the seven cardinal principles are functions the school performs to reinforce other institutions. For example, health, worthy home membership, and ethical character are primarily aspects of socializa-

[7] Bureau of Education *Bulletin,* "Cardinal Principles of Secondary Education," 1918, Number 35.

tion, and therefore are aspects of one of the primary functions of the family. Further, these other functions are not usually taught directly, but left to indirect methods, with the exception of a few types of vocations. Clerical work, through typing, shorthand, and bookkeeping, and shop are taught directly. But the relationship between the school and most of the other vocations is one of indirect teaching through attitudes toward quality in work. This problem of transfer of training deserves closer inspection.

What Should the Schools Teach?

The content of the school curriculum is a subject of continuous discussion and controversy in a democratic society. In the performance of its major function the institution of education must have its goals clearly defined, because the curriculum is the means through which the established ends are attained. We have already indicated the major function of education to be the transmission to the young of the knowledge, skills, and values requisite for successful life as a community member. The question, then, is what specific subjects will best accomplish these ends. There are many schools of thought on this matter, two of which will illustrate well the relationship between school and community.

The controversy has to do with the problem of "transfer of learning." [8] This phrase refers to the theory that learning in one field prepares individuals to meet situations in another. For example, training in mathematics, it is held by one side, will train the individual to be logical in his thought habits. Similarly, a thorough grounding in Latin was supposed to cultivate the mind so well that the individual would be able to meet practical life situations which seem far removed from the study of Latin. This so-called classical curriculum has been subjected to severe criticism by various groups including both the "citizens" who say there is no "practical" value in Latin or mathematics—beyond simple arithmetic—and by a strong professional education group. Since World War II there has been a mounting volume of criticism of the drift away from the old standards and a call for reinstatement of more mathematics and science and Latin in the curriculum. But the old controversy remains unsettled. The proposition is difficult to demonstrate and prove either way. If it does occur, then the emphasis on the revision of the curriculum is not of great importance, but if transfer does not occur, then it is a serious matter for the schools to devise a curriculum that will meet the needs of life in the contemporary community.

[8] See, for example, Robert C. Craig, *The Transfer of Guided Learning*, Bureau of Publications, Teachers College, Columbia University, New York, 1953.

There is much reason to believe that transfer of training does occur among the better students, and it occurs to a greater degree as it is encouraged by teachers in pointing out to the students where particular kinds of information or skills may be applicable. Naturally, students who are brighter are more likely to recognize situations in which a skill learned or information learned in entirely different contexts may be applicable. This would mean, in terms of practical considerations in correlating the school with the community, that those subjects which are mainly offered for the purpose of transfer of training might be limited to the brighter students who might make such a transfer. It would also mean that many courses such as Latin might not be given for purposes of transfer to most students, since the relationship between Latin and most life problems that students would meet is very distant, therefore making transfer very difficult. This is not to say that Latin should not be offered, but rather that if Latin is offered, it should be defended on its legitimate grounds, namely, that of interest in the arts and humanities courses. It is probably true that the trend toward practical courses such as manual training, vocational agriculture, homemaking, and so on was helped along by the fact that most of the liberal arts and humanities courses were defended on practical grounds, thus making practicality a value criterion without any question being raised by anyone as to its legitimacy.

The same point may be made regarding much of the literature which is taught in the school. While the literature in itself may promote the skill of reading, it is likely that courses which include the difficult works of Shakespeare and some of the major poets are singularly unrelated to the worthy use of leisure time. The point here is neither in defense of, nor opposition to, the offering of such literature at the high school level. Rather, it is the point that for school and community to be well correlated, there must be realistic assessment of the consequences of the courses offered as well as the teaching methods—consequences then examined in terms of values in the community. In the short run, this is not so effective as propagandistic techniques and may result in unfavorable decisions about such courses; but in the long run, the person who is desirous of including such courses in the curriculum may find it better to build a realistic rationale for each course in terms of the consequences that might really accrue to the offering of such a course. A good case in point is the offering of courses in mathematics. In the very small community, where there are no universities and most of the students either migrate to blue collar jobs or accept positions within the community, the argument for mathematics just does not make sense. In very recent years, the emphasis upon the shortage of engineers and physical scientists, for whom mathematics is a requirement, should show that the arguments during the 1930's and 1940's on mathematics should have been to increase the alternatives offered to the students in selecting college courses.

It was pointed out above that transfer of learning is more likely to occur if it is deliberately promoted by the teacher. One of the difficulties here is the subject-matter orientation of most courses. Teachers are in danger of personal insecurity if they fail to teach effectively the concrete facts and skills of their subject, since strong sanctions for this coverage are effected through statewide tests, where a teacher's results may be compared with the state average. The achievement of students is measured quantitatively, so that teachers are encouraged, although not deliberately, to emphasize the factual content of their subject to the neglect of the attitudinal objectives. Certainly, the achievement of students on information and skill learning is a basic function of the school, as evidenced by the existence of legislation and policy regarding the statewide tests. But the consequence of such tests to other value objectives in the educational institution must be recognized if the community is to organize its school to meet the requirements set by the community.

THE SCHOOL AND SOCIAL CHANGE

Intergenerational Change

In addition to the function of the school in teaching and in transfer of training from subjects taught to later life, the school operates in an important way in social change. Much social change undoubtedly occurs through the process of the younger generation taking over positions. In this sense, regardless of control of the school by community powers, much goes on in a classroom which brings about attitudes different from those traditionally held in the community. This modification may occur through interaction between teacher and class, but more likely occurs among students themselves. Thus, conflict between the individual student and his parents may be generalized and reinforced through the fact that the adolescent culture is different from that of adults. Since the school brings adolescents together, this may be viewed as a latent function of the school. Insofar as these adolescent values are carried into adulthood, they represent social change.[9]

[9] See Kingsley Davis, "The Sociology of Parent-Youth Conflict," *ASR*, Vol. 5, No. 4, pp. 523–34.

School Goals

More directly, the school and the community may be found closely related in social change problems, and will differ according to whether they reinforce each other or are in conflict.[10] To the school, more than other institutions, are deliberately assigned aims by other people and by school personnel themselves. This is perhaps the main difference between the school and other institutions. Most of the basic functions of the school are not amenable to deliberate change over a short period of time without disorganizing the society. This, of course, would mean that rapid change could not be produced even if everyone decided that it should be. At the secondary level of functions, however, many of the particular aims of the school are changed from time to time or are at least strongly encouraged either by school personnel or by people in the community. At this level of functioning, the question becomes one of deciding who should define the social goals of the school. The one extreme position in this matter is that the community should decide the goals for the school. The other extreme is that the school personnel, since they have made more intensive study of the school situation, should assess the goals and set them independently of community influences.

The result of giving the responsibility to define goals for the school solely to members of the community means that the talents and knowledge of those who are best informed on the potentalities of the school and limitations of the educational process are not utilized in the definition of the aims. The consequence of this would be that the school would be given some goals which it cannot perform and on the other hand, many potentialities in the school would not be realized because they were not recognized by those who defined the aims. The other position, namely, that the social goals should be defined entirely by the school personnel, would mean that since the school teachers often come from subcultures quite different from the community in which they teach, the likelihood of inappropriate goals is high.

Selection of Textbooks

One important aspect involving the relationship between the school and community in social change is in the selection of textbooks. For the most part,

[10] Raymond J. Young, "The Problem of School and Community Relationships," in Grinnell and Young, *op. cit.*, Chapter 1; see also Albert I. Oliver, Jr., "Community and Curriculum Correlation," *ibid.*, Chapter 2.

textbooks which deal primarily with factual information and skills are of little concern to the community, so long as the content is well defined. It is in subjects where the attitudinal content in relation to information is high that the selection of texts becomes an issue between school personnel and the community. This is found in the area of social studies, where there is often either a lack of information and skills in the community or at least a lack of attention to them, so that a heavy emphasis is placed on attitudes in the content for the course. Conflict between school and community over appropriate texts may result because much of the emphasis and many expectations defined by the community in the area of social studies are attitudes. For example, loyalty to community, to state, to nation, and to the mores generally is considered important. One will find treatment of the Civil War in the high school history books in Northern schools somewhat different from that used in the South. Factual events in the area of social studies are colored with certain attitudinal frames of reference which give more than informational content and in some cases actually prejudice the selection of information to be presented.

Teaching Democracy

It is usually found that citizenship education is largely limited to social studies, but that the expansion to occupational effectiveness is found in those courses which are highly specialized. Thus, if democracy is to be learned in school, it is learned as subject matter in the government classes and in some of the extracurricular activities. It is seemingly obvious that democracy itself, while it is a subject content, must involve training as a skill and as an attitude in day-to-day living. But democracy is isolated from day-to-day living when taught merely as an idea rather than as a way of life. This probably follows from the fact that democracy itself is an extremely difficult way of life. It requires an intelligent citizenry, a leadership which does not dictate courses of action, and often more time in arriving at decisions than does authoritarian government. The pressures on the school teacher to cover a certain amount of content in his field, particularly in preparation for some kind of state examination on which his effectiveness is to be rated, impose tremendous difficulties if the time is taken to teach by democratic methods.

If democracy is to be taught "by doing" in the classroom, the teaching method and the content to be covered presupposes decisions by students themselves. But if students knew enough to make a decision on content and methods, they would not need to take the course. This is a real argument against teaching by democratic methods, and yet, if democracy is to be learned, it must be learned as it becomes applied to all areas of life. As one school teacher put it, "Citizenship is an elusive subject . . . [and] like hygiene, it is a collection of habits which you learn by doing. The use of local material is undoubtedly a common practice in almost every school but it seems to me that we miss a golden opportunity in citizenship training if we offer such material just for information." [11]

Academic Freedom and Leadership in Change

The school situation is traditionally thought of as one in which the free play of imagination can bring about new ideas either in the intellectual world or in the world of affairs. It is the area in which much social invention can occur, although it is not the only institution in which new means and new ends may be articulated for the community. The freedom of the teacher and of the students to be creative in these areas of life is usually referred to as academic freedom.[12] At the college level, it applies mainly to research problems, to methods of study, and to disseminating new ideas among students who may be tomorrow's scientists and scholars, even though such ideas may go counter to those commonly held. At the high school level, academic freedom is more difficult to define. It is applied to methods of teaching thought to be productive of a better learning situation. The definition of academic freedom in content has not been clarified. There are many factors, however, which operate to limit it as it applies to content. Some of these have already been mentioned.

Watson [13] suggests five changes or aspects of the problem which bring about less academic freedom in the public schools. The first of these is the restraint imposed through laws or rules for the assurance of teacher loyalty or freedom from subversive tendencies. No law can be so specific that it operates in such a narrow sphere, and therefore the freedom of the teacher is sacrificed to this desire to assure teacher loyalty. The second source of difficulty listed by Watson is that of subsidized attack by various organizations opposed to certain types of freedom in education. This difficulty usually begins with a specific type of problem, such as some particular emphasis in

[11] Matt Lagerberg, "Two Local Units on Practical Citizenship," Clearing House, XXIV (October, 1949), pp. 11–12.

[12] Lloyd H. Elliott, "Freedom in Teaching and Learning," ibid., Chapter 6; Howard K. Beale, Are American Teachers Free? Charles Scribner's Sons, New York, 1936; Education Policies Commission, The Education of Free Men in American Democracy, National Education Association, Washington, D.C., 1941.

[13] G. Watson, "The Public Schools Retreat from Freedom," The Nation, CLIV, June, 1928, 1952, pp. 53–57.

the curriculum, cutting costs in the budget, or certain textbooks which should be changed. Usually such attacks come from more outspoken individuals and often a small minority in the community. A third factor, particularly notice-able in the 1940's and 1950's, was the increased precautions or self-censorship against possible charges of subversion. This included avoidance of debatable issues in all school matters, such as course content, methods, library materials, or speakers. A fourth factor is the decreasing vigor with which defenses for academic freedom are argued. Compromise is often used instead of vigorous defense and argument, with the result that freedom is infringed. The fifth factor listed by Watson is the growing influence of religious doctrines on the schools.

MASS SOCIETY AND THE COMMUNITY SCHOOL

As is the case with most institutions in the community, there are pan-community influences which prevent the local community from determining the nature of its schools. Some of these influences have been mentioned previously, including state-controlled examinations, state-adopted textbooks, teacher certification, and the influence of certain national organizations which seek to promote or discourage certain contents or methodolgy used in the school. In addition to this, of course, there are several other rather obvious influences which severely limit the local school, including textbook publishing companies, distributing corporations, national professional edu-cation organizations, the requirements for matriculation in colleges and uni-versities, and accrediting groups, all of which tend to shape the schools in the direction of homogeneity rather than making them unique to each com-munity.

There are many adult organizations with educative structure and functions that influence the school. Some of these are community organizations, al-though they may be organized formally on a pan-community basis and in-formally on a neighborhood or friendship group basis.

Social Trends and the School

In a dynamic society such as that of the United States, the elements of the community are constantly undergoing modifications. The relations between and among its institutions and other components are subjected to influences from without as well as within the community. One of these society-wide influences is the increasing urbanization of the population. Even rural society is undergoing transition from a relatively simple group life characterized by informality and intimacy to one which is more formally organized, more impersonal, and vastly more complex.

Technology, which has helped to erase some of the differences in thought and behavior between rural and urban people, has also increased their interdependence and placed them in daily contact. It has also helped to increase the farmer's feeling of insecurity by enforcing his dependence upon the behavior of other groups. This feeling of insecurity has led farmers to make aggressive efforts to achieve greater stability of income through agricultural legislation, the establishment of cooperative marketing agencies, and the formation of more effective national farm organizations.

Meantime, labor and business have been similarly engaged in protecting their group interests, with the result that American society is segmented into three major pressure groups; business, labor, and agriculture. Belshaw notes the results of such competitive practices in the following statement: "Agrarian protectionism as it was practiced between the wars, . . . although it may have improved the lot of an *existing* rural population producing within a *given* pattern of production, . . . reduced the incentive to those structural changes and shifts in occupation distribution which were necessary for improvements in productive capacity and for any substantial betterment of rural welfare in the long run." [14]

Education should aim to resolve the conflicts between farm and non-farm groups by promoting a better understanding of the nature of present-day society and the various groups which compose it. Above all, it should seek to develop in people a sense of their social responsibilties as citizens in a democracy. Specifically, greater emphasis should be placed on the interdependence of all groups and on the principle that the general welfare is promoted when each group makes its maximum contribution and is impaired when any group seeks to gain maximum advantage with minimum contributions. The pulling and hauling of pressure groups (farmers, workers, business men, veterans, the aged, and so on) may thwart rather than promote the welfare of all. The only alternative is education for a citizenship which will display a broad sense of social responsibility.

In the schools, through instruction appropriate for each age level, children and young people can gain an understanding of the effect which the new technology has upon them personally and upon their homes and communities. This instruction should be concrete and practical and be brought about through experience on farms, in factories, and in offices. Such a program was in existence at one time in Gary, Indiana.

[14] H. Belshaw, "Foundations of Rural Welfare," *International Labour Review*, LI: 282, March, 1945.

Two major considerations have accrued from technological change: youths who will remain in agriculture and youths who will migrate to the city must both have opportunity to achieve vocational competence. Clearly, farming is a much more exacting occupation under present conditions then it was in the "horse-and-buggy" days. The successful management of a family farm, the capitalization of which may equal that of a country bank, is not a job to be taken lightly. The farm operator in the more highly mechanized areas must know how to utilize the available resources of land, labor, and capital for efficient production, how to market the product, and how to conserve and enrich the soil. In a rapidly changing world, he must be alert to take advantage of new methods as they become available through research and experience.

Vocational education is needed at the adult as well as the high school level. For example, the Smith-Hughes vocational program functions through the high school for the benefit of various age groups. The program includes:

(*a*) *Adult education for established farm operators.* This deals largely with technical and economic problems of farming.

(*b*) *Young farmer education.* This is a continuing program of directed learning experiences for young men who are out of school but not yet established in farming or some other occupation.

(*c*) *High school education in vocational agriculture for farm boys enrolled in the secondary schools.* This is based on the program of the Future Farmers of America and seeks to assist in promoting citizenship, leadership, and progress toward establishment in farming or some other occupation.

Preparation of the potential migrant for the adjustment he or she will have to make to town or city life and work is a problem that has long been familiar to rural educators. The number who migrate, though greater in some areas than others, will exceed 50 per cent for the nation. In any case, education through high school will be the responsibility of the local school. For some, the goal will be preparation for college and professional careers. For others, the need for terminal courses at the high school or junior college level is apparent.

For those who will be forced to seek employment away from home but do not plan to enter a profession, the school should provide training for jobs in industry and business. Even in the case of a boy or girl who later decides to remain on the farm or return to the farm after some time spent in the city, business or industrial training will be useful in modern mechanized farming.

For all pupils guidance is essential. Each one should make his vocational decision on the basis of all the factors in the individual case. With the help of a competent counselor he should explore his personal satisfactions and interests, his abilities, the possibilities of employment in the city and in the country, the prevalent trends, and the social usefulness of different kinds of work.

Education for Home and Family Life

The art of homemaking takes on new meaning as science reveals more knowledge of nutrition and household management, and as electricity with its manifold applications in the household becomes more generally available. The techniques and skills of using electric appliances safely, economically, and efficiently for various purposes is something all children, both boys and girls, will need to be taught. The uses of electricity in preparing and preserving food and in providing adequate light for conservation of eyesight in both the home and the school are certainly topics for education.

As the production and processing of items consumed by the family are taken out of the home, there is need for more emphasis on the use of money income. Budgeting and keeping accounts of expenditures are of increasing importance in the rural family. Methods of keeping simple accounts can be taught at many points in the curriculum, as can some of the fundamentals of wise purchasing. Moreover, as the dividing line between "men's work" and "women's work," or between "boys' work" and "girls' work," becomes less rigid, the need becomes apparent for training both boys and girls in the activities of homemaking.

The Use of Leisure

One of the outstanding developments of our age is the rapid expansion of commercialized recreation. Moreover, mechanization of farming and industry under wise planning should provide more leisure for people. Obviously, leisure time can be an asset or a liability. Training in the wise use of leisure is an oft-stated objective of education and one which takes on new meaning with the rapid advance of technology. Enjoyment of good music, art, and literature has to be learned. Children who derive satisfaction, while still in school, from creating with the hands or the mind, as well as from participating in wholesome play activities, are likely to pursue these satisfactions as adults. These wholesome recreational interests are fostered by making the school a social center of creative leisure activities for old and young.

Relieved of much of the drudgery of the home and work, people might well channel their energies into creative and satisfying activities in the community. There has always been a shortage of leaders in the community. One reason for this in the past was the exacting requirements of work and home; continuous and intense physical labor left little time or energy for social participation. One solution for the present lack of leadership is to provide girls and boys with opportunities early in life to develop their leadership capacities. Adults, too, can be helped, through local, county, and state educational agencies, to discover their latent capacities and to find appropriate places of leadership in their communities.

Among reasons for lack of active interest in community affairs is the high mobility of our population; many families do not reside in one community long enough to become participants in its activities. Perhaps people can be educated to sink their roots more quickly into a new environment. Certainly some earnest attention should be given to this problem.

The decline in the farm population and the increase in that of rural trade centers emphasize again the need for cooperative action on the part of both the farm and the village in arranging schools for the future. Creation of a village-centered educational system which will serve the farm as well as the town is often the desirable solution from the administrative angle. Though this cooperation of town and country is especially desirable with respect to the high school, in many cases the elementary units are also involved. In the immediate future, school facilities must be expanded for the lower grades; need for enlarged facilities in the higher grade levels will appear as the young group grows up. The fact that the child load will continue to be heaviest in the poorer areas underlines the need for equalization of costs by state and federal aid. The fact that farm prices have declined more rapidly than prices of industrial commodities in spite of the price-support program is a further reason for financial aid to rural areas.

The threat of atomic warfare has laid new emphasis upon the need for the decentralization of industry. However, there has long been a need to prevent the undue pyramiding of population in urban centers by providing jobs for the excess population in rural areas. Some efforts have been made in certain sections of the country to stimulate rural handicrafts, notably in New England and in the Southern highlands. In many cases, the schools have taken a leading part in this development. At the college level, Berea and Antioch are notable examples. Training children in the arts and crafts lays the foundation for the development of rural industries. The larger problem of decentralizing industries already established in urban centers calls for action at higher levels than the local community, but some industries can be attracted to areas where there is a labor force with the requisite skills to do the work involved. There are other enterprises, of course, which have to choose a location with primary reference to the availability of raw materials and a sufficiently large labor pool to meet the needs of the enterprises as they expand and contract.

The changes in the life of the family which lead its individual members toward increased participation in activities outside the home shift more of the responsibility for child rearing to the other institutions of the community, notably to the school. This new freedom which removes children from the immediate surveillance of their parents and relaxes many of the older controls upon behavior emphasizes the need for laying a strong ethical basis for self-control. Education in morals and in the values of family life in the new social order are of vital importance. The responsibility of the family under the new conditions, though not fully understood, is surely very heavy; prospective as well as present parents need to appreciate it. Freedom with responsibility should be the watchword of the times.

To meet its added responsibilities for many of the controls formerly exercised by the family, the enlarged community must secure cooperation among its various agencies and institutions. The school can appropriately take the initiative in building this cooperation; always with a view, however, of promoting and maintaining the integrity of the family. Most Americans aged fifty years or more who were born on farms attended grade school only three or four months a year. Today most rural boys and girls attend school seven or eight months, and many of them nine. Moreover, the school-attending age is longer; children enter earlier and remain later. Thus, the school has in its charge a large and growing portion of the lives of children; the home a correspondingly smaller portion.

The transition of the family from the patriarchal to the democratic type of control is paralleled by a similar transition in the teacher-pupil relationship. Schools today emphasize pupil participation; the teacher functions more as a *guide* than as the *general*. The school has the opportunity and responsibility to educate children in the processes of democratic living.

The rising living standard of farm families is in large measure the result of education, formal and informal. Since patterns of living tend to be socially inherited, new ideas must penetrate the "cake of custom" before improvements can be achieved. Schools in areas where standards are low can teach people manifold ways of making improvements without spending very much money, often without spending any.

With the growing centralization of governmental functions in the state and national units, attention tends to be focused on those more remote bodies. However, the assumption of responsibilities by federal agencies should not cause local initiative to atrophy. The virtues of local initiative, so widely cherished in the American tradition, are worth preserving. While it is clear that there are many goals which can be achieved only by action on an ever-broadening scale, there remain many objectives which call for local action. The quality of the community will depend, in the last analysis, upon what the people do for themselves. The kinds of schools, churches, and local government which people have, and the ways in which people use their leisure time, are very largely determined at the local level.

PRINCIPLES

1. *The means used by the educational institution are more open to community consideration than are those means of other institutions.*

This is doubtless due in part to the newness of the institution, so that the concept people hold of the school is less sacred and more rational. The means used by the school in performing its functions are less institutionalized; this does not mean, however, that some are not institutionalized, as would appear from the complaints over changes in the grading system, the furor over the emphasis or elimination of athletic programs, and the pride in a "new" band.

2. *The educational institution is placed in the structure of the community in varying relations with other institutions and with formal organizations.*

The relations between the educational institution and the political institution are carefully formalized. Thus the school budget comes through taxes, and limitations are placed upon the school by state legislatures and by local political authority. These limitations are not too restrictive, however, and the school is largely apolitical in that changes in party do not ordinarily bring changes in educational policy. The religious institution and the school are separated, but the separation is less precise than that between the school and the political institution, although the separation of church and state in American society has a considerable carry-over from the parent political institution to the school. The differing relationships among these three institutions gives rise to problems of significance, such as the use of public money for parochial school buses.

The family and the school have identical and overlapping functions in the socialization of the child. Yet the relationship between the two has been highly informal. The only formal relationship was through the very indirect and limited channels of the political institution; however, in recent years the PTA has become another link. The relationship between the educational and the economic institution is complex and varied. The school serves primarily as a social selector for the labor force, and the economic institution supports and influences much of the school operation.

3. *In most small communities the school is the largest single enterprise in the community, both in terms of the budget and number of people involved.*

The faith in education reflected in this concentration of effort has resulted in expanding the educational institution to lower age groups (kindergarten and nursery school) and to adults (educational programs for adults).

4. *The original function of the educational institution, that of training in basic skills of communication, has been supplemented by functions extending into almost every phase of the individual's life.*

Traditionally, the school's assignment was training in the three R's, but the school's function now supplements and reinforces the functions of the other institutions, such as the vocational (economic), conformity to basic values (religious, family, political), and worthy use of leisure time.

5. *The school's function in social change is poorly defined in the structure of the community.*

It may be that this is a case where the issue has not been faced and a definition worked out. Or it may be that any given person, group, or organization may have quite definite ideas on this matter, but that these ideas differ so much that no community position can be determined. Only the question, not the answer, can be accurately phrased: Does the school lead the community in social change, building change into the next generation, or does the school follow the community, avoiding the role of descriptive influence?

6. *The authority to make school-related decisions is carefully defined, with certain decisions resting with the school and some with the community.*

Matters requiring immediate drastic action by the community rest with the community, as for example in building or not building a new school. Matters of more long-range, steady action are left to the school, with broad limits set by the community or pan-community structures, as, for example, in the selection of textbooks.

7. *The educational institution is not well integrated at the post-school level with many relatively independent and specialized organizations performing overlapping functions.*

The provision of organized educational opportunities for adults is assumed by many community organizations. This is usually determined by demands made by the adult population upon the organization for educational opportunities or by the utility of adult education programs to the manifest function of the organization. This results in duplication and wasted efforts and in an imbalance between community needs and opportunities for adult education.

SELECTED REFERENCES

Bear, Robert M., *The Social Functions of Education,* The Macmillan Company, New York, 1937.

Brookover, Wilbur, "Sociology of Education: A Definition," *ASR,* 14:407–14, 1949.

Grinnell, J.E., Raymond J. Young, and others, *The School and the Community,* The Ronald Press Company, New York, 1955.

Havighurst, Robert J., and Bernice L. Neugarten, *Society and Education,* Allyn and Bacon, Inc., Boston, 1957.

Mercer, Blaine E., *The American Community,* Random House, New York, 1956, Chapter 10.

Nelson, Lowry, *Education in a Changing Rural Life,* reprinted from the 51st Yearbook of the National Society for the Study of Education, Part II, 1952.

Robbins, Florence G., *Educational Sociology,* Henry Holt and Company, New York, 1953.

Sanders, Irwin T., *The Community,* The Ronald Press Company, New York, 1958, Chapter 15.

Smith, T. Lynn, *The Sociology of Rural Life,* Harper and Brothers, New York, 1947, Chapter 17.

Vidich, Arthur J., and Joseph Bensman, *Small Town in Mass Society,* Princeton University Press, Princeton, New Jersey, 1958, Chapter 7.

Williams, Robin, *American Society,* Alfred A. Knopf, New York, 1952, Chapter 8.

American Journal of Sociology, Vol. 48, May, 1943. Issue devoted to a symposium on education.

The Economic Institution

The economic institution is represented by those norms and structured behaviors which center around the production and distribution of goods and certain services. The production of goods includes food, shelter, and luxuries, and therefore may be seen to be the most important condition in human behavior, for all else falls away if this is not satisfied. This fact has led many, however, to believe that since the satisfaction of economic needs is a *necessary* condition for other forms of human behavior, it is *sufficient* to explain all other forms. For several reasons this is not so, as will be explained later. Nevertheless, the economic needs, if left unsatisfied, strongly shape all other structures, and even if satisfied are among the most important conditioning factors in the community.

While the production and distribution of goods necessary or wanted in living are clearly economic functions, the description of services which are economic is more difficult. In American society, the cultural meanings of many services which once were economic have now become goals of the political institution. This means merely that the political institution has taken over many economic functions, although these functions are no less economic. For example, in Russia the economic functions are largely performed by the political institution, which may be conveniently viewed as merely one type of variation in the economic institution. Thus, one principle of economic institutions is that concerned with its varying relation of freedom from, and control by, the political institution. Likewise, the same relationship could be viewed for other purposes as a variation in political institutions, with the variable being the amount of control exercised over economic functions.

No attempt will be made here to classify services as economic or otherwise, although at times assumptions will be made implicitly as to the economic nature of certain services. More research is needed before any such classification can be made with the precision necessary to a complete understanding of the economic functions in community structure. For example, does the concept of "physician" pertain to an economic status and role? It is certainly concerned with the distribution of services, but its end product is probably better understood by separating the health-oriented behaviors into a separate class of phenomena. The concept of "banker" would certainly be considered economic, but again many loans are not for material goods but for doctor bills. Research may show the assumptions made in the present chapter to be wrong, but in the meantime analysis must proceed.

In foreign community work, many of the problems are economic.[1] The very concept of "underdeveloped" country implies usually a failure to realize the potentials of production and distribution of the necessities of life. But even a narrowly economic project would not succeed without modifications shaped by the other community elements and dimensions.[2] The reverse is also true, however, namely, that work on noneconomic problems must usually be modified in terms of the economic institution and particularly in two aspects: resources and the prescribed relations between the economic component and the community elements and dimensions.

The relationship between the economic and other institutions may be understood in the same way as other aspects of community structure, but one point of distinction must be kept in mind. Like the political institution, the economic is often similar to community development in the immediate goals for which it is designed.[3] Also like the political institution, the economic differs from the community development structure in the institutional nature of the former. Thus the possibilities in the economic institution are limited more by the mores and folkways and therefore are less amenable to change than are the possibilities in community development. If social action of a radical nature is demanded by the discrepancy between value goals and achievements, the community must weave in and out, supplement, and support the existing economic institution. This is particularly difficult in communities in many present-day societies because of differences in value orientations. In authoritarian societies, the economic institution is based upon involuntary behavior, with the political institution in formal authority over it. In community development, structured behavior follows means based on voluntary action. More particularly, in capitalistic societies, the means prescribed by the economic institution follow competition, while the means of community development are cooperative. In neither case is community development completely irreconcilable with the existing norms, but it would be

---

[1] See especially Phillips Ruopp, *Approaches to Community Development*, W. Van Hoeve, The Hague, Bandung, 1953, Part II.

[2] Edward H. Spicer, editor, *Human Problems in Technological Change*, Russell Sage Foundation, New York, 1952.

[3] Carl C. Taylor, "Community Development Programs and Methods," *Community Development Review*, December 31, 1956, pp. 34–42.

folly to attempt it without modifying the program greatly to fit in with the different norms.[4]

STRUCTURE

It is difficult to compare the economic institution with other institutions in terms of the amount of autonomy within the community structure held by the local organizations. It is obvious that possibilities of variation in economic behavior are limited and conditioned by pan-community forces. Thus, a chain store, a local labor union, or a large production establishment which is part of a national or a statewide industry has very narrow limits within which it can operate at the community level. This means, in essence, that the economic organization is determined by institutional norms not established with the community. Nevertheless, the relationships between the economic organization and other organizations are community elements, even though the causal conditions exist outside or above the local area. Prices, the amount of donations given to the community, both in terms of money and time and other resources, are thus determined by the policy of the industrial enterprise exercised from outside the community.

The structure of the economic institution also varies according to the way in which large aggregates relate themselves to each other. For example, the economic organization is based upon three large statuses: production, distribution, and the labor force. The relationships within the economic institution may often be quite important at a given time in understanding community structure. For example, strikes, which represent a form of interaction within the economic structure between the labor force and the producer and retailer, may completely disrupt community affairs at any given point in time. Examples exist within the communication system, the transportation system, and at certain times in the employment of consumer functions. Similarly, the relationships between retailers may often have a strong effect on community structure. In many types of products the community has changed largely because of changing patterns of consumption resulting from relations between retailers. For example, clothing purchases, banking, and appliance purchases have become largely centralized either in large nearby cities or through mail order houses. These services were once part of the local community, but now divert attention away from it to a larger service area. The trend toward centralization of purchases in other areas, such as groceries and hardware, is not noticeable, although the commuting of non-farm workers in the rural area may be a move in this direction insofar as

[4] See various examples in Spicer, op. cit.

their weekly shopping is done in the center where they work. The change noted in appliances and clothing results in part from the requirements of heavy investment in the case of appliances and from price competition in the case of clothing. Small community business men cannot compete in prices and cannot make the initial investment necessary to maintain the kinds of services desired by consumers. Thus, economic competition may be judged to be largely conditioned by size of the community in terms of the number of people who may be viewed as consumers.

Another aspect of the relationships within the structure of the economic organization itself which affects community structure is the relative amount of autonomy left to the local representative of a centrally controlled business. For example, insurance agents sell insurance with techniques appropriate to their own community, but often adjustments for claims are made at a pan-community level. The problem is particularly acute at the local level because in most areas of economic activity the locally controlled establishment cannot compete with those which are part of a pan-community chain such as a statewide or nation-wide industry. This means that more and more the trend is, and will continue to be, toward control at a level higher than the community. This also bears upon the problem of community development activities, since cooperation with the economic institution is essential but may be more difficult to get because of lack of familiarity with, or interest in, the community by those who hold the controls. There are examples, however, of nation-wide industries which have an explicit policy of promoting cooperation at the local community level.

The Gap Between Want and Level of Satisfaction

There is perhaps no area of human activity where the discrepancy between the aspiration and the achieved is more noticeable than in the economic institution.[5] This is not due to the existence of a greater discrepancy in the economic activities, but is due to the more concrete nature of the goals of the economic organization. Material comfort items are easily observed and any desire for them is easily manifested, so that the observer may become aware of them immediately. The transfer of attitudes from the basic necessities of food and shelter to luxury items may also attract attention to the discrepancies in economic behavior. Another point is that the aspiration is usually placed above past achievement. Again, since much economic activity is directed at quantitative goals, such as a number of material comfort items in the home, the discrepancy may continue. This is due to the fact that the

[5] For a discussion of the concepts of standards and levels of living see Carl C. Taylor, "Social Theory and Social Action," RS, 5:16–31, 1940.

purchase, say, of a refrigerator may lead immediately to a desire for a purchase of some other item. It is easier for the aspiration to stay beyond the achieved in the search for quantitative goals.

ECONOMIC DETERMINISM

In the first paragraph it was mentioned that satisfaction of certain economic needs is a necessary but not a sufficient condition to explain other activity. There are several reasons for this. In the first place, in American society most of the necessary aspects of the economic needs are met fairly well in most families. This has not been always so, as, for example, in the 1930's, but in recent years there is a relatively small proportion of families who have levels of living far below minimum standards. Many of the economic needs defined in the American value system as necessary are luxury items insofar as they are shaped by other than physiological needs. Thus, while they may appear to be necessary conditions, they are so only because of the value system. The value nature of economic needs is a second reason, therefore, that the economic explanation of social forms is not sufficient.

A third reason that the economic explanation is not sufficient rests in the fact that research has shown a two-way relationship between economic structure and other structures. Long ago Max Weber showed that the Protestant ethic was a prior condition to the rise of capitalism in many societies.[6] Furthermore, much of the economic activity in American communities results from a pan-community concern for defense which results not from economic factors but from the political institutional activity of other nations, such as Germany in the 1930's and 1940's and Russia in the 1950's. In summary, it may be said that the single-factor explanation of social forms as a result of economic structure and need is insufficient, but that certainly the economic institution and economic activities are very important in explaining any structure.

FUNCTIONS

The two most important functions of the economic institution, by definition, are production and distribution. This means in essence that the style of life of families, community, and nation is limited by the economic system. Goals, since they are usually toward some object, are as often toward the

---

[6] See Chapter 14 of present work; Max Weber, *The Protestant Ethic and the Spirit of Capitalism*, George T.F. Unwin, London, 1930; and R.H. Tawney, *Religion and the Rise of Capitalism*, the New American Library, New York, 1947.

objects of material welfare as upon any other type. Thus, the economic structure, if it is not satisfying the defined goals in the community, may be a central problem for community action. This has been evidenced at the community level in recent years by programs to attract industry to the local communities.[7] This is more observable of middle size communities than others. Constellations of communities such as New York City, Los Angeles, and Chicago seem to have little difficulty in attracting sufficient industrial development and service trade to effect adequate production, retailing of goods, and employment opportunities. Small communities have an insufficient labor force to attract some types of industry, and this means that there are often fewer jobs than there are people, which in turn reduces the labor force further through migration.

This community level activity, however, has little influence upon the availability of goods as such for the families. If a certain type of goods is not produced in the local community it is produced elsewhere and shipped in. But such goods have price tags fixed at the pan-community level which is likely to be higher than would be the case if locally produced. Yet with low employment opportunities for the supply of labor, the wages and therefore the purchasing power are depressed below the pan-community level. In short, the ability of small communities to supply economic needs is sorely limited. Under such conditions the level of living cannot be expected to rise to the pan-community level.

The attraction of industries is one way in which communities may provide release from such an economic strait jacket. Action programs usually take the form of special development corporations deriving funds from private subscription. They may advertise local advantages for certain types of industries, and even purchase land for industrial expansion and construct buildings to lease to an interested corporation.

The Trade Center and Farm Relation

The goods and services required by farm families residing in the open country have traditionally been supplied by the villages or trade centers. The mutual interdependence of these two segments of the rural community has increased as farming has become more and more commercialized and mechanized. While the number of farm consumers has declined over the years, the introduction of technological innovations on the farm has required more and more new types of services from the villagers. At the same time, some services have become obsolete, such as that of the village blacksmith. Also, the

[7] Arthur E. Morgan, *Industries for Small Communities*, Community Service, Inc., Yellow Springs, Ohio, 1953.

electrification of farms since 1935 has created demand for all kinds of electrical appliances, along with the function of servicing them. Thus, in spite of the drastic decline in the farm population since 1940, most of the rural trade centers have been able to maintain their numbers and many of them have grown. Nevertheless, the future of these centers is tied up quite largely in the possibility of attracting industry from the outside, or of developing it from local resources. One attraction for industry is the flexible labor supply which the village and its agricultural hinterland offers. For an industry which requires a large supply of labor on a seasonal basis, the farm population is an attraction, since some employment may be had on the farm during the slack season.

It is important to point out here also that the trend toward greater specialization in farming also modifies the economic structure of the trade center. Whereas, formerly a farmer may have expected to raise all of his own feed for his dairy herd, he now purchases feed from the mill located in the village, and depends less and less on his own production. Also, the trend is for farm families to forego keeping of enough cows and chickens to supply their needs for milk, butter and eggs, and to go to town each day or two to purchase these from the local grocery. In this and many other ways, the economic relations between farm and village are being increased in number and made more binding.

Economic Considerations as Basis of Power

In Chapter 9, the economic basis of power was analyzed and it was seen that the greatest power in large urban centers rests in the hands of economic organizations and personnel at the top of economic structures. At a smaller community level this is probably less the case. In the traditional community it was assumed that the ultimate power rested neither in the economic nor political organization, but with the religious institution. It is probable that at the small community level today, ministers and church elders still exercise a great deal of power and even authority. Even so, in American communities church elders are often selected because of their economic position. In a money economy it takes money to run a church, and it is therefore likely that the authority and power to control the program of the church may rest in those who have the economic resources to sponsor the activities.

Financial Support for Noneconomic Institutions

The economic institution may be described as a separate entity, but actually it exists in many specific relations between it and other organizations.

This general function is that of furnishing the budget for various activities such as the church (already mentioned), welfare organizations, and the political institution itself through taxes and bond issues. Likewise, the educational institution is strongly conditioned by the economic resources of the local community. In the chapter on education it is pointed out that in most small communities the school has perhaps the largest single budget of any organized activity. The availability of funds and the willingnes of economic authorities to pass them along to the schools is a strong conditioning factor in the quality and nature of the school.

Economic Determinants of Status

As was seen in the chapter on stratification, general status is transferred from economic position. It has already been mentioned that power is given in large urban centers and in many smaller communities on the basis of economic status, but it might also be said that the prestige and the more conspicuous parts of the style of life are strongly conditioned by the ability of the local economic structure to provide the economic wants of people in the community.

Economic Changes Affect Community Structure

It has been found in studies of change that the production of goods can bring about modifications in the noneconomic structure of the community. In one study it was shown that the structure of a community varied tremendously with the rise and decline of the growing of hopes. Even false hopes at times gave rise to a change in community structure.[8] It can also be shown that the very location of community centers is often largely determined by economic considerations at the pan-community level.[9] For example, changes in transportation have often fostered or inhibited the growth of communities. At a time when transportation was by waterways, the location at central points on the routes was very important in determining whether a given community would grow, or remain relatively stationary, or decline. Later the railroads were a decisive factor, although sometimes the railroads went to centers which had previously been determined by waterways. The present emphasis on air travel is perhaps another case in point, although again the air centers are those which are already urban industrial loci.

---

[8] W.A. Anderson, "Social Change in a Central New York Rural Community," *Cornell AES Bulletin 907*, 1954.
[9] William F. Ogburn and Meyer R. Nimkoff, *Sociology*, Houghton-Mifflin Company, Boston, 1950, pp. 281–82.

Consumption Levels as Related to Activity

Changes in the level of consumption produce a change in the value system and in certain types of activities. Perhaps this is best illustrated by two cases at the extremes in the economic level. At the very low level of consumption where even the necessities are not met, most human activity is economic in nature. Eskimos are a case in point, as are also certain low status people among the sharecroppers in the South or slum dwellers in New York City. It would hardly be appropriate for an organization to expect high participation in any activity not concerned with making a living and getting the bare essentials. At the other extreme one may see certain communities where the extremely high level of consumption produces a change in aesthetic values. It would be fairly easy to show the relationship between the status of the family and the type of landscaping done around the home. One might, for example, compare a community largely populated by Negroes and poor whites in the South with an elite section of Atlanta. The same thing can be done in most large urban centers in the country, North, South, and West, where within a one-block distance one may find extremely "high-class" landscaping in close proximity to houses with no grass and bushes at all. E.L. Kirkpatrick reported a high degree of correspondence between the appraisal of the economic status of farm families, as judged by the appearance of the house and grounds, and the levels of consumption of the same families.[10]

The increase in the level of consumption can be expected to be associated with extension of activities into other realms of life, and therefore would function in terms of participation, leadership, and attendance at meetings as well as interest in other forms of activity. It is not only the amount of money which makes for a better school in a community where the level of consumption is relatively high, but also the ability of the families to relate themselves closely to the school in time and effort because their attention is not centered entirely upon ferreting out the bare essentials of physiological need.

Given a constant economic level of consumption, differences in status within the economic structure can produce important differences in other activities of life. This has already been implied by the descriptions of change above, but is very important in understanding the relationships presented in Table 1 in Chapter 8 between occupation and other types of characteristics. Most of the relationships are partly due to the economic aspect of occupations. It is also true that there are several other characteristics resulting from

[10] E.L. Kirkpatrick, "Rating Marginal Homes from Observation," *RS*, 2:51–59, 1937.

status in the economic structure which bear upon community-individual and community-family relations. One aspect of this is communication, insofar as the community can exist as a structure only through communication among the families, individual members, and organizations. This is extremely important in shaping the community structure. People of lower status have less intense relationship to the community structure and fewer communication facilities; thus, it would be expected that they are less aware of alternatives for their own behavior and are, perhaps, less well oriented toward current events. It has long been established that lower status people are less well educated and therefore probably have less knowledge of the long-term resources available to them for raising their status in either economic or other activities. Recent research has also shown that lower status families adopt fewer new farm practices and probably change less in other ways, such as family practices or rearing children. This is probably due in part to the communication system, to the cost of some new practices, to a lack of knowledge of some alternatives, and partly to their concentration of efforts in obtaining the minimum essentials.

ECONOMIC ORGANIZATION AND FREEDOM

A major part of the economic organization centers about the work world. In the traditional community, work is unspecialized and each person to a large extent is his own boss. There are very few truly *gemeinschaft* communities left in the world today, as was indicated in the chapter on values and social change. In pioneer America the frontier household was a farm family in which food, clothing, and whatever luxuries they had were for the most part produced at home. This condition has disappeared almost entirely from the American scene, with even the farm family producing almost none of its food. This means that the trend of American society is toward specialization, by which is meant that a person, such as a school teacher, fulfills a job role which may not bear directly upon any of the necessities of life. Teaching as a profession can exist only when there is such specialization that other people produce all the necessities. Education obviously is not a necessity in the sense that food, clothing, and shelter are. It should be pointed out again, however, that even the physiological necessities are matters of value judgment, since only through a value placed on life and health can such a product be considered necessary. Nevertheless certain of the occupational conditions in American society do not bear directly upon these necessities.

Perhaps the major trend in American economic organization is the trend toward industrialization. In an industrial society there tends to be elaborate specialization. A whole hierarchy of white collar jobs is added to those of the assembly line. This means in the first place that those who actually produce goods work on an assembly line of some sort where not only the job they do but the speed with which they do it is determined and prescribed by the assembly line. Second, the clerical aspect concerned with keeping books on the amount of distribution, production, and so on is again highly specialized and jobs are prescribed as to detail through written rules. These are referred to as bureaucracies.

Since much of man's life is concerned with his work, these job descriptions mean that much of his life in the system is prescribed by rules which cannot be varied to any great extent. The secretary, the bookkeeper, the man who fastens wheels on automobiles, and so on must work specified hours at a given pace with routine, unvaried job roles to fulfill. Out of the approximately sixteen waking hours of the American citizen, approximately eight are concerned with the work world. This question then arises: Even though the political structure is democratic, how much freedom does the American citizen actually have?

Achievement and Freedom

The answer to the question is not an easy one to give, but here are certain things that appear evident from research on industrial sociology and bureaucracy. It is apparent that certain values have been substituted for the value of freedom, since freedom is practically impossible, at least in the lower status in bureaucracy and the production line. The values of achievement and security have taken precedence in the work world over the value of freedom. Of course the value placed on achievement in itself probably leads to freedom, since those few who succeed in achieving a very high position in a bureaucracy have considerably more freedom than the large majority of petty bureaucrats who merely follow rules. But even those who succeed in reaching those positions where they appear to be largely their own bosses find a new norm coming into being. This norm centers on the tremendous responsibility given to them. The general truth that psychosomatic illnesses, such as heart disease, mental disorders, and the like, are found more frequently among vice-presidents and higher status officials in a bureaucracy is not an accidental correlation between physiological conditions and status. Rather it is a product of a job in which there is relative freedom with tremendous responsibility and very few norms to guide one in making a judgment.

This point perhaps needs some elaboration. Let us say that a decision must be made with respect to a certain policy for advertising. The responsibility for a successful and effective decision is placed squarely upon the shoulders of a vice-president in charge of distribution. Yet there are very few precedents for such a decision. This is especially so when a relatively new invention within the field of advertising and propaganda comes into being. Should the great expenditures involved be directed at the new technique or should one wait and see how it works for other industries and competitors, with the risk of lagging behind those competitors? Furthermore, with the many decisions that the high status person must make, he does not have time to make a thorough and scholarly investigation into the possibilities of the technique of advertising. Thus, he must make a quick decision with tremendous implications for not only his company but his own job. It is small wonder that such jobs produce nervous tension and psychosomatic disease. More relevant to the immediate problem, however, is that even though this same vice-president may be free to leave in the afternoon to play golf, one can hardly say he is free when his economic security and self-respect, as well as the respect of others, depend upon decisions which are practically impossible to make on any rational and studied consideration.

Security and Freedom

Another substitute for the value placed on freedom is security, although this may always have been relatively high in the American value system. There are many cases of first sergeants in the Army who refused to accept a commission, and many cases of foremen who refused to move into the white collar end of industry merely because they do not wish to accept the responsibility which might risk their security.

The conclusion then is, tentatively, that in the work world, which is a large share of man's experience, freedom is almost a thing of the past, and it is a serious question as to whether real freedom can ever exist in this portion of man's life in an industrial society. Since community development as defined in this treatise is largely aimed at increasing the amount of lay participation and democracy in man's affairs, it must always contend with the fact that freedom and democracy seldom get into the work world. Insofar as work norms and general value orientations are learned from the work world and deemed realistic there, they may be transferred to the type of activity we are calling community development.

The Expert and Freedom

In the case of specialization, the role of the expert in American society is an interesting one. The physician, for example, has largely been accepted as the authority over health decisions. Doubtless if a lawsuit concerning a medical decision had to be decided with studied care, the patient would be considered to have the freedom and responsibility to make any decisions regarding his own health, but it is also more than accidental that the expression "ordered by my doctor" has come to have real meaning in behavior. This idea of the expert has been transferred to many areas of life. One example, interesting for community development work, is that of the relationship between the educational and other institutions. The teacher knows his job, is well trained, and is expected to perform miracles without any help from parents. When he falls down he is blamed, even though the integration of all the forces of the community toward teaching of values, knowledge, and skills may still be insufficient to achieve the object in mind. Reliance on the expert helps to avoid dealing with problems about which very little may be known. (See the section on stereotypes in the chapter on communication and public opinion.)

Another interesting area in which expertness has become an excuse to avoid facing a problem is that of juvenile delinquency. It is likely that as time goes by, more and more community development projects will center around this problem. There is some question as to whether delinquency is actually increasing, but there is no question as to the greater awareness of it on the part of the American citizen. Since delinquency is largely a community problem with community solutions seemingly more reasonable than those of other social units, one might predict that future community development will include increasing consideration of juvenile delinquency problems. Here the cause probably rests in the greater complexity with which the family in its socialization function, and the school in teaching values, have to contend. However, the problem of juvenile delinquency is defined as a problem of crime and is left to the experts, namely, the judge, the lawyer, and the social worker.

In the first place, juvenile delinquency is quite different from crime in its nature, its causes, and probably in its treatment. Exactly how it is different is not known, since the causes of juvenile delinquency have not been well isolated. Thus the so-called expert is not well trained to handle juvenile delinquency problems and there is even a question as to whether he could be so trained, because the knowledge of the causes and cure of juvenile delinquency is yet to be developed with any degree of completeness and precision. Since the causes probably lie in the nonlegal institutional framework of the community, it is small wonder that judges, lawyers, and social workers find themselves faced with an almost insurmountable problem.

Another interesting transfer of values from the work world which may be found to deter any deliberate action programs in community development is that of the definition of status structure. As indicated previously, in a bureaucracy the "boss" is the man who has both the authority and the responsibility to make decisions. He does not ordinarily consult his subordinates in making such decisions, since his subordinates do not have all the necessary knowledge. Insofar as this value is transferred to community development, it is very likely that the president of a voluntary organization or a person of high prestige in the community will be given the task of making decisions which in themselves belie the end or goal of democracy. This problem has already been considered in another chapter on the transfer of expertness from the work world to general community problems.

In the large community the economic basis of power is generally greater than other institutional bases and the main concern of the economic power is often extended far beyond the economic problems. This is probably a trend in American society that will continue, since more and more the budgetary concern in organization of any sort, including voluntary community-wide organizations for development purposes, is becoming more important. Holding the purse strings of a community organization or institution within the value framework in the modern-day American community gives a great deal more power than in the past. The trend from power based on religion and ethical goodness to power based on economic means is a definite trend in the American community. This means essentially that the relationship between the economic institution and other institutions and organizations in the community will become closer, with the economic institution becoming more and more a controlling factor. This still does not imply economic determinism but points out the varying importance of the economic institution in explaining other behavior. This influence is sometimes greater and sometimes smaller in importance, but the general trend is toward more economic control.

PRINCIPLES

1. *The economic institution is the structuring of behavior and norms around the production and distribution of goods and certain services.*

2. Since most value systems consider food, clothing, and shelter as essentials, the structure and change of the economic institution produce changes throughout the elements and dimensions of community structure.

This has often led to the conclusion that the economic system is the basic factor in structure and change. Evidence indicates that it is a basic factor, but that changes in the economic system may be produced by changes in other substructures, such as the religious ethic.

3. In addition to the manifest functions of production and distribution, the economic system has several latent functions, one of the most important of which is that it gives to important positions within the economic institution itself high status which carries over into noneconomic relations. Power and authority is often associated with economically based status.

4. Since budgets to community programs are limiting factors, the economic system often sets the range within which action programs must operate.

5. The economically related activity of man is a large share of his day's activity, and therefore will have much to do with determining his style of life with respect to freedom, rcreation, community responsibility, and participation and leadership.

SELECTED REFERENCES

Davis, Kingsley, *Human Society*, The Macmillan Company, New York, 1949, Chapter 17.

Hoover, Calvin B., and B.U. Ratchford, *Economic Resources and Policies of the South*, The Macmillan Company, New York, 1951.

Hunter, Floyd, Ruth C. Schaffer, and Cecil G. Sheps, *Community Organization: Action and Inaction*, University of North Carolina Press, Chapel Hill, 1956, Chapters 3 and 4.

Meadows, Paul, *The Culture of Industrial Man*, University of Nebraska Press, Lincoln, 1950.

Mercer, Blaine E., *The American Community*, Random House, New York, 1956, Chapter 12.

Ruopp, Phillips, editor, *Approaches to Community Development*, W. Van Hoeve, Ltd., The Hague, 1953, Part II.

Sanders, Irwin T., *The Community*, The Ronald Press Company, New York, 1958, Chapter 13.

Vidich, Arthur J., and Joseph Bensman, *Small Town in Mass Society*, Princeton University Press, Princeton, New Jersey, 1958, Chapters 3–5.

Whyte, William H., *The Organization Man*, Doubleday and Company, Inc., Garden City, New York, 1957.

CHAPTER 18

Health Organization

Institutions arise out of human needs. The need for treatment and cure of disease is universal in time and place. However, each society develops its own ways of dealing with this problem. In primitive societies treatment developed out of human experience without the benefit of scientific knowledge, so that it took the form of exorcism of malignant spirits thought to be the cause. In Western society, where scientific processes have become an important element in the culture, the means of treatment or prevention are sought according to the rules of science.

This is not to say that all magic has been eliminated from the general area of treatment of disease. The persistence of faith in folk remedies among rural and urban people alike is evidence of this, and it is one of the deterrents to scientific health practices.

THE NATURE OF HEALTH ORGANIZATION

The means by which contemporary communities seek to achieve good health are many and varied. However, they always require *trained personnel,* including physicians, dentists, nurses, and technicians; *physical facilities,* such as hospitals, clinics, sanitoria, and the increasingly elaborate equipment involved in diagnosis and treatment; and finally, *organizations,* whether governmental or nongovernmental, which diffuse knowledge regarding health matters, establish controls to prevent unhealthful practices, and facilitate the treatment of disease by insuring access to, and adequacy of, health services.

In American communities the responsibility for public health is assumed by governmental organizations, while the responsibility for personal health is left to the individual. When individuals are unable to assume this responsibility, it becomes a matter of public concern because of the potential danger to the health of the public at large. Public health measures then assume the form of free medical care for the indigent and public programs and services

362

for prevention of disease or medical care. In general, however, personal responsibility in matters of health is handled through a relationship established between the individual and the medical and health resources.

The most prevalent type of relationship is a private one based upon what is called fee-for-service, in which the patient chooses a physician when in need of service and pays him the charges made for it. While the fee system is universally accepted, it has proved to be an inadequate means of insuring adequate medical care, from the point of view of both the patient and the physician. Unexpected medical expenses are often beyond the financial abilities of the patient, and the personal values attached to medical care may militate against adequate utilization of services. As a result, the growth of prepayment and insurance plans during the past thirty years has been so rapid that a large portion of the population is now "protected" against the hazards of a catastrophic medical bill. But in a free democracy there is room for much experimentation, and the variety of forms of payment for medical care in the United States is remarkable.

Following is an indication of this variety:

Methods of Paying for Medical Care

I. Fee-for-service, the prevailing system
II. Voluntary Sickness Insurance
    A. Commercial insurance, health and accident.
    B. Fraternal societies, unions, and other sick-benefit associations.
    C. Industrial plans: Mines, lumber companies, manufacturing plants, and others have had such plans many years, paid for by payroll deductions, sometimes by joint payments of labor and management, occasionally paid for entirely by industry.
    D. Consumer cooperative plans: a group of families form an association and contract with physicians to furnish medical services, either on a salary or fee-for-service basis, and assess each family a specified amount per month to cover cost.
    E. Blue Cross Hospital plan: provides benefits in any registered hospital for prepaid monthly premiums.
    F. Blue Shield plan: minimum costs of surgery and physicians' care in hospital.
    G. Private group clinics: a group of doctors offer specified services to consumers for a monthly fee.
III. Compulsory plans
    A. Tax-supported medical care: the plan is in operation in the United

States on a limited basis. Medical care is provided for veterans, the armed services, Indians, prisoners, inmates of other institutions, and the indigent. One-fifth of all general and special hospital beds are under state and local government control. The number under federal government control is steadily rising because of its expansion of facilities to care for veterans.

B. Compulsory health insurance: the plan proposes the deduction from payrolls of employed workers, and contributions from the self-employed, to pay costs of complete medical care, including hospitalization and sickness benefits while disabled. It would be an integral part of the social security system.

C. State socialized medicine: under this system the total cost of medical care would be paid out of taxation in a manner somewhat similar to that for providing public education. Doctors would be on a civil service basis as regards salary, tenure, certification, etc. Hospital and clinical facilities would be provided by tax funds. There would be no need to preclude the private practice of medicine.

In the United States the prevention of disease has become a manifest function of public health services. Each state, in cooperation with the federal office of Public Health, has a Board of Health which inspects water supplies, food-processing and distribution, restaurants, and other public food services; carries on programs of immunization and vaccination in the schools; informs the public through educational programs of preventive measures; and maintains records of vital statistics. For value received the funds invested in public health services undoubtedly yield higher returns in good health than any spent otherwise.

With the expansion of the concern for public health and the increasing involvement of government in the field of community health, the study of the sociology of health is also rapidly expanding. The reasons for this are related to two significant social changes: the increasing value placed on scientific health practices and the concentration of medical personnel and facilities in the larger urban areas. This centralization of resources is true of most of the institutional aspects of the community, as indicated in the centralization of schools, the assumption of many traditional family responsibilities by other institutions, and the increasing centralization of government itself. However, there are few areas of community structure where centralization has been felt more keenly than in the area of public health. The nature of this trend and its implications for the rural community are illustrated by the following excerpt.*

* John H. Lane, Jr., "What Has Happened to the Country Doctor?" *Missouri AES Bulletin No. 594,* Columbia, Missouri, 1953. Research on which this article is based was

What Has Happened to the Country Doctor?

How It Is in Farmville

When ten-year-old Johnny Carter fell off the barn roof, his worried father couldn't drive from the farm into the nearby village of Farmville for a doctor to set Johnny's broken arm. When the postman in Farmville complained of chills and fever, his family couldn't telephone the doctor for help. There is no doctor in Farmville, nor within miles of Farmville.

It was not always like that. Forty years ago, Dr. Blank's office nestled close to the village drug store. It was a small office without running water or electricity. It boasted no electro-cardiograph, no X-ray equipment, no present-day medical facilities of any kind other than those which Dr. Blank could pack up in his little black bag. But Dr. Blank set the broken bones and treated the sick in the Farmville of 1910, and he was a reassuring figure to the villagers and farmers within the few square miles of his medical domain.

No one has taken Dr. Blank's place since he died twenty years ago. The way it looks now, no one will.

Farmville Is Typical

But Farmville is no exception. Rural people everywhere are faced with the same problem. Like Farmville, many small towns have had no doctor for a long time, while others are just now losing theirs. In other words, the country doctor has not disappeared overnight. Instead, he has been slowly, but steadily, leaving the American rural scene for the past forty years. Thirty years ago it was already plain to see that the automobile was going to have a lot to do with where doctors located in the future. As farm people began to own cars, they found the physicians in larger towns were within easy reach. The result was that the doctor back home began losing his practice. He just couldn't compete with the specialists located in the larger towns and trade centers.

The doctor, too, has been influenced by such things as automobiles, telephones, and better roads. Now he can be called more quickly and get there faster. He can cover a much larger territory and visit far more bed-ridden patients than the "horse-and-buggy" doctor ever could. Or by means of a short, comfortable ride in a motor car, many more patients than formerly can now be treated in the doctor's office.

Consequently, many of our village doctors have moved to larger communities. But they have not been alone. A lot of other villagers have also been moving to the cities, and for about the same reasons. Good roads and motor cars have brought the farmer closer to the advantages of the trade center. More and more he passes up the limited services of the village. We can see that the smaller towns

done by C.E. Lively, Robert L. McNamara, and their associates at the University of Missouri.

have not only been losing doctors, but they have been losing other services as well. Villages that forty years ago had five or six business houses may now have only one or two.

For these reasons, many thoughtful people do not consider the loss of country doctors a serious problem. They point out that rural people are coming to depend more and more upon towns and cities for more and more services of all kinds, including health services. There is probably much truth in this argument. There is little doubt that the concentration of doctors and hospitals in the cities is only a part of the general movement of both people and services toward the economic and social advantages of large towns.

Nevertheless, the problem of readily available medical service is not solved for the country dweller. . . . Doctors are far apart, and many persons seriously ill or injured cannot safely make a long trip. Elderly people who choose to retire in the open country must face these facts.

Many small town and farm people still look upon the shortage of country doctors as a serious problem. The people of Farmville felt that it was a problem when there was no doctor around to set Johnny Carter's broken arm, or to treat the village mail carrier when he became ill. Country people still have their day-to-day health and medical problems just like everyone else. If their need for medical service is not being met, they do, indeed, face a serious health problem.

Population Is Outrunning the Supply of Doctors

Before centering our attention on the disappearing country doctor, let us look at the supply of doctors for the whole nation. One important fact stands out. The supply of doctors in the United States, especially those in private practice, has failed to keep up with the nation's population increase and the growing demand for health services. No more doctors are being graduated from medical schools today than there were forty to fifty years ago.

Why is this? For one thing, the question of quality as well as quantity has been of great importance. At the turn of the century, a great many second and third-rate medical schools were operating all over the country, turning out hundreds of doctors every year. A degree in medicine was cheap and easy to get. Of course, by the standards of that day, there were good doctors then as well as now. But the "medical diploma mills" were keeping our standards of medicine low by turning out thousands of second-rate physicians.

To remedy this situation, some such-needed reforms were applied to our medical schools between 1910 and 1920. These measures resulted in fewer schools of medicine and fewer medical school graduates. Now, though we are getting fewer doctors, we are getting better ones.

But there is another side to the question. The reforms improving our medical schools have now been in effect many years. We can't go on blaming these changes of several decades ago for the continuing doctor shortage. In Missouri, for example, the decline in the number of physicians has continued for the last forty years. During this period the state has suffered a net loss of about 1,000 doctors—from more than 6,000 in 1912 to about 5,000 today. But the loss is far greater than these figures show. For during this same forty-year period Missouri had a population increase of more than 600,000 persons.

The rural areas of the state have been particularly hard hit by the decline in the number of doctors. A recent study of physician supply in twenty Missouri counties, most of which are rural, reveals a drastic change in the number of physicians. In 1912, a total of 539 physicians resided in the twenty-county area; in 1950, there were only 158. This represents a loss of about 70 per cent during the last forty years. Furthermore, the greatest percentage loss has taken place during the last ten years. Since 1940, the twenty-county area has lost more than one-third of its doctors.

Missouri Medical Services Are Moving Cityward

While the over-all supply of Missouri physicians has been decreasing, the number located in our larger cities has been steadily increasing. In this respect, what the rural folks have lost, the city dwellers have gained. Today, nearly three-fourths of all the Missouri physicians listed in the American Medical Directory are located in the four city counties of Jackson, Buchanan, St. Louis, and Greene. This is almost the reverse of forty years ago when less than half the doctors in the state lived in these same four areas. Clearly, the trend has been toward greater concentration of physicians in our larger cities.

Many Doctors Are Not in Private Practice

If you are sick, not all of the 200,000 physicians in the United States stand ready to be called to your bedside. Some are on full-time duty in hospitals, sanatoria, and other institutions. Some are in federal service or in public health departments. Some are full-time or part-time teachers in medical schools. Some are retired. Without these, about 150,000 M.D.'s are left to serve John Q. Public. That means there is about one practicing physician for every 1,000 Americans.

In Missouri, the picture is much the same. Of the 5,000 M.D.'s in the state, only about 3,800 are available to the public either as general practitioners or specialists engaged in private practice. The result is a ratio of one practicing physician for every 1,073 persons who live in Missouri. But even this is a misleading figure. The two largest medical centers—St. Louis and Kansas City—are so located that many out-of-state patients from Illinois and Kansas compete with Missourians for the use of hospital beds and doctor services. And because these cities are well-known medical centers, many patients come to them from other states for the treatment of difficult cases. When these people are considered, it is clear that Missourians can count on far less than 3,800 physicians to keep them well.

When we consider that one doctor per thousand people is the figure generally quoted as a good, practical ratio, and one per 1,500 as the limit, Missouri, as well as the nation, appears to have a fine average. But like most averages, it does not apply everywhere. It is small comfort to the many Americans in the same plight as those in Farmville. A good national or state average doesn't give them a doctor to set a farm boy's broken arm or to treat a village pneumonia patient.

Within the nation's borders, states vary in their physician population from one practicing physician for every 626 citizens to one for every 1,761. And within state borders, available medical services range from completely staffed city centers to rural and small town areas with no medical help at all. As many as thirty-seven Missouri counties have more than 2,000 persons per physician, and almost half of these counties have more than 3,000 for each physician.

Yes, the Dr. Blanks are disappearing from our rural places. And from the looks of things, they will continue to do so.

What Has Happened to the Dr. Blanks of 1910?

Dr. Blank remained in Farmville until death ended his career of over forty years of personal service to the community. In 1910 he was in his prime, forty-five years old and in robust health. Farmville had been his home since graduation from medical school in 1890. He knew everyone in and around the village. His advice was much sought after by the villagers in all sorts of matters, medical and otherwise. By 1910, he could boast of having delivered most of the village's children into the world. His practice was good—and it was all his.

Twenty-two years later, Dr. Blank died at the age of sixty-seven. In his later years he was still making a fairly good living, but his practice was on the decline. Many of the villagers now owned automobiles and some were driving fifty miles to the county seat for their medical services. Dr. Blank managed to keep most of the older folks around Farmville coming to him, but the young people were getting a lot of new ideas about what they wanted in a doctor.

Nevertheless, the people of Farmville felt a deep personal loss when the old doctor finally passed away, a loss that was felt even more deeply when no one took his place. Even though they could now get into the county seat more easily for many of their medical needs, accidents still happened, and people still got suddenly ill. Death had robbed Farmville of the man they could turn to in such times of crisis.

Dr. Blank's case shows what has happened to many of our country doctors. They moved into small rural villages back in the days when the United States was still pretty largely rural in its make-up. More people lived on farms, and levels of living were not so high. Less equipment for the practice of medicine was required. Farm villages provided a thriving practice for a doctor. Like Dr. Blank, many doctors remained with the villages of their choice until death or retirement ended their careers.

A community can lose its doctor in any one of three possible ways: death, retirement, or his moving away. The first two, death and retirement, are perhaps the most common in rural places because the country doctor is rapidly becoming an old man. By this we mean that the average age of the rural physician in all states is steadily increasing. The reason is that too few young doctors are moving into the rural areas to bring the average down.

Take a look at rural Missouri. Today, one out of every two rural physicians in the state is over sixty-five years of age. In the study of twenty Missouri counties, it was found that in 1912 only one doctor in fourteen was over sixty-five; now more than one in three are past that age. In fact, the proportion of doctors over age sixty-five in this sample area has nearly trebled in the past twenty years.

Doctors at the age of sixty-five are approaching retirement. Most of them are unable to serve as many patients as they did at an earlier age. For effective service, one hundred doctors past age sixty-five are equivalent to about thirty-five doctors aged forty. Furthermore, the doctors' death rate, like that of other people, increases rapidly after sixty-five. Within ten years only about one-third of today's elderly physicians will still be living.

A fresh supply of younger doctors is the only way the rural physician can be prevented from disappearing. Moreover, the replacements needed are greater than one might expect. In the twenty sample counties studied it would not be enough to replace the older doctors as they die or retire. These counties would need to start by meeting a minimum standard of one doctor for every 1,500 persons. To do this, twenty new physicians would be needed at once, and seventy additional physicians would be needed by 1960. In all, ninety new doctors would be needed in the present decade. This is three times as many as have moved into these counties during the last ten years.

Even though the rural population may decrease still further, it will require effort that is little short of heroic to meet the minimum standard. Furthermore, there are other similar areas in Missouri. Without careful study and planning, there seems little likelihood that the situation will improve. Local communities should study their problem and initiate practical measures for its solution.

And so, as the established rural physicians die or move away, and young doctors fail to take their places, the practice of medicine in the country keeps balancing a heavier load on the shoulders of fewer and older doctors. With even a moderate load, the country doctor needs more time to make trips among his widely separated patients.

The heavy demands of the rural doctor's widespread practice make it a losing battle for him to try to keep up with the fast pace of modern medicine. He lacks time during his busy days and nights to get at the reading of his current medical journals. He finds few chances to get away from his patients to visit medical centers where new techniques and refresher courses might keep him up-to-date. He seldom has hospital or laboratory equipment nearby. Frequently he must act as his own nurse or laboratory technician, and he seldom has enough professional contacts to keep abreast of cases which demand a specialist's skill.

The New Doctor Sets Up Practice

The young doctor who has spent at least seven long, expensive years preparing to write "M.D." after his name has definite ideas about the kind of place where he would like to live and work. Of course, he wants to make a good living and establish a pleasant home. But he wants more than that. Hospital and nursing facilities, laboratories, and technicians must be within easy reach if he is to make use of his up-to-date training. He doesn't want to do his surgery on the kitchen table. And for the benefit of his patients, he shouldn't have to do so.

He needs stimulating professional contacts with other doctors. He wants to be able to refer to the proper specialists the rare or difficult cases that seem to call for skills more highly developed than his own. Also, he is not likely to be equally interested in all types of illness. Often he, too, would like to have a specialty.

Specialists Belong in the Larger Centers

More and more doctors are leaving Dr. Blank's realm of general practice to become specialists in various medical fields. But specialization takes them to the city. For example, a heart specialist in a small town of a few hundred, or even a few thousand, cannot expect to be kept busy in his chosen field. He needs to practice where greater numbers of heart cases will demand his skill.

As they think these things over, both newly trained specialists and general practitioners are turning to the cities to practice their healing arts. Even some doctors already established in country areas and small villages have packed up and left for centers where they can serve a large number of cases daily because more patients are close by. Only twelve out of every hundred doctors leaving the armed services after World War II looked forward to rural practice as civilians.

Many Country People Now Do Without

The migration of rural physicians to city practice, the small number of young doctors taking their places, and the increasing age of rural physicians have cut deeply into the medical care available to rural people. Also, the low money income of many farm families puts a hurdle in the path of proper treatment for their ills. Travel expenses to the larger centers and the higher fees usually charged by city doctors amount to more than many families can afford.

As a result, rural folk get in the habit of doing without doctors. With no medical prescription for their ills, they treat themselves with home remedies or with patent medicines suggested by a neighbor, the local drug store clerk, or perhaps by some published advertisement. When there are no nearby hospitals in which they may have their babies, they have them at home—often with only a midwife attending. Many a rural American has never been a patient in a hospital, and he thinks of one as a place to die rather than as a place to get well.

Army Rejections Tell the Story

Wartime rejections of farm youth brought into the open the results of this scarcity of good medical service. Farm folk could not help but notice that the old notions about the healthful life in "God's country" did not keep the rejection rates for their young people from climbing fully 10 per cent above those for the nation as a whole.

Digging a little deeper into the well-being or ill-being of the nation's rural population, we find that the number of farm and small town Americans who die too young from diseases which advanced medicine can cure also tops the national figure.

Typhoid, for instance, in spite of its sharp downward trend as a killer, claims more than three times as many victims in the country as in the city. The diphtheria death rate is twice as high among farm and small town citizens. Rural mothers die from childbirth and its complications 50 per cent more often than do city women. Anemia, malnutrition, bad teeth, and impaired vision are more common among farm and small town residents. Farm boys and girls get only about half the medical attention of city children.

The findings in Missouri are not unique. For example, a study conducted in Louisiana came to approximately the same conclusions regarding the availability of dentists and nurses, showing the problem to extend to all health careers.*

The Availability of Medical Personnel in Rural Louisiana

The Availability of Dentists

In 1948 there were 976 dentists in Louisiana who were certified by the State Board of Dentistry. The ratio of persons per dentist for the state was 2,667. The ratio in 1946 was 3,738. In comparing these figures with the standard established by the Committee on the Cost of Medical Care, an extremely large deficiency in the state is evident. The Committee estimated the optimal ratio to be between one dentist per 556 persons and one per 1,000 persons, depending upon the backlog of dental defects to be corrected. The ratio of persons per dentist for Louisiana in 1948 was almost three times greater than this estimated minimum for optimal dental care. The 976 dentists who were attempting to care for the dental needs of more than two and one-half million Louisianians obviously were numerically insufficient to cope successfully with the task.

The most favorable situations, as far as the number of persons per dentist was concerned, were found in Orleans parish (1,414) and Caddo parish (1,952). No other parish had a persons-per-dentist ratio of less than 2,000 in 1948. Even in these parishes, the number of dental personnel relative to population is far above the one to 1,000 minimum for optimal dental care. In general, the same relationship previously pointed out between the degree of urbanization and the availability of physicians is also true for dentists. The more urban parishes had lower ratios than the more rural ones. Both parishes named above as having a persons-per-dentist ratio of less than 2,000 contain large urban centers. On the other hand, three rural parishes did not have a single dentist. The residents of St. Bernard, Plaquemines, and St. Helena parishes in 1948 were obliged either to do without dental care or to incur considerable expense and inconvenience in traveling to a city in some other parish in order to secure it. Besides these situations, in each of five parishes, there was one dentist for the entire population. Assuming dental care is obtained only within a parish, one finds that in West Feliciana parish, one dentist was responsible for the dental health of 10,378 persons; in Red River parish,

* Paul H. Price and Homer L. Hitt, "The Availability of Medical Personnel in Rural Louisiana," *Louisiana AES Bulletin No. 549*, 1951.

one for 12,850 persons; in Grant parish, one for 14,561 persons; in Livingston parish, one for 19,397 persons; and in Sabine parish, one for 21,388 persons.

The twenty-three totally rural parishes taken collectively had a ratio of persons per dentist of 5,768 in 1948. Compare this with the parishes having more than 40 per cent urban population. In the latter group, there were 1,789 persons per dentist, which simply means that, assuming that parish lines are not crossed, a dentist working in the rural parishes would have about five times as many potential patients as a dentist in the more urban parishes. The intermediate group of parishes, those with some urban population but less than 40 per cent, had a persons-per-dentist ratio of 3,824. A dentist in these parishes would be responsible for the dental health of three times as many people as a dentist in the more urban parishes. These data indicate that there is a significant relationship between urbanization and the availability of dentists—the more urban the parish, the lower the persons-per-dentist ratio and vice versa.

As in the case of doctors, persons-per-dentist ratios by themselves do not give a complete picture of the availability of dentists to rural people. The great majority of the dentists in a parish may be concentrated in an urban center, with the result that the rural areas not immediately adjacent to this center are seriously handicapped.

The Availability of Registered Nurses

In 1949 there were 6,060 registered nurses located in the state who were certified by the Louisiana State Board of Nurse Examiners. The persons-per-nurse ratio was 435 in 1949, as compared to 513 in 1946. Since no optimal ratio of nurses to population has been established, a standard of this type is not available for comparison. However, in order to make possible some sort of evaluation of the adequacy or inadequacy of the supply of nurses in Louisiana, the national average of persons-per-nurse in 1940 has been used as a basis. The persons-per-nurse ratio in Louisiana in 1949 was considerably higher than the national average in 1940. The actual ratios were 435 and 370, respectively. This indicates that Louisiana in 1949 remained considerably below the position of the nation in 1940 as far as the supply of registered nurses was concerned.

The lowest persons-per-nurse ratios followed the same general pattern as that for doctors and dentists. The most urban parishes were characterized by the smallest number of persons per registered nurse. Orleans parish has 218 persons per nurse; Caddo parish, 235; Rapides parish, 266; East Baton Rouge parish, 280; and Ouachita parish, 291. No other parish had a person-per-nurse ratio of less than 300. Parishes showing the largest number of persons per nurse were predominantly rural. In West Feliciana parish, there were 5,105 persons for each nurse; Catahoula parish, 6,013 persons; Red River parish, 6,236 persons; and Cameron parish, 6,332 persons. If parish lines were not crossed and the services of nurses were used to the same extent in all parishes, a nurse in the above parishes would be responsible for the care of twenty-five times as many persons as a nurse in the five parishes recording the lowest number of persons per nurse.

The twenty-three totally rural parishes in the state had a collective persons-per-nurse ratio of 1,438 as compared to a corresponding figure of 259 for the parishes with over 40 per cent urban population. This means that a nurse in the rural parishes would be responsible for the health needs of six times as many persons as a nurse in the more urban parishes, provided, of course, that parish boundaries are not crossed. The intermediate parishes in 1940 (those having some but less than 40 per cent urban population) together had an average of 744 persons per nurse in 1949. Again assuming that parish limits are not crossed, a nurse in these parishes would have three times as many potential patients as one in the more urban parishes. These figures indicate a direct correlation between urbanization and the facility with which the services of a nurse can be obtained—the more urban the parish, the lower the number of persons per nurse.

These studies in Missouri and Louisiana bring out the essential points relative to the changing rural-urban distribution of medical personnel—points which are substantiated by many studies in other states and for the nation as a whole. It is well to caution the student that studies of distribution based upon arbitrary county units do not give a complete picture of the problem of availability. Some counties with no physician located within their boundaries nevertheless may have comparatively easy access to clinics and physicians located in adjacent counties.

The fact is well established, however, that the country doctor is moving to the city. Physicians and other medical personnel are increasingly concentrated in urban centers. While it is comforting to rural families to know that there is a family physician within a reasonable distance in case a home call is necessary, it is increasingly rare for them to enjoy such comfort. More and more, the patient goes to the doctor's office for treatment, rather than having the doctor come to the patient. The exodus of medical practitioners from the small towns does not mean necessarily that they become less accessible than their predecessors of a generation ago. They may be more accessible, even though the distance separating them from their clientele is much greater.[1]

THE USE OF HEALTH SERVICES

The other side of the coin is the utilization of health services and facilities by the "consumers." This is the subject matter of the selection * to follow.

[1] For a delineation of medical service areas of the United States which disregards political boundaries, see Frank G. Dickinson, A Medical Service Areas Map of the United States, Bulletin 67, Bureau of Medical Economic Research, American Medical Association, Chicago, 1949.
* Olaf F. Larson and Donald G. Hay, "Hypotheses for Sociological Research in the Field of Rural Health," RS, 16:225–37, 1951. Used by permission.

Factors Influencing Use of Health Facilities

This exploratory study had a threefold purpose: (1) to determine the extent of the use that rural people are now making of health care resources such as physicians, dentists, hospitals, county health departments, and school health services; (2) To determine factors, such as availability of personnel and facilities, which influence the use of these resources; and (3) To develop and test methods of effectively obtaining data from families on their use of health care resources.

Data on use of health care services were obtained for 250 representative rural households in Cortland County and for 283 households in Oswego County.

The sample consisted of all households located within geographic areas selected systematically from a list of all sampling units for all rural portions of each county. This selection was designed to give proportionate representation from open-country and village areas.

The two counties were selected because they were similar in several agricultural, population, and social characteristics, but were considered to differ as to availability of health care resources within the county.

Availability of health care services was measured by an index based on the unweighted average rank of the forty Dairy Belt counties in New York State with respect to five items: (1) physicians per 1,000 population; (2) hospital beds per 1,000 population; (3) dentists per 1,000; (4) registered nurses per 1,000; and (5) proportion of births delivered in hospitals. Cortland ranked twentieth among the forty Dairy Belt counties; Oswego ranked thirty-seventh.

Patterns of Use of Health Resources

The importance of health care services in the lives of New York rural people is evident in the high incidence reported of use of one or more type of such services by one or more household members. Over nine-tenths of the households and about four-fifths of all persons one year of age and over in each county had used one or more types of health services during the twelve-month period ending September 30, 1949 (hereinafter referred to as "1949").

Out of every ten households in each county about nine used a general physician during 1949, six used a dentist, over five used some type of public health service for individuals, a little less than three used a hospital, fewer than two used a medical specialist, and less than one used an osteopath or other health care personnel including chiropractors.

About four-fifths of the households in each county used two or more types of service.

Of every ten persons one year of age and over in the sample households, about six used a general physician in 1949, over three used some type of public health service for individuals, three used a dentist, and less than one used either a hospital or a medical specialist.

Nearly two-fifths of the persons in each county limited their use to a single type. Slightly over two-fifths in each county used two or more of these services.

Major Purposes of Present Paper

Certain hypotheses were formulated prior to the study under consideration. Analysis of the data and planning for further studies in the field of rural health have stimulated the formulation of other hypotheses. These hypotheses are of three types: (1) hypotheses of relationships, (2) hypotheses of trends, and (3) hypotheses of method.

The remainder of the paper is devoted to the statement of selected hypotheses of the three types and an examination of the test data available from the two-county study.

Hypotheses of Relationships

HYPOTHESIS 1—*The utilization of private health resources by the rural people within a county is closely related to the availability of these resources located within the county as measured by county indices of availability.* The evidence from the two New York counties fails to prove this important hypothesis.

The data for the use of these crucial health resources—physicians and dentists in private practice and hospitals—with the one exception of the percentage of persons using a dentist, show county differences in the use patterns by rural people which are either (1) statistically not significant or (2) run exactly opposite to what would be expected on the basis of the index of availability.

How may this *contrariness* be explained? One possible explanation might be that the composition of the sample population in the two counties was different enough from the factors which affect use rates to give the results indicated. However, without presenting detailed supporting data here, it appears that the contrariness in results cannot be adequately explained by variations in the composition of the sample for the two counties. Neither is there evidence to suggest any important difference in the need for health service during the period covered by the study.

However, the data available do suggest an explanation for the contrary behavior described. The explanation seems to rest largely in the *ecological distribution of these resources in relation to the potential rural consumer.* Thus, for the general physician, while Cortland had the advantage in the county index, when one examines the distribution within the county, the advantage disappears. Over four-fifths (83 per cent) of all general physicians in Cortland were located in the two urban-centered communities, while only two-thirds (66 per cent) of those in Oswego were located in the two city-centered communities of that county. One of Cortland's four village-centered communities are but three miles apart, while the two in Oswego are eleven miles apart. Although less than 10 per cent of the persons in the sample in either county were more than eight miles from a general physician, the mean distance was greater in Cortland (3.8 against 3.3 miles).

When the effect of this distribution pattern is analyzed in relation to utilization, one sees (1) that although in each county about 80 per cent of the use of a general physician is with a physician within the county, Cortland individuals go a greater distance—1.2 miles farther on the average (mean), (2) only 50 per cent of the general physician use in Cortland is with a physician located in a village under 2,500 population compared with 62 per cent in Oswego, and (3) finally, only 45 per cent of the general physician use in Cortland is with one located at the usual trade center as compared with 60 per cent in Oswego.

In both counties all medical specialists were in the urban centers. Here Cortland had a marked advantage in the ecological distribution for this type of service by virtue of its more favorable ratio. For this service the advantage is comparable to that held by Oswego in its distribution of general physicians. This shows up in the fact that 47 per cent of the Cortland County use of a specialist by individuals was within the county as compared with 20 per cent for Oswego.

Oswego had not only a higher index value for dentists but also a much better distribution. Only one of the four village-centered communities in Cortland against five out of the seven in Oswego had a dentist. Consequently Oswego persons were closer to a dentist on the average (mean distance 6.1 in Cortland, 3.7 in Oswego) and were much more likely to use one located at their usual trade center (42 per cent in Cortland, 68 in Oswego).

The case seems to be clear that rather than place full reliance upon a county index of the availability of private health resources, the distribution of resources among the communities within a county and the availability of services outside the county lines must be more fully considered. Sociologists have a contribution to make in the delineation of the service areas for these resources.

For the sake of brevity, other hypotheses of relationships will not be elaborated upon.

HYPOTHESIS 2—*The utilization of public health resources is closely related to availability of services within the boundaries of a local governmental unit.*

This hypothesis is one of those "common-sense" observations whose pertinency can be easily supported. For example, in Cortland County, which has a county health department, 9 per cent of the sample rural households reported one or more visits by a public health nurse, whereas in Oswego, with no county health department but a combination of local health officer and a district office of the state department of health headquartered outside the county, no such nursing visits were reported. A "freezing" effect is associated with public health services provided by local units of government, since utilization is largely restricted to what resources are provided by the local governmental unit of residence—town, village, school district, county, etc. A free flow of consumers across boundaries of these units does not take place for service of this type, as is the case with use of private resources. One might add that there is evidence that within the larger units, such as counties, availability of public health resources within the local community affects the utilization pattern.

HYPOTHESIS 3—*Rural families, with prevailing distribution of physicians, system of medical care, and transportation and communication arrangements, are generally exercising free choice of physicians.* This hypothesis is given here because of the statement sometimes made that such free choice is not actually available because of the distribution pattern of physicians in rural areas. That data for these two New York counties supports the hypothesis. For example, in one county the mean distance to the general physician used was 10.5 miles as compared with the mean of 3.8 to the nearest physician available. In the second county the comparable means were 9.3 and 3.3.

HYPOTHESIS 4—*The utilization of health resources, both private and public, is positively associated with family income; that is, use increases with an increase in income.* The evidence shows this relationship to be one of the most marked and consistent of any, generally holding true for the use of the general physician, medical specialist, dentist, hospitals, and public health services for individuals.

HYPOTHESIS 5—*Satisfaction with existing health resources is positively associated with (a) family income and (b) utilization of resources; that is, the probability of being satisfied increases as family income and utilization of health resources increase.* The evidence *does not* support this assumption.

From the fact that income and utilization are so closely and positively related, one might draw the inference that increasing the income of low groups or providing services without cost or at a reduced cost would bring the utilization level and pattern of this group up to that of the higher income groups. Such an inference would be a mistake, at least for New York rural people, if the data from this study are correctly interpreted. Such an inference overlooks the basic sociological-psychological fact that most use of medical resources is a form of voluntary participation and therefore is dependent upon the whole complex of factors which motivate people to participate.

The evidence for one count, for example, shows that only 39 per cent of the low income group (and 20 per cent under $1,000 net) expressed the opinion that some things should be done in their area to improve the health and medical care for the people as compared with 64 per cent of the high income group (the 29 per cent with $3,000 and over net). The second county reveals almost identical percentages. In the county having the health department, the percentage of low income families using specified public health services (including schools)—which are free—was only half that of the higher income families. In the same county 56 per cent of the low income households had heard of the county health department, and 42 per cent reported contacts with it compared with 73 and 65 per cent, respectively, for the high income families. Use of health resources is not only a matter of availability and dollars.

HYPOTHESIS 6—*Age, sex, and family member roles are significantly related to utilization of health resources, knowledge of them, and opinions about them.* The evidence shows some marked variation in use of the various resources by age and sex. . . .

HYPOTHESIS 7—*The general physician occupies the key position in rural health care from the standpoint of role and status.* The study and supporting evidence from studies in two communities in other counties support this hypothesis, and therefore reinforce the importance of continued consideration of the general physician in any program for improving the health care of rural people.

Hypotheses of Trends

HYPOTHESIS 1—*The trend has been for rural people to increase their use of professional, scientific health resources such as physicians and hospitals.* If folk health practices have decreased with a growing regard for scientifically based practices, as is commonly assumed, and if health education has been effective, then the use of professional personnel and significant resources—such as hospitals—should have increased.

Fortunately for our purposes, Dwight Sanderson made a health study in Cortland County in 1923 and 1924 and published the data in such form that some qualified inferences may be drawn as to the trends over the last twenty-five years.

While it is not possible to make a comparison as to the proportion of households or individuals receiving a physician's services, a comparison is possible as to the average number of home and office calls per person (thus eliminating any effect of the difference in household size). Compared with the 3.6 average for 1949 for home and office calls of general physician and specialist was the 1.8 for 1923–24. For the general physician the average number of calls per person was 1.5 in 1923–24 against 3.2 in 1949. For the specialist the average was 0.25 in 1923–24 against 0.4 in 1949.

Concerning hospitals, it appears that the rate of use has perhaps quadrupled; 2 per cent of the individuals in 1923–24 were reported as having used a hospital during the past year as compared with 8 per cent in 1949. About 30 per cent of the births were in a hospital in 1923–24 compared with over 90 per cent in 1949. The average length of stay was longer for the earlier period (seventeen against thirteen days).

With respect to dentists the use has also grown; in 1923–24, 35.5 per cent of the households reported expenditures for dental care as compared with 58 per cent in 1949 having one or more members reported as using a dentist.

While there are limitations on the earlier data for making these comparisons, the over-all trend is supported.

HYPOTHESIS 2—*In rural medical practice there has been a shift (a) from home calls to office calls and (b) from the general physician to the specialist.* The comparative data from the Sanderson study clearly support the first part of this hypothesis. Of all physicians' calls in 1923–24, 49 per cent were at the home as compared with 11 per cent in 1949. Considering only general physicians, which is more appropriate, the shift was from 50 per cent home calls in 1923–24 to 12 per cent in 1949. Memory of this earlier pattern may well help explain some of the present-day opinions expressed by rural people about wanting more home calls.

As for the second point, while as many as 4 per cent of the individuals may have used specialists in 1923–24 as compared with 6.5 per cent in 1949, the available data do not clearly indicate a corresponding shift in the total proportion of calls to or from a physician accounted for by [those involving] a specialist.

The nature of health organization, then, may be described as highly specialized, and therefore centralized, with increasing use by a clientele.

These characteristics promote not only pan-community organization, but cooperation among communities, such as the support for a hospital in a large community given by small surrounding communities.

It is no small wonder that we must look to the large urban center for effective action programs in the main. The next section presents one such plan.

ACTION PROGRAMS

The provision of health facilities and personnel can no longer be achieved by the community acting alone. It has become a problem of such magnitude that pan-community action is necessary. This is not to say that there are no areas left in which the local community can operate alone; numerous American communities have organized themselves to obtain the services of a physician or other personnel. At least one large urban center, New York City, has provided a medical service program which in terms of services offered and the scope of coverage is without equal in the country. Before describing some of the national-state activities in this field, a brief account of the New York experience is appropriate.

New York's Health Insurance Plan *

The Origin of the H.I.P.

The Health Insurance Plan of Greater New York, generally known as the H.I.P., grew out of the concern of former Mayor Fiorello LaGuardia about the inability of people of modest income to meet the rising costs of adequate and competent medical care. He was especially concerned about city employees, though his concern did not stop with them. He was seeking a community-sponsored insurance plan to which the city as an employer might turn for the purchase of such prepaid medical care. In April, 1943, he appointed a committee of sixteen citizens representing organized medicine, consumer groups, and the general public to investigate the subject and, if possible, to outline a plan. This committee worked during the next sixteen months to find a plan that would be acceptable.

The plan proposed by the committee sought to combine the advantages of prepayment for medical care, the group practice of medicine, comprehensive service, family coverage, capitation as the basis of reimbursement to groups of physicians, and group enrollment of persons under contracts made with employers, union welfare funds, and other types of associations. Under the insurance law of the State of

* Health and Medical Care in New York City, a report by the Committee for the Special Research Project in the Health Insurance Plan of Greater New York, published for the Commonwealth Fund by Harvard University Press, Cambridge, Mass., 1957, pp. 4–7. Reprinted by permission of the publishers and the Commonwealth Fund.

New York an insurable group must be composed of persons whose group adherence arises from conditions not related primarily to insurance; in a medical care plan this meant not related directly to the specific medical needs of its members. The Health Insurance Plan embodying these features was incorporated on September 28, 1944, over the signatures of some eighty leading citizens who signed as incorporators.

Another two and a half years were required to get the plan into actual operation. New state and municipal legislation was required to remove legal obstacles to the group practice of medicine and to enable the city to purchase this type of insurance for its employees. Sanction by the State Insurance Department and the State Department of Social Welfare had to be obtained. Meanwhile, Mr. LaGuardia had retired from office and a new municipal administration had to satisfy itself through an independent study that the benefits offered by the plan justified its cost to the city.

Once the plan had been incorporated, it was possible to approach the medical profession in New York City with a concrete proposal. This stipulated that contracts would be made with groups of physicians who organized themselves and met the professional requirements of a Medical Control Board composed of a representative body of physicians to be set up by the Corporation to formulate and enforce standards of medical care. It was not difficult at that time to attract the interest of many well-qualified, excellently trained physicians who were being released from military duty and who had become habituated to a form of group practice in the Medical Corps.

When it became apparent that there would be sufficient interest among qualified physicians to insure the formation and operation of medical groups to implement the plan, an intensive period of preparation both in developing the medical groups and in establishing the administrative headquarters of the H.I.P. followed. Premium rates had to be set. Administrative methods for premium collection and payment of capitation rates had to be worked out, enrollment and accounting procedures had to be devised, and physician efforts to form medical groups had to be encouraged and guided to assure compliance with the requirements of the Medical Control Board. These groups, in turn, had to establish partnerships, adopt names, find offices, develop administrative staffs, set up procedures of referral between general physicians and specialists, and arrange for all the needed ancillary medical services.

Benefits and Restrictions in H.I.P. Contract

By March 1, 1947, the technical and administrative details had been sufficiently organized to enable the H.I.P. to begin operation. On that date twenty medical groups scattered throughout . . . four . . . boroughs of New York City with approximately 472 physician members were prepared to accept responsibility for the care of patients insured under the H.I.P. contract. This meant that each group had to have within its partnership or otherwise affiliated with it the requisite specialists and a staff of general physicians to enable each H.I.P. subscriber to have his choice in the selection of personal or family physician.

The medical services accepted by the groups as their responsibility were described in the insurance contract as including:

Medical Services: A person while insured under this Contract shall be entitled to the following medical services provided by the Medical Group in which he is enrolled:

a. General Medical, specialist, surgical, and obstetrical care.

b. Laboratory procedures, diagnostic procedures.

c. Periodic health examinations, immunizations, and other measures for the prevention of disease.

d. Physical therapy, radiotherapy, and other therapeutic measures.

e. Professional services for the administration of blood and plasma.

f. Eye refractions.

g. Visiting nurse service at the residence of the insured person, as prescribed by a physician of the Medical Group.

h. Ambulance service from the residence of the insured person to a hospital, when ordered by a physician of the Medical Group.

The subscriber's certificate further explained that such medical services were to be available and provided at such times as were deemed necessary and practicable by the medical group and to be in accordance with standards adopted by the H.I.P. Medical Control Board. These services were to be available in the offices of the medical group, at the insured person's residence, or elsewhere within the area served by the medical group, as specified in the contract between the medical group and H.I.P. The medical group was also to furnish the services of physicians in a hospital to which the insured person was referred by the medical group. In addition, the insured person had a right to benefits consisting of medical indemnity not to exceed $150 for each instance in which such an insured person, while away from home and not able to be served by his medical group, had an accident or an emergency illness that required hospitalization.

It will be noted that the H.I.P. benefits do not include hospital services per se. This omission is mandatory under the state insurance law which prohibits a corporation from offering insurance for both hospital care and physicians' services. But the H.I.P. has from the beginning required all subscribers to carry Blue Cross or other hospital insurance to make sure that there will be financial provision for the H.I.P. physician to place the patient in a hospital.

Before H.I.P. came into operation the contemplated provision for comprehensive care with no physical examination as a requirement for acceptance, no waiting periods, no age restrictions, and no exclusions of pre-existing conditions was generally viewed with apprehension. Critics predicted adverse selection of risks and such excessive use of the services available as would destroy the quality of the service, if not the total functioning of the plan. The originators of the plan, however, depended on group enrollment to insure adequate spread of risk.

Premium Rates

The setting of premium rates was originally envisioned as a process of harmonizing the factor of the ability of families of moderate income to absorb in their budgets a regular payment for medical care (half the premium rate with the other half paid by the employer) with the expense involved in providing a comprehensive program of first-class medical care and operating an efficient insurance mechanism. The upper limit of a moderate income was placed at $5,000 for a family. Decisions and agreements as to premium rates and capitations were reached in June, 1946. The following month the Office of Price Administration went out of existence and the index of the cost of living in New York City began a rapid ascent. But the plan could not jeopardize its inauguration by trying to adjust its rates at that moment.

It was not long before another condition began to make itself felt. The rising costs of living with the ensuing wage adjustments, together with the employment of married women, carried many family incomes over the $5,000 limit. It became very difficult with such a limitation to enroll city departments as well as other employed groups. This problem was finally met by accepting families of higher income on an adjusted premium. The limits for the base premium were put at an annual income of $5,000 for a person insuring himself only and $6,500 for a family group. Premiums for persons and families with incomes above those amounts were set at 50 per cent higher than the base rate.

H.I.P. Medical Groups and Subscriber's Choice of Physician

Before the H.I.P. offers the services of a group of physicians to H.I.P. subscribers, the medical group has to meet the standards of the H.I.P. Medical Control Board and enter into a formal contract with H.I.P. to supply the services set forth as guaranteed to subscribers through medical groups. These standards relate to the qualifications of the physicians, their group organization, and the facilities and equipment of the group's medical center. Each group must be a medical partnership composed of family physicians and representatives of the twelve basic medical specialties. Each group defines the area from which subscribers are accepted by it. Some medical groups provide all of the office services at the medical center, while others decentralize the family physicians (and in a few instances the pediatrician's services) and use the medical centers largely for the specialist services.

When a person has signified an intention to join H.I.P., he is supplied with a directory of medical groups that lists their names and addresses, gives the names of the physicians composing the group, indicates which are family physicians, and gives the address of any office they may have away from the medical center at which they are prepared to see patients. The person is not enrolled until he has chosen a medical group. Beginning with his effective date, that medical group receives semimonthly capitations for the subscriber and each of his dependents. New subscribers are instructed to visit their medical groups promptly in order to select their family physician from the several who are in the medical group, to arrange for check-ups, and to become acquainted with their doctors and the H.I.P. system before an emergency occurs. Subscribers are free to choose any medical group that serves their area of residence and to change their family physicians and, in some groups, their pediatricians at any time. When a subscriber moves out of the area served by his medical group, he transfers to a group serving his new location.

From the beginning, the H.I.P. subscriber has been urged to think of his affiliation with the H.I.P. medical group as the election of a team of doctors engaged in medical group practice and designed to meet, with very few exceptions, all of his medical needs. Utilization data show that about half of all the physician services rendered are those of specialists. H.I.P. subscribers are free to use outside physicians, but such physicians will receive no compensation from H.I.P. or the medical group for assistance in diagnosis and treatment. Subscribers who are devoted to a family physician they have had prior to joining H.I.P. may continue with him and use their medical group only for X-ray, laboratory, and other specialist services. Conversely, some subscribers may continue with a specialist they have previously had and use their H.I.P. affiliation for any other medical needs that they or their dependents may develop. Women pregnant at the time of enrollment often continue with the obstetrician they have previously engaged.

The New York plan, in its origin and development, well illustrates the possibilities of community action where imaginative and effective leadership is able to mobilize the groups, formal organization, and institutions and direct them toward the achievement of the goal of improved health facilities. Action on the scale of the New York experience is, however, beyond the reach of the smaller communities. Their needs can be best served by action at the county, state, and national levels. It is in the construction and operation of hospitals that achievement has been most marked. While prepayment plans for medical services under government sponsorship have met with the determined opposition of organized medicine, similar sponsorship of hospital construction and maintenance has met with approval, as has also the prepayment plan for coverage of hospital expenses.

The Blue Cross hospital prepayment plan has spread rapidly to all parts of the United States and Canada since its humble origin in Baylor, Texas, in 1929. Blue Shield, the prepayment plan for surgical expenses, has also experienced rapid growth, but has not so widespread a membership as Blue Cross. Both, however, illustrate the point that pan-community action in the health field is the most common method of dealing with its problems.

In the construction and maintenance of hospitals, the community-state-federal relationship is again manifest. The passage of the Hill-Burton Act by the Congress in 1946 set the stage for nation-wide planning for distribution and construction of hospitals. Aimed in part at redressing the imbalance between urban and rural hospital facilities, the act provided that each state which wished to participate in its benefits must submit a state plan for hospital construction to the Surgeon General of the Public Health Service for his approval.

A state report prepared in Virginia under the auspices of the Department of Rural Sociology of the Virginia Agricultural Experiment Station is similar to those of other states which were done under the sponsorship of official state committees. Twelve subcommittees prepared reports on different aspects of the problem.[2] All the states, including Virginia, were guided in developing a hospital service system by the plan proposed by the United States Public Health Service. This plan in brief would provide facilities as follows:

(1) Base hospitals, of 500 beds and up, located in larger cities, and providing teaching, research, and consultation on a wide range of disease problems; staffed with the most skilled personnel and capable of handling the most difficult cases.

(2) District hospitals, of 100 beds or more, and capable of handling ordinary and fairly complicated illnesses and usually located in regional centers.

(3) Intermediate area hospitals, usually of 50 beds and up—the type usually found in small cities handling ordinary illnesses.

(4) Rural area hospitals which ordinarily have about 50 beds and a supporting base of up to 50,000 people.

(5) Health or community medical service centers which serve as headquarters for public health work. Health centers are sometimes enlarged into community clinics or medical service centers, which in addition to quarters for public health work have up to 25 hospital beds, office space for local doctors, and equipment for their joint use.

The committee calculated that in order to meet the standards of an adequate hospital service for rural and urban populations, the following beds would need to be added to those in service in 1952: general hospitals, 6,236 beds; mental, 9,681; tuberculosis, 1,535; and chronic disease, 6,380 beds. This meant that to the total of 16,322 beds in use in 1952, 23,832 additional beds were needed. Already, though, with the Hill-Burton grants-in-aid, the state and its communities had complete or had under construction facilities which would add 2,299 general hospital beds and 936 for tuberculosis.[3] Upwards of thirty hospitals aided through Hill-Burton funds were either completed, under construction, or authorized in 1953. Still, the gap between needs and resources remained great.

Among the most interesting parts of this report, which are of special concern in connection with this book, are two committee reports that deal with "health-related programs of other public agencies" and "volunteer organizations concerned with health problems." [4] A mere listing of these agencies and

[2] This summary is based on the elaborate report of twelve subcommittees edited by W.E. Garnett, "The Road To Health In Rural Virginia, 1900–1952," *Virginia AES Bulletin 466*, 1954.
[3] *Ibid.*, p. 28.
[4] *Ibid.*, pp. 39–46.

organizations will reveal the vast extent to which one basic community need (health) affects the functioning of so many components, and therefore the elements and dimensions of local life. These are the public agencies with health-related programs: the State Department of Education and the local school systems; the Agricultural Extension Service; the Agricultural Experiment Station; the State Department of Agriculture; the University of Virginia Extension Service; the college; the State Department of Labor; the State Compensation Board; the State Highway Department; the Department of Professional and Occupational Registration; and the Commission for the Blind.

The report itself summarizes the ways in which each of these public agencies functions in the field of health, but simply listing them is enough to enable the reader to infer what each one does.

The voluntary organizations concerned are as follows: the Medical Society of Virginia; the Old Dominion Medical Society (the Negro doctors); the state Dental Association; the Virginia Hospital Association; the Graduate Nurses' Association; the Practical Nurses' Association; the Mental Hygiene Society; the State Veterinary Medical Association; the American Red Cross; the Virginia Tuberculosis Association; the Virginia Division of the American Cancer Society; the National Foundation for Infantile Paralysis; the Virginia Heart Association; the Virginia Society for Crippled Children and Adults; the Society for the Crippled of Southwest Virginia; the Virginia Cerebral Palsy Association; the Safety Council; the Virginia League for Planned Parenthood; the Virginia Council on Health and Medical Care; the Congress of Parents and Teachers; the Federation of Women's Clubs; the League of Women Voters; the State Grange; the Farm Bureau Federation and Associated Women; the Negro Organization Society; the District Ruritan Clubs; the Agricultural Conference Board; the Virginia CIO-AFL; the Dietetic Association; the Home Economics Association; the Adult Educational Association; the Federal of Business and Professional Women; the State Chamber of Commerce; the State Conference of Social Work; churches of all denominations; and the Hospital Service Association.

These are only the statewide organizations. When to these are added their various county and local branches, plus those which are strictly local, one begins to appreciate the vast scope of volunteer organized effort in American society. Many of the formal organizations listed here are dedicated to the solution of specific problems, but some of them have added the health function to those for which they are especially designed. This would be true, say, of the churches and the educational institutions.

PRINCIPLES

1. *Health facilities are organized to serve the needs of a much larger population base than that found in most small communities.*
This type of organization is brought about by a greater value placed on specialization and efficiency. The rewards are likewise passed on to personnel for conformity to this type of organization. Hence the small community may well be without a physician as well as a hospital.

2. *The value placed by the mass society on health and long life as ends and physicians and hospitals as means have been subscribed to as much by families and persons in small communities as in large ones.*

3. *The discrepancy between the goal of adequate health facilities and social resources represents a community and pan-community problem.*

4. *This problem of nonavailability is partly ameliorated by better trans-portation facilities, which permit ready contact with a physician in case of serious illness.*

5. *The availability of hospital services in rural areas is being improved in their construction and maintenance by the joint cooperation of federal, state, and county governments.*

6. *Health and long life are goals so generally held high in the scale of values that numerous public and private agencies and organizations con-tribute to its achievement.*

SELECTED REFERENCES

Ensminger, Douglas, and T. Wilson Longmore, "Rural Health," in Carl C. Taylor and others, *Rural Life in the United States*, Alfred A. Knopf, New York, 1949, Chapter IX.

Foster, George M., *Problems in Intercultural Health Programs*, Social Science Research Council Pamphlet 12, New York.

Hunter, Floyd, Ruth C. Schaffer, and Cecil G. Sheps, *Community Organization: Action and Inaction*, University of North Carolina Press, Chapel Hill, 1956, Chapter 6.

Miller, Paul A., *Community Health Action*, Michigan State College Press, East Lansing, 1953.

Paul, Benjamin, editor, *Health, Culture, and Community*, Russell Sage Foundation, New York, 1956.

Sanders, Irwin T., *The Community*, The Ronald Press Company, New York, 1958, Chapter 16.

Smith, T. Lynn, *The Sociology of Rural Life*, Harper and Brothers, New York, 1947, Chapter v.

Health and Medical Care in New York City, a Report by the Committee for the Special Research Project on the Health Insurance Plan of Greater New York, published for the Commonwealth Fund by Harvard University Press, Cambridge, Mass., 1957.

PART FOUR

Community Change

The analysis presented in Part I concerned the influence of outside factors on community structure. In Parts II and III the internal operation of structural relationships within the community were analyzed, with particular reference to change. It is now left to consider more directly some aspects of change. The interest here is mainly in terms of practical programs of deliberate change.

The first chapter of Part IV is devoted to the fundamental questions in understanding, predicting, and controlling change. This is a frame of reference within which action programs must be understood. The analysis is mainly composed of questions, but moot points concern us more in action than does established knowledge.

The overview of social change is next considered more directly in community development. By this is meant the restructuring of community decisions in terms of democratic action in order to assure greater human happiness. The pitfalls of unplanned change may be recognized and taken into consideration in community development. They may not be so considered in power decisions. The structure and process of democratic community decision is discussed in Chapter 20.

The last chapter attempts to describe some of the

more obvious trends which have relevance to community structure and change with an eye to some educated guesswork as to the problems of the future, concerning both necessary action and ways and means of getting action appropriate to the need.

CHAPTER 19

Social Change

SOCIAL CHANGE AND SOCIAL PROBLEMS

Most of the problems of man involve social change in one way or another. In the first place, almost any kind of change produces problems if for no other reason than that it represents a deviation from that to which one is accustomed. It should be obvious by now, however, that the nature of social structure is such that a change in one dimension or element is likely to produce change in another. The resulting problems are likely to extend beyond that of mere deviation from the usual. A second relationship exists between social change and social problems.[1] When man faces problems, he adjusts his relations to ameliorate them. This adjustment in his relations is also, in fact, social change. Because of the nature of social structure, it will produce changes in relations which he did not intend or even anticipate. It is easily seen that this interaction is a continuing one, since one problem will produce changes which in turn create more problems and so on.

Difficulties in Understanding Change

The fact of change does not need elaboration, but the understanding of it, its prediction and control, is not so easy. There are at least three difficulties in understanding it. First, change is coterminous with structure, for in any but the rare, ideal-type, traditional (sacred) society, most dimensions and elements are changing and all are capable of it. Therefore, the difficulties of understanding the total structure of the community may be multiplied many times over those involved in understanding or describing a particular structure at a given time. A second difficulty arises from the fact that there are many types of change, and the generalizations which are valid for one type

[1] Don Martindale and Elio D. Monachesi, *Elements of Sociology*, Harper and Brothers, New York, 1951, Part IV; and Edward H. Spicer, editor, *Human Problems in Technological Change*, Russell Sage Foundation, New York, 1952.

do not hold for another. A third difficulty comes from the lack of knowledge based upon rigorous research. Before change can be understood, it is necessary to have a base line from which to measure it; that is, it is first necessary to understand structure at the beginning point from which change is to be measured. That this is difficult to accomplish is never denied by those who have begun to grasp the subtle nature of the power structure,[2] the dualism in the value system,[3] the shifting and ill-defined obligations of the family to the community,[4] and the elusive pressures exerted on the community from mass society.[5]

Interest in Change Is Both Scientific and Practical

Despite the difficulties mentioned above, change must be taken into consideration, whether the interest in the community be scientific or practical. From the scientific point of view, it is only half of the picture to describe and analyze structure at a given time. Indeed, it may be less than half since only through understanding the changes occurring over a course of time can prediction and scientific control be realized. From the practical point of view, change is of major interest because of its relationship to social problems. Community development is intimately bound up with this relationship. Because of its importance to both scientific and practical interest, change in elements and dimensions has been considered an integral part of the analysis throughout this book. It is now important to regard social change as a separate form.

THE NATURE OF SOCIAL CHANGE

The definition of change presupposes the definition of structure, but it is important to distinguish it from process. In a sense all human relations and structures are processual, in that they form and exist through time. Cooperation is obviously a process, but it is not social change. The assignment of status develops through time, and it operates in any concrete way only as men relate themselves to one another differentially. The elements of the

[2] Floyd Hunter, *Community Power Structure*, University of North Carolina Press, Chapel Hill, 1953.
[3] Robert S. Lynd, *Knowledge for What?* Princeton University Press, Princeton, New Jersey, 1939.
[4] William F. Ogburn and Meyer F. Nimkoff, *Technology and the Changing Family*, Houghton-Mifflin Company, Boston, 1955.
[5] Arthur J. Vidich and Joseph Bensman, *Small Town in Mass Society*, Princeton University Press, Princeton, New Jersey, 1958.

community are also processual. The family's functions have concrete meaning only so far as, in day-to-day living, the remainder of the community can depend upon the family to socialize the next generation, to participate in community affairs, and to propagate the race.

Change and Process

The first relation between process and change, then, is a logical one. Change is one of the social processes in that it is one form that human relations take through time. However, sociologists in the main have considered process in a very narrow sense. They have referred chiefly to four and sometimes five as if these were the only processes. These have been cooperation, conflict, competition, and accommodation.[6] Sometimes assimilation is added. Some theorists add many other processes, although there is no general agreement regarding them. Accommodation and assimilation are by their nature social change, and the other processes may be results or causes of change. To have meaning, change must involve more than this narrow concept of process. It must alter the form of human relations and structures, such as moving from competition to conflict, or from competition to cooperation.

In a given community situation, however, competition may exist quietly for years and suddenly flare up into conflict. After a period of time, the fires may die down and the old relation may be restored. Similarly, codes of conduct, such as rules of dress, may change for a while. Fundamentally, women's dress in American society remains much the same, but length and other minor features vary from time to time. It is desirable at present to exclude these fluctuations from the analysis, since the generalizations which are valid for social change are not applicable to many of these short-term cycles.

However, it is impossible at present to ascertain in all cases when a given sequence of behavior patterns is change and when it is some other type of process; when it is change and when fluctuation. More research is needed to show exactly what conditions are necessary for given generalizations. Nevertheless, much insight into social change can be gained without a precise definition. At least some of the criteria of social change can be observed and recorded.

[6] Robert E. Park and Ernest W. Burgess, *Introduction to the Science of Sociology*, University of Chicago Press, Chicago, 1921, Chapters 8–11; Louis Wirth, *The Ghetto*, University of Chicago Press, Chicago, 1928; Pitirim Sorokin, *Contemporary Sociological Theories*, Harper and Brothers, New York, 1928, Chapter 6; Lowry Nelson, *Rural Sociology*, American Book Company, New York, 1955, Chapters 8–10; and T. Lynn Smith, *The Sociology of Rural Life*, Harper and Brothers, New York, 1947, Part IV.

Types of Social Change

The first type is the long-term trend. It can be seen clearly that the level of living in American communities has been steadily increasing since the beginnings of American society.[7] This trend has been reversed on occasion only slightly and only temporarily. A second type of social change is the apparently permanent transfer of a function from one social unit to another. The family has surrendered the function of producer to the economic institution. This change came about slowly and is relatively permanent. A third phenomenon which may be considered social change is the shift in a fundamental aspect of one or more of the dimensions of the community. By "fundamental" here is meant those aspects which are least amenable to fluctuation. For example, the mores and folkways do not fluctuate and therefore the shift in one of these fundamental codes of conduct always is relatively permanent. Likewise, an occupation may increase or decrease in influence. There might be a question as to whether this is social change or merely fluctuation, but if authority is given less importance for a long period of time in determining status, then social change has occurred. The status of the doctor in income, prestige, authority, and so on has risen from negative sanctions to one of the highest status positions in the community. This is likely to remain the case for a long time and probably represents social change. The soldier in American society was low in status before World War I, high during World War I, low again from 1919 until about 1940–1941, and then high again. The generalizations of social change probably do not apply to the status of the soldier during these periods, but they may be valid for the change in status of the physician.

The common factor in distinguishing change from mere fluctuation thus far is the length of time over which the change persists. However, man is not concerned with such long-range changes in his decision-making. Problems are problems today, and the man who views consequences of alternative solutions for ten to twenty years ahead is indeed far-sighted and rare. It follows that short, as well as longer, terms must be considered. How, then, can an immediate shift in human relations be viewed as social change? Perhaps the best criterion is some basis upon which it can be predicted whether this shift will persist or will return to yesterday's form. The nature of social structure gives a clue. If a given shift is tied up with many other dimensions and elements it may be expected to remain for a longer time. For the im-

[7] Margaret Jarman Hagood, *Farm-Operator Family Level of Living Indexes for Counties of the United States 1930, 1940, 1945, and 1950,* United States Department of Agriculture, Bureau of Agricultural Economics, Washington, D.C., 1952.

mediate situation, therefore, generalizations about social change may apply if a shift in one aspect involves shifts in other dimensions and elements of community structure.

The Problem of Social Change

Social change may be viewed several ways within the frame of reference of the present treatise. One meaningful view is the negative one of preventing change in one part of the community structure from producing problems in other elements or dimensions. Thus when, say, the family breaks down in its function, it produces problems for the legal, educational, and economic institutions in performing their functions. The response to the problem of socialization may then take several forms. The legal institution may deviate from its established procedure in the function of assuring order and justice. It may do away with trial by jury, right to defense counsel, and so on. The educational institution may extend its functions to include instilling respect for life and property. The economic institution may support the expenses of playgrounds and recreational directors. The religious institution, always functioning to instill basic mores and folkways, may intensify its efforts not only in its basic functions but also in extending them to include recreational programs which give direction to leisure-time activities for youth. Thus the gap between expectations from the family and achievement of those expectations is closed and the main problem at the moment may be ameliorated. However, the solution pictured here involves a higher budget, more personnel, activity in an area where experience is lacking, and closer ties among the institutions of the community. It may be seen, then, that change is produced throughout the elements of the community by virtue of what happens in one element.

Social change may also be viewed as an effort to meet problems, while at the same time maintaining a clearly understood agreement on function. Is it really the role of the school to socialize the child? There is disagreement on this point. Is it really the obligation of the economic institution to support playgrounds and recreational directors through direct contributions rather than through taxes? These are all points of contention and indicate the confusion which exists when patterns of behavior deviate from those expected and when long-established understandings are broken down.

In summary, social change is the modification of structure to maintain stability and consistency.[8] Social problems must be solved in anticipation of new problems which may be created by their solution.

[8] Kingsley Davis, *Human Society*, The Macmillan Company, New York, 1948, Chapter 22.

WHAT IS IT THAT CHANGES?

There are four levels of structure which may change. The first and most important level is the total community. Change here is always slow and may occur only over many generations. In the course of time, a community may shift from a sacred-folk to a secular-prescribed structure.[9] Such change will occur in a short time only when it is in response to some disaster or some tremendously important event. The location of a very large plant near a relatively small community in which most codes of conduct are largely unwritten, where the status system is based mainly upon personal characteristics, and where the relations among the institutions are clearly understood by everyone, may change within two or three years to a buzzing confusion of anonymity, written laws, a status system based on position rather than acquaintance, and tremendous pressure on institutions to attain even partial success in fulfilling functions.

A second important point where change occurs is at the pan-community level. Since the community is made up of relations between other area-bound social units, like the school district and the township, the relations between it and nearby communities, as well as with the Great Society, will change as schools are consolidated or voting districts are altered. If a sufficient number of these changes are made, a small community may be swallowed up by a larger one, but ordinarily it will only surrender some of its functions. In addition, it is important to observe that the operation of mass communication as well as legislation enacted by state or federal governments will tend to remove from the local community many unique features it possesses. The local units become homogenized in the mass.

A third level of change is in dimensions and elements of community structure. It has been seen that dimensions are community-wide and thus may usually be expected to produce changes in more of the remainder of the community than would elements. However, both of them change within themselves and cause other social changes as well. The value system may change from being homogeneous to being heterogeneous; or from use of unwritten codes to written ones. The stratification system may change from being personality-based to one based on position. The relations between the family and the school may change from apathy to close cooperation. The relations between the church and the school may change from independent

[9] For example, see Howard Becker, *Through Values to Social Interpretation*, Duke University Press, Durham, North Carolina, 1950, Chapter 5.

operation to closer ties and reinforcement in functions through released time for religious instruction.

The fourth level where change may occur is in a component, such as the family or the organization of the school itself. These changes in substructures become important to understanding the community only when they imply changes in function. For example, the working mother represents a change in family structure, but this implies at least two changes in community elements. The increase in the labor force is assured and the breakdown in the socialization function is threatened. In the first case, the relationship between the family and the economic institution is involved, and in the second case, that between the family and the total community. Change in the structure of the family is not community change as such, as was the case with changes in elements and dimensions, but may be significant in producing community-wide change.

THE DIRECTION OF SOCIAL CHANGE

Trends

Change usually may be observed quantitatively, as when there is a rise in the level of living and increased specialization.[10] Only occasionally is it necessary to make qualitative observations, as, for example, in the situation in which the judge, the social worker, and the parent cooperate in a delinquency case. This introduces a new element of structure. Observation here is qualitative rather than quantitative. Even this kind of change may be viewed as a trend, however, if a look is taken at the number of communities adopting the practice.

It will be recalled that throughout this book particular trends have been noted: loss of family functions, rise or decline in participation, and so on. However, there are general trends which are reflected in these specific ones and which are important as a frame of reference for the study of the community.

From Sacred to Secular

First to be noted is the change in the total value system from sacred to secular. In this process more codes of conduct come to be written. These

---

[10] Carl C. Taylor, "Significant Trends and Direction of Change," in Taylor and others, *Rural Life in the United States,* Alfred A. Knopf, New York, 1949, Chapter 30. This chapter is of almost as much relevance to urban as to rural communities.

codes are more specific, and are based on rational considerations rather than upon tradition, as in the past. The content of the codes is probably little changed in the area of fundamental mores and most folkways. Group perpetuation is still the most serious code to violate, and security orientations still are fundamental. But decisions are more often made in terms of consequences than in the past. Precedents, or tradition, still weigh heavily, but external conformity is more and more the criterion if rationality cannot be used.

From Homogeneity to Heterogeneity

Very close to the change from sacred to secular is that from homogeneity to heterogeneity.[11] Homogeneity of values and behavior is a standard characteristic of sacred communities. The increasing segmentation of the value system, the increasing tolerance for different points of view, and the increasingly specialized codes, accepted by everyone but assigned only to particular positions, produce a heterogeneity in belief and behavior which is of great importance. The old categories of "upper" and "lower" classes and the later ones of "upper," "middle," and "lower" are largely broken up, with a status continuum now characteristic of most American communities. The result is a degree of heterogeneity probably unparalleled in world history.

The Role of Communication

Improved communication facilities have also been an important force in bringing about other changes in the community. A small community in California learns what is happening in a community in Florida and another in Maine on the same day the events occur. This trend is closely associated with the increasing facility of transportation, making for much less social isolation.

Mass communication media give to all people the same information, the same entertainment, the same suggestions. Its ally, transportation, allows great facility for personal contact.

So it appears that people in the modern world are being pressured by many opposing forces, some leading to heterogeneity and wider differentiation and others toward increasing homogeneity and likeness. The conclusion appears inevitable that differences will increase in some respects and decline in others.

[11] The classic statement of this theory was made by Herbert Spencer, *First Principles*, D. Appleton Company, New York, Sixth Edition, 1924.

From Folklore to Science

Associated with the shift from sacred to secular is the substitution of scientific thoughtways for folk beliefs and practices. This change is well established in the physical and biological worlds and is now involving the social world as well. It is obvious both from general observation of the number of new practices used and the number of people using them.

The Decline of Primary Group Influence

Human relations are less a function of primary groups and familial institutions than they are of the market place and the political institution. Friends and families are less influential in producing conformity. The economic institution and the government have more control and furnish more of the services previously assigned to the family. Retirement systems of business enterprises and the government social security system have largely taken over from the family the responsibility of care for aged and dependent members.

A decrease in individualism is also noticeable. While people differ from one another more than formerly, they do not exert as much control over the nature of this difference as was true in early America. This trend would not be so marked in some parts of the United States as it is in others, and certainly is not characteristic of all parts of the world. Where a feudal economy formerly prevailed, the trend is probably toward more freedom. However, the American frontier community is usually believed to have been highly individualistic, whereas present conditions, controlled more by the assembly line and by bureaucracy, inhibit individualism.

There is an increasing number of large formal organizations which are structured around specialized community problems that had not occurred previously and therefore were not within the province of existing institutions. With time, these organizations tend to take on the characteristics of institutions so that individual influence upon organizational affairs becomes negligible. This is illustrated by the Red Cross, the Community Chest and the Parent-Teachers Association, among others.

The picture in the American community is indeed a confusing one, with contradictory trends occurring side by side. It is nevertheless within this context that community development programs must operate, latching on to this trend and competing with that one.

Components of Social Change: Qualitative Change [12]

At any given point in time the necessary condition of social change is an *accumulation* of social and cultural traits. These may be dimensions, elements, or even material cultural items. From this accumulation certain ones are combined into a new social or cultural practice. William F. Ogburn refers to this as an *invention*, which he defines as a new combination of existing components. While the term "invention" carries the connotation of material items, there are social inventions as well. Examples of social inventions are the Constitution of the United States, the rectangular system of land surveys, the United Nations' compact, the marathon in political campaigning and promotion of causes, the labor union, the assembly line, and so on.

Inventions accumulate and it is a law of social change that inventions occur at an accelerating rate. Put another way, accumulation tends toward geometric rather than arithmetical progression. Since an invention is a new combination of the accumulated traits, the more traits that become available the more the inventions that can be made.[13]

These inventions go through the process of *diffusion* from one community to another; that is, they are borrowed from their point of origin and, sometimes with certain alterations, they become part of the structure of the community. In this process some *adjusment* is necessary, since any change produces new requirements from other dimensions and elements. Adjustment occurs more readily in material than non-material practices, and this is referred to by Ogburn as *cultural lag*. Cultural lag appears in more than one way. First, if an invention happens to be material in nature, the non-material culture lags behind in adjustment. Second, the secondary changes brought about by any invention are more rapidly assimilated in the material than in the non-material world. For example, adjustment to the consolidation of schools requiring longer distances of travel for children was facilitated by the invention of the school bus. On the other hand, the need for a greater tax base to provide the expensive visual aids, better-paid teachers, library materials, and costly laboratory equipment that modern education requires was much less readily acceptable to the people. Anticipated adjustment as well as defined need accounts for much of the differential acceptance among practices.

[12] William F. Ogburn, *Social Change*, the Viking Press, New York, 1952, Part 6.
[13] For a full discussion of the theory of innovations see H.G. Barnett, *Innovation: The Basis of Cultural Change*, McGraw-Hill Book Company, New York, 1953.

THE RATE OF SOCIAL CHANGE

Measurement of change is a very important problem for social scientists. A rigorous test of the cultural lag hypothesis (that non-material culture changes more slowly than does material culture) must await the devising of comparable units for measuring material and non-material culture. Similarly, change in some substructures cannot be ascertained with any precision, because the bench-mark description of structural variables at any given time is imprecise. How can one determine how much bureaucracy is present in a given company, or how much division of labor exists? Crude indices are the best measures available.

Measurement techniques are being developed, but in the meantime rates of change are so important in community development that some effort must be made to estimate them, at least on a relative basis. Within dimensions, as we have said, there appear to be varying rates of change. For example, mores change more slowly than folkways, and both more slowly than customs. Any human structure that is institutionalized changes more slowly than what is not institutionalized. Dimensions change more slowly than elements, but both change more rapidly than the community as a whole.

The generalization may be made that the more a given relationship is tied up with other relationships and beliefs, the less likely it is to change; and in any case the more slowly it will change.

Not only are relative rates of change of practical and scientific importance, but some absolute standard of expectation is particularly helpful in community development programs. How long should it take to be able to observe some progress in a community development program when it is concerned with a change in mores or in a stratification system? How long, if it is concerned with a new type of conduct for which there are not presently any definitions of right and wrong in the value system? How long should it take in either type of concern to achieve the major objective? How long before unanticipated consequences can be isolated and assessed as desirable or undesirable? The nature of institutional programs, where budgets often run from year to year and a change in policy can be made any time, requires some estimate of these programs. For example, how soon can the United States Congress expect to see concrete effects as a basis for deciding whether or not to continue the International Cooperation Administration program? There are almost no answers or even approaches to answers to these questions. Apparently sure-fire programs may fail while in some cases ill-designed programs succeed.

One approach to the study of this question is to distinguish between changes from one generation to another and those which come within a generation. The individual is a carrier of mores and folkways. If he believes wholeheartedly in these deep-seated codes of conduct he will instill them in his children. However, if change in a code of conduct is occurring, reinforcement from other dimensions and elements of the community will not occur and as a result the code will be less deeply internalized in the child. But the older person will be unlikely to change. In situations of this sort, effective change can be brought about only over generations.

The point made immediately above is not an ironclad conclusion. For example, during the depression of the 1930's, many families which were unemployed resisted accepting relief from the government for a considerable length of time owing to the value orientations toward individualism and the husband-father as the provider. Charity was shameful. But this did not last for a generation, since most of these families had come to regard relief as a necessary evil, but acceptable in view of the fact that so many other families were receiving relief.

No answer to the question of how much time may be needed for programs to succeed or even to take hold can be given. There are two points, however, which can be accepted with some assurance. The time needed for change depends upon how fundamental the attempted change is to the community structure. Second, none but the most superficial changes can be expected in a budget year. For example, reports on educational programs often use numbers of contacts or visits—in essence, the amount of effort—in evaluating effectiveness. Numbers are beguiling, and it is small wonder that personnel who have to think of such reports to gain support for the next year tend to think of the criteria of effort rather than objectives and consequences in evaluating their work to themselves and in deciding between alternatives.

FORMS OF SOCIAL CHANGE

Many grandiose efforts have been directed at describing the forms of social change. In considering trends earlier in this chapter, the assumption was made that during the last two centuries or so the changes specified were straight-line trends. Other concepts include the cyclical, such as movement from the idealistic to the ideational to the sensate and back again. No com-

pletely satisfactory scheme has been described, either from the point of view
of forms or of precision. It seems evident that no one form will describe
long-range social change in all or even most cases. It is unlikely, for example,
that secular communities will again become folk-sacred in nature. Other
types of change, such as conservatism and liberality, seem to follow a
pendulum-like cycle.

The Context for Community Development

Community development programs are deliberate efforts to bring about
social change. The launching of such programs involves many operations,
including not only the original design, the recruitment and training of
leaders, and the steps in implementation, but also a careful appraisal of the
situation with regard to the points presented previously in this chapter. Is
the problem one of change or fluctuation? The introduction of change requires careful anticipation of consequences. Is it quantitative or qualitative
change? If it is quantitative, is the program merely speeding up a trend or
trying to get one started? If it is qualitative, then one may ask, Is the community structured so that a new dimension, a new element, can be added
successfully? If so, will it help people achieve their goals or merely create a
new social and cultural diversity to confuse people? What form of social
change is being introduced—a linear trend which will gain momentum in
the same direction, or a cyclical trend which will return to former situations
after it has run its gamut? If it is linear, is there a point where there may be
too much of a good thing? If so, how do you stop the trend? These are only
a few of the relevant questions, and none of them can be answered in the
near future because much more research is needed.

The first known fact which may serve as a context for community development is the fact of structure. Elements and dimensions are interdependent.
What the status system is depends upon what the value system defines it to
be. What the value system is depends upon the willingness of the power
structure to support it. A change in one cannot successfully be accomplished
without a change in the other. But the status system and the value system
are equally related to the other dimensions of community structure. They
also are related to the elements of the community—the performance of functions by groups, large formal organizations, and institutions in the community
at large, and the relations between any of the substructures. Social change
is not introduced in a vacuum but in a structure of human relationships, a
veritable network of subtle and yet undeniable forces operating to maintain

the status quo. Without a thorough assessment of these dimensions and elements the success of a community development program is left to chance and probably doomed to failure.

The value system of most professionals in the field of community development would taboo a program which created more problems than it solved, or created a more serious problem than it solved. The fact of structure then gives cause for caution not only from the desire for success but from the desire to help. A program may succeed if it is supported by most elements and dimensions of community structure. Even with most careful planning a serious problem may be initiated in an unanticipated area of community structure.

Another factor involved in deliberate social change is the state of readiness of the community structure. Unfortunately, as yet, the assessment as to readiness must be done without devices for measurement. By contrast, an assessment of an individual for a job may be partially made by an aptitude test, an interest test, and a personal adjustment test. While such measures of individual characteristics are far from complete, they have been developed in a relatively short time. Few measures are available for the measurement of structure, and as a consequence, the only recourse is to a common-sense judgment made by skilled observers.

Closely associated with inadequate means of measurement is the problem of diffusion of information itself, of the particular concepts of structure and change which will at least give some insight. Community development workers must know technical aspects of the problem as well as having insight into the structure of the community. Further, the concept of community development implies ultimately the determination of the courses of action by the lay people of the community itself. How can lay people be trained in the business of self-assessment when tools for the purpose are lacking or difficult to use, when concepts of self-assessment are fairly difficult to understand, and, most important of all, when the structure of the community is implicitly understood rather than explicitly stated?

Knowledge as a basis for exact predictions as to what to expect from social change is not available to give to the layman.

The foregoing discussion considers several points which warrant caution in embarking upon deliberate social change of the community. The points thus far add up to a rather formidable array of difficulties: known difficulties and unanticipated consequences. What, then, is the warranty for community development programs, with the accompanying effort of universities to train people to work as resource experts in the community? If there are so many difficulties in the assessment of community development, would it not be better to divert intellectual and practical energies to less risky programs?

PLANNING CHANGE

The answer to this question must be based upon the generalization that change is bound to come. Once change has begun and there is movement away from the sacred-folk community, the problems created by the original change multiply, and as adjustments are made, they multiply again. If change is to happen to the modern community, is it not better to plan for it? Will there not occur fewer unanticipated consequences if directed effort is made to plan for them? Will there not be fewer rampant changes, if all possible features of the community are considered as reorganization and modification of structure are made? Will there not be more even changes throughout the dimensions and elements of community structure if one change is limited until adjustments in the remainder of the structure can be planned? The answers to these questions are matters of principle derived from the concept of structure. However, the implication of this principle for community development work is a matter of value judgment. If one values stability, as little culture lag as possible, and greater adjustment among the interdependent dimensions and elements of community structure, then the need for some deliberate action program such as community development should clearly be defensible.

Sources of Community Change

The source of change most easily grasped is that of swift and radical alterations in the environment of the community. For example, depletion of resources, heavy in-migration, changes in labor opportunities, resettlement projects, large defense plants which spring up within a few months, and other large projects of construction all may induce rapid change in structure. Somewhat more slowly comes the change which follows from altering the route of a major highway, but it still occurs rapidly enough to be seen within a single person's experience. Many communities plan for these kinds of changes by attempting to attract job-giving industry. Even a small plant can do a great deal to bring prosperity to a small community. There are other changes to be expected from the introduction of a new industry in a small community, such as changes in the power and authority structure, the value system, and the communication system. Changes in elements of community structure involving the relation between the economic institution and other substructures are practically inevitable.

Another important source of change is the increased communication facilities from one community to another through radio and television. By learning of achievements in other places, new alternatives will be seen by the local people and new problems recognized and defined. Similarly, increased transportation makes possible first-hand experience, which exposes members of one community to the value system and social organization of others. It has been noted in previous chapters that television may itself be a problem in some communities where it may interfere with participation and activity in organizational work.

Change is no more rapid in any aspect of social structure than in the legal codes of conduct. The community is not usually coterminous with a legal unit, but in most cases overlaps with several—the village or city, the township, and the school district. Since government performs a function in the community, changes in the legal structure will change its relations to other substructures. The case was pointed out earlier where one community was half in one county and half in another. A sales tax was adopted in one county but not in the other. One could hardly avoid seeing the immediate effect upon the entire community structure due to changed relations between the government and other substructures as well as the institution toward which the legislation was directed.

Not all legal changes are as dysfunctional as the illustration used above. Many community problems can be solved through governmental action, especially where the legal and community boundaries roughly correspond. Federal and state legislation also are important sources of amelioration of problems in the community. State legislation regarding delinquency prevention and treatment of the offender, conditions for, and amount of, help for buildings, such as hospitals, and assistance in problems of highways and sewage disposal are cases in point.

National and regional modifications in economic organizations serve as another source of change at the community level. The chain store and the large company with many local plants either deter or foster development programs, but always introduce change. The recent sensitivity to community relations found among large companies has probably done much to foster change of the types considered in community development.

The religious institution, while usually a force for stability, often promotes change as well. The religious sect may be an adjustment to diversions from the traditional faith in a community, and in turn may set up new relations between the religious institutions and the remainder of the community. In the beginning, Protestantism was such a change. Protestantism has splintered into many denominations, and in their beginning each represented new values, new relations with other institutions, in short, new structural elements. Cults, as new faiths are often called, may fulfill the felt need of a minority of community members for changes from the theology of the fundamentalist churches of the community.

Science, in its applied aspects, also induces change. Technology has had far-reaching consequences to community structure. Improved farm practices have allowed greater productivity, and through increasing the size of the farm enterprise have increased the relative advantages of the large over the smaller farmer. This means, on the one hand, that a larger population can be supported by a much smaller proportion of farmers than formerly, and on the other, that farm children must move to the non-farm, occupational world. Technology has also produced the assembly line. This has meant less freedom and craftsmanship value in the work world. It has reduced the work week until the emphasis upon the recreational substructure has assumed major importance. Many communities are almost entirely organized around the recreational function. Technology underlies many of the economic changes heretofore discussed, but not all of them. Technology itself must be introduced into a structure which is ready for such development.

The sources of change just discussed may be summarized as changes in size, in physical environment, increased contact with the mass society, and in the institutional make-up at the pan-community level. The institutional source requires some explanation, since it is often seen to operate at the community level. The kinds of changes discussed, however, are reflected at the community level, although the source of the change is at a higher level, such as a state or federal government, or a business only one of whose factories or stores is in any given community.

This discussion is not meant to imply that substructures are not sources of change in community elements and dimensions. The governmental change, the economic decision, the sect, and the educational unit may make internal changes affecting their relations with other substructures without having the change originate outside the community. Local laws are passed, locally owned businesses change production, employment, or selling practices, a sect may be unique to a given community, and so on. Changes between or among these substructures bring change, ipso facto, to the community, but also have ramifications extending to other elements or dimensions. It seldom happens that these changes are as fundamental as those which originate outside the community, since local changes in the mores are not often permitted by mass society. Even pressures upon an entire state to conform to mores, such as monogamy, have been known in the history of the United States, and it is much less likely that the less powerful unit at the community level could long endure against great societal pressures.

At any given time, however, there are quite important, although not fundamental, changes originating at the community level. Community development programs and other large formal organizations unique to the given community are cases in point. A particularly successful solution to the delinquency problem can be initiated and carried through by a community. Further, there is the local side even to many of the changes which originate in pan-community sources. Unless a law is mandatory, the community, or some component of it, may decide or refuse to build a hospital or sewage disposal plant, or put up a stop sign at a dangerous intersection. These represent community initiation of state or federal projects. Two sources of community change then come, not from the community structure as such, but from the mass society and some substructures within the community.

The Economic Source of Change

Many changes of importance in the community originate with, or are related to, the economic institution and its involvement with other substructures of the community. Doubtless, the economic basis of problem solution involves more consideration than most other bases in modern American communities. This is partly so because of the importance of budgets in community structure, but it also results in part from the high place that the economic values have in the total value hierarchy at the community level. In other words, economic determinism is in some sense a self-fulfilling prophecy. If people define economic problems as most important, then they will be most important. This is not a mechanical and automatic process, but results from the value system. In cases where the economic basis of change is a result of the value system defining it as most important, then change originates in the value system, not in the economic institution. However, change may result from an economic institution not explicitly defined as the basic problem in the value system. The problem as defined by local values may be schools, but to attract better teachers and build bigger and better school buildings will require money. Therefore, the economic institution is important in change as it relates to the remainder of the community structure.

Religion and Community Change

In many societies, social change or lack of it may be almost completely controlled by religious mores. This situation can prevail for many centuries. It appears that once social change gains momentum, the religious mores take on less importance in the value hierarchy of the people. In the modern American community, the religious institution has lost much of its earlier importance in controlling human behavior. Materialism, leisure time, and work have superseded the church in importance in many cases, and most fundamentalist doctrines particularly have suffered losses in membership, interest, and control. However, there are some fundamentalist churches which have increased tremendously in membership over the last fifty years, but whether this change has been due to the factors of increases in population, "worldliness" of the other and older churches, and an increasing frustration on the part of those who do not succeed in achieving middle class values is difficult to say. Whether the church is doomed to lose control in a changing social structure is a matter of controversy. Many churches have broadened their programs to include such concerns as adult education and the control of delinquency. Decision as to whether this will have the consequence of regaining lost influence will have to wait until these programs have had an opportunity to show their effects. The religious institution is a substructure whose relations with other substructures are important in social change, regardless of the decrease in importance. In underdeveloped societies, as has been said, the community structure may well be centered around the religious institution. In modern American society, the politician, the educator, and often even the business man all need sanction from the church. Regardless of how much the prayer in a political campaign may be a useful fiction to the campaigner, the universality of the practice of invoking the deity indicates that with the common man the church is still relatively important.

Local Government and Change

The political institution is a good candidate for an initiator of social change. For one thing, laws express mores and folkways to a large extent, and changes in laws often express changes in mores and folkways. Whether the law may violate the unwritten codes of conduct and therefore initiate change in fundamental dimensions of community structure is still a bone of contention among sociologists and anthropologists. The answer to the question of law versus mores is probably not an all-or-none proposition. For example, separation of the races in schools was certainly among the basic mores in southern communities of the United States when the Supreme Court's famous decision on integration was made. Many local communities did integrate, including ones which had no previous intention of doing so. This indicates that under some conditions the mores may be legislated. However, whole states had not yet moved in the direction of integration by 1959, and had devised various alternatives for circumventing the Supreme Court decision. Private schools, since they are not under federal jurisdiction, provided one attempt at a solution. To go to the extent of abolishing public schools is to indicate that under certain conditions the mores win over law. One rather obvious hypothesis would be that the more fundamental the mores, the more difficult it is for written codes to be enforced when there is a contradiction between the two.

While the answer to law versus unwritten code cannot be given, it is clear that the state is not the sole factor in change. But the fact that it can bring about change in the face of great adversity indicates that it is important. The definition of the political institution is that it has a monopoly on the ultimate use of force. Therefore, if the persons and groups making up the government were so inclined, the political institution could probably ultimately force any change desired. But the real issue is not whether it could, but whether it does. The facts are that it does not, and through the informal pressures in governmental operations probably never will. Even in a totalitarian regime, compromises are reached with the church and the economic institution.

At the community level, the political institution is even less likely to be the sole initiator of change. In addition to the general principles given above, it should be noted that the community is not coterminous with the political unit, and therefore change may occur in the government without producing change throughout the community. Similarly, there are changes in the community which leave the political institution relatively unaffected.

Over the long range, social change may result more from the functions of the family and school than from any other institutions. Through socializing the child in folkways slightly different from those of the older generation, the school may produce at least more willingness to change and at most specific attitudes favorable to change. The family, too, through a closer interpretation of the folkways as a result of more leniency and less contact with the child than formerly, may produce similar results. Such changes are long-range for the most part, with only slightly different belief systems occurring in the immediately succeeding generation. The family and school, like the stratification and value systems and the communication structure, are probably mechanisms through which changes occur (the diffusion process) rather than initiators of change. The value system, in its strain toward consistency, may promote adjustments to changes already happening, but for the most part produces conformity through sanctions against nonconformity. The stratification system is an initiator of change only when a lower status grouping gets sufficient power to increase its life chances in other realms of life. However, for the most part the powers that be can remain powers most securely through the status quo. The communication system may bring to one community alternatives from another, but this is a mechanism of diffusion rather than an initiator of change.

It should be apparent, then, that to understand change, one must understand lack of change. The institutional relations and value system primarily promote stability through their resistance to change. The context against which community development must be understood includes not only factors in the social structure which promote change and can be used by community development programs, but also factors deterring change. Looked at from the point of view of immediate success, these stalwarts of the status quo are barriers to change, but from a more comprehensive standpoint, the dimensions and elements resisting change are safeguards against random and often tragic consequences. Their demands for compromise promote stability and organization, and so often avoid the ill effects that uncontrolled change can have upon human happiness.

SELECTED REFERENCES

Allen, Frederick Lewis, *The Big Change: America Transforms Itself, 1900–1950,* Harper and Brothers, New York, 1952.

Barnett, Homer Garner, *Innovation: The Basis of Cultural Change,* McGraw-Hill Book Company, Inc., New York, 1953.

Becker, Carl, "Progress," *Encyclopaedia of the Social Sciences,* Vol. 12, pp. 495–99, The Macmillan Company, New York, 1934.

Becker, Howard, *Through Values to Social Interpretation,* Duke University Press, Durham, North Carolina, 1950.

Bossard, James H.S., "Social Change in the United States," *Annals of the American Academy of Political and Social Science,* 265:69–79, 1949.

Heberle, Rudolf, *Social Movements*, Appleton-Century-Crofts, Inc., New York, 1951.

Leighton, Alexander H., *Human Relations in a Changing World*, E.P. Dutton and Company, New York, 1949.

Malinowski, Bronislaw, *The Dynamics of Culture Change*, Yale University Press, New Haven, 1945.

Mannheim, Karl, *Freedom, Power, and Democratic Planning*, Oxford University Press, New York, 1950.

Nisbet, Robert A., *The Quest for Community*, Oxford University Press, New York, 1953.

Nordskog, John Eric, editor, *Contemporary Social Reform Movements*, Charles Scribner's Sons, New York, 1954.

Ogburn, William F., "The Great Man versus Social Forces," *Social Forces*, 5:225–31, 1926.

———, *Social Change*, Viking Press, Inc., New York, 1950.

———, *The Social Effects of Aviation*, Houghton-Mifflin Company, Boston, 1946.

Ogburn, William F., J.C. Merriam, E.C. Elliott, *et al.*, *Technological Trends and National Policy*, Report of the Subcommittee on Technology to the National Resources Committee, Government Printing Office, Washington, D.C., 1937.

Ogburn, William F., and Meyer F. Nimkoff, *Technology and the Changing Family*, Houghton-Mifflin Company, Boston, 1955.

Poston, Richard W., *Small Town Renaissance: A Story of the Montana Study*, Harper and Brothers, New York, 1950.

Redfield, Robert, *The Primitive World and Its Transformation*, Cornell University Press, Ithaca, New York, 1953.

———, *A Village That Chose Progress: Chan Kom Revisited*, University of Chicago Press, Chicago, 1950.

Sims, Newell L., *The Problem of Social Change*, Thomas Y. Crowell Company, New York, 1939, pp. 91–186.

CHAPTER 20

Community Development

The study of the community is as closely linked to practical problems of everyday living as any other field within social science. Most students have tended to identify social problems and issues as products of group living. Brownell suggests that the ideal community is to be identified with human values.[1] Buber considers the small community to be the answer to the great problem of centralization which is a barrier to freedom and democracy.[2] Park, Burgess, Wirth, and their school of urban sociologists have seen social disorganization as a product of increasing size.[3] Wirth speaks of the large urban community as a way of life in which a blasé attitude is taken toward all of life. Urban life is characterized by anonymity, which fosters the breakdown of social control and solidarity.

Whether their concern is with freedom, democracy, or other human values, most students seem to conclude eventually that the community is the locus for at least some causes of most social problems. If this be so, one must conclude that it is also the locus for the solutions to those problems. Thus, the many efforts to resolve basic social problems through active programs for social advance are centered in the community.

Action programs designed for community improvement have evolved with the unfolding of knowledge about the nature of structure and change. At the turn of the century poverty was a major social problem in London, and this led to the famous *Survey of the Life and Labor in the City of London* which inaugurated the survey technique of community study and sparked the formation of the charity organization movement.[4] Since that time there has been an increasing efficiency both in research methodology and in the design and conduct of programs for the improvement of condi-

[1] Baker Brownell, *The Human Community,* Harper and Brothers, New York, 1950.
[2] Martin Buber, *Paths in Utopia,* Routledge and Kegan Paul, Ltd., London, 1949.
[3] See for example, Robert E. Park and Ernest W. Burgess, *The City,* University of Chicago Press, Chicago, 1925.
[4] See Sidney Dillick, *Community Organization for Neighborhood Development, Past and Present,* Woman's Press, Whiteside, Inc. and William Morrow and Company, New York, 1953.

tions in the local community. As a result of this process the scientific study of the community has developed into numerous, fairly well-defined disciplines such as ecology, rural and urban sociology, and others. Action programs, too, have divided into several facets or approaches of which that known as *community development* is the primary concern here.

THE MEANING OF COMMUNITY DEVELOPMENT

Community development has come into being in recent years as one of the most significant techniques for the application of research findings to the resolution of major problems. The more rapid application of this invention has been retarded by some confusion in meaning and the term has become a catchword without clear meaning. This results, in part, from the confusion that has grown out of the indiscriminate use of the term by people who have not known its real meaning and thus are careless with its use.

In some areas, community development is conceived as a function of government that necessitates the establishment of a department or bureau appropriately designated.[5] It is, most certainly, a function of government, but not one to be so easily delegated. In theory, when government is conceived as the servant of the governed, community development is the process whereby the governed make known their will to their chosen governors. In practice, however, government has assumed an identity somewhat removed from the governed, particularly in colonial or trust territories. As an action process, community development must permeate all relationships within the government and between specialized agencies and the people. Development is not achieved through the creation of a department or bureau charged with that specific responsibility, while the remaining structure continues to operate untouched by the concept. The establishment of such a department acknowledges responsibility, but lacks the integrated approach essential to community development. The acceptance of community development as a method of operation imposes limitations upon the authority and power of the public servant, for both of these are retained by the people directly. Actually, of course, the security of the public official is strengthened by the spread of authority and responsibility upon the broadest possible foundation.

In some fields of activity, the term "community development" is applied

---

[5] This is illustrated in the case studies published in *The Community Development Bulletin* (University of London), in *Adult and Fundamental Education* (UNESCO), and in official papers by various UNESCO Bureaus and the British Colonial Office.

to methods utilized in effecting certain forms of *social organization*. Such use is seen in expressions like community development *for* social welfare, *for* recreation, or *for* public health. Since these terms deal with some specific aspects of the common life, their use immediately identifies the ideas behind such use as pertaining to social organization rather than community development. The only possible application of the word *for* in this context has to do with community development *for the community*, but this is redundant and therefore unnecessary.[6]

The term "community organization" is often used to refer to the study of existing patterns of community structure and interrelationships, and may be confused with the process for effecting changes in structure and relationships so as to achieve some self-determined condition in the future.[7] Through the scientific study and analysis of patterns, form, structure, and function of activities in community life, community organization provides the basic data that are the foundation upon which any community development must depend for its validity. Since it is not a pattern of continuous action for change as is implied by the word *development*, it is important that a clear distinction between the two terms should be maintained. Both are useful concepts with a definite place in the vocabulary of social study.

Sometimes the expression "community improvement" is used, but the connotations of the word "improvement" are too restrictive to represent the broader concepts contained in *development*.[8] Certainly the ultimate improvement of the community is the goal of any action program. Improvement, however, does not include implications as to method, while development implies growth and self-generation from within the structure, which is more accurate in meaning.

In far too many instances, community development is used to disguise *techniques for manipulation*. This is the most invidious misapplication of the term and potentially the most dangerous. The numerous techniques of community development lend themselves to manipulation. This depends upon the intent of those employing the techniques, and it may occur quite

[6] See, for example, the works of such authors as Wayne McMillan, *Community Organization for Social Welfare*, University of Chicago Press, Chicago, 1945, and Gerald B. Fitzgerald, *Community Organization for Recreation*, A.S. Barnes Company, New York, 1948.

[7] Dwight Sanderson and Robert A. Polson, *Rural Community Organization*, John Wiley and Sons, New York, 1939, provide a particularly good example of the earlier lack of precise differentiation.

[8] Frank Farrington, *Community Development: Making the Small Town a Better Place to Live in and a Better Place in Which to Do Business*, The Ronald Press Company, 1915, New York. This is incidentally the first book with this title. Many subsequent publications take the "improvement" point of view, particularly publications issued by Chambers of Commerce.

unconsciously. Those engaged in community development should constantly guard against slipping from democratic group action into group manipulation. The distinction between group self-determination and manipulation is difficult to clarify but everyone should guard against this confusion in meaning, whether it is consciously or unconsciously employed. The distinction rests on whose goals are being pursued.

Definition by Implication

It seems characteristic of an aging democracy that as individuals become habituated to the conditions of a free society, they assume freedom to be an inherent right rather than recognizing it as a constantly recreated product of social will and action. The result is that they neglect their responsibilities for preserving it. It is essential that people be made aware of their interdependence and that they have such unity of purpose as to accept willingly the full responsibility of citizenship. An educational process that integrates knowledge and provides the mass of people with a maximum degree of common understanding and purpose is the only means of achieving the acceptance of responsibility. Such a process must have real meaning and validity in terms of its application to the recurrent problems which individuals face in living within their experience world.

One of the most convenient and manageable parts of that experience world is the community. Education, therefore, must occur in the community as a whole community program seeking solutions to the problems of the individual in his total environment. In this way, individuals are trained in the ways of responsible citizenship by becoming actively involved in the evolution of their social environment in such a way that they react to conditions in their environment and effect changes therein. This is such an extremely flexible and variable process that it is not easily reduced to any patterned methodology, for it simultaneously involves learning by individuals and changes in their interrelationships. This quality of learning and living involves a dynamic methodology that is a continuous stream of deliberation and action. Thus, to pinpoint this process of cooperative interaction, the term "community development" has come into existence.

Confusion in meaning between this and the other types of social action is due principally to the lack of clear distinction between the educational process involved in the cooperative interaction of people in their social environment on the one hand and changes effected in the social environment not involving the education of the citizens to achieve that change on the other. Emphasis in community development, then, is on the education of the citizen rather than upon the factor of change itself. Changes will occur in the society almost inevitably. However, education for change admits the possibility that the citizens may have some share in determining the direction which that change will follow. Thus the society becomes a planned society rather than one whose destiny is left to chance. Participation by the people in the planning and control of change determines the democratic quality of the society.

Approaches

There are three distinct approaches to community development, involving the point of view of the participants, the position of professional community leadership, and the standpoint of a research scholar seeking understanding of this educational process. This tripartite approach within the discipline accentuates existing confusion.[9]

For the participant, community development is the normal means of solving group problems and achieving common goals. If, as frequently happens, custom, tradition, and convention supersede this dynamic adaptation to change, the process breaks down. In the complex societies of today, nondemocratic traditions have so engulfed the social processes that it is necessary for participants to learn new ways of reinstituting this essentially democratic process of achieving group goals. This is the function of community development as an education-for-action process. It can equip people with the ability to admit and identify common problems, accumulate the knowledge essential to their solution, and plan and follow a course of action leading to achievement.

The function of professional leadership, then, is to assist participants to gain control over this process. This imposes a change in methods of operation differing from the traditionally accepted ones. The leader becomes an agent constructing learning experiences rather than the proponent of a program for community improvement. It is the process itself which is of primary importance rather than the results which might be achieved. While the *process*, not the *product*, is important, as long as it is in operation valuable results will usually be achieved. In other words, emphasis is not placed upon the building of bridges, the planning of schools, or the development of additional social organizations. Primary importance is attached to the individual in terms of what happens within his consciousness to mold him into an intelligent participating member of a democratic society.[10]

[9] Gordon Blackwell, "A Sociologist on School-Community Relations," *The Annals*, Vol. 302 (November, 1955), pp. 128–35.
[10] Ronald Lippitt, Jeanne Watson, and Bruce Westley, *The Dynamics of Planned Change*, Harcourt, Brace and Company, New York, 1958.

The concept of community development involves three considerations in community change. The first of these is that community development is an approach to the solution of some specific problem which can be resolved at the community level; that is to say, one that is unique to a local area. Examples of this are education and recreation programs and facilities, public utilities, or local health and welfare programs. Quite different from the local area problem, but equally appropriate for community development, is the pan-community problem which may be solved community by community. The level of living, which is not usually a uniquely local area problem, is an excellent example of this. Since families live in the community and since some of the solutions to a low level of living seem to lie within changes in the community structure, such as the introduction of a new industry into a community, this matter comes within the scope of a local community development program.

A second aspect of the concept of community development is that the means employed in the solution of a community problem is more important than the solution itself. Thus, while the immediate problem may be juvenile delinquency approached through the establishment of supervised teenage recreation, the principal objective of the community development program is that of helping local people learn how to solve their common problems rather than the establishment of a single facility. Here is the basis for continuity in the solution of community problems. Such continuity may take the form of a permanent organization for community development, or the skills learned in one situation may lie dormant until another problem is confronted.

A third aspect of the concept of community development was discussed earlier in relation to social change. It is often difficult to separate community development from other types of change in the structure of the community. There is no doubt that community development is deliberate and purposive change. Roupp says that "social development, as distinct from social change, is the purposive alteration of conditions." He states further that "development signifies change from something thought to be less desirable to something thought to be more desirable." He suggests that development is the rational direction of structure toward goals implicit in the value system.[11] While this is a very good definition of community development, it must be pointed out that there are deliberate and purposive changes other than through community development, which Roupp recognizes as social development. In addition to this it must also be recognized that the relationship between purposive and nonpurposive change is a very close one and adjustment is

[11] Phillips Roupp, editor, *Approaches to Community Development*, W. Van Hoeve, Ltd., The Hague, 1953, p. 16.

required from both types. Purposive development, with all of the structural barriers to it, is a controlling factor in change generally; therefore, it can be seen that community development must be viewed within the total context of change as one of several types of purposive change.

THE PROCESS OF COMMUNITY DEVELOPMENT

The process of community development has not yet been studied empiri-ically with sufficient intensity to permit valid generalizations; nevertheless, students of the subject are able to develop hypotheses about the process. The first delineation of such hypotheses about the process of community develop-ment was enumerated by Edward Lindeman in his book *The Community* in 1921.[12] All subsequent attempts to describe the process have followed the pattern set by Lindeman with only minor variations. In his original state-ment, Lindeman describes, in sequential order of occurrence, nine steps in the process. These nine steps or stages have been refined by Taylor as fol-lows: *

The first step in community development is systematic discussion of common felt needs by members of the community. Unsystematic discussions of various kinds and on various topics are continuously going on among persons and families who literally live, as they do in rural villages, all the time in each other's pres-ence. Such discussions are, however, either mere gossip or concerned with com-plaints. It is only when discussions are systematic, even though among a relatively few representative persons or families, that analysis of important commonly felt needs is accomplished. Such discussion is readily induced when local villagers have cause to believe that any organized self-help efforts on their part will be en-couraged and assisted by their government or some other dependable agency. This simple but necessary first step is not taken when community councils or other vil-lage bodies are created by law or overhead administrative directives, as has been done in some underdeveloped countries which are trying to initiate community development programs. It is not taken when some technical agency or welfare or-ganization decides to initiate some improvement just because it has the consent, or even the invitation, of the Headman of the village to do so. It is not taken by finding one willing innovator who will try out one improved practice.

Sound community development programs, now in operation in a number of underdeveloped countries, provide both personnel to stimulate systematic discus-sions among villagers and technical, sometimes material, assistance to organize community self-help undertakings.

[12] Edward Lindeman, *The Community*, Association Press, New York, 1921, Chapter 9.
* Carl C. Taylor, "Community Development Programs and Methods," *Community Development Review*, Community Development Division Office of Public Service, Inter-national Cooperation Administration, December, 1956.

The second step in community development is systematic planning to carry out the first self-help undertaking that has been selected by the community. The most important things learned by the community in taking this step is that nothing by way of community development occurs if a project is nominated the carrying out of which is totally beyond the local community's self-help capacity. The community may think its greatest need is canal water for irrigation, which water can be provided only by constructing a great dam a hundred or more miles distant from the village. This it cannot do or even help do. Or it may think that its greatest need is for more commercial fertilizers which would require the construction of a factory and the development of a market distribution system. The first of these is an undertaking for national or state governments and the other an undertaking for government or some business entrepreneur.

Systematic planning for aided self-help community undertakings leads to the selection of the [initial] project which, because it is practically feasible, will mobilize the local manpower and ingenuity of those living in the community. It leads to the actual task of enlisting persons who will contribute their labor and talents, and often materials and money, to carry out the project. It accomplishes realistic and responsible thinking about what should be and what can be done. It is a step that starts to mobilize the community to do something for itself.

All kinds of experiences have been had and are being had in the task of mobilizing local communities for effective action in those underdeveloped countries which are promoting programs of community development. In some countries, however, the government jumps in and does the job which the Headman or some small local group specifies as the first basic need. It may employ local laborers and pay them wages, thus using the community's manpower by developing no local community-group responsibility. It may pour in so much material assistance and so many outside technical experts that the undertaking is in no sense even a demonstration of what local communities themselves can do. There are other countries which are encouraging local communities themselves to take this second step. It is always, by necessity, taken by doing relatively small community improvement projects. With a small amount of technical assistance and the very minimum of material assistance, local communities are building hundreds of miles of village feeder roads, building hundreds of schools, digging hundreds of wells to supply both domestic and irrigation water, improving sewer systems, etc., etc. As important as, or more important than, these accomplishments is the development of the responsibility, initiative, and self-confidence of village community groups.

The third step in community development is the almost complete mobilization and harnessing of the physical, economic, and social potentialities of local community groups. Once a goodly sized organized local group starts working on a project which if completed will yield obvious and early benefits to the whole community, members of the community who have thus far been only mildly interested or even skeptical start contributing to its successful completion. There are so many examples of this that what happens time after time no longer constitutes feature stories in the newspapers in some of the countries where community development programs are in successful operation.

Unfortunately, some state and national leaders who have witnessed one or more local communities mobilize in this way jump to the conclusion that a whirl-wind nation-wide propaganda campaign, offering of community improvement prizes, or some other mass stimulation and mobilization technique, can be used to start a rash of community development activities. Many experiences in this type of undertaking have also been had. They teach almost as much as sound programs of community development. What they teach is that there is no substitute for what have been described here as the *first and second steps* in community development. Even more important, they teach that the next and most important step is seldom taken as the result of furious campaigns of propaganda and competition.

The fourth step in community development is the creation of aspiration and the determination to undertake additional community improvement projects. Until this step is taken, the universal problem of how to get local villages and villagers to desire and initiate improvement is not solved. Many community organizations promoted by outsiders never take this step. But there are both good physical and sociological reasons why the majority of community groups, which have come into existence and progressed by taking the three previous steps described here, do take this four step. The physical reason is, there are other improvements which need to be understaken which are within the now developed competence of the group. The sociological reason is that every human group that has successfully accomplished worthwhile undertakings is proud of itself and tends to seek out and do other things to justify and feed its group pride. It has developed team spirit, esprit de corps, patriotism, or, in simpler terms, group sentiments. Even Charles Darwin asserted that sentiment is the cement of groups. This cement, because it is sentiment, not only holds groups together but makes them seek to perpetuate themselves. When they have developed it they seek things to do the undertaking of which will effectively perpetuate them as functioning, aspiring groups.

There are plenty of examples of community groups which never have taken this fourth step and there are plenty of examples of groups which have. Two specific examples will serve to show why some so-called community projects have not led to the taking of the final step in community development. One is the experience of a country where the central government urged local communities to build community halls. In order to induce them to do so it paid one-half the costs. A number of communities organized campaigns which involved a large per cent of all members of the community in one or another type of participation. In most cases these campaigns were sponsored by the most prominent citizens in the community. In most of the communities where halls were built the community has done nothing more in an organized way and has even been unable to stimulate any great community use of the halls.

In another experience, in a different country, an enterprising and altruistic government official tried to convert a dilapidated village of very low income families into a model community. By providing all types of technical advisers and a great deal of financial aid, he stimulated the villagers to clean up their streets, change their methods of sewage disposal, and even build new homes. The official now testifies that in less than ten years the village was just as dilapidated as when he started to change it. In this example, as in the other, the whole community helped in the project and some community improvement was accomplished. In neither case did the community seek out and accomplish other community improvement projects.

But there are examples in underdeveloped countries where the final step in community development has been and is being taken. A community which started by building a small but badly needed foot bridge across a stream, built a half mile of feeder road out to a highway, constructed a school with crude poles, straw, and mud, cleaned out a spring to provide a clean domestic water supply, or made some other simple improvement which met a commonly felt need has gone on to more and larger undertakings. These communities went on from the first project to another and another. Because of self-motivated, self-help experiences they developed not only self-confidence and competence, but group pride and aspirations.

BARRIERS TO COMMUNITY DEVELOPMENT

The process of community development is impeded by a variety of factors and forces that are inherent in the very nature of the community. The value system, the interdependence of elements and dimensions, powers, and the institutional and organizational structure of the community all serve to retard the process of change. Yet, at the same time, these factors may strengthen the process of development.

The value system of the community strains toward consistency and the maintenance of the status quo.[13] This can be utilized in the community development process because tradition can serve as a check against hasty, unstudied changes in which unanticipated consequences might violate the value system. It can be useful, furthermore, in identifying precedents justifying change from similar or dissimilar situations in the past. Like tradition, external conformity is a barrier to community development because it rejects deviations from the norm. Since decisions promoting changes are made by the group rather than by individuals in the community development process, the power of external conformity as an inhibiting factor is alleviated somewhat.

The power structure in any community is generally resistant to changes not of its own selection if such changes impose any threat to its power. In the study of Regional City, Hunter found that when any program of purposive change in any way threatened the basic mores or the self-interest of the power structure, mobilization of community resources against the change

[13] T.R. Batten, "Social Values and Community Development," in Roupp, *op. cit.*, pp. 80–86. See also his *Communities and Their Development*, Oxford University Press, London, 1957.

was accomplished through diversionary tactics or some other means.[14] The power structure will recognize, however, that the source of its power lies in the people and it will often support a community development program that is based on the general community will in order to continue in power.

Groups and Institutions as Barriers

Community structure includes a variety of patterns of relationships ranging from small friendship groups and cliques to large formal organizations and institutions. Each individual is a member of a number of different substructures, from the morning *Kaffeeklatsch* to a church circle. To each such group the individual owes his allegiance in varying degrees and each exercises an influence on his decisions, with the result that decisions are made in terms of a complex of influences acting on the individual that may be wholly unrelated to the matter at hand. The origin, form, and power of such indeterminate group influences are difficult to assess, yet they can decide the success or failure of the community development program.

Informal social groupings within a community may combine into a constellation of groups that can become a significant aspect of the power structure.[15] Such constellations are rarely continuous, so that different alignments of groups may develop around each issue. As a consequence, it is almost impossible to anticipate or predict the behavior of informal groups in response to community problems. This complicates the community development process, yet it acts as a safeguard at the same time, for such an informal power alignment can counteract the formal authority structure of the community.

The institutional elements in a community are so closely tied into the basic mores and folkways of the community that they can be expected to resist changes affecting community structure. They are reinforced by rituals and symbols in maintaining their position and generally have attained a level of institutional sophistication that results in the institution becoming an end in itself without regard to its manifest function. Purposive changes that result from the community development process are usually in response to needs that fall within the area of existing institutional functions but which the institutional structure has failed to meet. As a result, such changes become a threat to the institution and are resisted. It is possible for the per-

[14] Adapted from Harry L. Miller's review of Floyd Hunter, *Community Power Structure*, University of North Carolina Press, Chapel Hill, North Carolina, 1953. The review appeared in *Adult Education*, 4:167–75, 1954.

[15] Hurley H. Doddy, *Autonomous Groups and the Community*, Bureau of Publications, Teachers College, Columbia University, New York, 1952.

ception of the need for changes to arise within the institutional structure so that support rather than resistance becomes the institutional position. Since community development is basically a process of education for change rather than an organization in competition with the established structure of the community, it can occur within and among institutions and gain their support.

Interorganizational Barriers to Community Development

The principal objective of community development is that of helping the community learn to act as a unit for the common good. The multitude of problems that arise in a community gives impetus to a vast complex of social organizations that seek to resolve those problems. As new problems arise, existing organizations are not often prepared to assume added responsibilities, so that still more organizations are formed. This results in an extremely complex network of organization and association with overlapping and often duplicating functions. In time it becomes essential for community welfare that some kind of coordination be developed.

The need for coordination and cooperation among community associations is illustrated by the variety of ways in which such coordination is attempted. This process is largely unstudied: however, it appears to follow four basic forms:

(*a*) *Informal community cooperation.* The most common form of interorganizational relationship is found in the informal exchange of services between organizations. Such exchanges are more apt to occur when they are removed from any competitive relationship between organizations and this rarely involves general coordination of all organizational activities nor is it often structured on a continuing basis. When two organizations are functioning within the same general content area and/or population group, cooperation is less frequent.

(*b*) *Formal interest councils.* Within any given community one is apt to find a network of coordinating structures that are largely unrecognized. The number of such structures is related to community size and, in general, they involve organizations with similar interests and structural patterns. Thus, one may find a County Home Demonstration Council, a Federation of Garden or Women's Clubs, a Council of Ministers, or an Intercivic Council. Such coordinating bodies are almost unknown beyond the organizations that compose them and not well identified even within the membership of those constituent organizations. They function primarily as a clearing house for the exchange of information and program plans. Coordinative bodies of this sort are generally successful because they are held together by the mutual bonds of a primary organizational interest; and while their interests are similar, their activities are essentially noncompetitive.

(c) *General community councils.* In some instances, communities have attempted to establish general community councils designed to coordinate all organizational activity. While this purpose is valid, such councils are rarely successful. This is due to several factors: (1) they attempt to coordinate a variety of organizations with widely divergent primary interests; (2) they are superimposed upon an existent coordinative system, which is interest-based; and (3) their manifest functions are not clear-cut and generally acceptable to the organizations being coordinated.

(d) *Professional councils.* In instances in which two or more organizations with professional staff personnel are working in the same general area of need but not in direct competition in terms of specific content or population groups, cooperative action is possible on the staff level. This pattern is more common among health and welfare agencies and sometimes among agricultural agencies in rural counties. The function of such councils is generally well defined and within the area of primary interests of the constituent agencies.

In the construction of coordinative devices in a community three major factors appear to determine the success or failure of such devices.

(a) *The interest factor.* For coordinative devices to succeed there must be an essential harmony of interests among the organizations involved. The interests of the organizations must be homogeneous and coordination must be structured around the main interest of the organization. Coordination is more likely to succeed where interests are closely related and less likely to succeed when the interests of the organizations involved are only distantly related. Furthermore, coordination is more apt to succeed when the purpose for coordination more nearly coincides with the primary function and purpose of the organizations concerned; conversely, it is less apt to succeed when the purpose is peripheral or subsidiary to the main interests of the organizations being coordinated.

The successful coordination of organizations appears also to be influenced by the scope of organizational activity within their interest areas. Thus, organizations with similar and related interests that are not competitive are more apt to coordinate their programs than are those organizations serving the same population groups in essentially the same way.

(b) *Clarity of function.* The successful coordination of organizations with homogeneous interests appears to depend upon the mutual identification and acceptance of the manifest function for which coordination is desired.

Since any coordinative body is a superstructure of the operating organization in a community, its function must be one that enhances and extends the functions of the constituent organizations.

(c) *The financial basis.* The necessary financial support of coordinative bodies must be shared by the member organizations. Such bodies rarely succeed when essential services are provided by making them added responsibilities of member organizations. Attempts to finance such structures through individual contributions or solicitations from the community at large bring the coordinative body into competition with its member organizations and thus defeats the principal basis of coordination.

Community development programs cannot hope to succeed when their emphasis is placed upon the establishment of a formal coordinative structure. In general, communities have a variety of systems for cooperation and coordination, but as yet no wholly satisfactory inclusive structure has been invented. By concentrating on the process of learning to work cooperatively rather than upon the establishment of yet another organization, community development can bring about effective cooperative action without the necessity for a permanent structure. In those communities in which no other coordinative structures exist, such a device may result from the operation of the community development process.

LEADERSHIP FOR COMMUNITY DEVELOPMENT

The process of community development is as yet imperfectly analyzed by social scientists, and one of the most persistent and puzzling problems is that of the role of leadership. It is not impossible for a relatively isolated community to conduct a continuous program of community development without contact with any form of professional leadership. On the other hand, it is possible to induce communities to undertake a program through the exercise of competent leadership. Since one objective of social science is to use the discoveries of science to solve community problems, and since the community development process is one of the better means for accomplishing this, it is imperative that competent leadership be developed.

Competent leadership is essential for at least three reasons. First, the latent power structure is a constant threat to democratic action, particularly in cultures or subcultures which are traditionally authoritarian. Second, few communities have sufficient understanding of the processes of community development to bring it to pass without skilled leadership. And third, since most professional leadership in a community is affiliated with, and oriented to, a specific institution, it rarely can assume leadership for change in a community-wide situation.

Short of establishing a new institution for community development with its own corps of specially trained specialists, which would then be in competition with all other existing institutions and organizations in the community, the safest approach to this problem of leadership appears to be through the better education of institutional leadership for community development. At the present moment, most of the emphasis on leadership development is in terms of underdeveloped countries and the various assistance programs in such countries. It is in this context that Polson describes a leadership training program in the following extract.*

Assistance programs to underdeveloped countries operate on a different basis for community development from that which exists in America. In such programs a special organization for community development is constructed, so that leadership can be trained for a specific role in the community. Experiences in such foreign cultures have application to American communities, but with the difference that what is learned about training village workers abroad needs to be applied to the training of professional institutional leadership for American communities. The training of professional leadership for America has become so specialized in terms of subject-matter specialties that the knowledge and skills essential for community development are ignored. Thus, agricultural or home agents, teachers, and health and welfare specialists, among others, are given intensive training in agricultural science, home economics, pedagogy, and other specialized areas of knowledge to the exclusion of adequate knowledge about the nature and structure of communities and the processes of working with adults in educational situations. The things that Polson has enumerated as essential components of the education of village workers are equally appropriate to the education of professional personnel for American communities.

The assumption is made that any particular training program will be adjusted to the cultural setting in which it occurs, to the type of community development program of which it is a part, to the bureaucratic organization within which it operates, and to the value orientations and preconceived notions of community development that the trainees bring with them.

Countries initiating new community development programs do not have readily available a body of trained professional workers. There are often inadequate numbers of supporting technicians, and those available are frequently without training and insight into the techniques of mobilizing group action and self-help projects. The first part of the training task is to select from among the individuals with

* Robert A. Polson, "Theory and Methods of Training for Community Development," *RS*, 23:34–42, 1958. Used by permission.

some training those most likely to succeed in community development work and then to instruct them in how to facilitate a program.

A training program should encompass all major categories of persons involved in a community development program.

The emphasis to date in training programs has been on the village level worker, with some attention being given to those who supervise him. However, since community development is problem-oriented and involves many branches of government and fields of technology, all who are to be intimately associated with a program need to be trained. For example, there is a need for training subordinates at all bureaucratic levels in effective supervision. Observers indicate that many supervisors have not been able to make a distinction between assisting village level workers with their job and giving them orders.

An adequate national training program should include selected organized learning experiences for the following:

Political leaders of the country: local, state, and national.

The administrators and supervisors of the community development program and the administrators and supervisors of cooperating government departments at local, state, and national levels.

The technical staff members of the community development program and cooperating agencies at local, state, and national levels. These are the agricultural extension agents, the veterinarians, the highway engineers, the public health doctors and nurses.

The multi-purpose village level worker.

Influential village leaders: both traditional officials and lay leaders.

The community development training-staff members.

While the village worker is but one of the categories of persons that need to be trained, he is the one upon whom training programs have centered, and justifiably so, since he is the key person at the village level. However, training officers will have to give more attention in the immediate future to the development of appropriate training experiences for the other categories listed above, particularly for political leaders and civil servants whose understanding of a program is necessary for it to continue.

The selection of those to be trained as village level workers should be based upon a program's operational requirements.

The method of selecting village level workers will vary from nation to nation, depending upon the supply of trained people available. However, there are difficult problems involved.[16] In some countries selection is currently done according to the traditions of a civil service that overemphasizes tests requiring skill in paper work and knowledge of law and ignores appropriate attitudes and human relations skills. Whatever selection process is used, it should obtain a person who likes villagers and whom villagers like and who has sufficient training to carry out the duties of a village worker. It is doubtful if at this stage we can claim that a village-born high school graduate is better than a village-born college graduate or a devoted city-born college graduate.

[16] Allahabad Agricultural Institute, *Experiment in Extension: The Gaon Sathi*, Oxford University Press, Bombay, 1956, pp. 57–62.

Community development workers need training throughout their professional careers.

The village worker in most programs obtains preservice training for a period of four months to a year. There is a tendency, as a program becomes established, to extend this period of training. There is greater need for a well-developed in-service training program and a skillful supervisory service if the preservice training period is brief. The multitude of problems that the village level worker encounters requires that he be given appropriate in-service training in sufficient amounts to support him in his position. A variation of in-service training to maintain competent village level workers might be entitled "refresher training." In this case the village worker is taken out of the village for a period of a few weeks or a few months to trade ideas with other village workers, usually at a provincial training center. Here he also receives training in new subjects and gains experience with new techniques. A village worker needs a continuous training program—preservice, in-service, and refresher training—if he is to meet the vicissitudes of his job and grow in his capacity to serve the villagers.

Another aspect of training is the instruction of technical staff members, such as health workers and agricultural agents, to participate with the village workers in community development teams. One of the training devices that has been used in the Philippines to facilitate this cooperative activity has been to train the agricultural agents and home agents in the same training center and in the same classes as the multipurpose village workers. True, they come to this training with different technical backgrounds and experiences, but they learn together the methods of doing community development work and of complementing one another's skills. This method has been particularly promising where classroom exercises and field practice have been organized on the basis of teams of three or four trainees composed of a village worker and technical agents. This type of training, however, works best when the members of the team are of about the same prestige level and when they realize they are going to work together in the field in a manner similar to that in the training center.

The content of community development and training is a unique combination of theory, human relations skills, and technical information.

Miss Lyra Srinivasan of the United Nations Community Development staff summarizes the content of community development training in three broadly defined areas of study: "(1) background knowledge, e.g., of human behavior, of society and of basic economic principles; (2) knowledge and skills applied to the program in its general aspects, including methods of 'reaching' people; (3) specialized knowledge and skills for particular services." [17]

The second area, that of the knowledge of, and skills in, doing community development work, deserves special attention from rural sociologists who possess experience and skill in translating social science concepts into techniques for group action. Following is a list of needed areas of training for group action summarized by Miss Srinivasan after examining a number of training curricula.

"All workers would benefit from at least an elementary understanding of the following:

[17] United Nations, Department of Economic and Social Affairs, "Study Kit on Training for Community Development," New York, 1957, p. 14.

1. How to approach people so as to win their regard and trust;

2. How to help people to express their felt needs;

3. How to impart knowledge and skills to people and help them to gain a better understanding of their problems;

4. How to encourage people to consider alternative ways of dealing with problems and to make decisions for themselves;

5. How to draw on the ability of individuals to participate in the solution of problems;

6. How to contribute to the development of community feeling.

"Some workers would, in addition, need to know:

1. How to develop leadership and to work with and through leaders;

2. How to help a group undertake cooperative action that stands a reasonable chance of success;

3. How to help ease tensions that may arise in connection with specific activities;

4. How to assist in the coordination of various field services.

"Some workers, with in-service professional guidance, might learn:

1. How to deal with resistance—e.g., what methods to use in approaching persons who feel hostile, neglected or superior or who for other reasons refuse to take part in community work;

2. How to maintain good relations, simultaneously, with opposing groups or interest in the community;

3. When and how to withdraw from community projects—i.e., how to recognize when the field worker is no longer need or not wanted by the people;

4. How to help people plan on a long-term basis, recognizing the cumulative economic change that can result from a number of related projects;

5. How to assist in aligning local projects with broader economic processes taking place outside the community." [18]

There are certain areas of training where social scientists can make particularly significant contributions. The first is training in the use of organized groups to promote village action and obtain the participation of citizens in cooperative activity. The potential of cooperation between voluntary groups and governmental agencies is not fully appreciated by many who have a responsibility for promoting village improvement.

The second area is teaching the use of citizen participation in local government to obtain more effective expression of desires and assumption of responsibility for problem solving. There is a heritage from the past in many countries for citizens to assume they can do nothing and to feel that all their problems have to be referred to higher authorities for solution. Until they see the possibility of doing otherwise, community development programs are handicapped.

The third is teaching the use of discussion groups, planning committees, and other group activities. This is particularly important in order to change those relationships that have traditionally operated on the inferior-superior or worker-boss basis. Community development workers need to learn the effectiveness of ra-

[18] United Nations, Department of Economic and Social Affairs, *op. cit.*, p. 16.

tional group action and the superior quality of decisions that are made by motivated participation in groups over those made by prestigeful individuals. In this same training area a contribution of great value to administrators and supervisors of community development programs would be to help them develop their skills for involving subordinate staff members in group decision-making.

The fourth area is fact finding for program guidance. The village level worker needs to know how he can secure dependable information to guide him in his work. His training should include methods for making simple surveys, identifying and using key informants, using official records, interviewing, and keeping an accurate record of his activities. He also needs to know how to use the information and records he collects for program planning and program evaluation.

The fifth, another contribution that will loom larger in the immediate future, is the training of lay leaders. Foreign students show much interest in this topic and become intrigued with the possibilities of training village leaders to be more proficient in the promotion of community development projects. They frequently warn that this work can not be initiated in formal training schools such as we use in the United States, but they suggest a variety of ingenious ways in which the training can be started, such as week-end camps, instruction associated with the planning and execution of community projects, training under the guise of committee work, and the village worker's joining informal discussion groups and skillfully directing the conversation to desired topics.

Douglas Ensminger, addressing the Indian Community Development staff, recommends training camps for village lays leaders:

"Since guiding village people for effective participation in development is new to village leaders, it is important for the block staff to organize village leader training camps. Each camp should be limited to no more than fifty leaders at a given time." [19]

The methods of teaching community development workers should be a demonstration of desirable community development procedures.

It is said that students learn to teach by imitating their professors. The customary use of lectures and quizzes is of relatively little importance in community development training as compared to more informal methods, if the instructor is to demonstrate the techniques the trainee can use with villagers. There should be a high priority on teaching methods that can be readily transferred to village situations. Consequently, discussion groups, seminars, demonstrations, and visual aids are important teaching methods to use. A student often has considerable adjustment to make when he first participates in discussion and disciplines himself to be a cooperative member of a group when his previous experience has led him to be competitive with his classmates. Likewise, the shift from a professor-student relationship to a group member-consultant relationship can have surprising repercussions. When a Filipino professor who was teaching group methods broke with tradition, established an informal first-name atmosphere, and gave his students considerable responsibility for planning classroom activities, the new-found power went to their heads. They suddenly addressed dignified gray-haired professors by their first names, they challenged self-conscious young instructors to permit dis-

[19] Douglas Ensminger, *A Guide to Community Development*, issued by the Ministry of Community Development, Government of India, 1957, Chapter 22, p. 167.

cussion of their lectures. This produced a variety of emotional reactions, including denunciation of the trainees for bad manners, before the various parties discovered what was going on and developed certain understandings.

Skills cannot be learned by listening to lectures about them. Even demonstrations are seldom adequate. Teaching village workers those skills they need to know must include opportunities for practicing them. A village worker who is to show farmers a new practice needs sufficient skill in that practice so that he does not make a fool of himself. If a young man is going to show villagers new tricks he had better know what he is doing, and know that he knows. Therefore, skill training means practice, and lots of it.

The group-related skills, such as working on a committee planning common activities or carrying out a group-work project assignment, are often innovations for the trainees and practice in these should be incorporated into the training program.

Another area in human relations skills that can be demonstrated and practiced in a training school is the skill of working with subordinates. One of the requirements of community development work is effective communication between subordinates and superiors in the civil service hierarchy and between government workers and villagers. If there is no effective two-way communication between these individuals of different status levels, it will be difficult to gather adequate information for decision-making or to arrive expeditiously at concensus on important issues. Skill in working with subordinates is crucial for supervisors in the community development bureaucracy as well as for village level workers.

An alternative method of training new workers is to apprentice them to an experienced and successful worker. The value of this turns on the apprentice's being involved in as wide a variety of learning experiences as possible during his stay in a village and on his having the opportunity to return to his training center with other trainees of similar experience to evaluate his experiences and to interpret their meaning for his future performance. Whether as apprentices or as other types of field workers, all trainees need supervised field practice before completing their training.

Perhaps the most important teaching method of all is that wherein the instructor moves readily from principle to application and from application back to principle. This requires that he know enough about village life and its problems to be able to relate clearly, accurately, and with some dramatic effect the manner in which principles are applicable to village problems. He may also be able to point out certain skills that can be used effectively in the application of the principles.

Operational problems affect the efficiency of community development training programs.

Certain recurring problems need to be overcome in order to integrate a training program into the over-all operations of a community development program.

First, the training of village level workers is sometimes so idealistic in comparison to the realities of field work that its value is discounted both by the village workers and by the supervising staff members. The nature and quality of instruction should prepare the trainees to face the hard realities of field work.

Second, training-staff members are often without sufficient operating experience to translate theory and method into specific applications. Instructors can be more effective if they possess a knowledge of program operations and bureaucratic behavior sufficient to answer practical questions and realistically to orient trainees to their future duties. For example, training-staff members are inclined to idealize a village level worker's position and to describe it as being that of a member of a team, the essential link between the people and the government; but on the job the trainee may discover he is the low man in the bureaucratic hierarchy. He is expected to do what his boss tells him irrespective of what the training school has taught him. Training-staff members should participate in village level work intensively enough to develop their practical skills and to test their theories of community development procedures. This experience is not only essential for staff members who are teaching methods, but also for those who are teaching technical subject matter.

Third, inadequate attention is given to training program supervisors to operate in a manner compatible with community development philosophy and methods. Supervisors are frequently transferred to the development program from existing governmental agencies. They are usually older, more experienced persons familiar with traditional supervisory procedures. The latter are frequently in conflict with the village level workers' training and in violation of community development theory. They are often based on a top-down order-giving, inspection-enforcing system, emphasizing status differences and compliance with a superior's wishes. Training supervisors and particularly retraining those with traditional supervisory experience requires more emphasis than it has received to date. The Indian in-service training seminar is a recognition of the need. A variation of it has been introduced into the Philippines. In many cases the entire concept of supervision has to be changed from one of bossing to one of facilitating.

Fourth, technical subject matter specialists working in community development programs frequently do not know how to integrate their specialty into a community development program. The subject matter specialist needs training in theory and methods just as does the supervisor and the village level worker, training that will permit him to function effectively in relation to the village level worker.

BROADENING PARTICIPATION

Community development depends not only upon professional and lay leadership, but also upon the inclusion of most of the individual members of the community in the decision-making process. The broad base of participation in decision-making will increase the likelihood of anticipating the consequences of change. This is especially important in the sense that changes made by one segment of the population, say, the power structure, are likely to violate the value system of other segments. The broader base of participation in democratic action assures that these opposing values will be heard, and probably will modify any decision.

Part of the broad base of participation is represented by membership in organizations, attendance at meetings, and formal and informal leadership. It has been shown previously that not all segments of the population are well represented in these three types of participation. Limited membership and individual apathy both contribute to the highly selective nature of participation.

It is possible, and it is often the case, that every person influenced by a community decision may attend a meeting, but the decision is still made by a select group. What a person does at a meeting is as important as being physically present. Therefore, it is of the utmost importance, if democracy is to be meaningful, to assure participation in the meeting as well as at the meeting. It is only then that democracy wins out over power. It is only then that the full consequences of actions taken are likely to be recognized, regardless of the level of the community structure in which they are to occur.

Participation in a meeting is not automatic. Fear, embarrassment, apathy, and the comforts of the safety in the mass help prevent full discussion by representatives of all segments of the population. Size alone prevents full discussion by all members in many organization meetings. The psychological factors as well as size are of course not characteristic of the very small group, particularly when certain features of the primary group may be introduced into the situation.

In a handbook for lay leaders, the principles of the small group type of participation were offered by Reeder for use in meetings where full participation would be difficult. The following excerpts describe some of the techniques which may be derived from the principles discussed previously, immediately above and in the chapter on groups.*

The Small-group Discussion

What Is It?

Small-group discussion is a teaching technique to divide a large group of persons into small subgroups for greater participation in the discussion. Its primary purpose is to increase interest, participation, and teaching effectiveness. The small-group discussion has been called: *Discussion 66,* the *buzz session,* and the *committee system.*

It is one of the oldest social tools in man's experience. It happens at the end of almost every interesting meeting. Folks just naturally gather in groups of three, four, or five to talk among themselves. When a group gets too large, it soon sub-

* William W. Reeder, *Some Methods and Tools to Increase Interest, Participation, and Teaching Effectiveness, Cornell Extension Bulletin 907,* 1956.

divides. This old natural technique has merely been revived for effective use in classrooms and groups.

Advantages

1. Small-group disscussion is a most satisfying tool from the point of view of students or group members.

2. It invites and encourages everyone to participate in a situation in which he feels free and comfortable to take part.

3. The members of the group stimulate each other to think, and this increases the flow of ideas in a setting where ideas can be challenged and freely batted back and forth without embarrassment to anyone.

4. It places responsibility on every individual to think about the problem and to make a contribution for its solution.

5. The students or members of the group work out the answers for themselves. Thus, they are more meaningful than ideas which are simply told by someone else.

6. Small group discussion saves time. It is a rapid technique for pooling ideas or experiences or for bringing out questions and problems of group members. If three or four problems are to be discussed, the group may split into smaller groups so that discussion proceeds on all questions at the same time. As each team or group reports on its question, the entire class or group can make any additions that it feels should be made.

7. Small-group discussion increases group unity. Everyone shares in the discussion and thus becomes more interested in what is going on.

8. It gives each individual member of the class or group experience in tackling problems as a member of a team and of expressing himself in the same kinds of situations that he will encounter as a citizen in a democracy.

9. As the group gains experience and sees how much it is able to accomplish, each member develops confidences in his own ability to handle problems and in the democratic process as an effective way to solve problems and to get things done.

How to Organize a Group

The content of the discussion and the length of the discussion vary widely according to the purposes of the group, but the method of organizing the group for discussion is much the same. The steps are the following:

1. Orient the group.

Tell the group briefly what you plan to do and how you plan to do it, so everyone will know what is going to happen. Here is a sample introduction indicating the kind of information they will want to know.

Our topic for discussion tonight is, *How to Get Participation in the Group.* To get everyone in the discussion we have decided to use the *small-group-discussion* technique which is both productive and enjoyable. Here is how it goes:

First, divide into groups of four to six persons—not more than six. Persons in the odd-numbered rows turn their chairs around so they face the even-numbered rows. Then count from the aisle, and let every three persons become one of a committee of six. Continue until all are in committees. As soon as you are in your committee of six, introduce yourselves by name and home town. Then select a chairman and a recorder. It is the job of the chairman to see that everyone gets a chance to express his ideas, and the job of the recorder to write the ideas of this particular group and to be prepared to report to the entire group after the discussion.

We have two questions, so one-half will take the first question, the other half the second question. The people on the right side of the room can discuss this question, *Why Do Some Persons Not Participate in Meetings?* The people on the left side of the room can discuss this question, *Why Do Some Persons Participate in Meetings?* Each group has 12 minutes to discuss this topic after which we will call on the recorders to report for their groups. Each group has a card on which to write, and I will write the two questions on the board so everyone can see them. Are there any questions? If you have a question after we start, raise your hand and I will come to you.

Such an introduction lets everyone know what is to happen and what to expect. Sometimes, in a large group of 400 or more, written instructions for the odd- and even-numbered rows help. The leader should always go over such written instructions with the group.

2. Divide the large group into subgroups.

The large group can be divided in several ways, depending on the room and the group:

Have the odd-numbered rows turn around to face the even-numbered rows. This works well in large meetings. If the seats are stationary, the persons on the odd rows may turn around in their seats.

In smaller groups, you can demonstrate with five persons who sit together and have the rest follow your example.

Have the persons count and let the *1's* form a group, the *2's* a group, and so on. This is most effective in some kinds of meetings, because it splits little friendship cliques and helps people to get acquainted and thus encourages a greater exchange of ideas.

3. Keep the subgroups small.

The size of the subgroups depends upon the topic to be discussed. If it is a topic that requires considerable thought, five or six persons provide more thought stimulation than a smaller group and make the members feel at ease because no one feels pressed to come up with an idea. If the topic is one that most persons are likely to have several ideas about, three- or four-person groups give more opportunity to participate and are more satisfactory. Six is about maximum size for best results. With a group of seven or more persons, some individuals are left out of the participation.

4. How much time should be given to discussion?

The length of time for discussion varies with the topic. It should be long enough for each group to put down several ideas but not long enough to exhaust the topic. As the ideas are pooled, the group can be invited to add points which they feel have been omitted.

5. Consolidate the findings and report back to the large group.

There are three or four ways to consolidate the findings and to report back. The size of the group and the purpose determine which procedure to select.

In raising questions for discussion following a talk, you can move from group to group asking each for its best question and allowing enough time for answers after each question. In this technique, it is well to call for questions from different parts of the room. The discussion period is usually not long enough to cover all of the questions, and the group feels better if you do not concentrate on one particular part of the room in calling for questions.

If the group is fairly small, the spokesman from each group may present the report for his group. This works best where the group is working out answers to a question or problem. In such a group, the repetition of answers adds emphasis and usually does not detract.

Sometimes, such as in a problem census, program planning, or where a problem calls for a large number of answers, it works well to have a blackboard and to have a recorder list all the questions or answers on the board. It is usually best to get all the points down before you discuss any of them.

One way to avoid repetition and still give some recognition to all the groups is to take a quick vote of the number of groups who have the same question or answer while the recorder is writing the statement. This also gives some indication of the relative importance of each question.

Where the group is large, more than 100 persons, it is sometimes advantageous to send the recorders of each subgroup into an adjoining room to consolidate the answers while the group goes ahead with other matters.

It is well to have someone prepared to lead in the consolidation and to have one of the recorders report the findings back to the group.

Occasionally, it may fit the purposes of the group best to collect the reports from the various groups, have a committee consolidate them, and report the findings at the next meeting. Usually, however, it is best to get a report back during the same meeting.

6. Have a discussion follow the report.

The reports are a consolidation of the suggestions of the small groups and do not represent agreement of the group. Some discussion is usually appropriate. The length of such a discussion depends again upon the topic and the purpose. Following the small-group discussion the members are more free to discuss the questions in the larger group than they would otherwise be.

7. Call the attention of the group to its accomplishments.

Frequently the group becomes lost in the process of participation and is not aware of how much has been accomplished unless it is called to their attention. Questions such as the following serve to make a group aware of their own productiveness, the quality of their own ideas, and the tremendous resource which exists in the experience of the group. "How do you feel about the amount that we have accomplished today? How do you feel about the quality of the ideas that have been presented? Do you think that we have gained more or less information than a speaker could have given us?"

8. When should you use small-group discussion?

The small-group discussion is one of several teaching tools. The effective teacher or group leader is the one who knows them all and uses the ones which best fit his situation. This technique has several uses. A few situations in which it has proved effective are the following:

To draw out people's ideas and to find what they want when planning the program of the organization.

To find what people want to know about a particular topic for a particular meeting. Frequently speakers spend most of their time telling people what they already know and little time on issues in which they are really interested. Give the speaker a list of questions for which the group would like to have answers. This assures the maximum use of the speaker's time.

To draw out questions after a speaker has opened the topic.

To pool ideas on a question or a problem.

To discuss the pro's and con's of a particular issue, theory, or proposed solution.

To divide a large topic into sub-topics and have different groups work on different sub-topics; then have each group report its conclusions.

9. In what part of the meeting should small-group discussion be used?

The small-group discussion can be the basis of the entire meeting or it may precede or follow a speaker, a film, a socio-drama, or a panel. Wherever discussion is appropriate the small-group discussion which gets total participation may save time and better serve part of the purpose. Usually, it is combined with the large-group discussion which follows the report of the small groups.

10. How to teach the small-group discussion to a class or group which has not used it before.

Select an interesting topic, a problem in which you know the class will be interested and will have ideas about. Give the class or group one or two experiences, using the method under your direction. After two or three times, they can do it themselves with the help of a few instructions. Do not tell them about it—*show them how to do it.* To see it done and to take part in it gives persons much more confidence in trying it when they are to lead a group.

11. Caution!

a. Do not over-use the small-group discussion or any other technique! Variety of method lends interest. You will have to guard against this, as there is a tendency to keep repeating a technique that is working well.

b. While this tool works well in many situations, it will not do everything. Other tools work better on those topics with which the group members have not had enough experience to formulate good answers or good questions.

The Large-group Discussion

What Is It?

The large-group discussion is the most common type known to most of us. A large-group discussion is carried on whenever a total of seven or more persons gather for discussion as one unit. Theoretically, the number of persons could vary from seven to a thousand or more. In practice, however, discussion tends to break down into a question and answer session in groups of forty, fifty, or more.

Where It Fits

1. To thresh over ideas as a total group following a small group discussion.
2. Groups with fewer than fifty persons in which the members are well acquainted and are familiar with the discussion method can use it fairly well following a talk, a panel, a film, or a symposium.
3. Groups of from seven to twenty-five persons can use it fairly well in exploring an idea, though it is more productive to combine it with the small-group discussion.

Advantages

1. Gets members more involved in thinking about the questions and issues than the speaker-audience technique, although not so much as the small-group discussion or the dramatic techniques.
2. Keeps the group together; everyone knows what is happening.
3. Gives the total group a chance to check on any particular idea that may be presented.

Disadvantages

1. Less productive of ideas than the small-group method.
2. Moves slowly and is likely to get side tracked.
3. Frequently a few talkers dominate the meeting.
4. The larger the group, the fewer there are who feel free to speak.
5. As the size of the group increases, participation and the feeling of responsibility on the part of the members decreases.

Some Suggestions for Leading Large-group Discussions

1. Choose a topic in which the group is interested.

A discussion technique may create some interest, but for the most part it simply facilitates it.

2. *If possible, have the group sit in a circle, square, or diamond shape arrangement and face each other.*

With such an arrangement all can see each other's faces and can talk to each other.

3. *Sit down in the circle like any other member, with persons on either side, if the group is small enough so that they can see you and hear you easily.*

This creates informality and helps the group to take more responsibility upon itself.

4. *Encourage people to speak loudly enough so they can be heard.*

In large groups of row seats or chairs it is sometimes necessary for the leader to repeat the statement.

5. *When questions are directed to you, as a group leader, bounce them back to the group for an answer rather than answer them yourself.*

If anyone in the group knows the answer, it is usually better to come from them than from you. This prevents leader domination, maintains member participation and interest, and keeps the discussion from disintegrating into a question-and-answer session. Withhold your own comment until others have expressed their ideas.

6. *Use a minimum of formality.*

The smaller groups need almost none. The best amount is that which makes for greatest productiveness. Too much kills interest and wastes time. Too little in a large meeting may let it get out of hand and thereby waste time.

7. *Encourage group members to talk to the group and direct their questions to the group.*

8. *Summarize at the end.*

Either a summary by the leader or a group summary stresses important points, helps them to organize the ideas and enables them to see how much they have accomplished. Often, it is well to call attention to this last point as groups are seldom conscious of how productive they have been.

PRINCIPLES

Whether one be involved as a participant, a professional worker, or a research scientist, there are certain fundamental principles inherent in community development. These are not basic principles of methodology or process so much as of the condition that must exist if a process of community development is to occur. The absence of any of these contributes to the failure of the program.

1. The local community is the unit in which individuals can make their most effective contribution to bring about change in the society.

The local community offers a social unit small enough for an individual to become an active participant in the deliberations leading to decision-making. In any larger unit individual thought and action have a tendency to become submerged and to lose their effectiveness.

2. Social progress has validity only in terms of total community change.

When development occurs in one aspect of the community at the expense of others, the fullest progress of the society is inhibited. All parts of the social structure should develop in reasonable balance with all others, so that progress is achieved in the whole structure.

3. Every program of community development should be characterized by its use of the processes of democratic action.

In this way individuals can learn the meaning and methods of democracy by being a part of the processes of democracy at work in their immediate environment, thus strengthening and perpetuating the basic democratic values of American society.

4. Members of a community should be encouraged to participate in the community development program.

When opportunities for participation are provided, an individual can make his most effective contribution in terms of his own abilities. The group discussion processes are effective means of encouraging fuller participation in deliberations leading to decisions.

5. Channels of communication among citizens and between them and their leaders should be maintained.

Participants should have free access to the facts and issues of common concern; to each other, so as to reach group consensus; and to the leadership in order to implement those decisions.

6. Leadership should be flexible.

Leadership in community development is changing constantly with individuals rising into or descending from leadership as the situation requires or rejects their particular skill. At the same time, leaders will be alert to the potentialities in others and provide training and experience to prepare them for the leadership role.

7. Continuous education is necessary for effective community development.

With society in a state of constant change, individuals continually must be acquiring information essential to making wise decisions. Furthermore, they need continuous education in the processes of effective group action.

8. *The organizational structure for community development should be functional.*

While some kind of organization is necessary for community development to succeed, it should be responsive to changing requirements for organization and not become an end in itself.

SELECTED REFERENCES: COMMUNITY DEVELOPMENT

Allahabad Agricultural Institute, *Experiment in Extension: The Gaon Sathi,* Oxford University Press, Bombay. 1956.

Allen, Harold Broughton, *Rural Reconstruction in Action,* Cornell University Press, Ithaca, New York, 1953.

Batten, T.R., *Communities and Their Development,* Oxford University Press, London, 1957.

Colonial Office, *Community Development: A Handbook,* prepared by a study conference on community development held at Hartwell House, Aglesburg, Buckinghamshire, September, 1957, Her Majesty's Stationery Office, London, 1958.

Dube, S.C., *India's Changing Villages,* Routledge and Kegan Paul, Ltd., London, 1958.

Hatch, D. Spencer, *Toward Freedom from Want from India to Mexico,* Oxford University Press, Bombay, 1949.

Hayes, Wayland J., *The Small Community Looks Ahead,* Harcourt, Brace and Company, New York, 1947.

Lippitt, Ronald, Jeanne Watson, and Bruce Westley, *The Dynamics of Planned Change,* Harcourt, Brace and Company, New York, 1958.

Mead, Margaret, editor, *Cultural Patterns and Technical Change,* World Federation for Mental Health, UNESCO, Paris. 1957.

Mosher, Arthur T., *Technical Cooperation in Latin-American Agriculture,* University of Chicago Press, Chicago, 1957.

Poston, Richard, *Small Town Renaissance,* Harper and Brothers, New York, 1950.

Ross, Murray G., *Community Organization: Theory and Practice,* Harper and Brothers, New York, 1955.

Sanders, Irwin T., *Making Good Communities Better,* University of Kentucky Press, 1953.

Spicer, Edward H., editor, *Human Problems in Technological Change,* Russell Sage Foundation, New York, 1954.

Taylor, Carl C., *A Critical Analysis of India's Community Development Program,* issued by the Community Projects Administration, Government of India.

Teaf, Howard M., Jr., and Peter G. Franck, *Hands Across Frontiers: Case Studies in Technical Cooperation,* Cornell University Press, Ithaca, New York, 1955.

United States Department of Health, Education and Welfare, Office of Education, *Education for Better Living: The Role of the School in Community Improvement,* United States Government Printing Office, Washington, D.C., 1957.

SELECTED REFERENCES: BROADENING PARTICIPATION

Klein, Josephine, *The Study of Groups,* Routledge and Kegan Paul, Ltd., London, 1956.

Strauss, Bert, and Frances Strauss, *New Ways to Better Meetings,* the Viking Press, New York, 1951.

Assessing and Reporting Training Needs and Progress, United States Civil Service Commission, Washington, D.C., 1956.

Leadership Pamphlets, Adult Education Association of the U.S.A., Chicago, Illinois, especially:

"How to Lead Discussions," No. 1, 1955.
"Planning Better Programs," No. 2, 1955.
"Understanding How Groups Work," No. 4, 1955.
"How To Teach Adults," No. 5, 1955.
"Supervision and Consultation," No. 7, 1956.
"Training Group Leaders," No. 8, 1956.
"Conducting Workshops and Institutes," No. 9, 1956.
"Conferences That Work," No. 11, 1956.
"Effective Public Relations," No. 13, 1957.
"Better Boards and Committees," No. 14, 1957.
"Streamlining Parliamentary Procedure," No. 15, 1957.

Various issues of *Adult Leadership.*

CHAPTER 21

The Future Outlook

The future is always viewed in anticipation of change. A planning project attempts to anticipate what will probably happen, whether from the standpoint of the individual or the community, whether for the short or the long run. No budget can be made by a private or public agency without some estimate of changes to be expected during the coming year. Such estimates are made on the basis of conditions which must be assumed. Planning a community budget must take account of the population that might be expected through the year. Will there be more, fewer, or about the same number of people? Will there be more, fewer, or about the same number of children in the schools? What income from taxes might be expected? A wide range of questions of this sort implicitly or explicitly concerns budget-makers.

But a budget is usually planned for only one year ahead. What about the longer trends that may affect the local community? These long-run expectations are the subject of this chapter. The authors can claim no special prescience, no special prophetic insight in this regard. Nor can they, or anyone, hope to forecast the long-time trends in any particular community; there are too many unique situations involved. Each community must do the best it can in estimating its own future course.

It has been shown that community structure changes over a course of time, in both its elements and its dimensions.[1] The changes may arise in various ways, either from within or without the community. Modern communities are part of the world society; they are influenced by what happens even in those areas most removed from them. Developments in national and world

---

[1] The student will recall that in this book the community is regarded as the social structure in the local area within which people satisfy their major needs. This satisfaction of wants is its major *function*. The *components* of the community are the informal groups, large formal organizations, and institutions. The relationships between and among these components or substructures constitute the *elements* of structure. These elements, or *relationships*, are influenced and controlled by pervasive, persistent, and on-going patterns of behaving and believing, which are outside the power of the individual or group to determine. These pervasive matters have been called *dimensions*, because they constitute the sociocultural limits and environment within which the *elements* exist and function.

society are simultaneously transmitted via mass communication agencies to every corner of the land. It is the purpose of this chapter to call attention to some of the changes taking place in the United States and the world which are beyond the control of any single community or even the national society itself, yet affect every locality both by what is taking place now and what will take place in the future. At this point it may be well to call attention to changes over the past generation.

The Road We Have Come

One may better focus the trend of events by contrasting the present situation with that of so short a time as a generation or two ago. Up to 1920, farm, town, and city were more or less discrete units in the American landscape. It is true that suburbs existed and were expanding at the close of World War I, but the expansion then, measured by present standards, was only rudimentary. At the other extreme, the farm households were still relatively isolated from the city, and contacts with the villages and towns were largely Saturday affairs. Farmers used horses and mules for power—tractors were still relatively uncommon. While many farmers had Model T's, roads were not paved and few were "all-weather." Farms were more on a diversified basis, except in the highly specialized fruit and vegetable areas and the cotton plantations. Each farm family aimed to provide itself with milk, butter, eggs, and vegetables from its own farm. Dependence on town and city for the essentials of living was limited quite largely to food staples, clothing, and other specialized goods and services needed by the family.

In 1920, there were no radios and few telephones. People got news of the outside world by the weekly paper or by letter. Spot news was not important then; the war was over and people were preoccupied with their own problems or those of their local communities.

Then came the depression of the early 1920's, followed by the great boom that ended in the collapse of 1929 and the Great Depression of the 1930's. The great boom of the 1920's was in the nonagricultural segment of the economy and was associated with continued depression in farming. There was widespread unrest among farm people, numerous proposals for "farm relief," and many attempts by Congress to enact legislation which would aid the farmer.

The most important development in nonagricultural industry was the vast expansion of the automobile industry. Mass production techniques, initiated by Ford, encouraged the production of cars at unprecedented low prices; thus, mass production with the accompanying low prices made possible a mass market for the product. The resultant industrial expansion triggered a migration from farms of a magnitude never known before.

States began vast highway construction programs at the demand of the ever-increasing number of car owners. Bonds for millions of dollars were issued by the states for road construction. The federal government worked out arrangements with state highway commissions in 1921 for a nation-wide system of interconnected roads and highways, with federal aid provided for their construction and maintenance; as a result, transcontinental routes were laid out and constructed under this federal-state cooperative arrangement.

During the 1920's also, the radio was further developed, so that sets became available to the public at reasonable prices. These early sets operated on battery power rather than on the usual electrical current, and often were not in usable condition; moreover, reception was poor compared with mid-century types of instruments. With the extensive highway construction program and the coming of radio, the old isolation of the communities was rapidly alleviated.

The various sections of the country were being tied together as they never had been before. Transcontinental railway travel had been possible since 1868, but railways were not by any means equal to the automobile in getting people—by entire families—from one place to another. What the automobile meant to the mobility of the American people was dramatized in the great migration of what Congress referred to as "destitute citizens" to the Pacific coast in the 1930's.

Yet the increased migration which accompanied the depression years was as nothing compared with the accelerated movement brought on by the outbreak of World War II. In addition to the mobilization of millions of men and women for the armed services, at least as many if not more millions were attracted to the factories making planes, ships, tanks, and other munitions of war. Entire new communities sprouted around the powder plants, the shipyards, and the newly constructed factories for making planes and tanks. The numerous factories of the Great Lakes and Northeastern industrial complexes were rivaled or excelled by those on the Pacific Coast. The many military bases of the South and Middle States expanded old communities and created new ones. People were milling about the land not by thousands or hundreds of thousands, but by millions.

Unlike the post-World War I period, which was characterized by general demobilization and a "return to normalcy," the times since VJ Day have bristled with the excitement of the "cold war." After a brief respite from military anxiety in the years between 1946 and 1950, the outbreak of the

Korean war dimmed hopes of a return to the prewar status quo. Subsequent international tensions have made for the continuation of what is essentially a war economy. Vast military bases have to be maintained at home and overseas; the cost of defense amounts to nearly half the annual national budget—more than half, if the appropriations for atomic energy, veterans affairs, and so on are included.

In no comparable period of history have so many disrupting influences disturbed the equanimity of world, national, and local community life as have characterized the past half century. The net result has been the breakdown of cultural and social isolation. Physical and associated social isolation gave way before the advance of the mass-produced and mass-consumed automobile and the construction of paved highways across the land, including those from the farm to town. The revolution in electronics brought everyone within earshot of all parts of the earth. War conditions forced individuals out of isolated places and thrust them into areas previously unknown to them. Millions saw other parts of their own country for the first time, while millions also saw at first hand other countries and strange people.

In the space of four decades the more than twenty million horses and mules on the 1920 farms have all but disappeared. Tractors have taken their places. The mechanization of farming has proceeded to a degree undreamed of in the horse and mule era. There is no need to detail these changes. During this period rural communities have undergone a drastic revolution, and all their social institutions have been affected. Farms have been reduced in number and, on the average, have increased in size. The population residing on and operating farms has been reduced by one-third. Ribbons of concrete lie in parallel lines up and down and across the country. Each year over a million acres of farm land are taken for highways and the expanding suburbs. But the acreage is not needed, for the surpluses of crops continue to mount because agricultural technology progresses at a more rapid rate than the growth of the population.

The major problems a generation ago were those of a domestic character; those of four decades later are international—war and peace. Communities today make their plans on the assumption that the cold war will continue. They do this consciously or unconsciously, but they do it. The cold war means continued full employment, high wages, inflation, or the threat of it, and high taxes. These considerations provide the background influencing the thinking in every community planning its future.[2]

[2] For a review of changes from 1900 to 1950, see Frederick Lewis Allen, *The Big Change*, Harper and Brothers, New York, 1952.

The Demographic Revolution

But the technological and communication revolutions make up only part of the story of this most dynamic half century. Population since 1940 has increased at an amazing and unexpected rate, not only in the United States, but in the world as well. From the low point of sixteen plus of the middle 1930's the birthrate zoomed to more than twenty-five per thousand, an increase of over 60 per cent. Many states more than doubled their population, not by natural increase alone, but by in-migration from other states. But the tremendous increase in births everywhere made possible such growth of individual states. Old core cities, bursting at the seams, soon saw themselves surrounded by mushrooming suburbs. This phenomenon is so well known by the casual observer as to need no statistical verification. It is clear to all that the farm population has declined drastically since 1940; and it is equally manifest that the cities and their hinterlands have dramatically increased. It is estimated that by 1975 the population of the United States will have increased by sixty million over 1950—maybe more. The birth rate remains high even with a decline in the number of marriages—as a result of the low birth rate years of the 1930's. This can mean only that families of this generation are larger than those of the previous one; that second or third births are being followed by fourth, fifth, and sixth or later births.

The increase in the population in all parts of the world since World War II has been so spectacular that it has been called an "explosion" or a "bomb." Truly it is a sobering thought that an estimated 5,500 new human beings are being added each hour to the world's already staggering total of over 2.7 billions. At such a rate of increase a population equal to that of Italy (forty-eight million) is added each year.[3]

Full Employment

The factors responsible for this unexpected increase in the birth rate are not readily discernible, but there can be little doubt that the opportunities for employment at good wages has been of considerable influence. The re-

[3] World population figures are assembled by the United Nations and published annually in *The Demographic Yearbook*. For an excellent analysis of the population changes in the United States, see Conrad Taeuber and Irene B. Taeuber, *The Changing Population of the United States*, J. Wiley and Sons, New York, 1958. On a percentage basis, the most rapidly growing population region of the world is South America. For an excellent review of the situation in both North and South America, see Kingsley Davis, editor, *A Crowding Hemisphere: Population Change in the Americas*, *The Annals*, Vol. 316, Philadelphia, 1958.

cession of 1957–1958 was accompanied by a slight drop in the birth rate, the first such decline in several years. Full employment has characterized the country since 1940. The war naturally called for the utilization of the total labor force, and the persistence of the cold war allows no let-up. While unemployment increased somewhat in certain postwar years, it has never reached the proportions of the 1930's. Moreover, in 1946 Congress passed the so-called full employment act which committed the federal government to the responsibility of seeing to it that the labor force was fully employed. While this is not the wording of the law, the intent is clear that the federal government assumes responsibility for keeping jobs open to the working population.

This "population explosion," together with the "ability to pay," has accounted for the housing boom and the rapid growth of suburban communities. It has been estimated that since 1950 over 90 per cent of the increase in the population has taken place in the Standard Metropolitan Areas. These areas, which have been so defined by the Bureau of the Census, contain several counties as a rule and several of them overlap two or more states. These magnetic poles of population are the focal points of numerous community problems including the provision of schools, churches, and, above all, transportation facilities. Freeways, thruways, skyways, are being constructed in practically all of these SMA's, often at staggering cost and chiefly for the purpose of getting people to their places of work and home again. For, strange as it may seem, despite all the talk about decentralization of industry, the jobs of the working force seem to be where it is most difficult to get to them.

The demographic revolution and the general up-grading economically of the nation's families, along with the marvelous developments in the arts of communication and transportation, should direct some attention to the possibilities of promoting increased job opportunities in the smaller places. While there has been a marked increase in local industries, either through decentralization or through the exercise of local initiative and inventiveness, the greatest proportionate increase has occurred in the larger centers.

Why this increasing concentration of population in metropolitan areas? The only answer would seem to be the very simple one that there is where the jobs are. As the population grows, the division of labor proliferates. Yet, as was pointed out earlier in this book, there are many examples of deliberate community action to create jobs in the smaller communities. The problems of the large centers are becoming so acute as to raise a real question as to future capacity to absorb more population.

The editors of *Fortune Magazine*, in addressing themselves to metropolitan problems, pointed out that it will never be possible to provide parking space for all the motorists who want to come into the cities, and that the problem of getting people into and out of these centers is not to be solved by more and more thruways and freeways. One thing to keep in mind in regard to transportation is that any increase of sixty million people in the United States population will inevitably bring an increase of thirty million or more motor cars. It is no longer a problem of standing room only for people, but for automobiles especially.[4]

What may prove to be the limiting factor in the growth of the metropolis is the supply of water—or lack of it. Water consumption per capita has increased enormously in the first half of the century, chiefly because of the expansion of industry. Industry in 1958 is estimated to use eleven times as much water as in 1900 and has increased almost 50 per cent since 1952. It has been reported by the chief of the Corps of Engineers that 1,000 cities were in real trouble during the drought of 1953. In fact, the condition is becoming chronic, no matter what the rainfall. Cities like Dallas, Miami, and others, which depend so largely on underground water, now find they have pumped out so much fresh water that salt water is oozing in to take its place.[5]

Communities of the future will be compelled to take water supply into account. It may well be that some will need to develop a system of controls over water use in order to prevent waste. People who allow leaky taps may be subject to fines in the future. Industries may have their water supplies rationed. From 65,000 gallons now required to produce a ton of paper, techniques may have to be found to reduce it by half, and similarly with the tremendous quantities of water which go into the making of a ton of steel. More houses are being equipped with air conditioners, completely equipped bathrooms, dish-washers and automatic washers, all of which increase the domestic consumption of water. Although domestic use is only 10 per cent of the total consumption, it may be crucial in the growth of a city. More land is being irrigated each year, not only in the West, but also east of the Mississippi. There will clearly be a limit to the supply of water which any one center can command.

With the problems of the metropolis so immense and becoming greater

[4] *The Exploding Metropolis* by the Editors of *Fortune:* Doubleday and Company, New York, 1958.

[5] See the report of the President's Water Policies Commission, which appeared in 1952. This report presents the problems of water supply, utilization, and pollution, and recommends the establishment of control commissions for each of the great river basins. For a brief presentation of some of the more salient facts regarding the problem, see Robert and Leona Rienow, "The Day the Taps Run Dry," *Harper's Magazine*, Vol. 217, No. 1301, 1958, pp. 72–78.

each day, why do not more people remain in the smaller places, or even move from the large to the small? This is the other side of the coin of employment prospects. But it is also more than that in the view of some thoughtful writers. There are many who are concerned with the values that presumably inhere in small-town living. Some even argue that civilization as we know it is a product of generations of living in small places; that is, as far as the moral and spiritual values of our civilization are concerned. They view with disquiet the decline of small-town life with its intimate person-to-person association and the rise of the large metropolis with its impersonality of relationship and the anonymity of the individual.[6]

Town and Country Converge

Even farmers commute to towns and cities to work. A third of the income of farm families was derived from non-farm sources in 1957, a fact which indicates the extent to which the nonagricultural job opportunities have expanded.

This rise in farm family income from non-farm sources is further evidence of the break-up of farm isolation, both physical and social. A rising proportion of farm families have either the operator, the housewife, or one of the children employed in some job other than farming. Whichever member of the family may be involved, it may well mean that union membership is required. The hostility often shown by farmers toward labor unions in the past is bound to be modified by a personal experience in them.

The decline in the farm population, together with the improvement in transportation, among other factors, has contributed to the necessity or desirability of closing thousands of the farmers' typical one-room schools. These schools, built and maintained by farm families for farm children, are seemingly destined to disappear almost entirely within a few years. This means that farm children will go to school with town children; it means that farm families will share with town, city, or suburban families the support of schools as a joint enterprise. The little school districts are being dismantled in favor of the larger area- and population-based units. Farmers are at last having to give up their "segregated" schools. The same is true of the farmers' churches in the open country. Open country churches are merging, or they are abandoning the open country by joining up with a town or city church.

[6] There is no opportunity now to follow this thought further, but the student may want to read Baker Brownell, *The Human Community, Its Philosophy and Practice*, Harper and Brothers, New York, 1950, and Arthur E. Morgan, *The Small Community*, Harper and Brothers, New York, 1942.

At the same time that the decline in the farm population is creating radical changes in the character of the rural community through the elimination of many familiar rural institutions, it creates new problems resulting from growth in urban centers. Agricultural technological advances and the resultant specialization in production tend to squeeze out the inefficient, submarginal, subsistence level farmer, forcing him to move from the land to the industrial center. With him go his rural attitudes and behavior patterns and his unfamiliarity with urban folkways. This immigration of the less educated and less efficient rural folk creates problems of some magnitude for urban communities, and will continue to grow in importance as rural-to-urban migration accelerates. The heterogeneous nature of urban life is not conducive to the rapid assimilation of these rural migrants, and they tend to cluster in urban slum areas much as foreign immigrants used to cluster at the turn of the century. Such a pattern of movement emphasizes the interdependence and integration of urban and rural society and accentuates the importance of the concept of integrated services for all people without distinction as to place of residence.

Rural-Urban Differences Fade

The great disparity between rural and urban segments of the population, which for so long has engaged the attention of social scientists, is rapidly disappearing. The old contrasts in the level of living, in the possession of electricity, a telephone, running water, indoor plumbing, and the like, are becoming less apparent. The differentials in education, both in amount and quality, are being leveled off. Each census shows less difference in the amount of education of farm and non-farm people. Soon they will be approximately the same. And this removal of differences in education is of the greatest significance to community life. Stauffer's study of farm and non-farm attitudes showed that when education held constant there was no difference between town and country.[7]

The Importance of Occupation

If the differences among families based on where they live—on a farm or in a town or city—are disappearing, does this mean that all people, rural and urban, will tend to behave alike? In some respects the answer may be

[7] Samuel A. Stouffer, *Communism, Conformity, and Civil Liberties,* Doubleday and Company, Garden City, N.Y., 1955. See also Lowry Nelson, "Rural Life in a Mass-Industrial Society," *RS,* 22:20–30, 1957.

in the affirmative. On such questions as religious and racial tolerance, or questions regarding labor unions, attitudes may be less fixed and more subject to moderate change. Political issues may be more subject to rational consideration than to traditional and emotional guidance. This is admittedly speculation, and only further experience will reveal whether such a generalization can be verified.

But while some forces we have discussed are making for integration and conformity, there are also forces which are contributing to increased diversity. As society becomes more complex and technology is elaborated constantly, new occupations come into existence. Of course, some also disappear—the blacksmith, the harness-maker, the livery stable operator—but these are few in number compared with the vast array of new occupations which have come with the invention of the internal combustion engine and the inventions in the field of electronics. Also, numerous new services come into being; there is no need to labor the point. Society is growing more complex from the standpoint of the tasks which are required and the different vocations which are open to people.

This occupational diversity, resulting from technological advance, the growth in numbers of people, and the complex needs accompanying modern existence, is one important aspect of the problem, but there is another. Increasingly, individuals who formerly may have performed several services now specialize in performing only one. This is well illustrated in farming. What is called diversified farming—the growing of several types of crops and livestock—is giving way to specialization. Thousands of farmers who formerly kept enough milk cows, chickens, and hogs to supply the family needs no longer do so. They buy milk, eggs, butter, and fresh meat from the grocery and butcher shop. The farm may be devoted to a single enterprise; dairying, poultry-raising, production of pure seed, and the like. The dairy farmer no longer expects to produce his own feed, but buys it from the feed mill which specializes in the production of balanced ration feeds. The poultry grower needs only a building, perhaps three floors high, to carry on his enterprise, since he, too, buys his feed.

In fact, the new movement called "vertical integration" would relieve the farmer of still more of the tasks or responsibilities which he carries on even under the degree of specialization mentioned. The situation is well illustrated in the case of the production of fryers. A poultry marketing corporation may agree to furnish the chicks to the farmer, supply him with the feed, and guarantee to purchase the poults when ready for the market at a stated price. All the farmer does is furnish the housing for the birds and perform the labor of feeding and caring for them. Similar arrangements are being made in the case of hog producers and other specialized operators. The arrangement has been common in sugar-beet production from the beginning of the industry, and is also practiced in the case of canning crops. In the case of sugar beets, the sugar factory supplies the seed, and will often lend money to pay for the thinning the plants in the spring and harvesting the crop in the fall. Supervision of the operation is provided during the growing season by a fieldman of the company. The contract usually calls for the company to purchase the beets at a specified minimum price per ton at harvest time, with additional compensation if the price of sugar justifies it when it is marketed. The more recent introduction of similar arrangements in other types of farm production is something of an innovation and raises many questions as to the role which the farmer will play in the productive process in the future.

This development has two aspects, as will be readily seen. In the first place, it promotes specialization and therefore adds to diversity of interests in the field of agriculture; secondly, it ties the farmer definitely to the non-agricultural interests. That is, he becomes a partner with non-farmers in the production process. Other illustrations of the trend toward specialization could be used, especially in the professions, clerical jobs, and skilled blue collar work.

Some Implications

Communities of the United States, then, in making plans for the future must consider these developments:

(1) The communication and technological revolutions have broken down the old lines separating farm, town, and city. Residential groups are of importance still, but their importance in a physical as well as a social sense has been greatly reduced. The linkage among communities will increase, willy-nilly, and ideas from one community will be implemented in another. The community which has a problem first may serve to call attention to the problem long before it happens elsewhere. The attempts at solution in one community may serve as experiments for another.

(2) As far as the town-country community is concerned, the basis for more complete integration now exists, and it remains only for the initiative and enterprise of local leadership to consolidate it. The small community might then experience an easier path to community development, with the old conflicts minimized.

(3) The rapid growth of population with its extraordinary concentration in metropolitan areas sets the stage for the emergence of vast problems to

provide goods and services, particularly in transportation and utilities. While these problems are rallying points for community development, they may be so pressing that the patience needed to restructure the community will be discouraged.

(4) While most communities are increasing in size, thus providing new opportunities as well as new problems, some are declining in population. The declining community has a special set of problems distinct from the growing one. But there are numerous examples of communities which have forestalled threatened decline by vigorous and ingenious action.

(5) The diversities along older lines are disappearing, but the rise of new occupations and further specialization within old ones create new possible lines of cleavage.

(6) The rising level of education of the mass of people, rural and urban, should make possible the growth of tolerance on lines of religion and race, and form a more secure base for future community development and action.

SELECTED REFERENCES

Allen, Frederick Lewis, *The Big Change*, Harper and Brothers, New York, 1951.

Barck, Oscar Theodore, Jr., and Nelson Manfred Blake, *Since 1900: A History of the United States in our Time*, The Macmillan Company, New York, 1952, Chapters 1 and 30.

Exploding Metropolis, The, by the editors of *Fortune*, Doubleday and Company, New York, 1958.

Hallenbeck, Wilbur C., *American Urban Communities*, Harper and Brothers, New York, 1951.

Morgan, Arthur E., *The Community of the Future and the Future of the Community*, Community Service, Inc., Yellow Springs, Ohio, 1957.

Mumford, Lewis, *The Culture of Cities*, Harcourt, Brace and Company, New York, 1938.

Saarinen, Eliel, *The City, Its Growth, Its Decay, Its Future*, Reinhold Publishing Corporation, New York, 1943.

Index of Subjects

Action Programs, 14, 30, 50, 70, 80, 82–83, 90, 237, 256, 351, 360, 379–385, 405, 413
Adolescence, 197–202, 212, 264
Adoption of Change (See Diffusion, Decision-Making)
Adult Education, 194, 250, 326, 339
Age, 193, 194, 202, 212; interpretation of, 194–195
Applied Science (See Science and Practice)
Authority (See Power and Authority)
Autonomous Groups, 219, 220

Beliefs (See Mores, Values)
Bureaucracy, 175, 356

Change, social and community: acceptance of, 252–253; adjustment to, 236, 257; causes of, 49, 68, 405–411; components of, 400; direction of, 397–400, 444–454; and education, 333–337, 339; effects of, 20–22, 353–354; forms of, 462–463; and government, 309–314; and groups, 221, 233; industrialization and population, 268–269; and planning, 405, 444; problem of, 395; and process, 142, 393; rate of, 401–402; and religion, 290–293, 298; and social structure, 2, 27–28, 49, 216; and technology, 351; types of, 394–395; and values, 114–115, 124, 132
Class, social, 93, 156–158, 166–170
Communications: and change, 398, 411; and community size, 36; channels of, 80–82, 139–142, 249; and diffusion, 136; and other elements, 90; and primary groups, 225; and training in skills, 366; function of, 135–139, 355; nature of, 133; principles of, 148–149
Community (See specific aspect of interest)

Community, definition of, 9–12
Community Development: and change, 403–405; and democracy, 357; and economic institutions, 347; and government, 321; and juvenile delinquency, 358; and leadership, 426–433; and leadership training, 427–433; and population, 87; and power, 182; and social problems, 392; approaches to, 417–419; barriers to, 275, 422–426; meaning of, 30–31, 414–417; objectives of, 94, 274; process of, 419–422
Community Organization, 29, 83, 90, 182, 183
Community School, 329, 337
Conflict, 173, 191, 242, 260
Conformity, 17, 182, 252, 269, 398–399
Culture, 56, 246, 333, 346
Customs (See Mores, Values)

Decision-Making, 90, 132, 142, 146–149, 182, 251, 255, 261, 273, 315, 326, 328–329, 344, 359, 389
Definition of the Situation, 146–148
Delinquency, 264, 358
Democratic Process, 19, 60, 105–106, 174, 183–191, 255, 261, 335–336
Demographic Factors, 3, 4, 12, 45, 51, 68, 70, 73, 267, 268, 448–451; function of, 70–71; sparsity, 74–76, 87
Determinism, single factor: geographic, 55–58; economic, 350–359, 408
Diffusion, 134–135, 142, 273, 400
Dimensions of Community, defined, 21–22, 89–91
Discussion, small group, 434–440
Division of labor (See specialization)

Ecology of Community, 1, 2, 3, 9–12, 24–27, 33, 34–45, 50, 55, 68, 448–452; trade center, 357

457

Author Index

460